A Post-WTO International Legal Order

Meredith Kolsky Lewis • Junji Nakagawa •
Rostam J. Neuwirth • Colin B. Picker •
Peter-Tobias Stoll
Editors

A Post-WTO International Legal Order

Utopian, Dystopian and Other Scenarios

Springer

Editors
Meredith Kolsky Lewis
University at Buffalo School of Law
The State University of New York
Buffalo, NY, USA

Junji Nakagawa
Faculty of Liberal Arts
Chuo Gakuin University
Chiba, Japan

Rostam J. Neuwirth
Faculty of Law
University of Macau
Taipa, Macao

Colin B. Picker
University of Wollongong
Wollongong, NSW, Australia

Peter-Tobias Stoll
Jean Monnet Chair, Institute for
International Law and European Law
Georg August University of Göttingen
Göttingen, Germany

ISBN 978-3-030-45430-2 ISBN 978-3-030-45428-9 (eBook)
https://doi.org/10.1007/978-3-030-45428-9

This Springer imprint is published by the registered company Springer Nature Switzerland AG.
The registered company address is: Gewerbestrasse 11, 6330 Cham, Switzerland

Dedicated to the memory of
Professor Sidney I. Picker, Jr., one of our field's early contributors from the Kennedy Round to the NAFTA, he served as a negotiator, drafter, dispute settlement panellist, teacher, researcher and mentor.

Preface

The collection of papers in this book is the result of a global project organised by Professors Junji Nakagawa and Colin B. Picker to explore what might be the consequences or potential responses if the World Trade Organization collapsed or became largely irrelevant—neither impossible to imagine given the relentless attacks on the institution in the recent years.

The project was premised on the view: (1) that the WTO and its commitment to a rule-of-law-form of multilateralism is worth saving, even if it is not perfect and even if it needs some substantial reform and (2) that the insights generated by exploring a post-WTO world, in both dystopian and utopian perspectives, would likely be helpful in trying to save the WTO from potential collapse or stagnation.

The project included a series of workshops held around the world, designed to ensure that a wide variety of perspectives could contribute to the project. As such, workshops were held at the University of Tokyo from 9 to 10 January 2019 (thanks to Professor Junji Nakagawa for hosting), at the Fletcher School, Tufts University on 26 July 2019 (thanks to Professor Joel Trachtman for hosting) and at King's College London from 18 to 19 October 2019 (thanks to Dr. Holger Hestermeyer for hosting). Over fifty academics from around the world participated in the three workshops, though due to the time constraints to publish this book, most were unable to commit to providing their presentations as completed chapters. Nevertheless, it is expected those not appearing in this publication will appear in journals and other fora over the next few years.

The editors wish to express their gratitude to Ms. Agata Daszko for her assistance in the publishing process and to all others who have assiduously helped to realise this volume and hope that it will inspire further conversations around the future of the WTO.

Buffalo, NY, USA — Meredith Kolsky Lewis
Tokyo, Japan — Junji Nakagawa
Macau, China — Rostam J. Neuwirth
Wollongong, NSW, Australia — Colin B. Picker
Göttingen, Germany — Peter-Tobias Stoll

Contents

About the Contributors

Elisa Baroncini is an Associate Professor of International Law at the University of Bologna. Currently, Co-Chair of the ESIL IG on International Economic Law and Coordinator of DIEcon, the Interest Group on International Economic Law of the Italian Society of International Law, Elisa holds a cum laude Bologna Law Degree and a PhD in EU Law from Alma Mater Studiorum - Università di Bologna. On 9 August 2018, she got the abilitation as Full Professor of International Law from the Italian Ministry for University. She teaches International Law and International Economic Law at the Law School of the University of Bologna, has been Visiting Professor at the China-EU School of Law, speaker in many international conferences and Visiting Researcher at the European University Institute. She manages and participates in international and national research projects. Her main fields of research include the crisis of the WTO Appellate Body and the reform process of the dispute settlement mechanism; the relation between free trade and non-trade values; transparency in International Economic Law; the role of the European Parliament and the European Commission in the conclusion of the international trade agreements; the new generation of EU Free Trade Agreements.

Leïla Choukroune is a Professor of International Law and Director of the University of Portsmouth Thematic Initiative in Democratic Citizenship. Her research focuses on the interactions between international trade and investment law, human rights, jurisprudence and social theory in the Global South (India, South Asia, China and East Africa in particular). She has vastly published in English, French, Spanish or Chinese and authored more than 10 books. She is the Editor of the Springer book series International Law and the Global South and the Routledge book series in Human Rights, Citizenship and the Law. She is Associate Editor of the Manchester Journal of International Economic Law. Together with Professor James Nedumpara, she is the Co-Chair of the South Asia International Economic Law Network (SAIELN).

Bradly J. Condon is the WTO Chair Professor at ITAM in Mexico City. He serves as Advisory Board Member for the Global Trade Law Series, Kluwer Law International, Editorial Board Member for academic journals such as the Latin American Journal of Trade Policy and the Journal of International Economic Law and has served as a peer reviewer for Cambridge University Press, Kluwer Law International, Oxford University Press and several international academic journals. His most recent book is Climate Change and Global Economic Governance (OUP, 2013), co-authored with Tapen Sinha and featuring a foreword by Nobel Laureate Robert F. Curl.

Yuka Fukunaga is a Professor of International Economic Law at Waseda University. She is a winner of the Waseda Research Award in 2017. She was an assistant legal counsel at the Permanent Court of Arbitration (PCA) and an intern at the Appellate Body Secretariat, World Trade Organization (WTO). She holds an LL.D. (2013) and an LL.M. (1999) from the Graduate Schools for Law and Politics, University of Tokyo and an LL.M. (2000) from the School of Law, University of California, Berkeley. She has published a number of articles and chapters in the field of international trade and investment law.

Gabriel Gari is a Reader in International Economic Law at the Centre for Commercial Law Studies, Queen Mary University of London and Academic Director of the LL.M. in International Economic Law. Prior to joining Queen Mary, Gabriel practised Employment and Commercial Law and worked for the Uruguayan Supreme Court of Justice. He holds degrees in Law and in Sociology from the University of the Republic (Uruguay), an LL.M. from the London School of Economics and a PhD from Queen Mary University of London. He is a member of the Latin American and Caribbean Research Network on Services, the Latin American Network on International Economic Law, the Society of International Economic Law and the European Society of International Law.

Tomohiko Kobayashi is a Professor of International Economic Law at Otaru University of Commerce. He has served as Visiting Professor at Jagiellonian University, Poland (2019), National Chung Hsing University, Taiwan (2016–2017) and the Far Eastern Federal University, Russia (2014). Before joining the faculty of Otaru, he was a deputy director at the Multilateral Trade System Department of the Ministry of Economy, Trade and Industry, Japan (2005–2007). He holds two LL.M. degrees from the School of Law, University of California, Berkeley (2015) and the Graduate School of Law, Kyoto University (2001).

Jaemin Lee is a Professor of Law at School of Law, Seoul National University in Seoul, Korea. His major areas of teaching and research are public international law, international investment law and international trade law. He has published articles and book chapters on various topics of public international law, international investment law and international trade law. Upon graduation from College of Law,

Seoul National University in 1992, he joined the Korean Ministry of Foreign Affairs as a foreign service officer. His post in the ministry included deputy directorship of the Treaties Division and the North American Trade Division. Between 2000 and 2004, he also practised law with Willkie Farr & Gallagher LLP (Washington, D.C. office) as an associate attorney of the firm's international trade group. During the period of 2004–2013, he taught international law and international economic law at School of Law, Hanyang University in Seoul, Korea.

Simon N. Lester is the associate director of the Cato Institute's Herbert A. Stiefel Center for Trade Policy Studies. Previously, he was a legal affairs officer at the Appellate Body Secretariat of the World Trade Organization. In 2001, he founded the international trade law website WorldTradeLaw.net. He has written articles for a number of law journals, including the Stanford Journal of International Law, the Journal of International Economic Law and the World Trade Review. In addition, he has taught courses on international trade law at American University's Washington College of Law, the University of Michigan Law School and Melbourne University Law School.

Meredith Kolsky Lewis is a Professor of Law and Vice Dean for International and Graduate Programs at the University at Buffalo School of Law, State University of New York and Associate Professor at the Victoria University of Wellington Law School. Meredith's research focuses on international economic law, with a particular emphasis on international trade law, free trade agreements and the WTO. She is a founding member and former Co-Executive Vice President of the Society of International Economic Law and is co-rapporteur of the International Law Association's Committee on Sustainable Development and the Green Economy in International Trade Law.

Chin Leng Lim is the Choh-ming Li Professor of Law at The Chinese University of Hong Kong and a barrister at Keating Chambers, London. He is a BIICL Honorary Senior Fellow and Visiting Professor at King's College London. Lim was previously a Professor of Law and a member of Court and Senate at Hong Kong University and the inaugural Lionel Astor Sheridan Visiting Professor at NUS in Singapore. His latest books include International Investment Law and Arbitration (Cambridge, 2018) by Lim, Ho and Paparinskis, with a Foreword by Gaillard and the forthcoming Cambridge Companion to International Arbitration, with a Foreword by Lord Neuberger.

Junji Nakagawa is a Professor at the Faculty of Liberal Arts at Chuo Gakuin University and Professor Emeritus of the University of Tokyo. He has B.A., M.A. and PhD, all in law, from the University of Tokyo. He is a chairperson of the Asian WTO Research Network and the Asian International Economic Law Network. His recent publication includes TPP Commentary, Japan Tariff Association, 2019, International Economic Law, 3rd edition, Yuhikaku, 2019, Asian Perspectives on International Investment Law, Routledge, 2019 and Nationalization, Natural Resource and International Investment Law, Routledge, 2017.

James J. Nedumpara is a Professor and the Head of the Centre for Trade and Investment Law established by the Ministry of Commerce and Industry at the Indian Institute of Foreign Trade. He has worked with leading law firms, corporate firms and also UNCTAD's India programme. He has appeared in various WTO dispute proceedings as part of the Indian delegation including the India—Agricultural Products (Avian Influenza dispute, DS 430) and India—Export Subsidies (DS 541). He has also represented the Government of India in three disputes at the consultation meetings in Geneva.

Rostam J. Neuwirth is a Professor and the Head of the Department of Global Legal Studies at the Faculty of Law of the University of Macau. He holds a PhD degree from the European University Institute (EUI) in Florence (Italy), a Master's degree in Law (LL.M.) from the Faculty of Law of McGill University in Montreal (Canada) and law degree from the University of Graz (Austria). Before joining the University of Macau, he taught in India at the West Bengal National University of Juridical Sciences (NUJS) in Kolkata and the Hidayatullah National Law University (HNLU) in Raipur and worked at the International Law Bureau of the Austrian Federal Ministry for Foreign Affairs in Vienna (Austria).

Colin B. Picker is the Executive Dean of the Faculty of Law, Humanities and Arts at the University of Wollongong in Australia. Previously, he was at UNSW Law in Sydney where he was Director (and founder) of the China International Business and Economic Law (CIBEL) initiative as well as Associate Dean (International). Prior to joining UNSW, he was the Daniel L. Brenner/UMKC Scholar and Professor of Law at UMKC School of Law. He entered academia in 2000, after practising in the DC law firm Wilmer, Cutler & Pickering. He was a founder and the first executive Vice President of the SIEL.

Sonia E. Rolland is a Professor of Law at Northeastern University School of Law (Boston, USA). She is the author of Emerging Powers in the International Economic Order: Cooperation, Competition and Transformation (with David. M. Trubek, Cambridge University Press, 2019) and Development at the WTO (Oxford University Press, 2012) and regularly acts as an expert for international and non-governmental organisations including the United Nations, the International Centre for Trade and Sustainable Development and the India Institute of Foreign Trade. She has held appointments at Columbia University, Georgetown University and the University of Michigan.

Engela C. Schlemmer is a Professor of Law (School of Law) and Assistant Dean: Academic Planning and Strategy at the Faculty of Commerce, Law and Management at the University of the Witwatersrand, Johannesburg. She is an assistant editor of the South African Yearbook of International Law and member of its editorial board; she is also an editorial board member of the Tydskrif vir Hedendaagse Romeins-Hollandse Reg/Journal of Contemporary Roman Dutch Law. She is a member of the

Society for International Economic Law (SIEL) and of the International Law Association (ILA). She is a member of the International Monetary Law Committee of the ILA and the Committee on the Rule of Law in International Investment Law. Her research focuses on international economic law and in particular the international law on foreign investment and WTO law as well as on real and personal security law.

Peter-Tobias Stoll is a Professor at the University of Göttingen and a Director of the Institute for International Law and European Law, where he heads the Department for International Economic and Environmental Law. He holds a Jean Monnet Chair for European Union and Global Sustainable Development Through Law and co-chairs the ESIL Interest Group on International Economic Law. His research focus is on international law, trade, investment and the environment. He has extensively published on international economic and environmental law and is one of the general editors of the Max Planck Commentaries on World Trade Law.

David M. Trubek is the Voss-Bascom Professor of Law and Dean of International Studies Emeritus at the University of Wisconsin-Madison and a Senior Research Fellow at the Harvard Law School. He is a world-renowned expert on law and development, with a regional focus on Latin America. He has published dozens of books and articles, including Law and the New Developmental State: the Brazilian Experience in Latin American Context (2013) and World Trade and Investment Law Reimagined: A Progressive Agenda for an Inclusive Globalization (2019).

Akshaya Venkataraman is a Senior Research Fellow at the Centre for Trade and Investment Law (CTIL), a centre which advises the Indian Government on issues in international trade and investment law. She obtained her B.A.LLB(Hons) from the West Bengal National University of Juridical Sciences, Kolkata and worked at a leading full-service law firm in India prior to joining CTIL.

Rolf H. Weber is a Professor of International Business Law at Zurich University acting as co-director of the Research Program on Financial Market Regulation, the Center for Information Technology, Society, and Law and the Blockchain Centre. Furthermore, he was Visiting Professor at Hong Kong University and he is a practising attorney-at-law in Zurich. He is a member of the Editorial Board of several Swiss and international legal periodicals and frequently publishes on issues of global law. His main fields of research and practice are IT and Internet, international trade and finance as well as competition law.

Brett G. Williams an Australian Legal Practitioner, is the principal of Williams Trade Law and an Honorary Senior Lecturer at the University of Sydney Law School where he has taught WTO law since 2001. His legal practice specialises in the law of the WTO and of bilateral regional trade agreements, including representation in WTO dispute settlement (e.g., acting for Indonesia in Australia—A4 copy paper DS529), and accession issues and also trade issues under Australian law. His publications include one co-edited book, China and the World Trade System (CUP2003) and articles on WTO negotiations on agricultural trade, China's WTO accession, trade in services and innovations in dispute settlement mechanisms in trade agreements.

Weihuan Zhou is a Senior Lecturer at UNSW Law and a member of the Herbert Smith Freehills China International Business and Economic Law (CIBEL) Centre. Weihuan publishes widely in the field of international economic law, particularly the laws of the World Trade Organization, trade remedies, free trade agreements and China's integration into the international economic order, including a recent monograph on China's Implementation of WTO Rulings and two co-edited books, one on the China–Australia Free Trade Agreement and the other on Non-Market Economies under the WTO. His work has been cited in research reports of the Productivity Commission, the Senate Economics References Committee and the European Parliament and also by leading experts in the field. He is a member of the Executive Council of the Society of International Economic Law (SIEL), the world's leading organisation for academics and academically minded practitioners and officials in international economic law.

Abbreviations

AB	Appellate Body
ASEAN	Association of Southeast Asian Nations
BITs	Bilateral investment treaties
BRICS	Brazil, Russia, India, China and South Africa
CETA	Comprehensive Economic and Trade Agreement
CPTPP	Comprehensive and Progressive Agreement for Trans-Pacific Partnership
DSB	Dispute Settlement Body
DSM	Dispute settlement mechanism
DSS	Dispute settlement system
DSU	Understanding on rules and procedures governing the settlement of disputes
FDI	Foreign direct investment
FTA	Free trade agreement
GATS	General Agreement on Trade in Services
GATT	General Agreement on Tariffs and Trade
ICSID	International Centre for Settlement of Investment Disputes
ICTSD	International Centre for Trade and Sustainable Development
IIA	International Investment Agreement
ITO	International Trade Organization
MFN	Most favoured nation
NAFTA	North American Free Trade Agreement
NT	National treatment
OECD	Organisation for Economic Co-operation and Development
PTA	Preferential trade agreement
RCEP	Regional Comprehensive Economic Partnership
RTA	Regional trade agreement
TBT Agreement	Agreements on technical barriers to trade

TPP	Trans-Pacific Partnership
TRIPS	Agreement on Trade-Related Intellectual Property Rights
TTIP	Transatlantic Trade and Investment Partnership
UNCITRAL	United Nations Commission on International Trade Law
UNCTAD	United Nations Conference on Trade and Development
USMCA	United States–Mexico–Canada Agreement
WTO	World Trade Organization

Part I
The Post-WTO: Introduction

An Introduction to Utopian and Dystopian Post-WTO Regimes and Environments

Junji Nakagawa and Colin B. Picker

Contents

1 Introduction

The collection of papers in this book originated from some of the presentations that were made at a series of workshops held around the world in 2019 on the topic of the "Post-WTO". We, along with local hosts at the different workshops,[1] organised a

Respectively, Professor at the Faculty of Liberal Arts at Chuo Gakuin University; and Executive Dean of the Faculty of Law, Humanities and Arts at the University of Wollongong in Australia.

[1]The first workshop was held at the University of Tokyo from the 9th to the 10th January 2019 (thanks to Professor Junji Nakagawa for hosting). The second workshop took place at the Fletcher School, Tufts University on the 26th of July 2019 (thanks to Professor Joel Trachtman for hosting).

J. Nakagawa
Chuo Gakuin University, Abiko, Japan and Anderson, Mori and Tomotsune LLP, Tokyo, Japan
e-mail: nakagawa@fla.cgu.ac.jp

C. B. Picker (✉)
University of Wollongong, Wollongong, NSW, Australia
e-mail: cpicker@uow.edu.au

M. K. Lewis et al. (eds.), *A Post-WTO International Legal Order*,
https://doi.org/10.1007/978-3-030-45428-9_1

series of workshops to explore what might be some of the possibilities or consequences if the WTO collapsed or became largely irrelevant in the international economic arena. As an initial matter, it needs to be stated that this chapter and indeed the entire project, including the other chapters in this collection as well as the presentations and discussions at the workshops held in 2019 and those to be held in the future, are premised on the idea that the project's ultimate goal is to try to help preserve the WTO or what it stands for—a multilateral rule of law regime for international trade. Thus, in no way should the work be viewed as supporting the undermining or denigration of the WTO. It was strongly felt that such serious discussion of a "post-WTO" as were held at the workshops and in the papers would help keep the current regime alive by showing how difficult and challenging might be the international economic legal order (IELO) in a post-WTO world or by showing, in its utopian scenarios, avenues for a future reform of the WTO.

Primarily, the participants were leading scholars in the fields of international economic law.[2] Government and international organisation officials were for the

The final workshop took place at King's College London from the 18th to the 19th of October 2019 (thanks to Dr. Holger Hestermeyer for hosting). It is expected that future workshops will take place, but they are obviously not reflected in this volume.

[2]The workshop participants (and their presentation titles) included: Pinar Artiran (Post-WTO lessons from EU-Turkey disputes at WTO v EU-Turkey FTA DS mechanisms); Elisa Baroncini (The EU Approach to overcome the WTO DS vacuum: suggesting arbitration on the model of Art. 25 DSU and activating bilateral dispute mechanisms under new EUFTAs); Tomer Broude (Early thoughts on Regulatory Liberalism and the WTO); Leïla Choukroune (The Concern with Non-Concerns: Beyond Trade, Power Rights); Kathleen Claussen (Trade's Enforcement Conundrum); Bradly Condon (To Dystopia and Beyond: The WTO in a Warming Megaregional World); Fernando Dias Simoes (Nothing Lasts Forever: The (im)permanence of the AB); Michael Ewing Chow (Between Legislation and Litigation: The WTO as the Missing Middle); David A. Gantz (Post-WTO State-to-State Disputes in FTAs: E.g. USMCA); Henry Gao (Being Digital: The WTO and Data Regulation); Gabriel Gari (A proposal to split the WTO in accordance with the nature of its obligations); Caroline Henckels and Elizabeth Sheargold (Reimagining Public Policy Exceptions in WTO 2.0); Holger Hestermeyer (Trade Dispute settlement without the WTO?); Tomohiko Kobayashi and Yuka Fukunaga (Like a Rolling Stone: Exploring Viable Options for Adjusting the WTO Dispute Settlement Mechanism to the Changing Environment); Qingjan Kong (The Discourse on Fair Trade and its Implication: From Domestic Rules to International Rules); Jurgen Kurtz (Past as Prologue? Historical Parallels and Discontinuities in Modern Trade Wars); Jaemin Lee (What Can We Learn from Our Struggling Nephew?—Recent Discussions on Reform of International Investment Law and Investment Dispute Settlement Proceedings); Simon Lester (The Return of Cordell Hull); Meredith Lewis (From an Omnilateral to Multilateral or Multilateral to Plurilateral Future); Chin Leng Lim (Geneva Still Inspires: The Idea of an Appellate Mechanism for Investment Arbitration); Tsai-yu Lin (Transforming WTO to play a ICSID-like function for FTA disputes in a decentralized trade order); Mitsuo Matsushita (The WTO Shares the Governance of International Trade with FTAs and Other International Organizations); Gregory Messenger (How not to trip over your robes: lessons for a post-WTO dispute settlement system); Andrew Mitchell and Tania Voon (Regulating Cross-Border Data Flows in a Post-WTO World); Junji Nakagawa (A Long and Winding Road toward WTO2.0: Focusing on Its Function as a Forum for Trade Negotiation and Rule-making); James Nedumpara (Rise of Import Substitution Subsidies/Local Content Requirements in Post-WTO Dystopian World); Federico Ortino (Incorporating foreign investment in a future/new WTO); Shin-yi Peng (A New Trade Regime for the Servitization of

most part not invited as the project sought to ensure that its findings and conclusions might not be viewed as tainted by state or organisational self-interests—even given that such presenters typically would note and believe that their presentations only reflected their own personal views and not those of their employers. It was also felt that such a hard subject, one that government officials cannot even begin to voice for fear it would hasten the end of the WTO, was one particularly suited to and indeed one that is the duty of academics to raise and discuss when others cannot do so.

Due to the different locations of the workshops, regional perspectives were explicitly and implicitly reflected in the explorations, though there is a need for further and deeper opportunities for perspectives from developing countries which may have been less well represented due to the lack of funding to support their participation at the workshops.[3]

The workshop participants were instructed that the workshops (and consequently this collection of some of the papers) were to presuppose (whether correct or not) that the WTO either:

a) Stagnates into the foreseeable future (Doha withers, no new Rounds, at best a few minor amendments, and little new jurisprudence (due to the effective collapse of the DSB)) or
b) Falls apart completely.

While all participants uniformly believed that neither of those possibilities would be desirable, it was generally conceded that neither is inconceivable. After all, the historic sudden collapse of the Soviet Union and the end of the Cold War tells us that anything is possible (in 1986 no one foresaw the end of the Cold War—a much bigger event than simply the demise of the WTO and the current IELO). Similarly, just a year or two before the COVID-19 pandemic, Brexit or the election of Trump

Manufacturing); Colin Picker (Conceiving Utopian and Dystopian Post-WTO Regimes and Environments: Methods, Theories, and Approaches); Rostam J. Neuwirth (GAIA 2048—A 'Glocal Agency in Anthropocene': Cognitive and Institutional Change as 'Legal Science Fiction'); Sonia Elise Roland and David Trubek (A Development Driven Post WTO World); Engela Schlemmer (The demise of multilateralism and the rise of sovereignty); Fiona Smith (Dystopian Food Trade: A Future Without the WTO); Peter-Tobias Stoll (Saving world economic order bottom-up: a network of RTAs/PTAs); Akihiko Tamura (How to Re-construct the Global Trade Order—Awaking a Normativity-aspiring Part of the Soul of the Global Citizens in the Time of Identity Politics and Sustainability); Lisa Toohey (A human centered system of International Economic Law—could we design a self-executing WTO 2.0 that was human focused?); Joel Trachtman (Addressing the WTO's Legislative Capacity Gap); Elizabeth Trujillo (Retaining Normative Impact Post-WTO through Fragmentation); Markus Wagner (The Re-Multilateralization of International Trade Law? Prospects for a post-WTO Era); Heng Wang (The Int'l Governance Crisis and Post-WTO: A China-US G2 FTA as a Solution?); Rolf Weber (A New Trade Regime for Digital Assets); Jason Webb Yackee (Diplomacy as an Alternative to Law: Lessons from French Investment Disputes in Post-Colonial Africa in the 1960s/1970s); Weihuan Zhou (Theory of Distortions and Welfare as the Backbone of the WTO: If We Lose the Form, Do We Lose the Essence?).

[3]The workshops had academics from Australia, Austria, China, France, Germany, Hong Kong, India, Israel, Italy, Japan, Macau, Malaysia, Mexico, Portugal, Singapore, South Africa, South Korea, Switzerland, Taiwan, Turkey, United Kingdom, United States, and Uruguay.

no one foresaw those eventualities and the significant consequences that would ensue from them. And so, the participants agreed that there is value in being prepared for a worst case or dystopian scenario for the WTO. Accordingly, it was felt that despite our commitments to multilateralism and specifically to a vibrant and dynamic WTO, it was nonetheless time that academics in our field began to seriously discuss what a post-WTO world could look like—both from utopian and dystopian perspectives. We thus could begin to contribute to what might be needed for the IELO in the future, or better yet, through these grim scenarios or idea of reform, actually help save the WTO and the commitment to a rule of law multilateralism for our fields.

Some papers can clearly be seen to have tackled the dystopian[4] or utopian[5] predictions, while others, reflecting the inevitable blurring of the ideas, straddle both utopian and dystopian perspectives.[6] The current collection comprises but a fraction of all the presentations and papers due to the tight timeframe employed for this book to ensure that a publication was able to be disseminated quickly so as to play a role in the ongoing development of the field at this critical time in its life. It is hoped that the other works prepared for the project will appear individually or perhaps even as a second later volume covering these issues.

This introduction will lay out some of the general parameters and methodological approaches that are relevant for this sort of work, by the current chapters in this collection, the other presentations at the workshops (an earlier version of this paper was available to them), and most critically by future scholars and policy makers that will be confronting this reality—a WTO under intense pressure, a WTO that might not survive. There is no question that scholars and policy makers will be tackling these issues in the years to come, regardless of the resolution of the current crises at the WTO, and hence this chapter is intended to provide some scaffolding that could be employed for those later works.

2 Project Conceptual Issues (e.g., Methodological and Theoretical Bases)

This project, as well as the works to come addressing the possibilities in a post-WTO world are and will not necessarily be trying to predict the future—clearly an impossible task.[7] Rather, what this project and related works are doing is to present possibilities of what a future for the international economic legal order (IELO) could

[4]See e.g. in this volume, Bradly Condon, To Dystopia and Beyond: The WTO in a Warming Megaregional World.

[5]See e.g. in this volume, Sonia Elise Roland and David Trubek, A Development-Driven Post-WTO World.

[6]See e.g. in this volume, Gabriel Gari, Narrowed Down Utopia: Adjusting the WTO to a Changing Trade Environment.

[7]Though, see Rescher (1998).

look like when just one factor, albeit a large one, is taken out of the equation. In this case—what the future could look like if a healthy or robust WTO no longer existed.

The consequence of such a change could result in all sorts of possible futures, from dystopian to utopian IELOs, or perhaps that the overall status quo within the IELO is not in fact altered! Indeed, it can easily be imagined that a future without a "live" WTO might rather continue largely as now, maintaining the rough status quo. Such a scenario leads to the somewhat tongue-in-cheek question of "whether anyone would notice if the WTO ceased to exist". But, by the way we have positioned our project, namely by seeking utopian or dystopian consequences of the demise of the WTO, the project is searching to explore two opposites from this thought exercise (a thought exercise that is perhaps becoming ever more real each year). Both are somewhat extreme sets of scenarios, even as the project seeks to explore what might be the consequences of a WTO-less world.

Hence, this project's approach, varying one factor within the environment, and seeing what the consequences may be, is somewhat akin to counterfactual analyses. Though, it should be noted that counterfactual analyses are usually set in the past (e.g., what would have happened had Hitler's parents never met). But, unlike the complex methodological demands for well-presented counterfactuals,[8] we have a relatively easy set of circumstances, namely, our timeline is sufficiently short and we can work with just one factor changed (the role or character of the WTO). We can also assume that the actors, principles and so on are largely consistent over the short time frame we are considering—say across the next 10 years. Nonetheless, scholars engaging in this sort of exercise might be well served to consider the many developed counterfactual methodological tools.

More directly, what of predicting the future? Clearly an impossible task, and yet in so many ways one which is repeatedly attempted—whether through academic exercises or through the machinations of forward-looking regulations and laws. But, for the explicit attempt, among the many approaches one could take three are briefly laid out below, though constrained to a 5–20 year time frame (otherwise it is too soon or too far off).[9] The three approaches consist of:

1. Identification of the choices (the 'forks in the road') the field faces in the future;
2. Identification of the complex questions (not the binary questions reflected in the "forks" above) the field must answer in the future which will help to lay out the ground upon which the future will unfold; and
3. Identification of the forces and pressures (by states, corporations, etc.) that will help to determine the future of the field.

[8]See e.g. Tetlock and Belkin (1996), pp. 1–39.

[9]These approaches (including explaining why the timeframe should be between 5 and 20 years) are developed more fully in a draft article available at SSRN. See Picker CB (2020) Predicting the Future of International Trade Law. Available at SSRN: https://papers.ssrn.com/sol3/papers.cfm?abstract_id=3542889.

Utilising these three approaches, and others,[10] can provide some rigour for such predictions in our field.

Of course, scholars investigating the consequences of a post-WTO world may draw on a wide range of methodologies and perspectives. Indeed, over the course of the three workshops a variety of those methodologies were utilised—though given that most legal research publications do not discuss their methodological approaches,[11] those approaches are more often not explicitly noted, and would need to be gleaned from the papers. Doctrinal approaches have been and would be the primary approach[12]—given that approach dominates legal research, even though employed it typically remains unstated in most legal research publications.[13]

Comparative methodologies were also commonly employed, particularly via comparison with how other fields have weathered similar environments (e.g. how has investment survived and thrived (or not) with no overarching multilateral organization or agreed rules).[14] Though, for those employing comparative methodologies, the usual pitfalls that should be avoided should be considered.[15] Empirical methods appear to be unlikely to be employed in the sort of studies considered here given the forward nature of the exercise. Other methodologies as applied to this project find bases in, among others, socio-legal,[16] technological,[17] economic,[18] and historical approaches.[19]

Of course, the methodological bases should not be (though too often are) confused with what might be the theoretical bases of the works. Though, we should note here that for purposes of this short introduction we will conflate theoretical bases of research with the perspectives brought to bear on the research or the paradigms laid over or around the research. We concede they are different from each other, but for the brief purposes presented here they are sufficiently akin to each other. Regardless, while the methodological approaches are typically less clearly presented in legal

---

[10]See e.g. the approach taken in this volume, Rostam J. Neuwirth, GAIA 2048—A 'Glocal Agency in Anthropocene': Cognitive and Institutional Change as 'Legal Science Fiction'.

[11]Picker (2013), pp. 21–48 (discussing potential reasons for death of discussions on methodological bases of research in IEL).

[12]While subject to different characterisations as to what is a doctrinal analysis, an example in this collection could be said to be that of Elisa Baroncini's work in Chap. 7. For an excellent explanation of what is and the role of doctrinal analysis in law, see Roux (2014), pp. 178 et seq.

[13]Shaffer (2008), p. 30. See also Trachtman (2008), p. 45.

[14]See e.g. in this volume, Jaemin Lee, What Can We Learn from Our Struggling Cousin? Recent Discussions on Reform of International Investment Law and Investment Dispute Settlement Proceedings.

[15]See e.g. Brand (2007), pp. 405–466; Reitz (1998), pp. 617–636.

[16]See e.g. in this volume, Leïla Choukroune, The Concern with non-Concerns: For the End of Trade Dystopia, could be said to include socio-legal perspectives and approaches.

[17]See e.g. in this volume, Rolf Weber, A New International Trade Framework for Digital Assets.

[18]See e.g. in this volume, James Nedumpara and Akshaya Venkataraman, The Rise of Import Substitution Subsidies and Local Content Requirements in a Dystopian WTO 2.0 Regime.

[19]See e.g. in this volume, Simon Lester Waiting for Cordell Hull.

research papers, the theoretical/perspective/paradigm bases are more often explicitly laid out or easily identified from their implicit centrality to the research output. Perhaps the more common theoretical/perspective/paradigms bases that will be present are liberal-economic, neoliberal, public choice theory, law and development, critical theoretical perspectives, feminist perspectives, and so on.[20]

3 Approaches

At a more tangible methodological level, the following are some of the potential approaches that were taken at the workshops and some that might be taken in future to tease out possible utopian and dystopian futures that result from the demise or stagnation of the WTO.

3.1 Utopian

To construct a utopian successor to the WTO there are, among other approaches, two fundamental directions that can be considered:

1. Identification of what might have been fundamentally negative aspects of the WTO and the environment that it propagated; and
2. Identification of the potential goals or objectives for any potential successor institution(s) to the WTO.

Each is considered in greater detail below.

3.1.1 Fundamental Negative Features of the WTO

Since even before it formally was launched there has been no shortage of criticisms of the WTO. The criticisms since have covered almost every aspect of the WTO. Perhaps most foundationally, is that some criticisms, most critically from some governments, have argued that there are fundamental, critical or fatal consequences within or around the WTO. In other words, and as described further below, those potential negative features of the WTO were a result of factors or characteristics belonging to or within the WTO (endogenous) or ones external or outside of the WTO (exogenous).

---

[20]Public choice theory is clearly a major part of the theoretical basis found in this volume, see e.g. in this volume, Brett Williams and Weihuan Zhou, If the WTO were to Break Down Completely, Would We Stoop and Build it up with Worn-Out Tools?.

As one considers the failure of the WTO leading to the post-WTO, identifying any relevant causes that might have been endogenous could be helpful in constructing a utopian successor regime that should ideally better manage any internal problematic challenges or not then include those contributing fatal characteristics. Concededly, it may have been difficult to establish a consensus on what issues or features were or are still fundamentally negative within the WTO. Views vary in this respect depending on normative perspectives, individual interactions with the WTO and the IELO, the ideological background of the critic, the timeframe or period under consideration, and so on. Indeed, it may be that some features noted as negative by one WTO expert might be considered by other WTO experts as actually being one of the WTO's positive attributes. Adding complexity is that experts may differ on the degree of negativity and harm, with some believing a feature's harm is so fundamental that it may be directly responsible for the current potentially fatal crisis facing the WTO. Indeed, given the list of possible negative characteristics of the WTO any such lists could be quite lengthy.

The below includes a partial list of some of the outward facing endogenous factors that may have led or are in danger of leading to the demise or stagnation of the WTO:

- It was an organisation based on outdated approaches (e.g., a 1980s approach to multilateralism or an early 1990s commitment to the international rule of law);
- It did not respond to changed and changing circumstances (e.g., much of the technological advances are largely unmanaged by the WTO);
- Many individual states felt left out or disenfranchised (e.g., smaller economies in particular);
- Developing states felt the WTO Agreements and processes did not adequately support their interests (e.g., failure to advance agricultural liberalization);
- Many civil society groups felt their interests were not reflected (e.g., trade and the environment);
- One or two countries or regional blocks dominated to the detriment of the rest (e.g., the US and the EU in particular);
- Businesses and industry were inordinately influential (e.g., in the areas of intellectual property);
- Trade in agriculture was insufficiently a part of the regime (e.g., little advance beyond the Agreement on Agriculture);
- Preferential Trade agreements ("PTAs") displaced the WTO and/or undermined the WTO (e.g., the focus on bilateral and regional agreements even as the WTO never advanced);
- It failed to properly address the trade linkage debate and/or include related/connected regimes (e.g. environmentalism, labour and human rights); and
- It did not address the uncompensated externalities of the IELO (e.g. environmental consequences);

No doubt the above list could be extended, but it is sufficient for this work and aspects of all of the above were found somewhere among many of the workshop presentations and in some of the works included in this volume, even as those presentations and the chapters provided additional examples or issues.

In addition, within the WTO Agreements, processes, culture and approaches there are potentially a whole host of very particular or specific issues and inward facing endogenous factors which may have had a disproportionate impact in producing some of the broad negative effects (and affects) on the WTO. Some might include:

- The "consensus rule" for "legislative" change or reform;
- The adherence to the "single undertaking" approach to negotiations;
- The "negative consensus" rule for adoption of DSB reports;
- Essentially no retrospective/retroactive compensation upon finalisation of disputes by the DSB;
- The many suggested failings of the AB and panels, which could provide a long list of its own here (see EU's recent reform proposal[21]);
- Lack or insufficient compliance of "reporting requirements" by some members (e.g., subsidies); and
- Failure to enforce GATT Article XXIV sufficiently (and the weakness of the RTA committee);

However, what if one felt there were no negatives or few negatives of any significance? And that the demise of the WTO was due to exogenous factors that undermined the WTO. In fairness, it could be argued that any successor regime would also have these forces acting on it and so then we need to consider how to structure a utopian successor that would then be able to manage those exogenous factors. To do so we need to understand what those exogenous factors might have been or are likely to be so that a successor regime could then be developed to cope with them. Among many others, they could have been things like:

- The rise of populism and populist leaders (e.g. the U.S.'s President Donald Trump and the U.K.'s Prime Minister Boris Johnson);
- The rise of RTAs/PTAs/FTAs (e.g., the Comprehensive and Progressive Agreement for Trans-Pacific Partnership (CPTPP or TPP11) or the East Asian Regional Comprehensive Economic Partnership (RCEP));
- Unanticipated technology related trade issues (e.g., the role of data in the economy);
- Globalisation of supply chains;
- The rise of internet platformers (e.g., Google, Amazon and Facebook)
- Geopolitical changes (the rise of Russia, India and China since the birth of the WTO);
- Lingering poverty and uneven economic development;
- Population movements and demographic challenges;

[21] WTO, Communication from the European Union, China, Canada, India, Norway, New Zealand, Switzerland, Australia, Republic of Korea, Iceland, Singapore And Mexico to the General Council (26 November 2018) WT/GC/W/752. Available at http://trade.ec.europa.eu/doclib/docs/2018/november/tradoc_157514.pdf.

- Aggravated climate change;
- Ideological challenges to market-based economic theories; and
- The “Great Recession” or Global Financial Crisis.

The above list merely records the past exogenous factors—all of which are still relevant and which would need to be taken into account in any successor regime. Many of these factors were raised in some of the presentations and in some of the chapters in this volume, even as they raised other factors. And so, in addition, any successor regime would need to anticipate or be constructed with sufficient versatility and agility to handle the unanticipated exogenous forces that will arise in the future. Of course, predicting what those would be and how they would be managed is a difficult task.

Once these endogenous and exogenous factors have been identified, and a hierarchy assigned to them (necessarily identifying which were most critical/least critical), then one can begin to develop how a successor regime would have to manage these, with those most critical being most important to be rectified in any new regime(s). Of course, what is really behind this project is the idea that the insights and conclusions developed by considering a post-WTO could actually be brought to bear to help save the WTO—and so any developments supposedly for use by a successor regime could hopefully be employed to help save the WTO.

3.1.2 Identify the Goals or Fundamental Character of the Successor Regime

Identifying the goals or character of a successor utopian regime is necessary in order to know how to properly construct it and to consider how best to develop/nurture it in order to ensure its viability and sustainability. Of course, one could simply take the goals of the WTO as the goals for the successor regime, but what if those goals were fatally too limited or overly expansive and hence were themselves tied up in the failings of the WTO? Reassessing the successor regime(s) goals would thus be a useful exercise.

The goals or character of the regime can span a wide range, with diametrically opposed goals or characteristics possible. The below show some of these opposed goals/characters—some of which may have been thought to have been resolved with the birth of the WTO, but which are today subject to debate again. Of course, the below reflect the extremes, and the goals or approaches could take any point in between those listed approaches:

- A purely economic focus versus a holistic focus for the organisation (e.g. including environmental or human rights);
- Rule-of-Law or legalistic dispute resolution versus diplomatic resolution of disputes;
- Elevation of the global or multilateral interests at the expense of state or local interests;

- A robust and dynamic legislative body versus strict retention of control by states for changes to the commitments;
- An institution of broad competence and coverage (e.g. including competition law, investment law, etc.) versus a narrow one or at the most minimal a simple treaty

Each of these and other goals formed part of the analyses of many of the presentations and in some of the chapters in this volume. The variety of goals proffered may itself be a major challenge for the current and any future regimes. Regardless, once the goals have been identified and ranked, if possible, then they too can be the basis by which aspects of a new regime could be constructed. And in keeping with the goal of saving the WTO, it might be relevant for reform of the WTO as well!

3.2 *Dystopian*

When considering a dystopian IELO following the demise or irrelevance of the WTO, among the many approaches that could be taken are the following three that get to the heart of the critical issues that should be considered:

1. Identification of those parts of the WTO that were successful and positive and hence likely absent in a dystopian future;
2. Identification of what might be the consequences if the positives delivered by the WTO were not replaced/substituted with approaches/regimes or devices that would have delivered an equivalent positive impact within the IELO; and
3. Identification of devices, institutions or approaches which might replace the WTO to deliver the equivalent role within the IELO.

3.2.1 Successful or Positive Aspects of the WTO

Again, like the above discussion of negative aspects of the WTO, determination of what was/is positive or successful in or by the WTO will likely be subject to considerable debate. There are differences of opinion once again varying with ideological, personal and experiential differences. Those differences were clearly visible in the different perspectives presented at the workshops and can also be found in the different perspectives found within this volume.[22] Regardless, the below list could be viewed as endogenous positive or successful aspects of the WTO that would then either be absent in an imagined dystopian future or if possible should be reproduced/replaced by non-WTO means in a dystopian future that had no or an irrelevant WTO:

[22]E.g. compare in this volume, the works of Leïla Choukroune, The Concern with non-Concerns: For the End of Trade Dystopia, with that of Simon Lester, Waiting for Cordell Hull.

- Peaceful resolution of international trade disputes;
- Rule of Law governing international trade regulation;
- Development of trade law through jurisprudence;
- Sustaining multilateral approaches in the face of plurilateral challenges;
- Stopping increases in trade barriers;
- Reduction in trade barriers;
- Maintenance of lower or minimal trade barriers;
- Non-discrimination in tariffs and other trade measures; and
- Transparency in domestic trade regulations;

Once the positive characteristics or activities have been identified, and a hierarchy assigned to them (which would be the most critical/least critical), then one can begin to figure out how they could be replaced or reproduced, or their absence mitigated in a post-WTO IELO.

3.2.2 Consequences of Not Replacing Those Positives

While the best approach would be to reproduce or mitigate the lost positive attributes of the WTO, it is not unlikely that a successor regime to the WTO would struggle to do so. This is likely to be the case, at least in the short term, as many of the critiques and critics of the current regime, the WTO, would stand in the way of constructing a robust successor regime. As such, a post WTO IELO will likely not include those positive attributes or not include them to the same extent or reach. Even PTAs, the most likely forms of successor regimes to the WTO as noted in some of the works in this volume,[23] while they may include the positive attributes, will only do so between the members of the PTA, and not even for them when they interact with states outside the PTA. Of course, it would also be absent for the IEL interactions between states who are not members of those PTAs.

Accordingly, when considering a dystopian IELO following the collapse or slide into irrelevance of the WTO each of the positive attributes lost would need to be examined in order to figure out the consequences for the IELO. It is likely that those consequences would be far reaching, not only within the IELO, but even intruding into local domestic economic orders. Indeed, there would possibly be knock-on effects into the non-IELO regimes including geopolitics, and so on. Of course, considering just the impact of the absence of one positive consequence of the WTO in the IELO (and within domestic economic orders) would be so complex that it alone would be sufficient to require a chapter or essay all of its own. Accordingly, researchers in the future could, if they wished, just pick one lost positive role of the WTO and examine the consequences to their logical, and perhaps even illogical or irrational, conclusions. I say illogical or irrational for when dealing with humans, governments and participants in economies we know that *homo*

[23]See e.g. in this volume, Engela Schlemmer, A Possible Hierarchy of Dispute Settlement Systems? and Peter-Tobias Stoll, Saving the World Trade Order from the Bottom Up: A Role for Preferential Trade Agreements.

rationalis (*homo economicus*) is only present in unrealistic and sterile economic models.

Of course, perhaps not all is gloom and doom. While there would certainly be negative consequences of the loss of those positive WTO attributes, there may also be offsetting positives from the loss of the negative attributes of the WTO (see Part 3.1.1 above). So, while still a dystopian IELO, the issues raised by the loss of the WTO and its negative sides should also be studied, and would also be sufficiently complex and far reaching to deserve their own study. And as repeatedly noted above, the insights from such dystopian analyses may ultimately help to save the WTO by showing the dire consequences of letting the WTO expire or become irrelevant.

3.3 Substitutes to Fill the Void Left by a Lost WTO

The identification of devices, institutions or approaches which might replace the WTO to deliver the equivalent role within the IELO is clearly a critical component when considering how the IELO will survive or function in a post-WTO world. Some of the chapters in this collection have taken this approach,[24] particularly through suggestions that international investment law should be looked at for possible models of a part of the IEL that has survived, perhaps even thrived, despite having a regime that is fragmented and mostly not multilateral.[25]

Another possibility to fill that void suggested in the collection focuses on the ability of the many different PTA regimes to both fill the substantive needs of the IELO (albeit on a non-multilateral basis) as well as stepping into the dispute resolution void that already exists given the current suspension of the WTO's AB to function.[26]

Future researchers may find that identifying substitutes to fulfil the roles of the WTO is the most critical and time sensitive part of the entire set of issues to be researched in a post-WTO world. After all, one should first ensure the IELO functions at a basic level, and then turn to restoring or building further the more sophisticated and progressive aspects of the IELO that is needed to ensure the most efficient and effective IELO.

Again, research and consideration of what might be replacements or substitutes for a lost WTO will actually help the WTO to survive its current challenges—for it becomes immediately clear that there are no easy or available substitutes to carry out the functions of the WTO, even as flawed or ineffective as one might have considered the WTO.

---

[24]See e.g. in this volume, Rolf Weber, A New International Trade Framework for Digital Assets.

[25]See e.g. in this volume, Chin Leng Lim, Reaching for Utopia, Geneva as Inspiration for Investment Disputes?.

[26]See e.g. in this volume, Tomohiko Kobayashi and Yuka Fukunaga, Like a Rolling Stone: Exploring Viable Options for the WTO Dispute Settlement Mechanism to Evolve Forward in the Post-WTO Era.

4 Conclusion

The above are merely some potential approaches to what is a somewhat difficult and different exercise for many of the academics in our field. While these exercises may push some out of their comfort zone, forcing them to consider worst-case (and, if they desire, best-case) scenarios resulting from the loss or irrelevance of a beloved institution (the WTO, warts and all), it is nonetheless a vital task. After all, the many different ideas, reflecting imaginations unleashed, that were generated at the workshops, some of which are present in this collection and those works that will be inspired by this collection, will be useful not only if one were ever to look to models for a successor regime, but they could also suggest avenues for reform of the WTO—rescuing it from irrelevance or destruction. And perhaps even more critically, the dystopian examples would hopefully show the horrors that might arise if the WTO is allowed to fail, encouraging our policy makers to redouble their efforts to save the WTO.

References

Brand O (2007) Conceptual comparisons: towards a coherent methodology of comparative legal studies. Brook J Int Law 32(2):405–466

Picker CB (2013) Comparative legal cultural analyses of international economic law: a new methodological approach. Chin J Comp Law 1(1):21–48

Reitz CJ (1998) How to do comparative law. Am J Comp Law 46(1):617–636

Rescher N (1998) Predicting the future: an introduction to the theory of forecasting. State University of New York Press, Albany

Roux TR (2014) Judging the quality of legal research: a qualified response to the demand for greater methodological rigour. Leg Educ Rev 24(1):177–204

Shaffer G (2008) A new legal realism: method in international economic law scholarship. In: Picker CB, Bunn ID, Arner D (eds) International economic law-the state and future of the discipline. Hart, Portland, pp 29–42

Tetlock PE, Belkin A (1996) Counterfactual thought experiments in world politics: logical, methodological and psychological perspectives. In: Tetlock PE, Belkin A (eds) Counterfactual thought experiments in world politics: logical, methodological and psychological perspectives. Princeton University Press, Princeton, pp 1–39

Trachtman JP (2008) International economic law research: a taxonomy. In: Picker CB, Bunn ID, Arner D (eds) International economic law-the state and future of the discipline. Hart, Portland, pp 43–52

Part II
The Post-WTO: Macro and Theoretical Perspectives

To Dystopia and Beyond: The WTO in a Warming Megaregional World

Bradly J. Condon

Contents

> There's no real way to know what will happen except by looking at roughly similar catastrophes in the past, which have left the Earth a graveyard of failed species. We burn some of them to drive our cars.—Roy Scranton[1]

1 Introduction

This chapter will highlight the linkages between the climate crisis and trade negotiations in a dystopic post-WTO world. It will argue that the window of opportunity to achieve an effective multilateral trade regime has closed and will be sealed shut by accelerating climate change. The post-WTO regime is a megaregional regime, and it will exclude those countries that do not get on board before the destabilizing effects

WTO Chair Professor, Department of Law of the Instituto Tecnológico Autónomo de México (ITAM).

[1]Scranton R (2019) Lessons from a genocide can prepare humanity for climate apocalypse. MIT Technology Review, Apr 24, 2019, https://www.technologyreview.com/s/613343/lessons-from-a-genocide-can-prepare-humanity-for-climate-apocalypse/.

B. J. Condon (✉)
Department of Law of the Instituto Tecnológico Autónomo de México (ITAM), Mexico City, Mexico
e-mail: bcondon@itam.mx

M. K. Lewis et al. (eds.), *A Post-WTO International Legal Order*,
https://doi.org/10.1007/978-3-030-45428-9_2

of the climate crisis make their inclusion impossible to achieve. Geopolitical shifts destabilized the WTO regime and have led to its collapse. The effects of the climate crisis will be even more dramatic. This chapter examines the (not even) worst-case scenario for the post-WTO twenty-first century, in order to highlight the importance of managing the risk of catastrophic economic, ecological and security consequences arising from the convergence of multilateral institution failure and the worsening climate crisis.

2 Climate Change and Its Impact on the Post-WTO Trade Regime

While scientists cannot predict the future climate with precision, the range of probabilities points to a global increase of the average temperature of between 2.6 °C (4.7 F) and 4.8 °C (8.6 F) between 2000 and 2100 (that is, in addition to the warming that already occurred up to 2000).[2] Land will warm faster than ocean, and the Arctic will warm faster than the tropics.[3] Climate change could cause abrupt changes, including to the Atlantic meridional overturning circulation (AMOC), Arctic sea ice, the Greenland ice sheet, the Amazon forest and monsoonal circulations, as it has in the past in periods of much slower climate change.[4] Melting of the Greenland and Antarctic ice sheets may accelerate into a sudden loss of large amounts of ice, leading to dramatic changes in sea level and ocean circulation.[5] Indeed, a catastrophic sea level increase is already unstoppable.[6] New measurements have increased estimates of vulnerable coastal populations (based on 2010 population numbers); under a high emissions scenario, up to 630 million people live on land below year 2100 projected annual flood levels of 2 m, the majority in developing countries across Asia.[7]

Melting Arctic permafrost could rapidly release methane, which would create a feedback loop of increased warming that releases further methane emissions. Recent research shows that eroding coastal permafrost (about one third of the Earth's total coastline) releases significant quantities of CO2, adding a new source of GHG

[2]Collins et al. (2013), pp. 1029–1136.

[3]Collins et al. (2013).

[4]Collins et al. (2013).

[5]Bamber et al. (2019), pp. 11195–11200; Holland et al. (2019).

[6]Englander J (2019) Rising Sea Level: The crisis on our doorstep, The Royal Institution – London, 11 February 2019. https://www.johnenglander.net/sea-level-rise-blog/my-royal-institution-video-goes-viral/.

[7]Kulp SA, Strauss BH (2019) New elevation data triple estimates of global vulnerability to sea-level rise and coastal flooding, 10 Nature Communications, Article number: 4844 (29 October 2019), https://www.nature.com/articles/s41467-019-12808-z.

emissions caused by increased warming.[8] In addition, when seawater becomes too saturated with CO2 to absorb any more, the rate of greenhouse warming will increase dramatically.[9] Sea temperatures are increasing at an accelerating rate (the five warmest years since 1955 were 2015–2019) and are now at their warmest in recorded human history, which is an indicator of accelerating global warming and poses high risks to biodiversity and fisheries.[10] The oceans store over 90% of warming and increased ocean temperatures lead to rising sea levels via thermal expansion and melting land ice. Interconnected tipping points in the climate system are more likely than previously thought and risk long-term irreversible changes. We could exceed the threshold for a cascade of tipping points between 1 and 2 °C of warming.[11] Since we are already more than 1 °C above pre-industrial levels,[12] the risk of unstoppable and catastrophic climate change is now a clear and present danger.

To meet the goal of the Paris Climate Agreement, to limit global warming "to well below 2 °C above pre-industrial levels and to pursue efforts to limit the temperature increase to 1.5 °C above pre-industrial levels", global emissions must peak by 2020.[13] The most recent estimate from the United Nations concludes that there is only a 66% chance that warming will be limited to 3.2 °C by 2100 (range 3.0–3.5 °C) if all unconditional Nationally Determined Contributions under the Paris Agreement are implemented.[14]

Science can observe the effects of catastrophic climate events, such as drought and floods. Human innovations can move the dial, for example with crops genetically modified to withstand more drought or improved irrigation systems. However, climate change threatens the four pillars of food security: availability (yield and production), access (prices and ability to obtain food), utilization (nutrition and cooking), and stability (disruptions to availability).[15] Recent research shows that rice yields will drop 39% further than previously estimated, due to climate-induced

---

[8]Tanski et al. (2019).

[9]National Center for Atmospheric Research/University Corporation for Atmospheric Research (2019) Predictions of Future Global Climate, https://scied.ucar.edu/longcontent/predictions-future-global-climate.

[10]Cheng et al. (2020), pp. 137–142.

[11]Lenton TM et al., Climate tipping points—too risky to bet against, Nature, 27 November 2019, https://www.nature.com/articles/d41586-019-03595-0.

[12]Climate Central, The Globe Is Already Above 1 °C, on Its Way to 1.5 °C, 9 October 2018, https://www.climatecentral.org/gallery/graphics/the-globe-is-already-above-1c.

[13]Revill C et al. (2017) The Climate Turning Point, http://www.mission2020.global/climate-turning-point/.

[14]UN Environment Programme (2019) Emissions Gap Report 2019, 26 November 2019, https://wedocs.unep.org/bitstream/handle/20.500.11822/30797/EGR2019.pdf?sequence=1&isAllowed=y, 27.

[15]IPCC (2019) Climate Change and Land, an IPCC special report on climate change, desertification, land degradation, sustainable land management, food security, and greenhouse gas fluxes in terrestrial ecosystems https://www.ipcc.ch/report/srccl/.

changes in soil arsenic behaviour and plant response.[16] More than half of the global population depends on rice for subsistence.[17] Infants will face potentially permanent effects of undernutrition.[18]

Science can attribute extreme weather events to climate change, such as the record-breaking heatwaves in Europe in June and July of 2019[19] and the catastrophic bushfires in Australia that began later the same year.[20] However, if technology develops effective approaches to mitigation and adaptation, we might experience less than the worst-case scenario. Recent research is not encouraging, since it tends to show that the climate crisis will be worse than previously thought. There are promising new technologies that can consume or remove CO2 from the atmosphere, but they are not yet fully developed. For example, genetically engineered *E. coli* bacteria can feed on CO2.[21] Scientists are developing materials that can convert CO2 into usable products.[22] There is also a process to convert atmospheric CO2 to fuel, but that only achieves net zero emissions.[23] We are also developing clean energy sources and zero emissions vehicles. Nevertheless, it is too early to tell how effective such technological solutions will be in a world with well over 400 ppm of CO2 in the atmosphere that is on the verge releasing a cascade of tipping points that lead to unstoppable and catastrophic climate change.

As a result of the ever-shifting range of possible climate change scenarios, the time frame for this chapter's predictions is not precise. Science can show us how to mitigate climate change, how to adapt to climate change and point to factors that make one country, or one population, more vulnerable than another. However, the degree of climate change and the speed with which it takes place will depend on political will and technological developments, as well as an unforeseeable magnitude of shifts in the climate system.

My predictions regarding the effects of the climate crisis are based on scientific evidence. My predictions for the world trading system are based on speculation

[16]Muehe EM et al., Rice production threatened by coupled stresses of climate and soil arsenic 10 Nature Communications, Article number: 4985 (1 November 2019), https://www.nature.com/articles/s41467-019-12946-4.

[17]International Rice Research Institute (2016) Leading Innovations, Annual Report 2016, http://books.irri.org/AR2016_content.pdf.

[18]Watts et al. (2019), pp. 1836–1878.

[19]Vautard R et al. (2019) Human contribution to the record-breaking July 2019 heatwave in Western Europe, https://www.worldweatherattribution.org/wp-content/uploads/July2019heatwave.pdf.

[20]Nature Editorial (2020), pp. 449–450.

[21]Gleizer et al. (2019).

[22]Nield D (2019) Scientists Create a Material That Captures CO2 And Turns It Into Organic Matter, https://www.sciencealert.com/scientists-create-a-material-that-converts-co2-into-useful-organic-matter.

[23]Conca J (2019) Carbon Engineering – Taking CO2 Right Out Of The Air To Make Gasoline, Forbes, 8 October 2019, https://www.forbes.com/sites/jamesconca/2019/10/08/carbon-engineering-taking-co2-right-out-of-the-air-to-make-gasoline/#334cf22f13cc.

regarding political responses to the likely consequences of catastrophic climate change, such as mass migration and catastrophic crop failures. Taken together, these elements reduce the likelihood of a successful round of multilateral trade negotiations, which in turn does not bode well for future of the WTO dispute settlement system.[24] However, the success of multilateral trade negotiations is likely to be the least of our worries in the near future. We are facing an existential threat to civilization and our survival as a species.[25] There are precedents in human history for climate-induced civilization collapse.[26] Those precedents pale in comparison to the magnitude of the climate risks we now face.

3 The Post-WTO Trade Regime and BRICS+ Countries

The rule making function of the WTO has migrated to megaregional free trade agreements, such as the TPP/CPTPP and the Trans-Atlantic Trade and Investment Partnership (TTIP). These megaregions include the group formally known as the "Quad": Canada, Europe, Japan and the United States (assuming the United States chooses to return to the CPTPP and TTIP negotiations restart and succeed). Prior to the creation of the WTO, the Quad led the rule-making function for the GATT. In that sense, the post-WTO rule-making regime for trade agreements resembles the GATT era. With the weakening of the WTO dispute settlement mechanism, the resemblance to the GATT era is complete.

The megaregional regime permits the Quad to evolve the trade system beyond the 1980s, without countries like Brazil, Russia, India and China (the "BRICs") blocking consensus. In the early years of the megaregional regime, there will be efforts to bring these countries, and other major emerging market countries like Indonesia, Nigeria and South Africa, back to the multilateral table. However, this will have to be preceded by their incorporation into the megaregional regime.

China will be the priority participant, since its trade dwarfs the others. China will be the only possible exception to exclusion from the Quad-led megaregional regime, because of the size of its economy and its geopolitical importance. Bilateral negotiations with the United States will set the stage for China's incorporation into (or exclusion from) the Quad-led megaregional regime.[27] Beyond those negotiations, climate-related trade barriers could be less likely to affect China, due to its progress addressing mitigation. China's total emissions from fossil fuel and

---

[24]Condon (2018), pp. 535–556.

[25]Spratt D, Dunlop I (2019) Existential climate-related security risk: A scenario approach, Breakthrough – National Centre for Climate Restoration | breakthroughonline.org.au, May 2019, https://docs.wixstatic.com/ugd/148cb0_a1406e0143ac4c469196d3003bc1e687.pdf.

[26]Sinha et al. (2019), p. 11.

[27]Brands H, Cooper Z (2019) After the Responsible Stakeholder, What? Debating America's China Strategy 2 Texas National Security Review (February 2019), https://doi.org/10.26153/tsw/1943.

industrial processes are projected to peak 5–10 years ahead of its 2030 target in the Paris Agreement, with carbon emissions peaking for most cities at a per capita GDP (in 2011 purchasing power parity) of US$19,000 to 22,000.[28] Moreover, China is seeking its own megaregional, in the form of the Regional Comprehensive Economic Partnership (RCEP) with the Association of Southeast Asian Nations (ASEAN), Japan, South Korea, Australia and New Zealand. However, India has chosen not to participate and it remains to be seen how the RCEP might take shape.[29]

Brazil, Russia, India, Indonesia, Nigeria and South Africa (BRICs+) will have to get on board or face the prospect of being left to drift into the past with the rest of the WTO membership that remains outside the Quad-led megaregional regime. It is not clear what these countries should have agreed to in order to achieve a successful outcome of the WTO Doha Round, and it is beyond the scope of this chapter to analyze this complex set of issues. Moreover, it is not clear what these countries could do differently now to forestall the dystopian outcome of a climate crisis in a post-WTO world. Indeed, it is likely too late to achieve a successful multilateral negotiation. Had these countries made greater concessions in 2008 to reach a successful Doha Round conclusion, they might have been in a better position today to adapt to future climate impacts, given the important role of trade in goods and services in disseminating technology for climate change adaptation and mitigation.

Mexico is already part of the megaregional regime of the CPTPP and the USMCA and also has free trade agreements with the European Union and Japan, among others. Mexico is likely to remain integrated into the North American market due to its strategic geographic position. Similarly, Turkey is likely to remain integrated into the European market, due to its strategic geographic position. However, their geographic positions are both a blessing and a curse. Turkey is already the country with the most refugees in the world, with close to 4.1 million refugees.[30] Mexico is under pressure to accept more refugees and to do more to prevent migrants from using Mexico as a bridge to the United States.[31] The impact of the climate crisis on migration, together with the changing legal landscape for climate refugees, will only

[28]Wang et al. (2019).

[29]Pant HV, Sarma N (2019) Modi was right. India Isn't Ready for Free Trade. Until the country can address its own economic problems, agreements like the RCEP may do more harm than good. Foreign Policy, 19 November 2019, https://foreignpolicy.com/2019/11/19/modi-pull-out-rcep-india-manufacturers-compete-china/. Also see Suneja K (2020) Govt yet to take call on RCEP meeting invitation, The Economic Times, 22 January 2020, https://economictimes.indiatimes.com/news/economy/foreign-trade/govt-yet-to-take-call-on-rcep-meeting-invitation/articleshow/73507779.cms?utm_source=contentofinterest&utm_medium=text&utm_campaign=cppst.

[30]UNHCR, Global Focus, Turkey, http://reporting.unhcr.org/node/2544.

[31]BBC, Mexico under pressure as asylum applications skyrocket, 15 October 2019, https://www.bbc.com/news/world-latin-america-50040477. Jordan M (2019). Trump Threatens Tariffs on Mexico. Have Any of His Immigration Measures Worked? May 31, 2019. https://www.nytimes.com/2019/05/31/us/border-tariffs-trump-immigration.html.

put Mexico and Turkey under greater pressure.[32] The recent case of the case of Ioane Teitiota has opened the door to considering climate migrants as refugees.[33]

With rule making already shifted to the megaregional regime, dispute settlement will follow. The megaregional dispute settlement system will be more acceptable to the United States than the defunct WTO dispute settlement system came to be. This system will provide the United States with carte blanche to use unilateral trade barriers as bargaining tools in negotiations. Canada and Mexico will harmonize their BRICs+ trade policies with the United States. Indeed, the USMCA requires consultations regarding trade negotiations with China.

A new multilateral global forum for rule making and dispute settlement would require a much greater effort on the part of BRICs+ to achieve consensus than they have made in the WTO context. Assuming that is unlikely, BRICs+ will have to demonstrate sufficient good will to be allowed to participate in the megaregional regime, which is now the only stepping stone available to return to a multilateral system. BRICs+ may try to build trade networks with African, Latin American, and Asian countries that also drift outside the Quad-led megaregional regime, such as the RCEP, but that is not an adequate long-term strategy for them to pursue. It is more of a negotiating strategy, but one that is likely to fail.

As the planet warms, the extent to which second-best international economic policy fails to achieve results will become more apparent to BRICs+. This could motivate them to adopt more flexible bargaining positions, but by then it would be too late. By the time BRICs+ understand the folly of their megaregional and multilateral bargaining positions, a climate-induced financial crisis could further complicate trade negotiations.[34] The stakes will only get higher for the financial system to avoid a climate-driven collapse in asset prices, as climate-related financial risks continue to rise with temperatures and sea levels.[35]

---

[32]The Slow onset effects of climate change and human rights protection for cross-border migrants. Human Rights Council, Thirty-seventh session, 26 February–23 March 2018, Agenda items 2 and 3, Annual report of the United Nations High Commissioner for Human Rights and reports of the Office of the High Commissioner and the Secretary-General, A/HRC/37/CRP.4 (22 March 2018), https://www.ohchr.org/Documents/Issues/ClimateChange/SlowOnset/A_HRC_37_CRP_4.pdf.

[33]United Nations, International Covenant on Civil and Political Rights, Human Rights Committee, Views adopted by the Committee under article 5 (4) of the Optional Protocol, concerning communication No. 2728/2016, Adopted by the Committee at its 127th session (14 October–8 November 2019), CCPR/C/127/D/2728/2016, 7 January 2020, https://tbinternet.ohchr.org/_layouts/15/treatybodyexternal/Download.aspx?symbolno=CCPR%2fC%2f127%2fD%2f2728%2f2016&Lang=en.

[34]Rudebusch GD (2019) Climate Change and the Federal Reserve, FRBSF Economic Letter 2019-09, 25 March 2019, https://www.frbsf.org/economic-research/publications/economic-letter/2019/march/climate-change-and-federal-reserve/. Technological change is likely to add to the risk see Zetzsche DA, Buckley RP, Arner DW (2019) Regulating LIBRA: The Transformative Potential of Facebook's Cryptocurrency and Possible Regulatory Responses (July 11, 2019). European Banking Institute Working Paper Series 2019/44; University of New South Wales Law Research Series UNSWLRS 19-47. Available at SSRN: https://ssrn.com/abstract=3414401.

[35]Carney M (2019) The financial sector must be at the heart of tackling climate change, The Guardian, 17 April 2019, https://www.theguardian.com/commentisfree/2019/apr/17/the-financial-

Climate change may have contributed to the war in Syria, which produced a flood of migrants that set the stage for Brexit and other destabilizing political movements in the EU.[36] Similarly, climate change may have played a role in the flows of migrants from Central America to the United States, which the Trump administration linked to trade by threatening Mexico with trade sanctions for failure to stem the flow of migrants.[37] The effects of the climate crisis will only accelerate from this point on, increasing the politically destabilizing consequences of mass migrations and financial crises.

Continued use of market-distorting subsidies and trade remedies will impede innovation and increase the cost of clean energy technology, slowing the spread of clean energy and hobbling mitigation efforts.[38] Similarly, intellectual property rights that favor the producers of climate-ready GMO crops over the users of this technology will hamper adaptation efforts and worsen the impacts of climate change on farmers.[39] In this scenario, regulatory capture of trade policy will combine with the diminished bargaining power of developing countries to create a negative regulatory feedback loop, in addition to the feedback loops of the natural world that will accelerate climate change.

The BRICs+ are likely to become increasingly marginalized. India will suffer from killer heat waves, floods, drought, and famines. This will only make concessions on agricultural subsidies and intellectual property rights for climate-ready plant varieties more difficult for India and prevent it from participating effectively in any megaregional regimes. Indeed, climate change has shifted agriculture and subsistence strategies in the Indian subcontinent before, to more drought tolerant crops, and served as a catalyst for the de-urbanisation of the Harappan civilization.[40] The modern equivalent would be a shift to GMO crops, but intellectual property rights, combined with terminator genes that make seeds infertile, could create an obstacle to access.[41] While richer countries can achieve some adaptation to killer heatwaves in their cities,[42] India is unlikely to fall into this category. Indian cities will struggle to

---

sector-must-be-at-the-heart-of-tackling-climate-change. Also see Network for Greening the Financial System (NGFS) (2019) First comprehensive report, A call for action: Climate change as a source of financial risk, April 2019, https://www.ngfs.net/sites/default/files/medias/documents/ngfs_first_comprehensive_report_-_17042019_0.pdf.

[36]Kelley et al. (2015), pp. 3241–3246. For a contrary view, see Selby et al. (2017), pp. 232–244; De Châtel (2014), pp. 521–535.

[37]Grant W (2019) US-Mexico talks: Trump hails deal on migrants to avoid tariffs, www.bbc.com, 8 June 2019, https://www.bbc.com/news/world-us-canada-48568389. Climate reality project (2019) How the climate crisis is driving Central American migration, 31 May 2019, https://www.climaterealityproject.org/blog/how-climate-crisis-driving-central-american-migration. Kuil et al. (2016), pp. 6222–6242.

[38]Condon (2017), pp. 675–690.

[39]Condon (2013), pp. 897–923.

[40]Sarkar et al. (2016); Also see Kathayat et al. (2017).

[41]Condon (2013).

[42]Vautard et al. (2019).

save lives because of economic inequality, even if wealth increases. It is the poorest and most vulnerable who die in killer heat waves in urban areas. As for subsistence farmers, we know that it would not take much money to solve that problem, given the political will.[43] While the links between climate change, migration and conflict are complex, the effects of climate change on subsistence farmers could produce waves of climate migrants from India that would dwarf the flows seen thus far from Syria and Central America.[44] Rising sea levels on India's coastline will be another source of migrants, but the complexity of interacting factors (infrastructure, sea level rise, climate change mitigation and adaptation) makes numbers difficult to predict.[45]

In Russia, forest fires in boreal forests will increase dramatically, with far-reaching ecological and socioeconomic consequences.[46] This will coincide with the massive release of methane gas from the previously frozen north. Devastating air pollution will combine with rising alcoholism and suicide rates to reduce life expectancy in Russia's shrinking population.[47] Russia's belligerence with its neighbours delayed its accession to the WTO.[48] The combined effect of the climate crisis and shrinking revenues from fossil fuels will only increase Russian security concerns. The result will depend on Russia's response to its changing circumstances. Increasing belligerence could make Russia's inclusion in the megaregional regime more difficult. At the same time, the security threat posed by Russia could motivate the Quad to push for its integration into the megaregional system. Russia's history in and out of the G8 demonstrates how difficult it is to predict how Russian aggression will play out in international institutions.

Brazil's status as an agricultural powerhouse will decline as the effects of climate change increase; the destruction of the Amazon is likely to accelerate that process.[49] The climate crisis will be devastating to Indonesia, South Africa and Nigeria as well.

---

[43] Condon and Sinha (2013).

[44] Brzoska and Fröhlich (2016), pp. 190–210; Reuveny (2007), pp. 656–673.

[45] Wrathall et al. (2019), pp. 898–901.

[46] Kelly et al. (2013). World Meteorological Organization (2019) Unprecedented wildfires in the Arctic, 12 July 2019, https://public.wmo.int/en/media/news/unprecedented-wildfires-arctic. RFERL (2019) Siberian Wildfires Set To Break Land Area Record, 12 August 2019, https://www.rferl.org/a/siberian-wildfires-set-to-break-land-area-record/30106388.html. NASA (2019) Boreal Forest Fires Could Release Deep Soil Carbon, 21 August 2019, https://www.nasa.gov/feature/goddard/2019/boreal-forest-fires-could-release-deep-soil-carbon.

[47] Burke et al. (2018), p. 723; Razvodovsky (2015), p. 22.

[48] Kimball S (2011) Compromise with Georgia clears way for Russian WTO membership, https://www.dw.com/en/compromise-with-georgia-clears-way-for-russian-wto-membership/a-15509704.

[49] USAID (2018) Climate Risk Profile Brazil, https://www.climatelinks.org/sites/default/files/asset/document/2018-April_30_USAID_CadmusCISF_Climate-Risk-Profile-Brazil.pdf. Deathwatch for the Amazon, Economist, 1 August 2019, https://www.economist.com/leaders/2019/08/01/deathwatch-for-the-amazon. The Amazon is approaching an irreversible tipping point, Economist, 1 August 2019, https://www.economist.com/briefing/2019/08/01/the-amazon-is-approaching-an-irreversible-tipping-point. NASA (2019) Wildfires in the Brazilian Rainforest Creating Cross Country Smoke, 21 Aug 2019, https://www.nasa.gov/image-feature/goddard/2019/wildfires-in-the-brazilian-rainforest-creating-cross-country-smoke.

Climate change is likely to increase economic inequality between and within these and other countries.[50] Moreover, in some of the countries most exposed to climate change, including India, Indonesia, and Nigeria, insurance penetration is less than 1%, making them more vulnerable financially.[51] A developed country like Australia is very vulnerable to climate change, as the 2019–2020 bushfires have demonstrated. However, a country like Australia has greater resilience than a country like Nigeria, due to its greater financial capacity, well developed insurance markets, and high level of technological development.

A recent study has estimated the economic cost of climate change by country, measured as the social cost of carbon per tonne of CO2 (tCO2). India's is the highest (US$86 per tCO2), followed by the United States (US$48 per tCO2), Saudi Arabia (US$47 per tCO2), Brazil (US$24 per tCO2), China (US$24 per tCO2) and the United Arab Emirates (US$24 per tCO2). Northern Europe, Canada and the Former Soviet Union are expected to have a net benefit because their current temperatures are below the economic optimum.[52] Another study predicts that the negative impact of climate change on economic growth, measured as the percent loss in GDP per capita by 2100 with no climate change mitigation, will be worse for the countries with the greatest temperature increases, which includes Russia (12.46%), India (13.39%), and the United States (14.32%).[53] India and the United States are the common denominators in these two studies, but the United States has greater adaptation capabilities than India and the United States will find itself inside the Quad-led megaregional regime; India will not.

It is possible that catastrophic climate change will motivate countries like India to make concessions that will lead to breakthroughs in trade negotiations. After all, international trade can facilitate access to and development of climate change mitigation and adaptation technologies. Unfortunately, history demonstrates that catastrophic climate change is likely to deepen existing divisions in society.[54] To put it another way, in times of crisis there is a tendency for humans to circle the wagons and start shooting inwards. Civilizations are not insulated from environmental change.[55]

There is every reason to think that the economic hardship and existential threat from climate change will lead to populism and the scapegoating of trade, migration,

---

[50]Diffenbaugh and Burke (2019), pp. 9808–9813.

[51]Carney M (2019) Fifty Shades of Green, Finance & Development, December 2019, 56:4, https://www.imf.org/external/pubs/ft/fandd/2019/12/a-new-sustainable-financial-system-to-stop-climate-change-carney.htm?utm_medium=email&utm_source=govdelivery.

[52]Ricke et al. (2018), pp. 895–900.

[53]Kahn ME et al. (2019) Long-term Macroeconomic Effects of Climate Change: A Cross-Country Analysis, NBER Working Paper 26167, August 2019, http://www.nber.org/papers/w26167.

[54]Marvel K (2019) Lost Cities and Climate Change, Scientific American, 29 July 2019, https://blogs.scientificamerican.com/hot-planet/lost-cities-and-climate-change/. Also see Büntgen et al. (2011), pp. 578–582; McCormick et al. (2012), pp. 169–220; Douglas et al. (2016), pp. 613–645; Kaniewski et al. (2019), pp. 1–11.

[55]Büntgen et al. (2011).

and "them". Humans have evolved to be a cooperative species within "tribes" and a competitive species between "tribes". As Karthik Panchanathan puts it, "The logic of between-group conflict to foster within-group cooperation, the very logic that may have got us into problems like global warming, surely cannot get us out of it."[56] Evolutionary psychology tells us that the influence of evolutionary forces on human intuitions decreases their reliability. Tribalism is a good example. Tribalism selects for racism, nationalism and xenophobia, indirectly influences political views, and affects the acceptance of scientific evidence on climate change.[57] The evolutionary forces that prevent humanity from addressing climate change are the same ones that will increase obstacles to successful trade negotiations because of the climate crisis.

In general terms, small and developing states will suffer the most in a warming post-WTO world. The most vulnerable of these face a higher cost of capital, which makes adaptation even more costly.[58] One view holds that the people most vulnerable to the climate crisis live in low-latitude, hot regions of the world, like central South America, the Arabian Peninsula and much of Africa, and relatively less so in India and China.[59] However, it makes more sense to categorize countries based on objective criteria that affect the economic impacts of the climate crisis, the likelihood that the country will be the target of climate-motivated trade barriers and the capacity to address the cost of mitigation and adaptation: the "Climate Sensitivity Index" (CSI). The CSI would include: (1) current per capita annual GHG emissions; (2) proportion of population who are subsistence farmers; (3) population of the country who are poor in absolute terms. Other criteria could be added, such as the per capita GDP and some measure of technological capacity.[60]

Higher per capita GHG emissions in a country increase its exposure to the risk of climate-motivated trade barriers. A high rate of emissions would override every other criterion in the CSI, since the risk of trade barriers would exceed the country's capacity to lower emissions.

Second, one needs to consider whether there is a significant proportion of subsistence farmers, as is the case with India.[61] This criterion measures both vulnerability to climate change and its related impact on the probability that a country would make sufficient concessions in trade negotiations to achieve consensus at the multilateral or megaregional level. Climate change will make farmers with less than 3 ha of land particularly vulnerable because they will be hard pressed to buy

[56]Panchanathan (2016), 2013, 280 pp, $24.95/£16.95 (paperback), ISBN:9780691158167, Book Review, Journal of Bioeconomics 18:229–232.

[57]Winter C (2019) Towards a Dual-Process Theory of Criminalization, Working Paper, https://www.christophwinter.net/s/Dual-Process-Criminalization.pdf. Greene (2017), pp. 66–77; Kahan (2012), pp. 732–735.

[58]Economist (2019) Costing the earth: Countries most exposed to climate change face higher costs of capital, 17 August 2019, https://www.economist.com/finance-and-economics/2019/08/17/countries-most-exposed-to-climate-change-face-higher-costs-of-capital.

[59]Samson et al. (2011), p. 532.

[60]The index presented here is a modified version of the one proposed in Condon and Sinha (2013).

[61]FAO (2018) India at a glance, http://www.fao.org/india/fao-in-india/india-at-a-glance/en/.

genetically modified seeds that would be able to withstand more variable weather as a consequence of climate change.[62] Countries with a significant proportion of subsistence farmers will find it more difficult to make concessions regarding agricultural trade and intellectual property rights.

Third, greater poverty increases the risk of mass migration of climate refugees. Average income is not an adequate measure, because it does not consider inequality in income among the population. One commonly used measure of inequality is the Gini coefficient. However, if everyone's income increases by tenfold, the Gini coefficient is not affected. Thus, the Gini coefficient would be meaningless as a measure of inequality that can be compared across countries. A more appropriate measure of inequality is to include people who are poor in the country in absolute terms. The more people there are below an absolute poverty level, the more difficult it is to pay for climate adaptation.

Poverty data is not as easy to find as one might think, and should be taken with a grain of salt. India accounted for 24% of the world's population in extreme poverty in 2015,[63] but it lost its position of the country with the largest number of people living in extreme poverty to Nigeria in 2018, and the number is projected to continue falling.[64] As of March 2019, 3.5% of India's population lives in extreme poverty, or 47.4 million.[65] In Brazil, the number of people living in extreme poverty increased from 13.5 million in 2016 to 15.2 million in 2017.[66] In Russia, while poverty is increasing, the available data is that none live in extreme poverty, which may refer to the availability of data rather than the real number.[67] In China, only 0.7% lived in extreme poverty in 2015, according to the World Bank, and only 0.4% in 2019, according to World Poverty Clock.[68]

If current trends continue, the climate crisis will only widen the gap between rich and poor, within countries and between countries, and increase the gap in bargaining power between countries. Brazil, India, Indonesia, Nigeria and South Africa are among the countries with the highest probability of economic damage from the climate crisis. Russia has the lowest probability, due to its cooler climate, and China

---

[62]Condon and Sinha (2013), Chapter 8.

[63]Katayama R, Wadhwa D (2019) Half of the world's poor live in just 5 countries, Data Blog, 9 January 2019, https://blogs.worldbank.org/opendata/half-world-s-poor-live-just-5-countries.

[64]Kharas H et al. (2018) The start of a new poverty narrative, Brookings Future Development Blog, 19 June 2018, https://www.brookings.edu/blog/future-development/2018/06/19/the-start-of-a-new-poverty-narrative/.

[65]World Date Lab (2019) World Poverty Clock, https://worldpoverty.io/.

[66]AFP (2018) Number of poor in Brazil grows by two million, https://www.france24.com/en/20181205-number-poor-brazil-grows-two-million.

[67]World Date Lab (2019); Ostroukh A (2016) Poverty in Russia to rise sharply: World Bank, Market Watch, 6 April 2016, https://www.marketwatch.com/story/poverty-in-russia-to-rise-sharply-world-bank-2016-04-06/.

[68]World Date Lab (2019); World Bank (2016) Poverty Data, http://povertydata.worldbank.org/poverty/country/.

is in the middle.[69] The climate crisis makes it likely that BRICs+ (minus China and Russia) will suffer from declining bargaining power in trade negotiations. Moreover, the climate crisis is an important cause of a biodiversity crisis that is a major contributor to economic damage, through environmental damage to key resources such as fish and water.[70] The combined climate crisis and biodiversity crisis will hurt economic growth and change priorities in the hardest hit countries.

The effects of accelerating climate change will have a destabilizing impact on trade negotiations, particularly for the worst-affected developing countries. The effects of the climate crisis will make it more difficult to make concessions in crucial areas, such as agriculture and intellectual property rights, due to the effects of the climate crisis on agricultural yields and the increased need for technology to adapt to a warming climate and reduce greenhouse gas emissions. Rising sea levels, droughts, floods, and killer heat waves will provoke mass migration, with impacts on domestic politics that makes trade concessions more difficult. In this context, multilateral trade negotiations are unlikely to advance in a significant way and megaregional trade agreements will become increasingly difficult to join. The result will be a warming world that is divided between those included in and those excluded from the megaregional trade regime. This will also hamper efforts to slow and to adapt to the climate crisis, due to the key role that international trade plays in addressing both. It is beyond the scope of this chapter to analyze the political links between the effects of climate change on each country's trade policy, as useful as that might be. We have seen how migration and trade policy have become linked in the public's minds in the United States and the United Kingdom. We have seen how large populations of vulnerable subsistence farmers creates obstacles to concessions on agricultural subsidies for India and among a broader set of developing countries with respect to intellectual property rights for new plant varieties. However, we have only begun to imagine how the multiplicity of impacts from accelerating climate change will affect the political feasibility of different trade policies in different countries as they grapple with unique combinations of food insecurity, catastrophic weather events, mass migration, health impacts, and risks to financial stability.

---

[69]Diffenbaugh and Burk (2019).

[70]Díaz S et al. (2019) Summary for policymakers of the global assessment report on biodiversity and ecosystem services – unedited advance version, United Nations, Intergovernmental SciencePolicy Platform on Biodiversity and Ecosystem Services, https://www.ipbes.net/sites/default/files/downloads/summary_for_policymakers_ipbes_global_assessment.pdf.

4 Conclusion

At the eleventh BRICS Summit, the Brasilia Declaration displays an apparent disregard for the predicament that the participating countries are in. They reiterate their commitment to the implementation of the Paris Agreement, "including the principle of common but differentiated responsibilities and respective capabilities, in the light of different national circumstances". They also urge developed countries "to scale up the provision of financial, technological and capacity-building assistance to developing countries to support mitigation and adaptation action".[71] These statements reveal a willful blindness to the realities of the post-WTO world order, in which trade and environmental policies become decreasingly supportive of each other, GHG emissions grow dramatically in China and India, and these large developing countries move into the league of the developed countries. Calls for a greater transfer of wealth from the Quad to the BRICS, based on the Twentieth Century notion of common but differentiated responsibilities and outdated ideas of where technological capacity is located, are not helpful. Such calls are particularly unhelpful in a post-WTO world that was brought about by the very geopolitical and economic shifts that make such claims so outdated. While some wealth transfer is necessary to improve access to technology, finance adaptation, reduce emissions and deal with the economic and human costs of the climate crisis, the needs and capacities of countries vary considerably from one to the next. Moreover, a successful multilateral trade regime, or participation in the megaregional alternatives, would help spur innovation and reduce barriers to technology, provided that countries are able to resist calls for excessive intellectual property rights protections in the case of technologies such as new plant varieties and provided trade regimes improve food security. It would be more helpful to categorize countries and technologies in accordance with a more sophisticated measure of vulnerability to climate impacts and financial and technological capacity. Indeed, in the case of the most vulnerable countries, such as small, low-lying island States, no amount of wealth transfer will prevent their disappearance. In such cases, resettlement is the only option, which raises very different issues from the case of a technologically advanced developing country such as China or India.

Of course, the ecological crises spawned by the climate crisis will also affect developed countries in northern latitudes, but they have greater adaptation capacities and a different climate base line. For example, while Canada is warming at twice the rate of tropical countries like India,[72] Canada's starting climate point means that this

[71]Brasilia Declaration (2019) 11th BRICS Summit, para. 10, http://brics2019.itamaraty.gov.br/images/documentos/Braslia_Declaration.pdf.

[72]CBC News (2019) Canada warming at twice the global rate, leaked report finds, 1 April 2019, https://www.cbc.ca/news/technology/canada-warming-at-twice-the-global-rate-leaked-report-finds-1.5079765. Regarding India, see Bal et al. (2016), pp. 353–369; Jaswal (2017), pp. 11–25; Chandler DL (2017) Deadly heat waves could hit South Asia this century. MIT News, 2 August 2017, http://news.mit.edu/2017/deadly-heat-waves-could-hit-south-asia-century-0802.

will bring benefits, not just problems, as the climate gets milder and arable land expands north. Moreover, Canada has greater adaptation capacity than India, as measured by the CSI.[73] Similarly, although Australia is highly vulnerable to climate change, it has greater financial and technological capacity to confront the challenge. For both Australia and Canada, membership in the megaregional regime also makes them more economically resilient and leaves them with better access to trade in goods, services and technologies for adaptation and mitigation.

The Quad-led megaregional trade order will combine with the climate and biodiversity crises to marginalize most of the major emerging markets. The only ones that have a chance to be included in the new trade order are China (due to its trade volume, strategic importance, and its relative resilience to climate change), Russia (due to its strategic importance and higher resilience to climate change), as well as Mexico and Turkey (due to their strategic geographic locations next door to North America and Europe and their current trade ties to the megaregional regime). Brazil, India, Indonesia, Nigeria, and South Africa will be excluded and suffer diminishing bargaining power as the climate crisis worsens.

Even though we cannot predict the effects with precision, science tells us that the effects of climate change will not be evenly distributed. The worst-case scenario for climate change is the collapse of human civilization and the extinction of millions of species. Humans probably will not be among the survivors in that scenario.[74] Technological innovation and political capacity are wild cards. Thus far, political incapacity has proved to be a stronger force than technological innovation. We are headed towards catastrophic climate change at an accelerating rate. The consequences for trade negotiations will convert trade into part of the problem, adding negative political feedback loops to the climatological feedback loops that already threaten to take us past the point of no return. Ironically, it is the very developing countries that have stalled WTO negotiations past the point of no return that will be the first to suffer the catastrophic consequences of a runaway climate crisis.

Acknowledgements I gratefully acknowledge ITAM and the Asociación Mexicana de Cultura for their generous support of this research. The opinions expressed in this article are the sole responsibility of the author and do not represent the views of the WTO. I am grateful for the helpful comments from Tapen Sinha, from the anonymous reviewers, and from colleagues at Paradise Lost of Found? The Post-WTO International "Legal" Order (Utopian & Dystopian Possibilities), Workshop Number 2 (Fletcher School, Tufts University), Friday 26 July 2019.

[73]Also see KPMG Change Readiness Index (2019), https://home.kpmg/xx/en/home/media/press-releases/2019/06/2019-change-readiness-index-launches.html.

[74]Ro C (2019) The animals that will survive climate change, BBC, 5 August 2019, http://www.bbc.com/future/story/20190730-the-animals-that-will-survive-climate-change.

References

Bal PK et al (2016) Climate change projections over India by a downscaling approach using PRECIS. Asia-Pacific J Atmos Sci 52:353–369

Bamber JL et al (2019) Ice sheet contributions to future sea-level rise from structured expert judgment. Proc Natl Acad Sci 116(23):11195–11200. https://doi.org/10.1073/pnas.1817205116

Brzoska M, Fröhlich C (2016) Climate change, migration and violent conflict: vulnerabilities, pathways and adaptation strategies. Migr Dev 5:190–210

Büntgen U et al (2011) 2500 years of European climate variability and human susceptibility Science. New Series 331:578–582

Burke M et al (2018) Higher temperatures increase suicide rates in the United States and Mexico. Nat Clim Chang 8:723

Cheng L et al (2020) Record-setting ocean warmth continued in 2019. Adv Atmos Sci 37:137–142

Collins M et al (2013) Long-term climate change: projections, commitments and irreversibility. In: Stocker TF et al (eds) Climate Change 2013: the physical science basis. Contribution of working group I to the fifth assessment report of the intergovernmental panel on climate change (2013). Cambridge University Press, Cambridge, pp 1029–1136

Condon BJ (2013) Climate change and intellectual property rights for new plant varieties. J World Trade 47:897–923

Condon BJ (2017) Disciplining clean energy subsidies to speed the transition to a low-carbon world. J World Trade 51:675–690

Condon BJ (2018) Captain America and the tarnishing of the crown: the feud between the WTO appellate body and the USA. J World Trade 52:535–556

Condon BJ, Sinha T (2013) The role of climate change in global economic governance. Oxford University Press, Oxford

De Châtel F (2014) The role of drought and climate change in the Syrian uprising: untangling the triggers of the revolution. Middle East Stud 50:521–535

Diffenbaugh NS, Burke M (2019) Global warming has increased global economic inequality. Proc Natl Acad Sci 116:9808–9813. https://doi.org/10.1073/pnas.1816020116

Douglas PMJ et al (2016) Impacts of climate change on the collapse of lowland Maya civilization. Ann Rev Earth Planetary Sci 44:613–645

Gleizer S et al (2019) Conversion of *Escherichia coli* to generate all biomass carbon from CO2. Cell 179(6):1255–1263.e12. https://doi.org/10.1016/j.cell.2019.11.009

Greene J (2017) The Rat-a-gorical imperative. Cognition 167:66–77

Holland PR et al (2019) West Antarctic ice loss influenced by internal climate variability and anthropogenic forcing. Nat Geosci 12(9):718–724. https://doi.org/10.1038/s41561-019-0420-9

Jaswal AK (2017) Increasing trend in temperature and moisture induced heat index and its effect on human health in climate change scenario over the Indian Sub-continent. J Clim Chang 3:11–25

Kahan DM (2012) The polarizing impact of science literacy and numeracy on perceived climate change risks. Nat Clim Chang 2:732–735

Kaniewski D et al (2019) 300-year drought frames late bronze age to early iron age transition in the near East: new palaeoecological data from Cyprus and Syria. Reg Environ Chang 19 (8):2287–2297. https://doi.org/10.1007/s10113-018-01460-w

Kathayat G et al (2017) The Indian monsoon variability and civilization changes in the Indian subcontinent. Sci Adv 3:e1701296. https://doi.org/10.1126/sciadv.1701296

Kelley CP et al (2015) Climate change in the fertile crescent and implications of the recent Syrian drought. Proc Natl Acad Sci 112:3241–3246. https://doi.org/10.1073/pnas.1421533112

Kelly R et al (2013) Recent burning of boreal forests exceeds fire regime limits of the past 10,000 years. Proc Natl Acad Sci 110(32):13055–13060

Kuil L et al (2016) Conceptualizing socio-hydrological drought processes: the case of the Maya collapse. Water Resour Res 52:6222–6242

McCormick M et al (2012) Climate change during and after the Roman Empire: reconstructing the past from scientific and historical evidence. J Interdiscip Hist 43:169–220

Nature Editorial (2020) Australia: show the world what climate action looks like. Nature 577:449–450. https://doi.org/10.1038/d41586-020-00152-y
Panchanathan K (2016) Culture, conflict, and the birth of a cooperative species. Samuel Bowles and Herbert Gintis: a cooperative species. Princeton University Press, Princeton
Razvodovsky YE (2015) Suicides in Russia and Belarus: a comparative analysis of trends. Acta Psychopathol 1:22. https://doi.org/10.4172/2469-6676.100022
Reuveny R (2007) Climate change-induced migration and violent conflict. Polit Geogr 26:656–673
Ricke K et al (2018) Country-level social cost of carbon. Nat Clim Chang 8:895–900
Samson J, Berteaux D, McGill BJ, Humphries MM (2011) Geographic disparities and moral hazards in the predicted impacts of climate change on human populations. Glob Ecol Biogeogr 20:532
Sarkar A et al (2016) Oxygen isotope in archaeological bioapatites from India: Implications to climate change and decline of Bronze Age Harappan civilization. Sci Rep 6:1–9. https://doi.org/10.1038/srep26555
Selby J et al (2017) Climate change and the Syrian civil war revisited. Polit Geogr 60:232–244
Sinha A et al (2019) Role of climate in the rise and fall of the Neo-Assyrian Empire. Sci Adv 5:11. https://doi.org/10.1126/sciadv.aax6656
Tanski G et al (2019) Rapid CO2 release from eroding permafrost in seawater. Geophys Res Lett 46 (20):11244–11252. https://doi.org/10.1029/2019GL084303
Wang H et al (2019) China's CO2 peak before 2030 implied from characteristics and growth of cities. Nat Sustain 2(8):748–754. https://doi.org/10.1038/s41893-019-0339-6
Watts N et al (2019) The 2019 report of The Lancet Countdown on health and climate change: ensuring that the health of a child born today is not defined by a changing climate. The Lancet 394(10211):1836–1878. https://doi.org/10.1016/S0140-6736(19)32596-6
Wrathall DJ et al (2019) Meeting the looming policy challenge of sea-level change and human migration. Nat Clim Chang 9:898–901

Narrowed Down Utopia: Adjusting the WTO to a Changing Trade Environment

Gabriel Gari

Contents

Reader in International Economic Law, Queen Mary University of London.

G. Gari (✉)
Queen Mary University of London, London, UK
e-mail: g.gari@qmul.ac.uk

M. K. Lewis et al. (eds.), *A Post-WTO International Legal Order*,
https://doi.org/10.1007/978-3-030-45428-9_3

1 Introduction

The WTO is facing its worst crisis yet. Stalled multilateral trade negotiations, rise of protectionism,[1] a full-blown trade war between its two largest Members and a dispute settlement system on the brink of collapse, are sobering reminders of the seriousness of the problem. Most observers point the finger at the structural transformation of political and economic power among WTO Members—epitomized by the surge of China against a defensive America—as the principal cause for this crisis. While its relevance is beyond doubt, this is not the only contributing factor to the crisis. Another significant reason has to do with the difficulty of the organization to adjust its obligations and institutional framework to a changing trade environment.

Right after the end of the second world war, there was not such a thing as a global economy, but fragmented and shallow international economic relations between some States. Trade flows were subject to high tariffs and discrimination. To address them, the drafters of the GATT opted for the negotiation of a package of binding bilateral tariff concessions extended to all contracting parties on a non-discriminatory basis by virtue of the MFN obligation.

With their tariff policy discretion taken away, governments gradually began to apply non-tariff barriers to protect themselves from foreign competition. By the mid-1980s, it became clear that tariff commitments alone were no longer sufficient to maintain an open and non-discriminatory multilateral trading system, prompting GATT contracting parties to launch a new negotiation round to update the GATT's legal weaponry. By the end of the Uruguay Round, on top of an improved package of reciprocal tariff concessions, a number of obligations of a collective or integral nature, were added to the rule-book. They were expressly designed to address the trade restrictive effects of non-trade policy measures adopted 'within the border' such as technical regulations, sanitary measures, services regulations and the protection of intellectual property rights.

Since then, the global economy achieved unprecedented levels of interdependence,[2] the information and communications technology revolution is offering new ways to manufacture, sell and deliver products and services[3] and the broader socio-economic context within which trade takes place has radically

---

[1]See WTO Report on G20 Trade Measures (Mid-May 2019 to Mid-October 2019). https://www.wto.org/english/news_e/news19_e/report_trdev_21nov19_e.pdf.

[2]Despite a protracted slowdown of world trade growth in the aftermath of the 2008–2009 global financial crisis, trade still stands at around 28% of world GDP. That's essentially double the 13.5% average share in 1947–1991, during the Cold War. See Stephen SR (2019) US, China and the myth of global decoupling. https://www.livemint.com/news/world/us-china-and-the-myth-of-global-decoupling-11577290013979.html.

[3]The rise of international value chains, by which firms organize their supply chain across different countries, has shifted trade policy makers' concerns from barriers to selling to barriers to making things. See Baldwin RE (2012) Global supply chains: Why they emerged, why they matter, and where they are going. CEPR Discussion Paper No. 9103.

changed.[4] The combination of these factors is exposing trade flows to non-trade policies adopted within the border like never before. The problem is compounded by the profound differences between WTO Members' standards, regulations and institutions.

In response to this new trade environment, a sub-group of WTO Members have launched plurilateral negotiations on services domestic regulation, investment facilitation and electronic commerce.[5] A common feature of the draft texts circulated in the context of these negotiations is the predominance of obligations of a collective or integral nature over those of a bilateral or reciprocal type.[6] This trend is even more pronounced at regional level. Recent Preferential Trade Agreements have expanded their remit to cover a wide range of non-trade policies, including the environment, labour, anticorruption and competition policy, consisting almost entirely of collective obligations.[7]

In principle, updating its rule-book with collective obligations should provide the WTO with the necessary tools to address the rising impact of non-protectionist policy measures on trade flows. However, the rise of collective obligations within an institutional framework designed for the negotiation of bilateral concessions and an enforcement system based on the suspension of concessions will be problematic. Bilateral obligations are adopted through a negotiation process where each Member is expected to give some protection away in exchange for improved market access elsewhere, leading to a mutually advantageous package of reciprocal concessions. The secrecy, tactical and predominantly bilateral approach that characterises trade negotiations, is unsuitable for the development of collective obligations. The latter require an institutional framework that fosters a non-adversarial environment of transparency, dialogue and mutual trust, suitable for identifying common objectives and developing cooperation mechanisms to achieve them. The enforcement process is also expressly designed for bilateral obligations, having the suspension of concessions as its main remedy. As explained below, this too is unsuitable for collective obligations that are meant to advance a common interest.[8]

Against this background, the aim of this paper is to unveil the inconsistencies between collective obligations and a rule making and enforcement process designed for obligations of a bilateral nature. It also suggests ways to overcome such inconsistencies with a view to ensure that the organization remains fit for purpose to ensure an open and non-discriminatory multilateral trading system within an

[4]The distributional effects of trade, particularly its impact on jobs and income distribution are now subject to intense scrutiny. In addition, consumers are increasingly concerned about the impact of products and process of production methods on a wide range of issues such as the environment, food safety and animal welfare, to name but a few. See World Trade Report (2013) Factors shaping the future of world trade, p. 268. https://www.wto.org/english/res_e/booksp_e/world_trade_report13_e.pdf.

[5]See below Sect. 3.

[6]See below Sect. 2.

[7]See below Sect. 3.4.

[8]See below Sect. 4.2.

evolving trading landscape, where both protectionist and non-protectionist trade restrictions are kept at bay. The paper argues that the best course of action for the WTO in years to come is to: (a) keep fighting trade protectionism through negotiations and litigation, (b) avoid expanding its rule-book with hard collective obligations and (c) address the trade restrictive effects of non-protectionist policies by strengthening its deliberative function.

The remainder of the paper is organized as follows: Sect. 2 outlines the criteria for the classification of WTO obligations. Section 3 applies such criteria to the disciplines included in the draft texts circulated in the context of the plurilateral negotiations currently going on at the WTO. Section 4 unveils some inconsistencies between collective obligations and the WTO's rule making and enforcement processes. Section 5 offers some suggestions for adjusting the WTO institutional framework to the new trading landscape and keep it relevant in years to come. Section 6 concludes.

2 Typology of WTO Obligations

There is an established typology that distinguishes between international obligations of a bilateral or reciprocal nature and those of a collective or integral nature.[9] The former refer to unilateral commitments made by one State to another, the performance of which is owed specifically to that particular State, e.g. those included in a bilateral treaty or in a multilateral treaty consisting of 'bundles' of bilateral relations such as the Vienna Convention on Diplomatic Protection.[10] The latter are those established in the collective interest, where the performance of the obligation is not differentiated or individualized, but owed generally to all the parties to a treaty at the same time, e.g. those included in Human Rights treaties.[11]

Applying this criteria to the WTO Agreements, Pauwelyn argues that WTO obligations remain essentially of the bilateral type.[12] The reasons invoked in support of this contention include the following: the nature of trade, which is and remains a bilateral happening; the way WTO obligations are negotiated and re-negotiated, which is essentially bilateral (although the bilateral reduction of trade restrictions is then multilateralized pursuant to the MFN principle); the fact that unlike the prohibition of genocide or the protection of human rights or the environment, trade

[9]See Pauwelyn (2003a), pp. 907–951. The author traces the origin and evolution of the distinction through a number of sources of Public International Law including the ICJ Advisory Opinion on Reservations to the Convention on the Prevention and Punishment of the Crime of Genocide (28/05/51), the International Law Commission (ILC) Reports on the Law of Treaties by Sir Gerald Fitzmaurice, the Vienna Convention on the Law of Treaties, and the ILC Articles on State Responsibility (2001), in particular the differences between Article 42(a) and 48.1(a).

[10]Ibid.

[11]Ibid.

[12]Ibid.

liberalisation is not a value, i.e. it is not sought after for the achievement of some 'global common' that transcends the sum of total individual states interests, but only an instrument to increase economic welfare of states: and the fact that that unlike collective obligations, not all breaches of WTO law necessarily affect the rights of all other WTO Members.[13] Pauwelyn concludes that most (though not necessarily all) WTO obligations are of a bilateral or reciprocal type and can thus be reduced to a compilation of bilateral treaty relations, each of them detachable one from the other.[14]

This section further develops Pauwelyn's criteria for distinguishing between WTO obligations of a bilateral and collective nature, by making some additional observations of WTO obligations' scope of application and content.

When looking at their scope *rationae materiae*, a common pattern emerges. Bilateral obligations are concerned with market access restrictions and discriminatory measures,[15] whereas collective obligations are concerned with the trade restrictive effects caused simply by the disparity of non-discriminatory internal regulations.[16] With respect to the scope *rationae personae*, obligations of a bilateral nature confer rights and prescribe obligations only on states. Typically, that would include Article II.1 of GATT 1994, which prescribes the obligation of each WTO Member to accord to the commerce of other WTO Members treatment no less favourable than that provided in its schedule of concessions. The flipside of this obligation is the right conferred to other WTO Members to receive a treatment to their commerce that is no less favourable that that provided by each WTO Member's schedule of concessions. By contrast, some WTO obligations closer to the collective or integral type confer rights to individuals. For example, Article VI.3 of GATS stipulates that when authorization is required for the supply of a service on which a specific commitment has been made, the competent authorities of a Member shall inform *the applicant* of the decision concerning the application.[17]

Typically, bilateral obligations are *negotiable*, in the sense that each WTO Member can decide the extent of such obligations, i.e. in the case of goods, the number of tariff lines bound by their schedule of concessions and the rate at which tariffs are bound and, in the case of services, the sectors and modes of supply to be included in Members' schedules of specific commitments and the terms, conditions and limitations that Members may want to introduce to qualify such commitments. By contrast, collective obligations are non-negotiable, i.e. Members have to comply with them in the exact terms as they are prescribed by the treaty. There is no room for WTO members to alter the content of these obligations other than by following the

[13]Ibid., pp. 928–936.

[14]Ibid., p. 940.

[15]E.g. Articles I, II, III, XI GATT 1994.

[16]E.g. Articles VI of GATS, Article 3 of SPS and 2.4 of TBT.

[17]This of course, does not mean that the treaty confers the individual a mechanism to enforce such right. As it is well known, the legal standing to bring claims under the WTO dispute settlement system is limited to states only.

process for the amendment of the treaty, which is subject to the observance of specific formalities and the attainment of qualified majorities.

Another feature associated with bilateral obligations is their *excludability*, i.e. the possibility that the Member undertaking the obligation has to exclude or limit third countries' access to the benefits generated by such obligation.[18] For example, without prejudice to its WTO consistency, it is perfectly feasible for a Member to confer a tariff preference to products originating in a certain country but not to like products from other countries. By contrast, the benefits stemming from collective obligations tend to be non-excludable. For example, products and services from every country can benefit from the minimum institutional requirements prescribed by Article VI.2 of GATS or X.3(b) of GATT. Even if the importing country would like to limit such institutional benefits to products from certain countries, for practical reasons, it would be difficult, if not impossible, to do so.

Bilateral obligations are typically *negative in character*. For example, the duty not to accord products from other WTO Members, a tariff treatment less favourable than that provided for in the importing Member's Schedule of Concessions.[19] By contrast, collective obligations tend to require *positive* actions. For example, the duty to administer measures of general application affecting trade in services in a reasonable, objective and impartial manner,[20] or the duty to administer laws, regulations, decisions and rulings of general application pertaining inter alia to the valuation of products for customs purposes or affecting their sale, distribution, transportation, etc. in a uniform, impartial and reasonable manner.[21]

Bilateral obligations are, by definition, *horizontal*, i.e. they are owed by a WTO Member *vis a vis* another WTO Member and refer to the horizontal relationship between them. For example, Article III.4 of GATS imposes an obligation on Members to respond promptly to requests from any other Member for specific information on any of its measures of general application affecting trade in services. By contrast, collective obligations tend to be *vertical*, i.e. the content of the obligation refers to the relationship between public authorities of a state and the individuals subject to that authority, i.e. it informs the vertical relationship between a government and its subjects. For example, Article VI.3 of GATS imposes an obligation on the competent authority to authorise the supply of services to inform the applicant of its decision regarding the applicant's application for authorisation to supply a service.

Finally, bilateral obligations are *closed* because WTO Members have exclusive control over their content. By contrast, some collective obligations that refer to recognized international standards, principles or guidelines are *open* because their

[18]See Pauwelyn (2014) and Mattoo A, Mulabdic A, Ruta M (2017) Deep trade agreements as public goods. VOX, CEPR's Policy Portal, 11 October 2017. https://voxeu.org/article/trade-effects-deep-agreements.

[19]Article II GATT.

[20]Article VI.1 GATS.

[21]Article X.3(b) GATT.

exact content depends on external sources of law which may change in a manner that rests outside WTO Members' control.

3 Rise of Collective Obligations

3.1 Services Domestic Regulation

Article VI.4 of GATS mandates to negotiate disciplines for qualification requirements and procedures, technical standards and licensing requirements and procedures. After a long impasse marked by protracted differences, in 2016 a subgroup of WTO Members called for the resumption of the negotiations.[22] Since then, negotiations are being conducted on a plurilateral basis and in accordance with open, transparent and inclusive principles. At the open-ended meeting of the plurilateral group of 19 July 2019, participants welcomed a draft Reference Paper on Services Domestic Regulations produced by the Chairperson of the group.[23]

The Reference Paper includes disciplines on the transparency, development and administration of domestic regulations, which feature most of the characteristics of collective obligations identified above. To start with, in terms of scope *rationae materiae*, they apply to non-discriminatory internal regulations affecting trade in services.[24] In terms of their scope *rationae personae*, many of these disciplines confer rights to individuals. For example, paragraph 14 confers a right to service suppliers or persons seeking to supply a service to file enquiries to the competent authority regarding measures affecting trade in services and get a response from them, and paragraph 17 confers interested persons an opportunity to comment on proposed laws and regulations of general application affecting trade in services. The disciplines relating to the processing of applications for authorisation to supply services also confer clearly defined and self-executable rights to individuals, such as the right to be informed of the decision concerning the application, the right to be informed in case the application is incomplete, and the right to be provided with the opportunity to provide the additional information that is required to complete the application.[25]

With respect to their content, the disciplines are not negotiable. There is an expectation that once it is agreed, Members will include the final text in their schedule of commitments without further limitations, conditions or qualifications. For practical reasons, the disciplines are non-excludable, i.e. they will apply, *de*

[22]Communication from Australia et al—Elements for Discussion. (JOB/SERV/231/Rev.1, 13/06/16).

[23]Draft Reference Paper on Services Domestic Regulation, Note by the Chairperson, 12 July 2019. Copy on hold.

[24]Para. 1, Section II.

[25]Para 7(d) and 7(e), Section II.

facto, on an MFN basis as it may prove impossible to exclude certain foreign suppliers from the benefits of an improved regulatory environment. Most of these obligations prescribe a positive conduct for their fulfilment. For example, on transparency, the duty to publish, to consult and to inform; on the development and administration of domestic regulations, the duty to ensure that measures relating to authorisation for the supply of a service are based on objective and transparent criteria; and the duty to process applications within a reasonable, to name but a few. Finally, the procedural standards to be observed when processing applications for authorisation to supply services refer to the vertical relationship between public authorities of a state and the individuals subject to that authority.

3.2 Investment Facilitation

In December 2017, during the Buenos Aires Ministerial Conference, a subgroup of WTO Members issued a joint statement calling for "beginning structured discussions with the aim of developing a multilateral framework on investment facilitation for development."[26] The aim of the discussions is not to negotiate market access, investment protection or dispute settlement, but "to identify and develop the elements of a framework for facilitating foreign direct investments that would: improve the transparency and predictability of investment measures; streamline and speed up administrative procedures and requirements; and enhance international cooperation, information sharing, the exchange of best practices, and relations with relevant stakeholders, including dispute prevention."[27] In July 2019, a working document with proposed disciplines on investment facilitation was circulated by the Coordinator of the structured discussions under his responsibility.[28] In November 2019 the document was endorsed by 98 economies.[29]

The disciplines target non-discriminatory internal regulations affecting the admission, establishment, acquisition and expansion of investments in services and non-services sectors.[30] They feature most of the characteristics typical of collective obligations: non-negotiable, positive and non-excludable obligations, mostly concerned with the vertical relation between public authorities and investors. For example, proposed disciplines on transparency include the duty to publish in advance measures of general application affecting the admission, establishment,

---

[26]Joint Ministerial Statement on Investment Facilitation for Development, 13 December 2017 (WT/MIN(17)/59).

[27]Ibid.

[28]WTO Structured Discussions on Investment Facilitation for Development Working Document (INF/IFD/RD/39, 24 July19).

[29]Joint Ministerial Statement on Investment Facilitation for Development, 5 November 2019 (WT/L/1072).

[30]Ibid.

acquisition and expansion of investments, and to provide investors and other interested persons an opportunity to comment on those proposed measures.[31] The working document also includes proposed disciplines aimed at streamlining and speeding up investment related administrative procedures and requirements such as the duty to establish a Single Electronic Window (SEW) as a single entry point for the submission of all documents required by the agencies or regulatory bodies involved in the admission, establishment, acquisition and expansion of investments, and a duty to ensure that fees charged by competent authorities for processing applications for authorisations to invest are reasonable, transparent, and not in themselves a restriction to investment.[32] The working document includes very detailed procedural standards to be observed by public authorities processing applications for authorisation to invest, which confer a number of specific and directly executable rights to applicants.

3.3 Electronic Commerce

On the second WTO Ministerial Conference, Members adopted a Declaration on Global Electronic Commerce that in turn resulted in the General Council's enactment of a comprehensive Work Programme on Electronic Commerce "to examine all trade-related issues relating to global electronic commerce."[33] In spite of its auspicious beginning, the work programme did not make any significant progress other than the successive renewal of the commitment of not imposing duties on electronic transmissions.[34] However, in December 2017, a subgroup of Members committed to "... initiate exploratory work together toward future WTO negotiations on trade related aspects of electronic commerce."[35] By January 2019, participant Members, including China, the EU and the U.S., decided to mutate the "exploratory work" into a fully-fledged negotiation on trade-related aspects of electronic commerce.[36] In July 2019, the G20 Members adopted the Osaka Declaration on Digital Economy that endorsed these negotiations and confirmed G20 Members' "commitment to seek to achieve a high standard agreement with the participation of as many WTO Members as possible".[37] Several proposals for disciplines on electronic commerce have been tabled in the context of these

[31]Ibid.

[32]Ibid.

[33]Work Programme on Electronic Commerce, WT/L/274. General Council, World Trade Organization, 30 September 1998.

[34]Updating the Multilateral Rule Book on E-Commerce, ICTSD Policy Brief, March 2019, p. 2.

[35]Joint Statement on Electronic Commerce, 13 December 2017 WT/MIN(17)/60.

[36]Joint Statement on Electronic Commerce, 25 January 2019, WT/L/1056.

[37]G20 (2019) Osaka Declaration on Digital Economy. https://www.wto.org/english/news_e/news19_e/osaka_declration_on_digital_economy_e.pdf.

negotiations, a number of which are publicly available.[38] Their content revolves around three main objectives: to secure an open and non-discriminatory digital environment, a sound transaction digital environment and a safe digital environment.

Obligations proposed to secure an open and non-discriminatory digital environment such as the duty not to impose customs duties, fees or other charges on a digital product transmitted electronically resemble features akin to bilateral obligations. However, proposed disciplines to secure a sound transaction digital environment (e.g. the duty of Members to maintain a legal framework governing electronic transactions consistent with the principles of the UNCITRAL Model Law on Electronic Commerce 1996), and proposals to secure a sound transaction digital environment (e.g. duty to adopt or maintain laws or regulations to proscribe misleading and deceptive conduct that cause harm to consumers engaged in online commercial activities), feature most of the characteristics typical of collective obligations.

To start with, none of these obligations are concerned with trade policy measures *strictu sensu*. They target internal rules and regulations which have, at best, an indirect impact on trade. They prescribe positive conducts and none of them are negotiable, i.e. Members will have to comply with them in the exact terms prescribed by the draft eventually adopted. For example, the duty of Members to maintain a legal framework governing electronic transactions consistent with the principles of the UNCITRAL Model Law on Electronic Commerce 1996 is not negotiable and clearly not excludable in the sense that the benefits stemming from having a modern legislative framework for electronic transactions apply, *de facto*, on an MFN basis. The obligation prescribes a positive behaviour, i.e. to adopt or maintain a piece of legislation and, to some extent, it is an open obligation to the extent that it refers to an external source—i.e. the UNCITRAL Model Law on Electronic Commerce—that can evolve in a manner that escapes WTO Members' control and have an impact on the contours of the obligation.

3.4 Evidence from Preferential Trade Agreements (PTAs)

Recent PTAs have extended their scope to a panoply of domestic policy areas which only have an indirect connection with trade, such as labour and environmental policies, competition policy, anticorruption, good regulatory practices and macroeconomic and exchange rate matters.[39] A few examples extracted from the environment, labour, competition and anti-corruption chapters of the United States—Mexico—Canada Free Trade Agreement (USMCA) illustrate this point.

[38]See INF/ECOM/ in WTO Documents Online. https://docs.wto.org/dol2fe/Pages/FE_Search/FE_S_S005.aspx.

[39]See Acharya (2016); Hofmann et al. (2019), pp. 365–398.

The vast majority of the provisions included in these chapters prescribe *positive* obligations relating to the Parties' domestic legal systems including, among others, a duty to legislate on certain matters (e.g. duty to adopt or maintain consumer protection laws that proscribe fraudulent and deceptive commercial activities, competition laws that proscribe anticompetitive business conduct and anticorruption laws that criminalise certain conducts), a duty to effectively enforce such legislation, and a duty to have in place minimum institutional requirements for their implementation and enforcement (e.g. duty to maintain a national competition authority responsible for the enforcement of national competition law and duty to adopt or maintain measures to promote integrity among public officials).

Many of these disciplines deal with procedural matters that inform the *vertical* relationship between a government and its subjects, such as the duty to guarantee minimum procedural standards applicable to enforcement proceedings dealing with alleged violations of environmental, labour or competition law. Most of these minimum procedural standards expressly *confer direct and self-executable rights to individuals*, such as the right to have access to administrative or judicial proceedings for the enforcement of these laws and the right to seek appropriate remedies or sanctions for violations of these laws; the right to public participation and consultation in the development and implementation of environmental protection measures.

Another pervasive feature of many of these disciplines is their *openness*, in the sense that their content is contingent on external sources of law that remain outside the Parties' control. Typical examples include, the Parties' duty to adopt, maintain, and implement laws, regulations and any other measures to fulfil its obligations under Multilateral Environmental Agreements or the ILO Declaration on Rights at Work, and the duty to base their fisheries management system on internationally recognized best practices such as those prescribed by UNCLOS and FAO Code of Conduct for Responsible Fisheries.

Finally, the disciplines referred above are *non-negotiable*, in the sense that individual Parties cannot condition, limit or qualify their duty to comply with them in any shape or form and, for practical reasons, they are *non-excludable* because Parties to the treaty cannot exclude third parties from the benefits stemming from the alignment of their domestic legal systems to the standards prescribed by these disciplines.

4 Inconsistencies Between Collective Obligations and the WTO Institutional Framework

4.1 Rule-Making Process

As a matter of practice, the WTO's rule-making process involves multilateral negotiations, in pursuance of a broad negotiation agenda, subject to a single undertaking rule where nothing is agreed until everything is agreed and everyone must agree to everything. Negotiations are driven by requests and offers, in pursuance of offensive and defensive interests whereby each party seeks to make 'gains' at the expense of others' concessions. The entire process, from the launch of negotiations to the adoption of its results is decided by consensus. As explained below, this rule-making process is inappropriate for the development of collective obligations.

The single undertaking rule makes sense when you are trying to achieve a final package that secures an overall balance of rights and obligations. It is less useful when the subject matter of the negotiations is not reciprocal concessions but collective obligations. Here, what comes to the fore is the common objective pursued. Members may agree to a common objective in one area but not in another. Forcing Members to agree to one common objective will not add much for the achievement of another.

The practice of decision making by consensus was adopted to prevent Members from being outvoted and dragged against their will to upgrade existing obligations or adopt additional ones in new areas. But the benefits stemming from collective obligations are non-excludable. Third parties who do not want to participate in the negotiations will not be worse off and will fully enjoy the benefits of the negotiation outputs.

Collective obligations are meant to advance common interests that are more than the sum of individual market access gains. A process based on the request and offer of trade concessions is unsuitable for identifying these common objectives and defining the disciplines necessary to achieve them. For example, the objective of ensuring a safe digital trading environment, requires an exchange of information to identify the status of regulations in each Member's jurisdiction, and dialogue to define a minimum set of disciplines which everyone would feel comfortable to adhere.

The political economy underpinning the negotiation of reciprocal obligations is driven by producers' interests, forcing trade negotiators to administer tensions between export interests in certain sectors against import competing defensive interests in other sectors. By contrast, the development of collective obligations is underpinned by demands from a wider range of stakeholders including industry, civil society and an extended network of public authorities, pursuing a broader set of interests. This is likely to raise more complex conflicting demands that cannot be managed simply by balancing trade offensive and defensive interests. Moreover, it needs an environment of openness, dialogue and mutual trust, rather than the secrecy and tactical approaches that characterise trade negotiations.

Finally, most collective obligations require to legislate in new areas or to improve procedural and institutional standards for the administration of domestic regulations. Inevitably, Members with less advanced institutional and legal frameworks would face higher implementation costs, and thus would be more reluctant to support the adoption of collective obligations unless they receive support to meet such costs. A rule making process that fosters mutual cooperation and facilitates the delivery of technical assistance is required to address these concerns and avoid early objections to new collective obligations.

4.2 Enforcement Process

The WTO dispute settlement system is aimed at "preserving the rights and obligations of Members under the covered agreements".[40] Accordingly, the entire process, including the legal standing for bringing a complaint, the breach of obligations and the available remedies, revolves around the concept of nullification or impairment (N or I) of benefits accruing to a Member under the covered agreements. This fits well for the enforcement of obligations of a bilateral nature but less so for those of a collective or integral nature.

First, the right of recourse to the dispute settlement system is conditioned on the N or I of benefits accruing directly or indirectly to the Member bringing the complaint under the covered agreements.[41] The Dispute Settlement Understanding creates a rebuttable presumption that the breach of WTO rules constitutes a prima facie case of N or I.[42] Only a Member at the other end of a bilateral relationship that has suffered N or I of their benefits at the hands of other Members' measures can bring a claim. This admissibility test sits uncomfortably with obligations that are meant to protect collective interests. Since everyone suffers as a result of the breach of a collective obligation, each and every Member should have a right to bring a complaint, whether or not the breach has nullified or impaired benefits accruing to it.

Second, the dispute settlement system entertains claims demanding the redress of the N or I of benefits, even when it is not caused by the breach of a treaty obligation.[43] By contrast, claims for breach of obligations that do not N or I someone else's benefits accruing under the agreement will not fly. This too is unsuitable for the enforcement of collective obligations. Unlike bilateral ones, collective obligations are not designed to protect the trade interests of specific Members, but for the collective interest. As Pawuelyn notes, when a bilateral obligation is breached, it is not necessarily breached as against all other parties, but only as against the one or more states towards whom the particular promise, allegedly breached, is owed, whereas a collective obligation constitutes a promise made to all state parties collectively, hence its breach is necessarily a breach against all of them.[44] Thus, a dispute settlement system suitable for collective obligations should focus on whether or not Members' actions have breached the collective interests protected by the obligations, irrespective of the specific impact of that breach on individual Members.

Finally, when the defendant fails to bring the measure found to be inconsistent with a covered agreement into compliance with the recommendations of a ruling, the WTO dispute settlement allows the claimant to suspend the application to the defendant of concessions or other obligations under the covered agreements.[45]

---

[40]Article 3.2 DSU.

[41]Article XXIII.1 GATT 1994.

[42]Article 3.8 DSU.

[43]Article XXII.1 (b) and (c).

[44]See Pauwelyn (2003b), p. 65.

[45]Article 22.2 DSU.

Only bilateral obligations consisting of reciprocal trade concessions can be suspended without affecting the interests of other Members. Collective obligations are not "suspendable" because their suspension damages the common interest they protect. Pauwelyn expressly objects the availability of countermeasures against the breach of collective obligations included in the TRIPS agreement.[46] He argues that WTO Members should reconsider whether trade retaliation can be taken under all possible WTO obligations, or whether it should, for example, be limited to commitments set out in country-specific schedules.[47]

Given these inconsistencies, it is not surprising that at regional level, many PTAs exclude chapters consisting predominantly of collective obligations from the dispute settlement system, or at least limit its application to them.[48]

5 Looking Ahead

5.1 Keep Fighting Trade Protectionism

The key task of the WTO, as enshrined in the preamble of its constitutional chart, is to combat trade protectionism by entering into "... reciprocal and mutually advantageous arrangements directed to the substantial reduction of tariffs and other barriers to trade and to the elimination of discriminatory treatment in international trade relations." Trade protectionist measures include trade policy measures *strictu sensu* such as tariffs and quotas and non-trade policy measures deliberately applied as disguised restrictions on international trade.

Fighting trade protectionism, was the key reason for the creation of the GATT/WTO. The recent rise in trade protectionism[49] should serve as a stark reminder of the need for the WTO to stay focused on delivering its core mandate. There is still plenty of room for improving market access on agriculture, non-agriculture products and services and for addressing trade-distorting domestic support in all these sectors. No effort should be spared in trying to resume multilateral negotiations to this effect. In addition, Members should step up efforts to unblock the appointment of new Appellate Body members or find alternative ways to ensure that trade disputes remain resolved through a rule-based system.

A basic package of bilateral tariff concessions supported by functioning negotiation and enforcement mechanisms, may seem unambitious to address the challenges stemming from the new patterns of trade in the twenty first century. But at a

---

[46]See Pauwelyn (2003b), p. 77 citing the *EC-Bananas* case, where Ecuador obtained authorisation to suspend its obligations vis a vis the EC under the TRIPs agreement.

[47]Ibid.

[48]See, e.g. Articles 27.8, 28.20 and 29.10 USMCA.

[49]See WTO Report on G20 Trade Measures (Mid-May 2019 to Mid-October 2019). https://www.wto.org/english/news_e/news19_e/report_trdev_21nov19_e.pdf.

time when the very existence of the multilateral trading system is threatened by deep structural factors, preventing WTO Members from descending into a vicious circle of unilateral protectionist and retaliatory measures should be regarded as a resound success.

5.2 *Avoid Expanding the WTO Rule-Book with Hard Collective Obligations*

On top of the escalation of protectionism, trade flows are increasingly affected by within the border non-trade policy measures.[50] This raises a difficult question about the remit of the WTO, i.e. how far should the WTO rule-book be expanded with hard collective obligations aimed at addressing these new type of barriers? The question is not new. Back in 1995, John H. Jackson put it in these terms: "A major question facing international trade negotiators, as well as theorists, is which non-tariff barriers are really trade barriers that should be regulated by international rules and which are barriers that affect trade but are really legitimate government policies that are not intended to discriminate against foreign products or are simply societal preferences that give one country certain advantages over another so that trade is possible in the first place."[51] Patrick Low lists a number of considerations that should be born in mind when answering this question.[52]

This paper argues that there is not a strong case for expanding the WTO agenda in this way. The WTO is neither a regulatory nor a standard setting body, and lacks any mandate over non-trade policies such as labour or environmental policies, consumer protection, anti-corruption or cybersecurity. The adoption of disciplines on non-trade policies *per se*, irrespective of their trade restrictive or discriminatory effect, falls outside its area of competence. The WTO should not follow the path of recent PTAs, which have clearly crossed this line, moving beyond the usual goal of eliminating trade restrictions, all the way up to the attainment of common regulatory standards for the protection of human life, health or safety, animal or plant life or health.[53]

For example, the only regulatory aspect of the internet the WTO should be interested in, is on measures that have a direct impact on digital trade such as

---

[50]See above n2, n3 and n4.

[51]Jackson et al. (1995), p. 378.

[52]Low (2009), pp. 327–334.

[53]For example, the USMCA includes an Environment Chapter whose objectives are: "to promote mutually supportive trade and environmental policies and practices; promote high levels of environmental protection and effective enforcement of environmental laws; and enhance the capacities of the Parties to address trade-related environmental issues, including through cooperation, in the furtherance of sustainable development." (Article 24.2). The objective of promoting high levels of environmental protection *per se* goes beyond the objective of tackling the trade restrictive impact of environmental policies.

taxes on digital products, restrictions on payments and transfers and measures blocking the cross-border flow of data necessary for conducting trade. And the only thing WTO disciplines should require from Members adopting non-trade policy measures having a direct impact on trade such as the protection of individuals' privacy is to ensure that, whatever the degree of protection chosen, it is implemented in the least trade restrictive way.

There are a number of reasons that advice against drifting too much away from the WTO's core mandate. To start with, it is very difficult to define the exact scope of non-trade policy measures to be disciplined by WTO obligations. There are wide regulatory and policy differences among WTO Members. Collective obligations on non-trade policies may end up forcing an undesirable degree of regulatory convergence among Members' operating in very dissimilar regulatory contexts. There is not sufficient evidence available to decide what policy areas should be added to the trade rule-book and how should they be disciplined.[54] Trade agreements are now subject to intense scrutiny by a civil society that now demands clarity on the costs and benefits of subjecting non-trade policy measures to market access considerations. When trade obligations target non-trade policy areas which are already subject to specific international regimes, there is a risk of creating overlaps, inconsistencies and even conflicts between incompatible rules that could exacerbate the fragmentation of international law.[55] Finally, as noted by Lester, in a world where nations compete for investment, there is a strong incentive for autonomous or unilateral reforms to provide investors with the assurances they seek, that weakens the case for mandatory international rules aimed at improving domestic institutions.[56]

5.3 Strengthen the WTO's Deliberative Function

To remain relevant in years to come, in addition to keep fighting protectionism, the WTO must address non-protectionist trade restrictions caused by non-trade policy measures adopted within the borders. But it has to do it other than by expanding its rule book with hard collective obligations. The WTO's deliberative function, also known as the WTO's 'missing middle',[57] i.e. everything done within the WTO other than negotiations and litigation—is the right tool to deal with this new type of barriers. It provides a non-adversarial institutional framework capable of fostering

[54]There is a trade-off between respecting differences in national preferences and exploiting the efficiency gains from regulatory convergence. See WTO (2013) World Trade Report 2013, above footnote 4, p. 281.

[55]See International Law Commission (2006) Report of International Law Commission on Fragmentation of International Law: Difficulties Arising from the Diversification and Expansion of International Law.

[56]See Lester (2011), pp. 209–278.

[57]See Pascal Lamy's speech on 1/10/10. https://www.wto.org/english/news_e/sppl_e/sppl173_e.htm. On the case for strengthening the WTO missing middle, see Evenett (2009), pp. 359–374.

an open, participatory and frank dialogue among Members suitable for identifying common objectives and developing cooperation mechanisms to achieve them. Four set of measures could be adopted to reinforce the institutional framework underpinning the WTO's deliberative function to this effect.

First, reinforce the functioning of the committee structure where deliberations take place. A significant amount of work is already being carried out behind the scenes by WTO committees such as the TBT and SPS ones.[58] With adequate support and minor changes on their way of functioning, more could be done by them and by others directly concerned with the interface between trade and non-trade policy matters such as the Committees on Trade in Financial Services and Trade and Environment and those involved in the Work Programme on Electronic Commerce. For example, regulators and public authorities could be encouraged to attend committee meetings in addition to trade diplomats. Regulators' face to face meetings can contribute to understand and sensitize parties to the needs, priorities, and perspectives of their counterparts, to foster mutual trust and to identify regulatory equivalences necessary for minimizing regulatory diversities. WTO committees could also develop more sophisticated consultation mechanisms with the private sector and civil society in order to gain non-governmental perspectives on relevant matters. Dialogue and exchange of information with external stakeholders can inform an evidence-based deliberation of the case for expanding the WTO agenda and to identify common objectives and formulate best practices or other type of soft commitments to achieve them.[59]

Second, reinforce the Trade Policy Review Mechanism, which plays a critical role in enhancing transparency and understanding of the trade policies and practices of WTO Members. The non-litigious environment within which the process takes place is particularly useful for monitoring compliance with good regulatory practices and other soft commitments that could be developed by WTO committees. There is plenty of room for extending and refining the role of this mechanism.[60] So far, reviews are focused on measures directly affecting imports and exports. There is nothing preventing Members from expanding the scope of the review to cover non-trade policy measures with a direct impact on trade such as environmental, labour or competition policies as well as regulatory and administrative practices. Given the importance of technical assistance for the implementation of soft commitments necessary for the attainment of common objectives, trade policy reviews should also be extended to cover the provision of technical assistance by donor Members and its use by recipient Members. In addition, the preparation of trade policy reports has a positive side effect: by encouraging the involvement of various economic ministries in the exercise of explaining and rationalising policies affecting

[58]See Bohnenberger (2019), pp. 30–31.

[59]Finally, mechanisms should be put in place to provide targeted technical and financial assistance for WTO Members who struggle to attend and influence the debate within these committees.

[60]See Chaisse and Matsushita (2013), pp. 9–36.

trade, it promotes greater coherence in economic policymaking at the national level.[61]

Third, reinforce cooperation with international organizations with competence on policy areas that interface with trade such as environmental protection, employment and health. They are better placed than the WTO to address the trade restrictive effects of non-trade policy measures. Effective cooperation with them can enhance coherence between the WTO legal system and regulations developed in other multilateral fora. It can also provide trade diplomats with valuable knowledge and experience for dealing with non-trade policies in a more trade friendly way. By the same token, these organizations could benefit from a better understanding of the intricacies of the multilateral regulatory framework for trade. There is also a strong case for reinforcing cooperation with Multilateral Development Banks and other agencies responsible for delivering capacity building and technical assistance for WTO Members in need for help to implement good regulatory practices and other soft commitments necessary for minimizing the trade restrictive effects of non-trade policy measures.

Fourth, it would not be possible to strengthen the WTO's deliberative function without the support of a stronger Secretariat. It should be better equipped to carry out technical studies on the interface between trade and non-trade policies. It should play an active role in facilitating cooperation between the WTO and other international organizations, civil society and the private sector. And it should be directly involved in the delivery of the technical assistance necessary for the implementation of soft collective obligations, coordinating between donors, beneficiaries and technical assistance providers. To do all this, it is essential to endow the Secretariat with a larger budget and give it more independence from Members to avoid being constrained by the shackles of consensus every step of the way.

6 Conclusion

The survival of the WTO in years to come will depend on its ability to secure an open and non-discriminatory rule-based multilateral trading system in a changing trading landscape. As outlined above, the threat of trade protectionism has not faded away but increased. In addition, an increasingly interdependent economy, the information and communications technology revolution and significant changes in the socio-economic context within which trade takes place, are exposing trade flows to non-protectionist policy measures adopted within the border like never before. To remain fit for purpose to discharge its core task, the WTO needs yet again to adjust its obligations and institutional framework to this new trading landscape. This paper unveiled the risks of doing so by expanding the WTO rule-book with hard collective

[61] WTO Secretariat Background Note 'Coherence in Global Economic Policymaking and Cooperation between the WTO, the IMF and the World Bank' (WT/TF/COH/S/7 29 April 2003), para 74.

obligations disciplining non-trade policies. Instead, it argued that the best course of action for the WTO in years to come is to keep fighting trade protectionism through negotiations and litigation, and to address the trade restrictive effects of non-protectionist policies by strengthening its deliberative function.

Acknowledgments The article has benefited from feedback provided by participants to the workshop "Paradise Lost or Found? The Post-WTO Int'l "Legal" Order, (Utopian & Dystopian Possibilities)" held at the Dickson Poon School of Law, King's College London), 18–19 October 2019, Joost Pauwelyn and an anonymous reviewer. The usual caveats apply.

References

Acharya R (2016) Introduction – regional trade agreements: recent developments. In: Acharya R (ed) Regional trade agreements and the multilateral trading system. Cambridge University Press, Cambridge

Bohnenberger F (2019) Between law and politics: WTO regime management as everyday diplomatic practice. Paper presented at 8th PEPA/SIEL Conference, King's College, London, 30–31 May 2019

Chaisse J, Matsushita M (2013) Maintaining the WTO's supremacy in the international trade order: a proposal to refine and revise the role of the trade policy review mechanism. J Int Econ Law 16 (1):9–36

Evenett SJ (2009) Aid for trade and the "Missing Middle" of the World Trade Organization. Glob Gov 15(3):359–374

Hofmann C, Osnago A, Ruta M (2019) The content of preferential trade agreements. World Trade Rev 18(3):365–398

Jackson JH, Davey WJ, Sykes AO (1995) Legal problems of international economic relations, cases, materials and text, 3rd edn. West Group, St. Paul, p 378

Lester S (2011) The role of the international trade regime in global governance. UCLA J Int Law Foreign Aff 16(2):209–278

Low P (2009) Potential future functions of the world trade organization. Glob Gov 15(3):327–334

Pauwelyn J (2003a) A typology of multilateral treaty obligations: are WTO obligations bilateral or collective in nature? Eur J Int Law 14(5):907–951

Pauwelyn J (2003b) Conflict of norms in public international law. How WTO relates to other rules of international law. Cambridge University Press, Cambridge, p 65

Pauwelyn J (2014) Taking the preferences out of preferential trade agreements: TTIP as a provider of public goods? In: Morin J-F, Novotná T, Ponjaert F, Telò M (eds) The politics of transatlantic trade negotiations: TTIP in a globalized world. Routledge, London

Waiting for Cordell Hull

Simon N. Lester

Contents

1 Introduction

The world trading system has been in some sort of crisis for at least two decades. After a remarkable expansion from the GATT to the WTO during the Uruguay Round, the system has been surprisingly stagnant. In 1999, the famous "Battle in Seattle" demonstrated the strength of the objections of civil society to certain aspects of the trade regime. Then came the developing/developed country divide that blocked progress on the Doha Development Agenda. And as WTO negotiations stalled, bilateral and regional trade agreements proliferated, undermining the WTO's central place in the trading system. Now we are in the midst of several challenges put forward by the Trump administration to fundamental aspects of the system, including China's participation in the WTO, binding dispute settlement and an appeals mechanism, the MFN principle, and the classification of countries as "developing."

Associate Director of the Cato Institutes's Herbert A. Stiefel Center for Trade Policy Studies.

S. N. Lester (✉)
Cato Institute, Washington, DC, USA
e-mail: slester@cato.org

M. K. Lewis et al. (eds.), *A Post-WTO International Legal Order*,
https://doi.org/10.1007/978-3-030-45428-9_4

While these developments should not cause outright panic, they should lead us to think about alternatives to the WTO and imagine how the WTO might be replaced if it were to disappear. What are the flaws in the system, and how can we address them in order to create a more stable and functional system?

The simplest answer for what to do in a post-WTO world is to re-create the WTO. We have a model that mostly works. The alleged flaws are not as significant as they may seem right now, and the Trump administration will not continue forever. If the WTO collapses, governments should replicate it when the opportunity arises.

But as it is sometimes said, "Why let a good crisis go to waste?" If the WTO disappears or is no longer functioning, and we then have the opportunity to start fresh, we should aim high. Why not strive for perfection, or, at the least, excellence, rather than just muddling through as we usually do? Why not try to create a "utopian" trading system?

One aspect of creating a post-WTO utopia is the substance of WTO 2.0. The principles, and the detailed rules implementing them, are a core part of the exercise.

But at this unique time in trade policy history, the role of individuals and their passions, beliefs, and personal leadership is just as important. Many years ago, the trade policy world saw such leadership with U.S. Secretary of State Cordell Hull. It may be that the only way out of the current mess is through someone with a similar enthusiasm for an open trade policy under a rules-based system.

Of course, there is a risk in putting too much faith in individuals, with the current U.S. political situation as perhaps the best evidence. Sometimes people are the problem, and we need strong institutions to constrain them. At the same time, institutions have problems of their own. Without a shakeup every now and then, they fall into dangerous ruts. Change becomes impossible as interest groups' relationships with institutions become entrenched. After too much time with a particular institutional framework, real change may require innovative personal leadership in order to limit the influence of interest groups over our institutions and refocus them on their core purpose.

This chapter discusses the major problems with the current U.S. trade policy-making process (which, given the size and role of the United States, has a big impact on the trading system experienced by the rest of the world), and considers how a trade liberalizing visionary might break the interest group stranglehold in order to replicate some of Hull's successes and create a better version of the WTO. This visionary does not have to be American, but U.S. leadership is vital, because a system without American participation will be much less valuable. Just as the P4 countries developed a trade agreement that was moved along by Americans (negotiations to expand the P4 evolved into talks to form a new agreement—the Trans-Pacific Partnership), any country or individual can lead the way. But someone must lead, because as of this moment, and for perhaps a couple decades now, the world trading system has been wandering aimlessly.

2 Interest Group Paralysis in Trade Policy

Trade policy, and trade negotiations and trade agreements, have always involved a battle of interest groups. Producers who mainly sell domestically tend to favor high tariffs, whereas exporters want to see tariffs reduced. These two groups have long been at the heart of fights over how high tariffs should be and how much liberalization should take place in trade negotiations.

In recent decades, though, the role of interest groups has grown. First, the scope of the trade regime was expanded through lobbying by these groups. For example, various intellectual property holders convinced developed country governments that their issues were "trade" issues and should be on the trade agenda. With that precedent set, the expansion continued, as business groups pushed additional issues (such as investment protection and regulatory cooperation), and civil society groups weighed in with their own concerns, such as labor rights, environmental protection, and gender issues.

Second, having expanded the scope, lobbying ensued over exactly what the rules in these areas should say. Now, instead of just haggling over which industries should see tariff cuts, interest groups face off in the trade negotiating arena over a variety of substantive policy matters. As noted, intellectual property holders succeeded in inserting their issues into trade agreements, but civil society then fought back, trying to narrow the scope of these rules.

The result has been an expanded trading system characterized by controversy and stagnation. Trade negotiations take longer and generate more debate than ever. Slight tweaks in one direction or the other have been tried, with the balance of interest groups who are favored and disfavored adjusted slightly, but progress remains challenging. In addition, perhaps in part because of too many interest groups and too many countries, negotiations have moved away from the multilateral arena to preferential trade deals at the bilateral, regional, or plurilateral level. The WTO's negotiating arm is barely functioning.

To restore the centrality of the world trading system, we need someone who can push interest groups aside and make the case for trade liberalization directly to the people and to the political class. In theory, this leader could come from anywhere, and ideally there would be more than one. The problem of interest group influence over policy is widespread and applies to all political systems. But there will need to be an American aspect to this, because it would be difficult for a foreign visionary to influence U.S. policy, and without U.S. participation and leadership, the system will be of far less relevance. What the world trading system needs is a new Cordell Hull.

3 The Cordell Hull Vision of Peace and Prosperity Through Trade

In the 1930s, the motivation for trade negotiations, at least in the United States, did not come primarily from industry. Rather, it was part of a general reformulation of trade policy-making in the U.S. government, the implications of which may not have been well understood at the time. To a great extent, the reciprocal trade agreements of that period were a response to the Smoot-Hawley tariffs of 1930 (and decades of Congressional mismanagement of tariffs), and an attempt to establish new procedures that would avoid a repetition of that protectionist failure. Rather than have members of Congress agree to each other's demands for protection for each one's constituents (log-rolling), the Reciprocal Trade Agreements Act put the Executive branch in charge of negotiating lower tariffs with trading partners.[1] With the Executive branch now taking the lead, the practical result was that trade negotiations were guided by certain influential government officials, such as Secretary of State Cordell Hull and his staff, based on the view that trade liberalization constituted good economics and would encourage peaceful international relations.[2]

Some industries supported the idea of trade liberalization, while others objected, but the main arguments took place in the context of whether to reauthorize the Reciprocal Trade Agreements Act (RTAA), rather than in the negotiations themselves. In fact, industry complained that it was shut out of the negotiating process that was being run by the Executive branch.[3] The structure of industry interaction with the trade bureaucracy and the negotiating process itself were designed to keep private interests at a distance.[4]

Thus, at this time, the initiative for trade negotiations, as well as their content, came mainly from government officials who were pursuing a particular policy vision, rather than from industry demands. It was perhaps a historical accident and an anomaly, but the role of interest groups was diminished during this transition period.[5] The dominant role of Executive branch officials in guiding the scope and

---

[1]Irwin (1998), pp. 325–352.

[2]Hull (1948), p. 352; Ikenberry (1993), p.170; Irwin et al. (2008), pp. 9–13.

[3]Aaronson (1996), p. 36 ("Workers, congressmen, and some business leaders complained that the process for determining tariff reduction was secretive and did not include representatives from the people or affected interests.").

[4]Haggard (1988), pp. 115–116.

[5]Irwin (1998), pp. 341–342. ("Unlike Smoot-Hawley, Congress's consideration of the RTAA attracted virtually no participation by interest groups. Haggard reasons that 'in contrast to 1930 . . . when interest groups were the main protagonists and specific tariff rates the issue, the most important issues at stake in 1934 were institutional, centering on the transfer of authority from Congress to the executive' (1988, 112). The RTAA was simply enabling legislation, and no one knew how the authority would be used, how successful the negotiations would be, or how extensive the agreements might be. When the RTAA was passed, Congress could not anticipate how important the legislation would become or even whether it would be sustained by future Congresses. In view of the many short-lived trade policy experiments of the past three decades, it was

content of trade negotiations continued through the planning for, and negotiation of, the GATT/ITO.[6]

4 Breaking Free from Interest Group Influence

Over time, domestic trade policy-making changed in the United States, with industry and other private groups exerting more influence. As everyone learned the new process, interest groups came to play a more important role. Congressional reform measures in the mid-1970s meant special interests had additional opportunities to weigh in during the legislative process.[7] But the most important change came on the Executive branch side, where the Advisory Committee system created a special channel for private actors to communicate their views with trade negotiators, from which they had been effectively shut out in the 1930s and 1940s.

Advisory Committees started tentatively as part of trade legislation passed in 1962, but were more fully developed as part of the 1974 Trade Act.[8] The new system had its first test in the Tokyo Round GATT talks. John Ikenberry argues that this system "institutionalized" private interests, thereby allowing the U.S. Trade Representative's Office to "co-opt" them, and in this way build a trade consensus for the Tokyo Round, which passed Congress easily.[9]

But the co-option of industry proved to be short-lived, and interest groups' relationship to the government moved in the other direction. In the next big trade negotiations, the Uruguay Round and the NAFTA, the scope of trade agreements expanded in terms of their impact on domestic policy-making. Instead of being mostly limited to providing constraints on discriminatory trade policies, there were now trade rules that, in and of themselves, constituted regulation of intellectual property, labor, and the environment, to name a few. To a great extent, this expansion was the direct result of lobbying by interest groups, including both industry and civil society. The general framework established for the trade regime

not obvious that the RTAA would necessarily bring a lasting, durable change in U.S. trade policy making. Perhaps this accounts for the minimal participation of interest groups, even among export associations, in the RTAA's passage.")

[6]Aaronson (1996), pp. 34–60. ("... State Department officials were overconfident of their ability to broker between various interests to develop American trade policies. After all, the Trade Agreements Division ... had the responsibility of recommending measures to implement Article VII of the Atlantic Charter. This, they thought, gave them alone, rather than with members of Congress or business leaders, the expertise to broker the national interest on trade policy through a multilateral trade negotiation." p. 54); Irwin et al. (2008), pp. 46–52.

[7]Destler (1995), pp. 68–69. ("More open floor procedures also offered new opportunities for special interests to press their proposals").

[8]Campbell (1976), pp. 379–386; Winham (1980), pp. 383–385.

[9]Ikenberry (1989), pp. 297–301. He explains that through these committees, "the role of interest groups was made more predictable."

was susceptible to the influence of interest groups who saw how they might use it to their advantage. These groups came up with theories as to why their issues belonged in trade agreements and were able to convince key governments that an expansion of trade agreements made sense as a matter of policy or politics.

One of the first big new areas to be included was intellectual property protection. U.S. companies and business groups saw a possible connection between intellectual property protection and trade, and convinced the U.S. government that this issue should be part of trade agreements. These groups also brought their European and Japanese counterparts on board with the effort, and together they were able to argue successfully for including IP protections in the Uruguay Round of the GATT negotiations (as well as the NAFTA negotiations).[10]

At the same time these negotiations were taking place, labor, environmental, and other civil society groups had begun to notice the impact of trade agreements on their issues and were often opposing trade agreements as a result. In response, rules to blunt the perceived negative impact were developed, often taking the form of requiring domestic regulation in these areas. Early rules were non-binding, but over the years, they became stronger.[11]

Importantly, when interest groups argued for favorable new rules it was not simply a one-off lobbying victory. Rather, in many cases, a permanent private sector-government connection was created, to be used to push the rules further at a later time. In this way, industries and civil society groups developed close ties to the trade bureaucracy.

For example, as intellectual property holders argued for the U.S. government to use trade policy to toughen intellectual property protections around the world, a special section within USTR was created, and later expanded, to handle these issues. In the early to mid-1990s, the relevant USTR office was made up of several individuals doing a mix of intellectual property, investment and services. Then in the 2000s, with the accession of China to the WTO, more serious concerns began to emerge related to intellectual property protection. By the mid-2000s, more power and more resources were devoted to these issues. In 2006, a separate intellectual property office was created, headed by an Assistant USTR for Intellectual Property, as well as a Deputy in charge of enforcement.[12] By this time, the intellectual property staff consisted of multiple, dedicated individuals.[13]

---

[10]The most detailed and comprehensive explanation of the role of IP companies in U.S. and global trade policy comes from Sell (2003).

[11]See, e.g., Charnovitz, Steve, An Appraisal of the Labor Chapter of the Trans-Pacific Partnership, Remarks Submitted to the Committee on Ways and Means Democrats, January 2016.

[12]USTR Schwab Announces New Office Focused on Intellectual Property, press release, 23 June 2006, https://ustr.gov/archive/Document_Library/Press_Releases/2006/June/USTR_Schwab_Announces_New_Office_Focused_on_Intellectual_Property.html Currently, the office is called the Office of Intellectual Property and Innovation.

[13]By the time of the Obama administration, it had 7–8 staffers working there. Conversations with U.S. government official.

Similarly, labor interests eventually pushed successfully for a permanent labor section at USTR to deal with their issues. A dedicated labor office at USTR was created towards the end of the Clinton administration, but it was the Bush administration that hired the first staffer. A second and third person were hired during that administration. A fourth staffer came during the Obama years, but one person then left. They have also had a number of "detailees" over the years, from the Labor and State Departments.[14]

The expansion of the trade regime, and the ties between interest groups and the government, has continued to play a major role in shaping the U.S. trade agenda over the years, regardless of which political party was in power. For example, with a general goal of gaining support for—or at least reducing opposition to—the TPP from environmental groups, during the Obama administration USTR pushed for a strong environmental chapter, and was looking for new issues to include. In response, as part of the notice and comment process for the TPP, several environmental groups raised the issue of shark finning, and argued that the TPP offers an opportunity to encourage domestic actions to prevent this practice.[15] In reaction to this request, USTR included provisions on shark finning in its proposals for the TPP environmental chapter.[16]

Taking the approach to the extreme, the Trump administration has put interest groups (e.g., long-time trade lobbyists for the steel industry) in charge of significant portions of U.S. trade policy.[17] The result has been a trade policy that gives priority to favored industries, such as steel and aluminum, who were the intended beneficiaries of the Section 232 "national security" tariffs imposed by the Trump administration.[18] The proliferation of tariffs (in these sectors and against China) then opened

---

[14]Conversations with U.S. government official.

[15]Oceana, Re: Request for Comments on the Proposed Trans-Pacific Partnership Free Trade Agreement, 74 Fed. Reg. 4480 (26 January 2009)" (PDF file), March 11, 2009, downloaded from Oceana website, http://oceana.org/sites/default/files/TPP_comments_3_11_09_FOR_FILING_2.pdf; Humane Society International, Re: United States—Trans Pacific Partnership Agreement, Docket #: USTR-2009-0041, (PDF File), 25 January 2010, downloaded from Humane Society International Website, http://www.hsi.org/assets/pdfs/tpp_comments_ustr_012510.pdf.

[16]U.S. Tables Parts Of TPP Environmental Text On Conservation Issues, *Inside U.S. Trade*, 1 April 2011, https://insidetrade.com/inside-us-trade/us-tables-parts-tpp-environmental-text-conservation-issues; See also: McGrath, Matt, Giant US trade deal might weaken shark fin ban, *BBC News*, 16 January 2014, http://www.bbc.com/news/science-environment-25743459.

[17]Peterson, Matt, The Making of a Trade Warrior, The Atlantic, 29 December 2018 https://www.theatlantic.com/politics/archive/2018/12/robert-lighthizers-bid-cut-chinas-trade influence/578611/; Markay, Lachlan, Trump Officials Oversee Trade Rules Gamed by Former Clients, Daily Beast, 15 July 2019 https://www.thedailybeast.com/trump-officials-oversee-trade-rules-gamed-by-former-clients.

[18]Unfortunately for those industries, the overall trade policy under the Trump administration has undermined domestic manufacturing and left them worse off. *See* Institute for Supply Management, November 2019 Manufacturing ISM *Report on Business*, 2 December 2019, https://www.instituteforsupplymanagement.org/ISMReport/MfgROB.cfm?SSO=1; Rabouin, Dion, The End of Trump's Manufacturing Renaissance, *Axios*, 5 December 2019, https://www.axios.com/trump-tariffs-manufacturing-job-losses-6c4841de-0c01-4c4f-99c5-6e2bf26d670e.html.

the door to lobbying for exclusions, with well-resourced and well-connected companies that could afford the lawyers and lobbyists who understood the system as the ones best able to avoid the harm.[19] And the Trump administration has even been balanced in its outreach to lobbyists, trying to appeal to important interest groups on the left as well.[20] Trump himself may very well be thinking about trade policy in a way that ignores special interests, as he simply believes tariffs are good,[21] which benefits interest groups without them having to lobby for anything. But his administration is taking a more traditional approach that caters to interest groups.

Further tweaks to the interest group balance may get a trade agreement or two passed, but they are not going to solve the current problems over the long term and they will not reinvigorate multilateral trade liberalization and institutions. Going back and forth between stronger investment protection or intellectual property rights for business groups, or more labor, environment, and gender rights for civil society groups, is not an answer. There is no configuration of interest group demands for global governance policies that, on its own, will make the trade regime permanently secure and stable.

In the years leading up to the Trump administration, we have had both technocrats and outsiders to trade policy running U.S. trade policy. They worked within the system in the normal way that all U.S. policies are conducted: They courted interest groups and counted votes. But that only works as a quick fix to get a particular piece of legislation passed, and it doesn't even do that in every case (the TPP is a good example of recent failure).

The only long-term answer is to find someone who believes in trade liberalization and has the willingness and ability to fight for it. We need a modern day Cordell Hull, who can make the case for free trade with the passion that Donald Trump makes the case for tariffs. We need someone who will explain why imports are good, why bilateral trade deficits are nothing to worry about (and why overall trade deficits are not necessarily a problem), and that our trading partners are not all cheating us. Someone with conviction who believes in the cause of trade liberalization.

Just like Cordell Hull responded to Smoot-Hawley with an overhaul of U.S. trade policy-making, someone needs to respond to the Trump administration's economic nationalism with a principled case for trade liberalization. Trade agreements should

---

[19]Swanson, Ana and Vogel, Kenneth, Trump's Tariffs Set Off Storm of Lobbying, NY Times, 16 March 2018, https://www.nytimes.com/2018/03/16/us/politics/trump-tariffs-lobbying.html; see also, McDaniel, Christine and Parks, Danielle, Tariff Exclusion Requests: A One-Year Update, Mercatus Center, 11 April 2019, https://www.mercatus.org/bridge/commentary/tariff-exclusion-requests-one-year-update.

[20]Markay, Lachlan and Stein, Sam, Donald Trump Is Quietly Building an Alliance With Liberals on Trade, Daily Beast, 16 November 2017. https://www.thedailybeast.com/donald-trump-is-quietly-building-an-alliance-with-liberals-on-trade.

[21]Schlesinger, Jacob, Trump Forged His Ideas on Trade in the 1980s—and Never Deviated, *Wall Street Journal*, 15 November 2018, https://www.wsj.com/articles/trump-forged-his-ideas-on-trade-in-the-1980sand-never-deviated-1542304508; and Donald J. Trump, Twitter post, 2 March 2018, 5:50 a.m., https://twitter.com/realdonaldtrump/status/969525362580484098.

no longer be just a collection of interest group favors. This approach is not a long-term way to convince people of the value of trade.

It may not be possible, of course, to exclude interest groups in the manner that occurred with the RTAA legislation. There is unlikely to be any institutional innovation that fools interest groups these days. They are well-resourced and can usually find a way in.

However, the Trump administration has demonstrated how particular interest groups can be ignored to an extent that has taken many people by surprise. While part of the administration's strategy is to cater to particular groups, another part is to challenge other groups, by standing up for principle and pushing ahead no matter the criticism. For example, for many years, pro-business Republicans have insisted that they wanted a broad system of investment protection with ISDS to allow foreign investors to sue host country governments. But the Trump administration has significantly scaled back the system of investment protection in the renegotiated NAFTA,[22] and business groups have gone along with the change, demonstrating that some interest group demands can be resisted. Whatever else one might say about Trump and United States Trade Representative Robert Lighthizer, they have the courage of their convictions. To revitalize the trading system, we just need different convictions.

5 What Might a Utopian WTO 2.0 Look Like?

What convictions should we hope for? The core principles of the GATT/WTO are good and remain essential: Tariff reductions, non-discrimination, and transparency. These are the foundation of the mutually agreed constraints on protectionism that have always been, and should remain, the focus of the WTO.

Non-discrimination includes the MFN principle, of course. That means putting the brakes on the proliferation of FTAs. They will not be abandoned entirely, as there are reasons for regional economic integration that is deeper than what can be achieved at the multilateral level. For example, complete tariff elimination or regulatory convergence may be possible between close neighbors with good relations and similar political systems (e.g. Australia and New Zealand). But FTAs should not be the focus of anyone's trade agenda. The Bush administration pushed FTAs in combination with a broad multilateral agenda; the Obama administration made the TPP and the TTIP the centerpiece of its trade negotiating agenda. The Trump administration has now put the emphasis squarely on bilateral negotiations, but they have made little progress even with this supposedly simpler approach. They

[22]Lester, Simon, The U.S.-Mexico-Canada (AKA the New NAFTA) Trade Deal: Investment Protection/ISDS, *International Economic Law and Policy Blog*, 1 October 2018. https://worldtradelaw.typepad.com/ielpblog/2018/10/the-us-mexico-and-maybe-nafta-trade-deal-investment-protectionisds.html.

have mainly scaled back existing deals (NAFTA and KORUS), and tried to make up for the withdrawal from the TPP with a very limited bilateral deal with Japan. Bilateral deals may have their place, but they are preferential and trade-distorting, and should generally be avoided. Truly non-discriminatory trade rules can only be effected at the multilateral level. Ultimately, what is needed here is a better balance. Rather than FTAs being the focus of trade negotiating activity, they should be a small supplemental component to a broadly multilateral system.

The scope of the trade regime also merits rethinking. As noted above, other issues have found their way into the trade regime over the years. They should be sent back where they came from. Intellectual property issues are interesting and important, but they have only a tenuous connection to trade. They should be sent over to WIPO to handle. Similarly, labor and environment issues should stay separate from trade agreements and institutions. Unifying global governance in one institution will have the dual problem of generating controversy and not working very well.

Trade rules should stay focused on traditional trade in goods and services. The scope of the goods rules is broad and the obligations are well-developed. No major changes are required here. By contrast, with services, there are significant gaps. International trade in services is growing, but only a small portion is effectively covered by trade disciplines. To expand the liberalization of trade in services, we should move away from the positive list approach of the WTO, and also away from the substantial and complex negative list carve outs in agreements such as the CPTPP. Instead, principles such as national treatment and MFN should apply to all services trade. For those worried about intrusion into domestic policy space, rather than carve out individual categories of trade in services through the use of positive or negative lists, a better approach would be to cover all trade in services and then use exceptions to preserve policy space (as is done for trade in goods). To make this work, these exceptions might need to be refined from the restrictive form they currently take in the GATT and the GATS. For example, instead of a closed list, there should be an open list applying to all "legitimate public policies." And the "necessary" standard should be replaced by a looser "related to" one. In this way, public policy exceptions can be effectively utilized in the area of trade in services, and broader coverage will not interfere excessively with domestic regulation.

In fact, the artificial separation of goods and services could be rethought. All goods have a services component (in their production and distribution), and the classification into one category or the other can be complex and contentious. A "General Agreement on Trade" that applies well-defined principles to all goods and services, and establishes exceptions for legitimate policies, would both simplify and expand the system.

Digital information flows are more complicated. Digital information crosses borders, but it is not usually traded in the traditional sense. As part of various trade agreements (CPTPP, the United States-Mexico-Canada Agreement (USMCA), the U.S.-Japan trade agreement), governments are developing detailed rules to deal with cross-border data transfers. The reality, however, is that these rules are about as well understood as was the GATT in 1947. They look like great principles on paper, but how will they apply to actual domestic laws and regulations?

What impact will the obligations and exceptions have on domestic policy?[23] It is worth pursuing this area, either in the context of trade agreements or outside of it, but we should not expect international governance to accomplish much any time soon.

One might think these foundations are all fine, but still wonder how the WTO 2.0 will work when WTO 1.0 seemed stalled for so long. That takes us back to our modern day Cordell Hull. For multilateral trade liberalization to move forward, the wealthy world needs to be willing to liberalize more. If governments will not agree to additional constraints on their own protectionism, there is not much point to trade negotiations. In order to make progress in this regard, wealthy governments need to address their own sensitivities (i.e., stand up to their entrenched interest groups). To take one example, the frequently abused anti-dumping process could be put on the table for negotiation. As another example, farm subsidies could be reduced. If the United States and others were willing to talk about these issues, it could spur developing countries to cut their very high tariffs.

But without a leader willing to make the case for liberalization, none of this will happen. The trade rhetoric of almost all U.S. political leaders focuses on the faults of other countries, and gives no indication that American policy has its own problems. In such an atmosphere, it becomes very difficult for U.S. trade negotiators to have the political cover to offer significant liberalization as part of a trade negotiation. (Making this effort even more difficult is that the "United States" is not just one entity on trade policy. There is the administration in control of the executive branch at any given time, but there will also be a role for Congress—with both the House of Representatives and the Senate—and two political parties.)

6 Trade vs. Foreign Policy

Finally, the trading system would benefit from the separation of trade policy and foreign policy. There are two aspects to this. First, as noted, most trade liberalization should be multilateral, with non-discrimination as the core principle. If this could be accomplished, governments would not be able to use FTAs to reward friends and punish enemies. While using FTAs in this way may achieve a higher number of trade deals in the short-term, it undermines the trading system in the long-term. To illustrate the problem, the United States negotiated a trade deal with Australia, but not with New Zealand, due to Australia's support for the Iraq War and New Zealand's failure to support it. The effort to reward Australia did lead to one more trade deal, but it also contributed to trade agreements being subservient to (bad) foreign policy.

[23]Lester, Simon, Will the New NAFTA Boost Digital Trade?, *National Interest*, 5 May 2019 https://nationalinterest.org/feature/will-new-nafta-boost-digital-trade-55707.

Second, more broadly, the U.S. government's pursuit of "economic statecraft"—"economic carrots and sticks to advance the national interest"[24]—interferes with trade and often causes more problems than it solves. Economic statecraft by the United States and other economic powers is likely to persist as long as their power does, but ideally it would be scaled back considerably. In particular, country-specific trade sanctions should be avoided in all but the most extreme circumstances. Using economic power to influence the policies of foreign governments through trade measures is rarely successful or desirable. (Sanctions on individual bad actors are less of a problem.)

It may not be possible to craft international trade rules to enforce this trade policy/foreign policy split. Rather, it will require a change in attitude from the major economic powers who use their economic leverage as part of an assertive foreign policy. The United States is probably the leading practitioner, but the European nations often participate in U.S. efforts; and China has its own foreign policy agenda relating to its "One China" policy, which it pursues by using the Belt and Road Initiative and other trade tools.

7 Conclusion

The creation of the world trading system was one of the most significant accomplishments in modern history. The exact moment of origin is debatable, but the groundwork was certainly laid by Cordell Hull during his long run as Secretary of State.

Despite the various crises, the world trading system created by Hull is not likely to collapse. The value of the exercise carried out by this book may not be in crafting a replacement for the WTO, but rather in imagining a system without the WTO, so that we are free to be more creative and to not feel bound by what has come before. That creative thinking can help solve many of the serious problems the system is facing today. Many participants in the system have been working hard on solutions. But it may take a person with just the right personality, background and vision to break away from the interest group dominance that has become entrenched and has contributed to the system's stagnation.

References

Aaronson S (1996) Trade and the American dream: a social history of postwar trade policy. University Press of Kentucky, Lexington, p 36

Campbell R (1976) The foreign trade aspects of the trade act of 1974, Part I. Wash Lee Law Rev 33 (2):325–393

[24] Drezner (2019), pp. 7–24.

Destler I (1995) American trade politics. Institute for International Economics, Washington, DC, pp 68–69
Drezner D (2019) Economic statecraft in the age of trump. Wash Q 42(3):7–24
Haggard S (1988) The institutional foundations of Hegemony: explaining the reciprocal trade agreements act of 1934. Int Org 42(1):91–119
Hull C (1948) Tearing down tariff walls. In: The Memoirs of Cordell Hull, vol 1. Macmillan Company, New York, p 352
Ikenberry J (1989) Manufacturing consensus: the institutionalization of American private interests in the Tokyo trade round. Comp Polit 21(3):289–305
Ikenberry J (1993) The political origins of Bretton Woods. In: A retrospective on the Bretton Woods system: lessons for international monetary reform. University of Chicago Press, Chicago, p 170
Irwin D (1998) From Smoot-Hawley to reciprocal trade agreements: changing the course of U.S. trade policy in the 1930s. In: The defining moment: the great depression and the American economy in the twentieth century. University of Chicago Press, Chicago, pp 325–352
Irwin D, Mavroidis P, Sykes A (2008) The genesis of the GATT. Cambridge University Press, Cambridge, pp 9–13
Sell S (2003) Private power, public law: the globalization of intellectual property rights. Cambridge University Press, Cambridge
Winham G (1980) Robert Strauss, the MTN, and the control of faction. J World Trade 14 (5):377–397

GAIA 2048—A 'Glocal Agency in Anthropocene': Cognitive and Institutional Change as 'Legal Science Fiction'

Rostam J. Neuwirth

Contents

1 Introduction

Why do we remember the past and not the future?[1]

We are writing at the end of the year 2048, and marking a period of efforts towards the establishment of a new and comprehensive global governance mechanism, known, for short, as "GAIA 2048". GAIA stands for "Glocal Agency in Anthropocene", and describes a project for a novel institutional framework to be set up with the objective of tackling humanity's most urgent problems and glocally governing and sustainably developing human affairs in the future.

The future is what matters the most right now, as the world is hoping to recover from the devastating effects of the time period known as the "Digital Dark Age". This is the era from 2030 until 2045 when—as the result of an Internet blackout (outage)—all prior digital resources, including records and archives, became inaccessible and, because of the wide prevalence of the Internet of Things (IOT), the

Professor of Law, Head of the Department of Global Legal Studies, University of Macau.

[1] Rovelli (2018), p. 3.

R. J. Neuwirth (✉)
University of Macau, Taipa, Macau, China
e-mail: rjn@um.edu.mo

M. K. Lewis et al. (eds.), *A Post-WTO International Legal Order*,
https://doi.org/10.1007/978-3-030-45428-9_5

same happened to most related technical applications and utilities.[2] In short, this dark period wiped out all digitally or electronically stored data. As a consequence, it not only paralysed all technical facilities and caused millions of casualties, but also led to a collective loss of humanity's memory, which, furthermore, caused a loss of identity. Many still speculate about what triggered the meltdown of the former information society based on the Internet, with the suggested causes ranging from scientific, economic, and political to cognitive and, notably, legal reasons.

For instance, scientific explanations range from a cyberattack using malware to a nuclear blackout caused by the detonation of an atomic warhead in outer space, an accident at CERN creating a black hole in Geneva following a malfunction of the Large Hadron Collider II, or a failure of the 5G network in combination with a data overload on the World Wide Web caused by states' geopolitical struggles and the monopolistic tendencies of various tech giants. Other people invoke politico-economic explanations, simply citing the second global financial crisis of 2029, which was caused by trade and currency wars that, inter alia, eroded the finances needed for the maintenance of the Internet's sophisticated infrastructure. Environmental factors are also often named, such as floods and rising sea levels, increased volcanic activity and earthquakes, combined with heatwaves and global pandemics, which disrupted or paralysed the energy supply by damaging its essential facilities.

Politics also played a role, as populism and racism increased, further fragmenting society into ever smaller units, down to its most vulnerable minority, the individual. Constitutional democracies came under threat from changes that were, at first, undetectably small but that eventually combined and posed a serious threat. In legal circles, the fragmentation of international law, the rise of norm conflicts due to bad regulation, overregulation and the automation that took over several fields of law[3] are mentioned as the prime causes of the inability of humanity to halt the dangers of the conditions it had created for itself. It again became obvious that the rule of law needed not just legal texts but also stable institutional guarantors at both the national and the global levels.[4]

It is more likely that the blackout was due to a combination of interrelated factors in an environment characterized by an increasing complexity and ever faster pace of change. Since time immemorial, humanity has struggled with change or, notably, with its perception of change, since this perception may itself have been subject to change.[5] However, since the last millennium many observers have noted an apparent effect of an acceleration of change or so-called "time shrinking".[6] This trend for change to accelerate started to pose a major threat to lawmakers and policymakers and, in particular, to law, as it became more difficult to "preserve its integrity over time, while managing to address the newly emerging circumstances that continually

[2]Petersen (2014), p. 283.

[3]Ashley (2017).

[4]Bacchus (2003), pp. 533–550.

[5]Wittmann (2016), p. 124.

[6]Ten Hoopen (1995), p. 577.

arise throughout our history".[7] Another threat to law came from unprecedented levels of technological innovation, which culminated in a situation in which the regulation of specific industries and technologies, such as those of artificial intelligence, nanotechnology, big data and genetics, failed to find a successful balance between their unknown risks and their expected benefits. In short, excessive levels of specialization, not met by an adequate general understanding, led technological progress to spin out of control.[8]

Thus, by the year 2020 the international legal order had witnessed the disastrous effects of a gradual loss of control caused by decades of neglecting first subtle and later obvious signs of multiple law and policy failures. These policy failures culminated in the failed attempts to reform the most important international institutions, the United Nations (UN) and the World Trade Organization (WTO), in a holistic and comprehensive manner. There was a failure to bridge the rift that was caused when the International Trade Organization (ITO) did not materialize; the ITO would have complemented the institutional balance between the three Bretton Woods sisters, the ITO, the IMF and the World Bank. In other words, the institutional failure of the ITO to materialize also meant that greater coherence, or to integrate trade and non-trade concerns, was renounced as an ideal for global governance. The separation between the UN on the one hand and the GATT on the other, can also be regarded as a further strong manifestation of a dualistic mode of thinking based on binary logic. Most of all, it was the beginning of a failure of cognitive modes of thinking to keep pace with technological changes in the context so as to provide a stable and coherent global institutional framework for the governance of global affairs.

Historically, the GATT 1947 was characterised as having found "itself without an inadequate legal and constitutional base and required to fill a vacuum created by the failure of the ITO".[9] The situation also meant that attempts to reconcile trade and non-trade concerns in both substantive and institutional terms was postponed to a distant day. This delay later led to the emergence of the "trade linkage debate", by which different pairs of "trade and ..." problems were supposed to be reconciled. Lacking their reconciliation, criticism of the WTO also became louder and culminated in the protests accompanying the 1999 Seattle WTO Ministerial Conference.[10] Since then, the failure to address non-trade concerns and to achieve greater policy coherence continued and provided further momentum to the procedural crisis affecting the WTO Dispute Settlement Body. In sum, a lack of political will as much as outdated cognitive modes framed by dualistic thinking led to the law being inadequate to meet the institutional and substantive challenges.

To exemplify the impact of cognition on whether the law meets the demands put upon it, the present chapter divides the time between the year 2020 and 2048 into two opposite scenarios. First, Sect. 1 traces the lost years by drawing up a dystopian

---

[7]Johnson (2007), p. 845.

[8]Harari (2017), p. 51.

[9]Jackson (1969), p. 51.

[10]DiMatteo (2003), pp. 95 and 102.

scenario, in which cognition remained largely static and dualistic, such that changes did not keep pace with the speed of technological and scientific innovation. Section 2 is more utopian, in the sense that it relies on a newly acquired cognitive mode of thinking as exemplified by synaesthesia, which not only allows for the development of actions as causes of change but also includes a review and evaluation of the consequences. The conclusion finds that an entirely new mode of cognition, triggered by linguistic changes that are reflected in a recent rise of oxymora and paradoxes, opens a new perspective on how lawyers can help to both predict and shape the future.

2 Dystopian Scenario: Specialization and 'Fragmented We Fail'

> In the world of theory, there are many dichotomies. In the real world, there are many divisions and divides. In the world of power, all too often, these divisions, divides, and dichotomies serve to maintain and reinforce existing imbalanced and skewed power relations between individuals, communities, governments, and nation-states. In the world of power, it is indeed divide and rule.[11]

In attempts to describe the evolution of the multilateral trading regime from 1995 until 2048, so-called "digital historians" have argued that 11 December 2019 marked the decisive moment and unofficial date of the decline of the World Trade Organization. Although aggressive regionalism, unilateral measures and resulting trade wars as well as inertia in addressing the trade linkage debate and interinstitutional linkages between the WTO and the UN had been eroding the multilateral trading regime for some time before, it was on that day that the WTO's dispute settlement system became dysfunctional following the expiration of the terms of two of the three remaining members of the Appellate Body (AB).[12] This left the AB with fewer than the three members required by Art. 17.1 DSU to serve on appeal cases.

As with many international organizations, nation states and other legal constructs before it, the official decline of the WTO and the multilateral trading regime as a whole started slowly and then ended abruptly. The decline was probably the result of a chain of missed opportunities for the reform and adaptation of the relevant system to changes in the context, which notably saw a strong trend towards greater convergence of various industries, technologies and products.[13] This convergence further increased the need for the consideration of non-trade concerns and greater policy coherence. For some time, the system lingered on and ministerial conferences were merely held without achieving tangible results, continuing the deplorable tradition that began with the launch of the Doha Development Round in 2001. Most WTO

---

[11] Dias (2007), p. 278.

[12] Lo et al. (2020).

[13] Neuwirth (2015), p. 31.

members engaged in either a relapse into unilateral measures adopted at the domestic level or a rat race to join numerous regional trade agreements. However, in both cases, the most important challenges faced at that time, in the form of institutional gaps, regulatory fragmentation and overregulation, were not tackled, either nationally or regionally, let alone globally. Numerous calls and suggestions for institutional reform to achieve greater policy coherence, under the aegis of the so-called "trade linkage debate" discussing various "trade and ... problems" or how to better link trade with non-trade issues, were ignored.[14] In this regard, more importantly, the cognitive and conceptual dimension of trade policy was not duly considered, as "transformational change in the institutions and politics of international trade" were found to go "hand in hand with *cognitive* change" as Andrew T. F. Lang wrote.[15] He also found a nexus between cognitive change and institutional reform being linked to the criticism of the WTO and notably the failure to address the trade linkage debate.[16]

As a result, from this time on, the international system, or, more accurately, the remaining "international systemic chaos",[17] was described as having moved "away from an assembly of distinct, territorial, sovereign, legally equal states toward different, more hierarchical, and in many ways more complicated structures".[18] Even though an attempt was launched in 2006 to reform the United Nations Organization in order to streamline the coordination of its many specialized organizations and to enhance the coherence of global policymaking by "delivering as one",[19] the management of this reform eventually proved to be an oxymoron before it failed altogether.[20] For a long time, the UN's work in its core areas, from development to the environment, was described as fragmented, and its inefficient governance structure contributed to "policy incoherence, duplication and operational ineffectiveness across the system".[21]

What could be framed as a "trade and technology" problem, the earlier US–China trade disputes (2017–2020), also caused frictions in the innovation of new technologies and especially in the realm of telecommunication and information technologies.[22] These frictions led to a further fragmentation of the Internet and the market for information and communication technologies (ICT). Russia initiated the creation of an alternate web, which was later also used by the remaining BRICS countries,

[14]Pauwelyn (2005), pp. 329–346.

[15]Lang (2007), p. 529.

[16]Lang (2007), p. 523.

[17]Hopkins and Wallerstein (1996), p. 226.

[18]Van Creveld (1999), p. vii.

[19]United Nations High Level Panel on Coherence (2006) Delivering as One. G.A. A/61/583 (9 November 2006).

[20]Baumann (2016), pp. 461–472.

[21]United Nations High Level Panel on Coherence (2006) Delivering as One. G.A. A/61/583 (9 November 2006), p. 10.

[22]Lawrence (2018), pp. 62–82.

with other countries following suit. Moreover, it was common for the governance gaps and frequent legal inconsistencies between the various fragments of laws governing international trade and commerce to be abused by artificial intelligence and unregulated algorithms, those lacking a kind of *lex algoritmica*, meaning that global business generally operated in a "black box" inaccessible to consumers and lawmakers.[23]

From a commercial perspective, the "world wide web" (*www*), which was intended to become a "wireless world wide web" (*wwww*) by virtue of the transition to the 5G network, became further fragmented by national and regional firewalls as well as restrictive measures known as geolocation measures.[24] Other conflicts, in the form of regulatory paradoxes framed as dichotomies, such as those of "goods versus services",[25] "free trade in data versus data localization",[26] or "regulatory fragmentation versus technological convergence",[27] were also ignored.

In the same way, in other sectors covered by the GATT, GATS and TRIPS agreements, the multilateral trading rules were further eroded by trade disputes in which different claims were met by defences made on the basis of national security concerns.[28] Known as the "trade and security" problem, questions about the self-judging nature of the security exceptions widened the institutional gap opened by the split between the UN system and the GATT/WTO system caused by the failure of the International Trade Organization (ITO) to materialize. This institutional rift had, since 1948, left the world with a conflict of norms in the form of a "catch XXI" or "trade and security" dilemma.[29] After the WTO ruling in *Russia – Measures in Transit* in 2019, in which the panel held that it had jurisdiction to determine whether the requirements of Article XXI of the GATT 1994 were satisfied,[30] other countries simply refused to respond to requests for consultations and boycotted the relevant meetings.[31] In the end, the invocation of the security exceptions further eroded belief in the WTO and accelerated its demise.

The broader conditions in the global economy also grew dimmer and were closely related to the "trade and energy" problem. From as early as 2005, the tipping point in the production of oil was reached, meaning that conventional crude oil production

---

[23]Pasquale (2015).

[24]Yu (2019), pp. 503–529.

[25]Smith and Woods (2005), pp. 463–510.

[26]Burri (2017), pp. 65–132.

[27]Neuwirth (2015), pp. 21–50.

[28]Request for the Establishment of a Panel by Qatar, *United Arab Emirates – Measures Relating to Trade in Goods and Services, and Trade-Related Aspects of Intellectual Property Rights*, para. 1, WT/DS526/2 (12 Oct. 2017).

[29]Neuwirth and Svetlicinii (2015b), p. 892.

[30]WTO Panel Report, *Russia – Measures Concerning Traffic in Transit*, WT/DS512/R (5 April 2019).

[31]Requests for consultations and establishment of a panel by Qatar, *Saudi Arabia — Measures concerning the Protection of Intellectual Property Rights*, WT/DS567/1 (4 October 2018) and WT/DS567/3 (19 November 2018).

was not rising to match increasing demand.[32] The "all-oil peak" meant that, after decades of controversy over its arrival, there was a drastic dampening in economic growth and, actually, the inauguration of an era of global depression.[33] Notably, for oil-producing and other resource-rich countries, the so-called "paradox of plenty" aggravated, and the ensuing economic disaster also led to, the collapse of their constitutional system, and also triggered new waves of political violence. Since human civilization was a sensitive "complex adaptive system", other countries too, and the globe as a whole, also were drawn into a downward spiral of economic recession and political instability.[34] Institutionally, the proliferation and fragmentation of energy organizations and the failure to address the "global energy governance gap" by reforming existing energy agencies or creating a global energy agency, further contributed to the resulting disaster.[35]

The complexity of the global economy could also be seen in the connection between trade, the environment and energy. In parallel, numerous efforts towards achieving greater sustainability in economic development based on renewable energies were also unable to offset the devastating effects of the disruptive consequences of the "all-oil peak" and the ensuing global energy crisis on economies and societies around the world. The result was a global energy crisis in 2033 that disrupted most global trade in both goods and services and caused stock crashes through inflationary pressures, and later accelerated the eventual collapse of the international monetary system as it had done during the 1973 oil crisis. Renewable energies were also incapable of averting the crisis, even though the impact of the 2015 Paris Agreement, adopted with the objective of responding to the threat of climate change, had no negative effect on the global economy or on countries' welfare gains. Because of the absence of a coherent global regulatory framework, renewable energies remained expensive and investments often did not materialize. In this context, it was also a failure when the WTO membership addressed the "trade and environment" problem by, inter alia, reforming the WTO subsidies agreement, which resulted in various trade disputes challenging green policies.[36]

The lack of global competition rules, as a result of the abandonment of a project in 2004 that was one of four "Singapore issues",[37] led to the emergence of various multinational tech giants, which widely abused their dominant positions, explored tax loopholes, and competed unfairly in courts, patent offices and markets. They were also crucial in meddling in elections and were accused of undermining democratic institutions.[38] No efficient dispute settlement system under the multilateral trading regime, and a lack of legal standing for private parties, both natural and legal

[32]Murray and King (2012), pp. 433–435.

[33]Hall and Klitgaard (2018), p. 109.

[34]Ahmed (2017).

[35]Downie (2015), p. 475.

[36]Cosbey and Mavroidis (2014), pp. 11–47.

[37]Demedts (2015), pp. 415–416.

[38]Ginsburg and Huq (2018), p. 198.

persons, in domestic or supranational courts caused further havoc and greater inequality among global citizens. As early as 2017, inequality was reported to be standing at unprecedented levels, and it was claimed that "just eight men own the same wealth as the poorest half of the world".[39] These inequalities, dividing societies around the world, not only perpetuated themselves but even increased, with devastating effects on the global economy and the environment.

Another aspect of inequality was found in the "trade and development" link, another complex and cross-cutting "trade and ..." problem. Cutting a long story short, the development discourse continued along the "developing versus developed country" dichotomy, despite calls to the contrary and even its abandonment by the World Bank in 2016.[40] Even though the definition of "official development assistance" (ODA) evolved, it continued to be understood as resource flows from developed to developing countries.[41] With the mindset unchanged, the language use of "developed-developing countries" also remained the same. As a result, the US and the EU continued, on the one hand, to subsidize their agricultural producers and to reap excessive benefits from royalties on various patented and copyrighted products, while on the other, they kept granting support through official development assistance programs to a large number of developing countries. This practice continued to impede the development of local industries in the targeted countries.[42] Moreover, the uncertainty surrounding the meaning of "development status" further eroded the WTO's status after the US began to challenge it in 2019.[43]

At the same time, the trade and development problem was closely tied to the "trade and finance" problem.[44] Generally, the trade and finance link suffered from the failure of the ITO mentioned above, and the absence of a coherent framework for both trade and finance became manifest in the problem of so-called "currency manipulation", that is, the depreciation of a country's currency relative to other currencies so as to develop a large global and bilateral trade surplus.[45] Despite the three organizations, the WTO, the IMF and the World Bank, having pledged to enhance their policy coherence, their inter-institutional dialogues did not yield tangible results and the use of policy coherence was criticized instead as a way to introduce policy conformance.[46]

[39]An Economy for the 99%. OXFAM Briefing Paper, January 2017. https://www-cdn.oxfam.org/s3fs-public/file_attachments/bp-economy-for-99-percent-160117-en.pdf.

[40]Neuwirth (2016), pp. 911–925.

[41]Hynes and Scott (2013).

[42]Moyo (2009), pp. 52–53.

[43]WTO General Council, *An Undifferentiated WTO: Self-Declared Development Status Risks Institutional Irrelevance (Communication from the United States)*, WT/GC/W/757 (16 January 2019).

[44]Thomas (2000), pp. 1249–1278.

[45]Staiger and Sykes (2010), pp. 583–627.

[46]Grabel (2007), pp. 335–341.

Put briefly, the "trade and finance issue" also remained unsolved, and the two respective regulatory regimes of trade and of finance continued to evolve side by side in dramatically different directions in spite of being mutually interdependent systems.[47] This had a serious impact on the world as the regulatory gap between them grew even more intense while the technological reality saw them increasingly converge notably with the emergence of the blockchain technology that underlies cryptocurrencies. Cryptocurrencies, from Bitcoin to Altcoin, proliferated and gradually disrupted business and financial services as well as the global economy.[48] This meant that, in parallel to the third currency war between the world currencies (the dollar, the euro and the yuan), which began in 2010,[49] a digital currency war also began to be waged. In this digital currency war, the traditional world currencies fought against emerging digital currencies backed both by state and non-state actors. The ensuing chaos of currency wars brought about a loss of state control over financial markets and a rise of a global underground economy thriving on tax evasion and criminal activities.[50] It all culminated in a collapse of global trade and finance and ended with the second global financial crisis of the twenty-first century, which began on "black Wednesday" of 24 October 2029.

Together with military conflicts, global health pandemics, like the large-scale outbreak of the novel coronavirus (nCoV) infectious disease, and various natural disasters, like large scales rainforest wildfires and bushfires, caused by climate change and other anthropogenic factors,[51] the total disruption of the global economy created a dangerous dynamic, causing a severe migratory wave[52] that increased the number of forcibly displaced people from about 70 million people in 2018 to 1.4 billion less than 15 years later.[53] The crisis of migratory flows was aggravated by national governments and courts, who denied the affected persons the status of climate refugees.[54] At the same time, after an erosion of the rule of law in the majority of countries around the world, ever more restrictive national policies regarding citizenship in general, and dual citizenship in particular, also increased the number of stateless persons, who were thus deprived of all fundamental rights within and across state borders.[55]

The European Union, paralysed by endless Brexit debates and the United Kingdom's final exit from the EU on 31 January 2020, made little progress in reforming

[47]Gadbaw (2010), p. 552.

[48]Tapscott and Tapscott (2018).

[49]Rickards (2011), p. 98.

[50]Rogoff K (2019) The High Stakes of the Coming Digital Currency War. Project Syndicate. https://www.project-syndicate.org/commentary/global-battle-for-digital-currency-supremacy-by-kenneth-rogoff-2019-11.

[51]Reuveny (2007), pp. 656–673.

[52]Beets and Willekens (2009).

[53]UNHCR (2019).

[54]Berchin et al. (2017), pp. 147–150.

[55]Weissbrodt and Collins (2006), pp. 245–276.

its institutions, the single market, the single currency or its taxation system. On the contrary, past achievements in the four freedoms were scaled down as the result of nationalist policies in many member states. The EU's so-called "Luxembourg Treaty", negotiated under the 2029 EU Presidency of Luxembourg, added nothing that substantively remedied the lost opportunity of creating a constitution for Europe in 2001. The EU's failure to become the world's most competitive market (the Lisbon Strategy) extended the lost decade of the EU, which began in 2000, when, to a lost near-half century.[56]

Many more regional integration projects worldwide also stagnated. For instance, the BRICS, representing 42% of the world's population in 2014 and initially set up as a "cooperation and dialogue forum" between Brazil, Russia, India, China and South Africa in order to defy differences and make a difference in global governance, saw no progress, such as by seeking greater policy coherence based on more closely coordinating institutionalizing their cooperation.[57] Similarly, the positive effects on infrastructure development based on the Belt and Road Initiative (BRI), initiated by the Chinese government in 2013, were largely neutralized by opposition from the US and several European countries. The African Union also failed to prevent the food security crisis that hit the African continent in 2030[58] and that pushed the achievement of the objectives enshrined in Agenda 2063 into an even more distant future.[59]

In sum, despite the emergence of a creative economy, which was initially fostered by the potential of new and innovative technologies, the 2015 Sustainable Development Goals were still not realized by 2030. Across the globe, political disagreements prevented action for greater regulatory harmonization, while centrifugal forces and fragmentation intensified. Legally, a patchwork of isolated areas of law continued to grow, as did the number of regional trade agreements, which were violated or withdrawn from faster than they were negotiated. Put simply, the so-called "global governance paradox", or the logical loop that a global platform was needed in order to create a global platform, proved a problem that was too difficult to tackle in conceptual and cognitive terms. With no consistent global legal order, fragmentation prevailed and led to the aggravation of the negative effects of "trade and ..." problems on global peace and welfare.

[56]Neuwirth (2020), p. 51.

[57]Neuwirth et al. (2017) and Neuwirth and Svetlicinii (2019).

[58]Onyutha (2018), pp. 1203–1219.

[59]African Union (2017) Progress Report on the Implementation of Agenda 2063 First Ten-Year Implementation Plan. Available at: https://archives.au.int/handle/123456789/2618.

3 Utopian Scenario: Synaesthesia and 'United We Sense'

The limits of my language mean the limits of my world.[60]

In 2048, historians are still pondering the reasons for the collapse of the WTO. Some attribute it to isolationist US trade policies and the political turmoil around Brexit, while others tend to focus on the rise of first Asian and subsequently African countries. However, a different view identifies this failure as the beginning of the end of "end of ... stories"[61] or a drastic paradigm shift in cognition. Cognition had reached a tipping point in human evolution following two centuries of rapid technological innovations, which "shaped consciousness directly".[62]

Linguistic changes also confirmed this cognitive shift, mostly through the rise of essentially oxymoronic concepts.[63] As a result of these external factors, epigeneticists found biological and cognitive changes occurring in parallel. New organs of cognition hence emerged, as humans were evolving biologically and consciously. As a visible result, even by 2025 97% of new-born children displayed conditions of synaesthesia, i.e. the ability to better connect stimuli received from different sensory organs, which improved the skills to foresee developments and solve complex problems as well as enhanced their abilities of abstract thought.[64]

Related changes in educational policies were implemented, with the goal of creating a "world brain", or "an enhanced educational system through the whole body of mankind", designed to "replace our multitude of uncoordinated ganglia, our powerless miscellany of universities, research institutions, literatures with a purpose, national educational systems and the like".[65] This goal was to be achieved by fostering oxymoronic learning methods and giving training in both bivalent and polyvalent logic, complemented by training in multilingualism and oxymoronic thinking.

For the trade and health link, the novel coronavirus (nCoV) pandemic underscored once more the strong links between international trade, public healthcare and the global economy. As a result, the global healthcare system was integrated with a future trading system and backed by a consistent set of global innovation rules consisting of competition rules, intellectual property laws and fiscal incentives, which prevented price discrimination in pharmaceutical products and secured global access to affordable medicines. Additionally, universal healthcare was provided freely by a combination of measures that combined both traditional and conventional medicines.[66] Based on further changes in perception, such as

---

60 Wittgenstein (1960), p. 149 (5.6).

61 Neuwirth (2019b), p. 15.

62 Kern (1983), p. 1.

63 Neuwirth (2018a), pp. 23, 52 and 243.

64 Deroy and Spence (2013), pp. 1240–1253.

65 Wells (1938), p. xvi.

66 Neuwirth and Svetlicinii (2015a), pp. 330–366.

through the development of technologies for the visualization of auras,[67] medical diagnosis improved and conventional, traditional and alternative medicines as well as mental health strategies were all integrated into a coherent set of laws and policies. Further changes in healthcare were influenced by discoveries in so-called "life after life studies", which transcended the life–death dichotomy as the result of a greater awareness of the missing link in a globally coherent health policy.[68] Research on near-death experiences scientifically confirmed popular and religious beliefs about life after life.[69]

Overall, a new cognitive mindset emerged in parallel with technical tools, leading to a new conception of the areas of economics, politics and law. For instance, the global economy became more sustainable, based on the spirit of "degrowth", which rejected the illusion of endless economic growth by advocating for a "democratically-led shrinking of production and consumption with the aim of achieving social justice and ecological sustainability".[70] At the same time, new and cleaner energy resources were derived from nuclear fusion developed by the ITER project, helping to decarbonize the world's energy system.[71] Various new and renewable energies complemented this.[72]

Since a G20 initiative formulated in 2019, the global community embraced an ambitious tax agenda to improve cooperation and transparency on the basis of a strategy for a global taxation system.[73] This initiative originally included a global financial transaction tax to fund the new global governance system.[74] It later included a digital tax on the world's tech giants, which levied taxes in the places where the goods and services were sold rather than the places where the company was based. It also introduced a global minimum tax rate to prevent a company from shifting its sales to a country with lower taxes. Finally, a robotic tax, aided by the creation of a single global cryptocurrency (SGCC),[75] covered all activities based on automation to compensate for the disruptive effects of automation on the global labour market.[76] Together, these measures helped to contain the outbreak of currency wars and related trade/finance disputes.[77] On the other hand, the changes in the taxation system also helped to reverse the former trend of higher income taxes as opposed to lower corporate taxes. The new system achieved an optimal balance, with

[67]See also Milán et al. (2012), pp. 258–268.

[68]Neuwirth (2018b), pp. 3–26.

[69]Flannelly et al. (2012), pp. 651–662.

[70]D'Alisa et al. (2015).

[71]Fiore (2006), pp. 3334–3341.

[72]Ongena (2018), pp. 114–432.

[73]G20 (2019) Ministerial Statement on Trade and Digital Economy. http://trade.ec.europa.eu/doclib/docs/2019/june/tradoc_157920.pdf.

[74]Tobin (1978), pp. 153–159.

[75]Ahmed (2018), pp. 697–740.

[76]Abbott and Bogenschneider (2018), pp. 145–175.

[77]Yi-Lin-Forrest et al. (2018), p. 567.

around 5% income tax, 25% corporate tax (including on digital activities) and 35% robotic tax, as measures towards greater global tax justice.[78] These and other fiscal policies were introduced in coherence with other incentives to end the poverty trap.[79]

The cognitive shift also remodelled the international multilevel governance system towards a "glocal" and holarchic system in which local, largely self-governing, entities were complemented by various regional regimes often organized into mega-regional blocks, with those of an inclusive global system enshrined in the GAIA Charter of 2048. Holarchy here means a system in which various self-regulating entities function as autonomous wholes in supra-ordination to their parts but, at the same time, also as dependent parts in subordination to controls on higher levels their local environment.[80] The foundation is a polyvalent logic by which the links between stakeholders at different levels are supported by a dynamic system of subsidiarity and an open method of coordination.[81] It is based on a set of different criteria that the best possible level of regulation is determined without any prior bias towards either the local or the global level of governance. The same method is also applied to territorial questions, such as national sovereignty is no longer fixed but where territorial boundaries are drawn based on a similar set of criteria. Thus, like in the quantum world, different political entities, and even national governments' competences, can overlap and even be superimposed without being perceived in conflict.

Changes in cognition facilitated the adoption of the GAIA 2048 Charter, as the global community finally found the "common language"[82] to tackle the "global governance paradox" successfully. The paradox was that, in order to create a global legal order, the world community needed a global governance platform that had not previously existed, confirming that linguistic and cognitive changes are quintessential to institutional change.

Structurally, the GAIA 2048 was based on an institutional setting in which every "trade and ..." problem was coordinated by a "coherence committee", with the competence to avoid conflict between different policy goals. The functioning of the institutional framework was aided by an e-governance system, which used intelligent algorithms to consolidate redundant norms and detect incoherent measures. However, artificial intelligence was considered not only to be hype but also to be an oxymoron, and, in relation to law and policy, artificial intelligence measures were strictly bound by the requirement inherited from the former EU General Data Protection Regulation that they could not be implemented and enforced "without any human intervention".[83]

[78]Brock and Pogge (2014), pp. 1–15.

[79]Thang Dao and Edenhofer (2018), pp. 253–273.

[80]Koestler (1967), pp. 102–103.

[81]Neuwirth (2020), p. 51.

[82]Halpin and Roeben (2009), p. 6.

[83]Art. 22 Regulation (EU) 2016/679, O.J. L 119/1 (4 May 2016).

In substantive terms, existing sources of global law were codified into a single legal document, the GAIA Code, a global constitutional text that reduced the previous disarray of international laws. In this way, former conflicts between norms that arose because of dichotomies that were too simplistic to account for real complexity, be it between electronic and traditional modes of consumption of goods (GATT) and services (GATS), between IP law and competition law, or between international trade law and various subfields of general public international law in the name of "self-contained regimes", were no longer unavoidable and irresolvable.[84] In this context, global competition rules were integrated and enhanced so as to not only guarantee the sustainable economic development of the global market but also "solve social problems ranging from unemployment to income inequality and indeed to improve the functioning of democracy itself".[85]

Other necessary changes simply came with changes in cognition and understanding, and did not require a change in language as they occurred earlier when a higher court reconsidered its established case law. For instance, in the field of global economic law, the national treatment provisions of GATT Article III, GATS Article XVII and Article 3 of TRIPS were now no longer merely interpreted as prohibiting discrimination between domestic and imported goods or services but also as encompassing "all measures having an equivalent effect on consumers in covered markets".[86] This became necessary to cover personalized price discrimination made possible by the data economy.[87] These cognitive changes, plus a seamless global wireless web, also ended the western failure of the territorial national state.[88] As a result, the "four freedoms" related to the free movement of goods, services, persons and capital, became recognized as ubiquitous civil right and a global reality.[89]

The various systemic changes resulting from cognitive changes were supported by, and helped to establish, an effective and inclusive global dispute settlement mechanism, which recognized the right to bring an action and to be heard in court (*locus standi*) of not only international organizations, states and multinational corporations but also natural persons.[90] It effectively aligned the former WTO Dispute Settlement system with investor–state arbitration.[91] Both systems were elevated to a "world trade court" embedded within a fully-fledged global judicial body, the GAIA Tribunal, that was vested with various constitutional powers to sanction and enforce the rulings it issued.[92] Overall, the new institutional design based on these cognitive changes was said to have helped to "improve and

[84]Jeutner (2017).

[85]Wright et al. (2019), p. 294.

[86]Neuwirth (2015), pp. 21–50.

[87]Townley et al. (2017), pp. 683–748.

[88]Strange (1999), p. 345.

[89]Nett (1971), pp. 212–227.

[90]Schwartmann (2005).

[91]Li (2018), pp. 189–232.

[92]Cottier (2015), pp. 12–14.

eventually overcome the perceived lack of legitimacy of international courts and tribunals in the eyes of the governments, the legal community and civil society".[93]

4 Conclusion: 'Dystopian Utopia' or Oxymora to Predict the Future by Creating It

> My project was retarded by laws of nature. The world was not prepared for it. It was too far ahead of time. But the same laws will prevail in the end and make it a triumphal success.[94]

A dystopian or a utopian future, does it matter? After all, from the "perspective of the brain, there's a thin line between a good decision and a bad decision".[95] It seems, though, that what matters to everyone is the future, because the future is "where we are all going to spend the rest of our lives".[96] However, perhaps this must also not be the case as, paradoxically, most (or all) dichotomies have a limitation in that they not only trade accuracy for simplicity,[97] but also provide an invisible barrier to a vision of the bigger picture. This is where subtle linguistic changes may gradually trigger cognitive changes and eventually bring in legal and institutional changes, in the same way as dripping water hollows out stone, even though the cognitive habits of binary or dualistic thinking are said to die hard.[98] Easy or difficult, it is a source of encouragement for everyone, as we may, *à la longue*, be able to bring about the change we desire, given that institutional change is possible once a cognitive change has occurred.[99]

The recent rise in the number of oxymora and paradoxes, however, seems to indicate this "creative" possibility. For instance, various concepts implicitly reflecting the tensions between prediction and destiny within the confines of past and present, such as science fiction[100] or free will,[101] have been qualified as oxymora. In their context (and possibly in the context of all paradoxes), time therefore appears as the clue, or the key we need to find to unlock the limitations inherent in our current linear perception of time. The fact is that the grammar of many modern languages, conjugating verbs in the "present," "past," and "future" tenses, was said to not be "well-adapted for speaking about the real temporal structure of reality, which is more complex".[102] Various "nostalgic visionaries",

---

[93]Dimitropoulos (2018), p. 569.

[94]Tesla (2016), p. 46.

[95]Lehrer (2009), p. xiv.

[96]Rescher (1998), p. 1.

[97]Kosko (1993), p. 21.

[98]Segal (2008), p. 101.

[99]Lang (2007), p. 529.

[100]Csicsery-Ronay Jr. (2008), p. 8 ("As its name implies, science fiction is an oxymoron.").

[101]Crewe (2008), p. 23.

[102]Rovelli (2018), p. 111.

like Herbert G. Wells or Jules Verne, however, transcended the past–future dichotomy in their writings, thereby anticipating many future inventions.[103] Lawyers, too, can act in this way, as their work is often similar to that of science fiction authors, given that they can help in translating fiction into legal fact[104] or turning dreams into reality by combining "the law as it is" (*lex lata*) with "the law as it should be" (*de lege ferenda*) perspectives.[105]

For lawyers to achieve this creative goal and to synthesize the two competing scenarios of the future beyond the WTO outlined in this chapter, it will be necessary, first, to work actively towards a cognitive change. Applied to legal reasoning, it means to transcend an exclusively dualistic mode of reasoning, which means to solely rely on the "law of the excluded middle" (i.e. "Everything must either be or not be.").[106] Applied to the regulation of global trade, this kind of "either/or thinking" or that something either belongs to the sphere of trade or is classified as a "non-trade concern" must be complemented by the law of the included middle. The law of the included middle can be achieved through oxymoronic thinking by way of which, for instance, trade and non-trade concerns are not opposed to each other but where their apparent contradiction can be resolved at a higher level of reality or complexity.[107]

More concretely, lawyers must be able cognitively to transcend the iron law of binary logic by also being versatile in reasoning based on polyvalent logic—a kind of multivalued logic in which there can be more than two truth values.[108] A good way to remind ourselves of this is given in the following quote: "laws may differ but they do not conflict: the only possible conflict is in the mind of the judge".[109] In this regard, legal education seems the best place to begin.[110] Thus, addressing problems by legally expressing them solely using dichotomies is no longer apt to deal with their underlying complexity. It also means that a purely static approach should be complemented with a more dynamic one to ensure that laws are adopted in a way that embraces change ex ante and makes them fit for the future. In institutional terms, a more dynamic approach is also needed, as otherwise we merely observe their initial rise and subsequent demise.[111] In this respect, discursive institutionalism provides an excellent complement, as it regards norms as "dynamic, intersubjective constructs rather than static structures".[112] Ultimately, it is submitted here that, based on this cognitive change, novel models of global institutions, like GAIA 2048, can emerge.

---

[103]Unwin (2000), pp. 18 and 31.

[104]Fuller (1967), p. 1.

[105]Virally (1981), p. 519.

[106]Russell (1912), p. 113.

[107]Brenner (2008), p. 4; Neuwirth (2018a), pp. 180–181.

[108]Jeutner (2017), p. 151; Neuwirth (2018a), pp. 234 and 255.

[109]Glenn (2017), p. 162.

[110]Neuwirth (2019a), p. 45.

[111]Chase-Dunn and Hall (1997).

[112]Schmidt (2008), p. 303.

Second, the cognitive changes of polyvalent or oxymoronic thinking, when combined with new organs of perception as symbolized by synaesthesia, will enable another important insight, which lies in the realization that *the best way to predict the future is by creating (and regulating) it.* This insight puts the theory of a self-fulfilling prophecy into a new light, one which proves that theory and practice are intimately linked and that sociological predictions are "products of an era, co-determinants of what they assert".[113]

When applied to humanity as a whole, *predicting the future by creating it (and regulating it accordingly)* means that if we plan something and act upon it coherently and persistently, it is more likely to happen, eventually. This, however, first requires a cognitive change in the understanding of humanity as a divided amalgam of different peoples or nations instead of an organic whole united in its diversity. Only then can an adequate global governance mechanism capable of putting the necessary global legal order into place be expected to be brought forth. In short, the global governance paradox and other apparent contradictions can only be successfully addressed by expanding our reasoning from bivalent to polyvalent modes of thinking, as reflected in synaesthesia or in new optimized ways to receive and channel information through our different senses or, in legal terms, different institutions.

Applied to the dichotomy of the past versus the future, a new cognitive mode may one day enable humans to recall the fundamental importance of the present, that is, the magical power of the present to rewrite both the world of yesterday and the world of tomorrow. By the same token, humans can then eventually use the same magic to control the outcome between the two apparently opposite scenarios, the dystopian and the utopian one. For now, the two scenarios outlined in this chapter cannot answer the questions of whether or not, in our perception, linear time exists, or whether or not we have free will or all fate (including the fate of the WTO) is already written in a comprehensive book of destiny. This chapter is equally unable to say whether a post-WTO legal order will be able to avoid global disaster and humanity's as well as nature's demise. However, the hope is that the chapter shows that the many "scientifically fictitious" developments described in both the dystopian and the utopian scenarios concur in essence or are—if at all—divided by a very thin line, one merely drawn in our minds. Nevertheless, this thin line determines how we will deal with the most urgent challenges in the Anthropocene, or at any given point in time (when no longer understood as the linear process from the past to the future), because it clearly proves that today we humans cannot say that "*we did not know (about the dangers and inherent consequences of our actions)*". On the contrary, we can only say "*we knew but did not care*".

[113]Neurath (1973), pp. 405–406.

References

Abbott R, Bogenschneider B (2018) Should robots pay taxes? Tax policy in the age of automation. Harv Law Policy Rev 12(1):145–175

Ahmed NM (2017) Failing states, collapsing systems: biophysical triggers of political violence. Springer, Cham

Ahmed S (2018) Cryptocurreny & robots: how to tax and pay tax on them. S C Law Rev 69:697–740

Ashley KD (2017) Artificial intelligence and legal analytics: new tools for law practice in the digital age. Cambridge University Press, Cambridge

Bacchus J (2003) Groping toward Grotius: the WTO and the international rule of law. Harv Int Law J 44(2):533–550

Baumann F (2016) United Nations management – an oxymoron? Glob Gov 22(4):461–472

Beets G, Willekens F (2009) The global economic crisis and international migration: an uncertain outlook. Netherlands Interdisciplinary Demographic Institute, The Hague

Berchin II et al (2017) Climate change and forced migrations: an effort towards recognizing climate refugees. Geoforum 84:147–150

Brenner JE (2008) Logic in reality. Springer Science+Business Media, New York, p 4

Brock G, Pogge T (2014) Global tax justice and global justice. Moral Philos Polit 1(1):1–15

Burri M (2017) The governance of data and data flows in trade agreements: the pitfalls of legal adaptation. Univ Calif Davis Law Rev 51(1):65–132

Chase-Dunn C, Hall TD (1997) Rise and demise: comparing world-systems. Westview Press, Boulder

Cosbey A, Mavroidis PC (2014) A turquoise mess: green subsidies, blue industrial policy and renewable energy: the case for redrafting the subsidies agreement of the WTO. J Int Econ Law 17(1):11–47

Cottier T (2015) The Common Law of International Trade and the future of the World Trade Organization. J Int Econ Law 18(1):3–20

Crewe D (2008) Will to self-consummation, and will to crime: a study in criminal motivation. In: Lippens R, Crewe D (eds) Existentialist criminology. Routledge-Cavendish, London, p 23

Csicsery-Ronay I Jr (2008) The seven beauties of science fiction. Wesleyan University Press, Middletown, p 8

D'Alisa G, Demaria F, Kallis G (eds) (2015) Degrowth: a vocabulary for a new era. Routledge, Oxon

Demedts V (2015) Which future for competition in the global trade system: competition chapters in FTAs. J World Trade 49(3):407–436

Deroy O, Spence C (2013) Are we all born synaesthetic? Examining the neonatal synaesthesia hypothesis. Neurosci Biobehav Rev 37:1240–1253

Dias CJ (2007) International relations and international law: from competition to complementarity. In: Biersteker TJ et al (eds) International relations and international law: bridging theory and practice. Routledge, Oxon, p 278

DiMatteo LA et al (2003) The Doha Declaration and Beyond: giving a voice to non-trade concerns within the WTO trade regime. Vanderbilt J Transnatl Law 36(1):95–160

Dimitropoulos G (2018) Investor–state dispute settlement reform and theory of institutional design. J Int Dispute Settlement 9(4):535–569

Downie C (2015) Global energy governance in the G-20: states, coalitions, and crises. Glob Gov 21 (3):475–492

Fiore K (2006) Nuclear energy and sustainability: understanding ITER. Energy Policy 34:3334–3341

Flannelly KJ et al (2012) Belief in life-after-death, beliefs about the world, and psychiatric symptoms. J Relig Health 51(3):651–662

Fuller LL (1967) Legal fictions. Stanford University Press, Stanford, p 1

Gadbaw RM (2010) Systemic regulation of global trade and finance: a tale of two systems. J Int Econ Law 13(3):551–574
Ginsburg T, Huq AZ (2018) How to save a constitutional democracy. The University of Chicago Press, Chicago, p 198
Glenn HP (2017) Choice of logic and choice of law. In: Glenn HP, Smith LD (eds) Law and the new logics. Cambridge University Press, Cambridge, p 162
Grabel I (2007) Policy coherence or conformance? The New World Bank–International Monetary Fund–World Trade Organization Rhetoric on trade and investment in developing countries. Rev Radic Polit Econ 39(3):335–341
Hall CAS, Klitgaard K (2018) Energy and the wealth of nations: an introduction to biophysical economics, 2nd edn. Springer, Cham, p 109
Halpin A, Roeben V (eds) (2009) Theorising the global legal order. Hart, Oxford, p 6
Harari YN (2017) Homo Deus: a brief history of tomorrow. Harper, New York, p 51
Hopkins TK, Wallerstein I (1996) The age of transition: trajectory of the world-system, 1945–2025. Pluto Press, Leichhardt, p 226
Hynes W, Scott S (2013) The evolution of official development assistance: achievements, criticisms and a way forward. OECD Development Co-operation Working Papers, No. 12. OECD Publishing, Paris. https://doi.org/10.1787/5k3v1dv3f024-en
Jackson JH (1969) World trade and the law of GATT. The Bobbs Merril Company, Indianapolis, p 51
Jeutner V (2017) Irresolvable norm conflicts in international law: the concept of a legal dilemma. Oxford University Press, Oxford
Johnson ML (2007) Mind, metaphor, law. Mercer Law Rev 58(3):845–868
Kern S (1983) The culture of time and space 1880–1918. Harvard University Press, Cambridge, p 1
Koestler A (1967) The ghost in the machine. Arkana, London, pp 102–103
Kosko B (1993) Fuzzy thinking: the new science of fuzzy logic. Hyperion, New York, p 21
Lang ATF (2007) Reflecting on 'linkage': cognitive and institutional change in the international trading system. Mod Law Rev 70(4):523–549
Lawrence RZ (2018) Can the trading system survive US–China trade friction? China World Econ 26(5):62–82
Lehrer J (2009) How we decide. Houghton Mifflin Harcourt, Boston, p xiv
Li S (2018) Convergence of WTO dispute settlement and investor-state arbitration: a closer look at umbrella clauses. Chic J Int Law 19(1):189–232
Lo C-F, Nakagawa J, Chen T-F (eds) (2020) The appellate body of the WTO and its reform. Springer, Singapore
Milán EG et al (2012) Auras in mysticism and synaesthesia: a comparison. Conscious Cogn 21:258–268
Moyo D (2009) Dead aid: why aid is not working and how there is another way for Africa. Allen Lane, London, pp 52–53
Murray J, King D (2012) Oil's tipping point has passed. Nature 481:433–435
Nett R (1971) The civil right we are not ready for: the right of free movement of people on the face of the earth. Ethics 81(3):212–227
Neurath O (1973) Empiricism and sociology. D. Reidel, Dordrecht, pp 405–406
Neuwirth RJ (2015) Global market integration and the creative economy: the paradox of industry convergence and regulatory divergence. J Int Econ Law 18(1):21–50
Neuwirth RJ (2016) Global law and sustainable development: change and the "developing-developed country" terminology. Eur J Dev Res 29(4):911–925
Neuwirth RJ (2018a) Law in the time of oxymora: a synaesthesia of language, logic and law. Routledge, New York
Neuwirth RJ (2018b) The quest for the "missing link" in a coherent global health policy. Med Law 37(1):3–26

Neuwirth RJ (2019a) On the origin of legal diversity by means of comparative law, or the role of legal education in the solution of legal conflicts. In: Singh MP, Kumar N (eds) Indian yearbook of comparative law. Springer, Berlin, p 45
Neuwirth RJ (2019b) The end of 'development assistance' and the BRICS. In: Puppim de Oliveira JA, Jing Y (eds) International development assistance, China and the BRICS. Palgrave, New York, p 15
Neuwirth RJ (2020) The European Union as an oxymoron: from contest via contradiction to constitution? In: Chaisse J (ed) 60 years of European Integration: perceptions, interactions and lessons. Hart, Oxford, p 51
Neuwirth RJ, Svetlicinii A (2015a) Law as a social medicine: enhancing international inter-regime regulatory coopetition as a means for the establishment of a global health governance framework. J Leg Med 36(3–4):330–366
Neuwirth RJ, Svetlicinii A (2015b) The economic sanctions over the Ukraine conflict and the WTO: "Catch XXI" and the revival of the debate on security exceptions. J World Trade 49(5):891–914
Neuwirth RJ, Svetlicinii A (2019) The BRICS-Lawyers' guide to BRICS texts and materials. The BRICS-Lawyer, Macau
Neuwirth RJ, Svetlicinii A, De Castro Halis D (eds) (2017) The BRICS-Lawyers' guide to global cooperation. Cambridge University Press, Cambridge
Ongena J (2018) Nuclear fusion and its large potential for the future world energy supply. Comput Nanotechnol 2018(1):114–432
Onyutha C (2018) African crop production trends are insufficient to guarantee food security in the sub-Saharan region by 2050 owing to persistent poverty. Food Sec 10:1203–1219
Pasquale F (2015) The black box society: the secret algorithms that control money and information. Harvard University Press, Cambridge
Pauwelyn J (2005) The Sutherland Report: a missed opportunity for genuine debate on trade, globalization and reforming the WTO. J Int Econ Law 8(2):329–346
Petersen H et al (2014) The role of the internet of things in network resilience. In: Giaffreda R et al (eds) Internet of things. IoT infrastructures. Springer, Cham, p 283
Rescher N (1998) Predicting the future: an introduction to the theory of forecasting. State University of New York Press, Albany, p 1
Reuveny R (2007) Climate change-induced migration and violent conflict. Polit Geogr 26:656–673
Rickards J (2011) Currency wars: the making of the next global crisis. Penguin, London, p 98
Rovelli C (2018) The order of time. Riverhead Books, New York
Russell B (1912) The problems of philosophy. Williams & Norgate, London, p 113
Schmidt VA (2008) Discursive institutionalism: the explanatory power of ideas and discourse. Annu Rev Polit Sci 11:303–326
Schwartmann R (2005) Private im Wirtschaftsvölkerrecht. Mohr Siebeck, Tübingen
Segal G (2008) Poverty of stimulus arguments concerning language and folk psychology. In: Carruthers P, Laurence S, Stich S (eds) The innate mind: foundations and the future, vol 3. Oxford University Press, Oxford, p 101
Smith F, Woods L (2005) A distinction without a difference: exploring the boundary between goods and services in the World Trade Organization and the European Union. Yearb Eur Law 24 (1):463–510
Staiger RW, Sykes AO (2010) Currency manipulation' and world trade. World Trade Rev 9 (4):583–627
Strange S (1999) The westfailure system. Rev Int Stud 25(3):345–354
Tapscott D, Tapscott A (2018) Blockchain revolution: how the technology behind bitcoin and other cryptocurrencies is changing the world. Penguin, New York
Ten Hoopen G et al (1995) Auditory isochrony: time shrinking and temporal patterns. Perception 24:577–593
Tesla N (2016) My inventions and other writings. Dover, Mineola, p 46
Thang Dao N, Edenhofer O (2018) On the fiscal strategies of escaping poverty-environment traps towards sustainable growth. J Macroecon 55:253–273

Thomas C (2000) Balance-of-payments crises in the developing world: balancing trade, finance and development in the new economic order. Am Univ Int Law Rev 15(6):1249–1278
Tobin J (1978) A proposal for international monetary reform. East Econ J 4(3–4):153–159
Townley C, Morrison E, Yeung K (2017) Big data and personalized price discrimination in EU competition law. Yearb Eur Law 36(1):683–748
UNHCR (2019) Global trends: forced displacement 2018. UNHCR, Geneva
Unwin T (2000) Technology and progress in Jules Verne, or anticipation in reverse. J Australas Univ Lang Lit Assoc 93(1):17–35
Van Creveld M (1999) The rise and decline of the state. Cambridge University Press, Cambridge, p vii
Virally M (1981) A propos de la lex ferenda. In: Reuter P (ed) Mélanges offerts à Paul Reuter: le droit international, unité et diversité. A. Pedone, Paris, p 519
Weissbrodt D, Collins C (2006) The human rights of stateless persons. Hum Rights Q 28 (1):245–276
Wells HG (1938) World brain. Doubleday, Doran & Co., Garden City, p xvi
Wittgenstein L (1960) Tractatus Logico-Philosophicus. Routledge, London, p 149
Wittmann M (2016) Felt time: the psychology of how we perceive time. The MIT Press, Cambridge, p 124
Wright JD et al (2019) Requiem for a paradox: the dubious rise and inevitable fall of hipster antitrust. Ariz State Law J 51(1):293–369
Yi-Lin-Forrest J, Ying Y, Gong Z (2018) Currency wars: offense and defense through systemic thinking. Springer, Cham, p 567
Yu PK (2019) A Hater's guide to geoblocking. Boston Univ J Sci Technol Law 25(2):503–529

If the WTO Were to Break Down Completely, Would We Stoop and Build It Up with Worn-Out Tools?

Brett G. Williams and Weihuan Zhou

Contents

> If you can bear to hear the truth you've spoken Twisted by knaves to make a trap for fools, Or watch the things you gave your life to, broken, And stoop and build'em up with worn-out tools—Rudyard Kipling, "If"

Respectively, Principal of Williams Trade Law; and Senior Lecturer and Member of the Herbert Smith Freehills China International Business and Economic Law (CIBEL) Centre, Faculty of Law, UNSW Sydney.

B. G. Williams
Williams Trade Law, Sydney, NSW, Australia
e-mail: williams@williamstradelaw.com

W. Zhou (✉)
The University of New South Wales, Sydney, NSW, Australia
e-mail: weihuan.zhou@unsw.edu.au

M. K. Lewis et al. (eds.), *A Post-WTO International Legal Order*,
https://doi.org/10.1007/978-3-030-45428-9_6

1 Introduction

We are asked to consider what a post-WTO world would be like. Let's take that to mean that the WTO breaks down completely, that the obligations expire in fact or for all practical purposes. What would happen to world trade and trade policy?

This chapter uses existing tools of public choice theory to predict how governments would behave after the cessation of WTO obligations, leading to significant protectionist behaviour and associated economic losses. Then it uses existing tools on the feasibility of trade agreements to discuss what States could do to overcome that tendency toward economic losses from protectionist behaviour. Any attempt to overcome such protectionist behaviour would need to incorporate a way of dealing with all of the politically difficult issues that have in the past been obstacles to trade liberalization, for example, maintaining sovereignty, policy space and how best to tolerate or transition politically sensitive sectors. The key contribution of this chapter is to stress how the multilateral trading system, including dispute settlement rulings, has served to discipline the choice of policy instruments by Member governments while leaving sufficient policy space for them to pursue non-protectionist regulatory goals according to their own needs and preferences. We believe that a focus on the discipline of the choice between policy instruments to achieve Members' policy objectives would be critical to the success of any new attempt to construct an architecture for regulating international trade.

2 The Tension Between the Economics and the Politics of Trade and the Choice of Policy Instruments

2.1 Public Choice Theory

That trade protection generally causes economic welfare losses for nations is not generally considered to be contentious, outside of exceptional situations. The discipline of economics has long had tools to describe and explain the transfers of welfare and the net economic welfare losses arising from trade protection. While the net economic welfare losses are often explained in simple terms of the net amount by which the transfers of economic welfare away from some people exceeds the transfers of economic welfare in favour of others, that is, the deadweight losses, the tools of economics can also explain how these static deadweight losses can understate the welfare losses from protection in a dynamic economy, taking into account, *inter alia*, situations where, over time, losses to some are more durable than the gains to others, where gains to some are dissipated in rent seeking, and where competition in markets may work more efficiently with trade liberalization than without it. The discipline of economics has developed to integrate considerations like these and other flow on effects to attempt to arrive at more accurate models, computer generated models, of the welfare losses from protection and the welfare gains from trade liberalization.

Government decision-makers[1] are usually knowledgeable about the economic cost of protection but they still have a tendency to choose protectionist policies in many countries, industries and situations. Why is there this opposition between the guidance that can be drawn from economic analysis and what government decision-makers actually do in regulating international trade? To answer that question, the critical point is that external actions of States are determined by the internal politics within States. There is a branch of economics, public choice theory, which proposes ways of describing and predicting the ways that governmental decisions arise from the internal politics of States.

Public choice theory characterizes elected officials as self-interested individuals who formulate policies to attract support and minimize opposition from domestic interest groups so as to maximize their chances of retaining power.[2] As the government choice of trade policies would likely change the economic payoff for these interest groups, they would be keen to offer political support with an aim to influence government decision-making on trade policies for their own benefits. That political support (or opposition) affects the political payoffs that will accrue to government officials as a result of the decisions they make. Accordingly, the economic payoffs to domestic constituencies from particular policies can be estimated and used to predict the payoff in terms of political support or opposition that accrues to government officials deciding whether to adopt or remove particular policies.[3] Governments tend to be much more responsive to the demands of import-competing producers than to the needs of consumers, given the significantly uneven influence of the two opposing forces in the political process. Thus, even though government officials are usually knowledgeable about the long-term economic costs of protection, they are highly tempted by short-term political gains obtainable from granting protection to influential constituencies (i.e. import-competing producers).

Just as public choice theory offers insights about why politicians adopt positive levels of protection, this theory can also explain why, to protect a domestic industry, politicians frequently opt for policy instruments which are less transparent, and more trade-restrictive and more distortive, imposing larger economic welfare costs on the country than are necessary to achieve a chosen policy objective. Trade economists rank various policy instruments according to their welfare effects. Where a transfer of wealth to certain producers is politically preferable, standard economic analysis shows that a production subsidy imposes a smaller burden on a national economy compared to trade policy instruments applied at the border (e.g. import tariffs and quotas). This is because while the production subsidy only entails a distortion on the

---

[1]We use government decision makers, government officials or politicians interchangeable in this chapter. This section is partly based on Zhou (2020), p. 9.

[2]The seminal work on public choice theory includes Downs (1957), Buchanan and Tullock (1962) and Olson (1965). These three pieces of work form the foundation of subsequent development of modern political economy theories. See, e.g., Baldwin (1982), pp. 263–286; Grossman and Helpman (1994), pp. 833–850; Grossman and Helpman (1995), pp. 675–708.

[3]There have been some important empirical tests of particular models based on public choice methodology, including, for example, Koujianou Goldberg and Maggi (1999), pp. 1135–1155.

production pattern of the economy, the tariff and the quota tend to cause net welfare loss associated with both domestic production and consumption behaviour. Furthermore, an import tariff is generally observed as a preferable trade policy to an import quota which tends to be more trade-restrictive and distortive and less transparent. In addition, an import quota completely insulates the domestic producers from changes in the world price so the size of the margin between the protected internal price caused by the import quota and the world price may change in size, changing the size of the wealth transfers from consumers to producers and changing the size of the deadweight loss.[4] In contrast, an import tariff causes a fixed margin between the protected internal price and the world price, so changes in market parameters do not cause the same changes as are caused when protection is in the form of an import quota.

However, the ranking in terms of likelihood of the political choice of the aforementioned policy instruments for protection would likely demonstrate a reverse order of the economic ranking.[5] An import quota, being the most trade-restrictive and distortive, tends to be the most favourable instrument from the perspective of producers while it attracts less awareness (and hence resistance) from consumers compared with a tariff. This makes an import quota politically attractive. In contrast, a production subsidy may be the least preferred politically as it involves matters subject to periodic parliamentary review and approval, such as raising taxes for the finance of the subsidy and the allotment of government budget. Comparatively, the imposition of a tariff does not involve budgetary transfers and therefore would generate less scrutiny. The administration of an import quota (i.e. the allocation of import licences) is an administrative activity which is not subject to parliamentary scrutiny and hence is relatively easy to maintain.

The brief overview of the literature above demonstrates the rankings of policy instruments on the basis of economic efficiency and political likelihood. While it only covers three policy instruments, it shows the unwillingness of government officials to follow the guidance of economic theories on the choice between protection and trade liberalization and on the choice of policy instruments for protectionist objectives. More specifically, it shows that the order of ranking of policy instruments from the instrument imposing the lowest economic welfare cost to the instrument imposing the highest economic welfare cost is inverse to the order of ranking of those policy instrument in terms of their likelihood of adoption. Governments are most likely to adopt the most costly instruments and least likely to adopt the least costly instrument for achieving a particular objective. Table 1 below summarizes the economic and political rankings of policy instruments.

Below, we will explain how WTO obligations create constraints and incentives to modify political payoffs so as to bring the political ranking more into line with the economic ranking.

---

[4]The same can also happen when domestic producers respond to changes in the domestic market knowing their behaviour cannot be constrained by any increase in the volume of imports.

[5]Roessler (1993), pp. 53–62.

Table 1 Economic and political rankings of policy instruments[a]

Policy instruments	Economic rankings	Political rankings
Production subsidy	1	3
Import tariff	2	2
Import quota	3	1

[a]Ibid., p. 59

2.2 *What If the WTO Breaks Down Completely?*

We can now answer our question as to what would happen to world trade and trade policy in the event of a complete breakdown of the WTO. In the absence of the set of constraints and incentives provided by WTO obligations, government decision makers would be in a position where in many, if not in most instances, they would increase their political support by granting protection and decrease their political support by removing protection. We would expect internal decisions of governments to become increasingly responsive to protectionist pressure in the formulation of trade policies. We would expect the positive level of protection to increase across many products and services. We would also expect the choice of policy instrument to implement that chosen level of protection to be more responsive to protectionist pressure from import-competing producers and suppliers, as outlined above. We would expect to see a variety of measures, including, *inter alia*, higher import duties, more quantitative restrictions, more restrictive import licensing schemes, the grant of more exclusive import rights, more local content rules, administered support prices buttressed by import barriers leading to sales at a loss on the world market, and other forms of export subsidies and more questionable technical standards and SPS measures. Liberalization that occurred would be likely to be discriminatory and politically motived with retention of tariffs and other restrictions on imports from outsiders and, for services, retention of quantitative restrictions on service suppliers of non-parties. In addition, without the WTO, protectionist trade policies would be followed by retaliatory measures by affected nations. Just like the initial protective policy, the retaliatory protection would also impose economic welfare losses on the country imposing it; and just like the initiating country, the retaliating country might also choose its retaliatory protection in the form of instruments which impose more economic welfare losses than other available policy instruments. The cycle may keep occurring as is modelled in a prisoners' dilemma model or trading nations dilemma model where after each retreat from cooperation, the parties begin a new interaction in which the new non-cooperative Quadrant IV becomes the cooperative Quadrant I in a new round of interaction resulting in successive shifts to less and less cooperative positions and more and more protection against imports from each other.[6] All of that protection and retaliatory protection would impose substantial economic costs

[6]See generally Abbott (1985), pp. 501–532.

on the whole world and on all individual countries. The deterioration in economic relations between nations could affect harmony among nations in other ways.

3 Constructing an International Economic Order

3.1 Counteracting Protectionist Interests

Faced with a world characterised by protection and retaliatory protection, governments might do as they did after the Second World War, try to avoid suffering those losses of economic welfare and accompanying deteriorations in relations between nations, by building new international regulation of trade which can overcome the tendency toward protectionist behaviour. To overcome this tendency of nations to adopt policies protecting against imports from each other, such a new scheme of international regulation of trade would have to be constructed in a way that changes the way that decisions are made at the domestic level. The international rules would have to change the payoffs that accrue to decision-makers within individual States from decisions to grant protection or to liberalize trade. We have seen the tendency for producer interests to outweigh consumer interests in influencing payoffs of political support and political opposition accruing to politicians. It is those political payoffs that lead politicians to choose protectionist policies and so any new international regulation of trade would need to change the way that decisions on trade policy result in political payoffs to politicians.

To change political payoffs to politicians, it is necessary to harness the interests of exporters. By exchanging obligations regarding reductions in import barriers with other nations, the political equation within any one nation is changed from a contest between import competing producers and consumers into a contest between local producers who want to avoid competition from imports and local producers who want other countries to reduce barriers to imports so that they can export to those countries. As the influence of exporters increases, domestic protectionist pressure is counterbalanced, at least to some extent. Moreover, in the face of increasing contributions and participation by exporters, more contributions must be made by import-competing producers so as to maintain their influence on government officials and secure their preferred trade policy and policy instruments. Finally, once a round of trade negotiations successfully leads to the reduction of the level of protection, the amount at stake under the remaining level of protection diminishes, thereby reducing the amount that import-competing producers would be prepared to expend in opposing a further round of reciprocal trade liberalization.[7]

The requirement of reciprocity is fundamental as it creates lobbying incentives for exporters who know that the only way to secure lower tariff rates in a foreign importing country is to persuade their own government to implement tariff

[7]See Zhou (2020), p. 17.

reductions. For politicians to be able to rely on the political support from exporters to offset political opposition from import-competing producers, those exporters must be able to rely on the opportunities for market access in foreign importing countries which have given trade liberalization commitments.[8] For the exporters to be assured that the market access received under the treaty is reliable, the scheme of international regulation should (a) discipline the re-imposition of the protection in another form, (b) limit derogations and exceptions from the rules to behaviour that preserves the negotiated market access to the greatest possible extent, and (c) require and promote transparency as to what measures other members are implementing. Disciplining the use of protectionist instruments in light of the economic ranking of policy instruments helps to ensure that the value of trade liberalization to exporters is reliable by making it difficult for members to reinstitute the protection with the most distortionary policy instruments and by minimizing unnecessary restrictions on market access.

3.2 *Balancing Non-Protectionist Interests*

Opposition to trade liberalization may arise from non-protectionist interests (or constituencies other than import-competing industries). That is, people may oppose a trade agreement if the content of the agreement prohibits governments from achieving desired policy objectives or excludes the choice of policy objectives that might be desired in the future. If this occurs, then it is reasonably likely that the political support from exporters arising from the trade agreement would not give the government sufficient political support for it to offset the opposition from import-competing producers and the opposition from domestic constituents concerned about the loss of policy space or sovereignty. This additional factor means that trade agreements need to provide the flexibility for governments to respond to non-protectionist interests. It follows that trade agreements must strike a balance between constraining protectionism and preserving policy space for governments to pursue non-protectionist regulatory goals.

The Generalized Theory of Distortions and Welfare provides the guidance for how to achieve this balance. The theory was brought together into a structured taxonomy when Bhagwati reviewed a range of theoretical work analysing the welfare effects of trade liberalization in the presence of externalities and market failures, and also work analysing the welfare effects of trade liberalization in the presence of non-economic objectives, finding that the conclusions from analysis of

[8] See generally Ethier (2004), pp. 303–320 (treating reciprocity as one of the necessary elements of a feasible trade agreement); Kyle Bagwell and Staiger (1999), pp. 215–248 (using a different model but also conclude that reciprocity is a necessary element of a trade agreement).

the two situations were identical.[9] Therefore, we could use the term distortion to refer to both market failures or non-economic objectives (or objectives that a particular economic variable should be changed in some way or set at some desired level).[10]

The theory offers two significant propositions.[11] First, in the presence of some domestic externalities or non-economic objectives, trade liberalization may either enhance or diminish economic welfare but would remain economic welfare enhancing if the externality or objective is addressed separately with an optimal or first-best policy instrument. Second, in response to the externality or objective, policy instruments can be ranked according to their economic efficiency. An economically optimal policy instrument is one which strikes most directly at the source of the externality or objective; this is known as the "specificity rule" or "targeting rule".

Thus, in the pursuit of a domestic non-protectionist policy objective, the first-best policy would generally be a domestic tax or subsidy which strikes directly at the locus of the problem. When an import tariff is used, it tends to entail a by-product loss to the economy and hence may or may not enhance national welfare.[12] This is because the tariff does not tackle the problem at its source. In addition to comparing the welfare effects between a domestic instrument and a trade instrument, the theory applies to the ranking of domestic policy instruments as well. For example, in the presence of a domestic production/output-related externality or a policy objective to bolster or curtail production/output, the first-best policy is a production subsidy or tax. The second-best policy is either a tax or subsidy on factor-use or a tariff. A tax or subsidy on consumption tends to make things worse as it adds a loss at the consumption side on the top of the existing distortion associated with the production activities. The same rule applies to a domestic consumption externality or a policy objective to encourage or discourage consumption, distortions in factor market or a policy objective to ensure optimal production feasibility and to alter the factor-use in a sector, etc.[13] When two or more externalities (or domestic objectives) co-exist, the first-best policy would be the use of two or more domestic policy instruments attacking directly at the source of each externality (or addressing each objective specifically).

A major qualification of the theory concerns the existence of by-product costs associated with the application of a first-best policy instrument. Corden examined four principal by-product costs that the imposition of a subsidy or a tax may entail, including (1) the distortion costs associated with raising revenue to finance a

---

[9]Bhagwati (1971), pp. 69–90. For a review of the historical development of the theory and its applications, see Bhagwati (2002).

[10]As Corden put it: "[by the theory of distortions and welfare] the link between the case for free trade and the case for laissez-faire has been broken." See Corden (1997), p. 4.

[11]This section is partly based on Zhou (2020), pp. 19–21.

[12]Deardorff and Stern (1987), p. 39 (observing that "Trade policy is like doing acupuncture with a fork: no matter how carefully you insert one prong, the other is likely to do damage.").

[13]See generally Bhagwati (1971).

subsidy, (2) the costs associated with collecting taxes, (3) the costs associated with disbursing a subsidy, and (4) the income distribution distortion costs associated with taxing and subsidising.[14] He concluded that only the costs in item (3) may affect the general applicability of the theory. Particularly, Corden was concerned about the disbursement costs in developing or least-developed countries, especially in their underdeveloped industries. Such costs may be so high that the theory suggesting direct subsidization no longer stands valid, and a tariff which incurs no disbursement costs may become a better solution. Nevertheless, Corden emphasized that empirical evidence related to the magnitudes of the disbursement costs is required in judging whether a subsidy remains preferable to a tariff.

The theory has profound implications for the construction of a multilateral trading system, which are set out below:

- International trade regulation and enforcement must distinguish between policy objectives and policy instruments and must not unduly limit the freedom of governments to pursue non-protectionist objectives. However, the existence of such objectives and the need for government intervention does not provide an economic justification for the resort to protectionist measures.
- The more specifically a policy instrument addresses a chosen objective, the more economically efficient it tends to be. This rule applies to situations in which two or more objectives exist. Given the political ranking of policy instruments, international cooperation on trade liberalization and regulation remains essential to effectively discourage the use of sub-optimal policy instruments for protectionist purposes.
- In disciplining the choice of policy instruments based on the "targeting rule", one must take into account whether the application of the first-best instrument would (1) be capable of fulfilling the desired objective as effectively as the chosen sub-optimal instrument; and (2) give rise to by-product costs which render it economically inferior to the chosen instrument.

Overall, the theory provides an approach to striking a balance between trade liberalization and domestic regulatory autonomy. It suggests that in determining whether a chosen policy instrument is justifiable by a non-protectionist purpose, one should, firstly, identify the genuine objective; and secondly, assess the appropriateness of the instrument according to the "targeting rule" taking into account the effectiveness and side-effects of an optimal instrument.

[14] Corden (1997), pp. 33–44.

4 Reflecting on the WTO[15]

If the WTO did break down completely and it were necessary to construct a new architecture to regulate international trade, and in particular to decide how the new scheme of regulation ought to discipline the choice of policy instrument, it would surely be instructive to consider the content of the existing WTO rules and their practical operation in modifying behaviour.

4.1 Selected WTO Rules

It has been argued persuasively that GATT/WTO rules are designed to address the political biases discussed above and to serve a "domestic policy function" by removing or reducing the constraints or pressure confronted by governments in formulating and implementing trade policies and policy instruments.[16] To do so, these rules impose an external influence upon domestic decision-making by making it politically costly to deviate from economically efficient and transparent policy instruments. The WTO performs this function by incorporating the interests of exporters into the domestic decision-making process, which counteracts the political influence of import-competing producers.[17]

As Petersmann has observed,

> GATT law ranks the various trade policy instruments according to their respective welfare costs in almost the same way as economic theory suggests: the less a policy instrument tends to distort trade, the less legal restraint GATT law places on its use.[18]

To understand this observation, a brief description of the basic GATT/WTO rules is warranted. Generally speaking, domestic measures are not regulated as strictly as trade measures. For example, domestic subsidies are not generally prohibited. A subsidizing Member is allowed to maintain domestic subsidies as long as it effectively removes the adverse effects to the interests of other Members or tolerates countervailing measures. Furthermore, non-specific subsidies (i.e. subsidies generally granted for all industries, say, in support of research and development) are permitted even though they may adversely affect trade. Finally, it is at the discretion of Members to impose domestic taxes and regulations so long as they do not entail discrimination against imports in favour of 'like' or competitive domestic products. Comparatively, trade measures such as tariffs and quotas are subject to stricter disciplines. Tariffs are allowed, but are subject to bound rates agreed in periodical trade negotiations. Quantitative restrictions such as an import quota are in principle

[15]This section is partly based on Zhou (2020).

[16]See e.g., Tumlir (1980), pp. 1–15; Roessler (1985), pp. 287–298; Petersmann (1991), pp. 95–138.

[17]See e.g., Hudec (1993), p. 316; Dam (2005), p. 96.

[18]Petersmann (1993), pp. 47–48.

prohibited. In addition, provisions aiming to ensure transparency of government regulations and policies spread across almost all WTO agreements.

In the meantime, it is also widely accepted that WTO rules do not require Members to sacrifice "the pursuit of any economic or social policy goal" for the pursuit of free trade.[19] Instead, the rules provide for a host of exceptions and recognize that non-protectionist policy objectives should take priority over trade liberalization and that WTO-inconsistent measures may be necessary to attain these objectives.[20] In *Australia – Salmon*, the Appellate Body highlighted the distinction between policy objectives and policy instruments, stating that what the WTO rules seek to regulate are the instruments, not the objectives.[21]

In short, WTO rules impose different degrees of constraints upon various policy instruments in conformity with the suggestion of standard economic theories. This design ensures that the WTO effectively performs the function of disciplining Members' choice of policy instruments. By allowing the use of GATT-inconsistent instruments to pursue an array of policy objectives unrelated to trade, the WTO recognizes Members' freedom to pursue non-trade policy objectives.

There are many instances of specific WTO rules which guide Members in the way that they choose policy instruments to achieve their objectives. We offer just a few examples:

- The Understanding on Balance-of-Payments Provisions of the GATT contains, in Articles 2 and 3, a commitment to give preference to price-based over quantity-based restrictions;
- The Agreement on Technical Barriers to Trade (TBT Agreement), in Article 2.5, requires that Members will, on request, explain the justification for apply or proposing to apply a technical regulation which entails identifying the legitimate objective the Member seeks to achieve and explaining why the technical regulation is not more trade restrictive than necessary to fulfil the Member's objective;
- Article VI:5(a) of the General Agreement on Trade in Services (GATS) accepts that Members may impose regulation to ensure the quality of services provided but obliges Members to ensure that such regulation is not more burdensome than necessary to achieve that objective; and
- even more specifically, paragraph 8 of the Disciplines on Domestic Regulation in the Accountancy Sector adopted under Article VI:4 of GATS, obliges Members, on request, to advise any other Member of the rationale of any domestic regulatory measures, which necessarily involves specifying the legitimate objective (s) the Member seeks to achieve. Paragraph 2 of the same instrument limits

[19]See e.g., Roessler (1985), p. 294; Petersmann (1991), p. 230; Sykes (1999), pp. 6–7, 23.

[20]It is beyond the scope of this chapter to identify and explain all of the elements of the various WTO agreements which allow for Members to choose objectives but limit the choice of policy instrument.

[21]Appellate Body Report, Australia – Measures Affecting Importation of Salmon, 199-200, WTO Doc. WT/DS18/AB/R (adopted Nov. 6, 1998).

Members' choice of policy instrument to those which are not more trade-restrictive than necessary to achieve a chosen legitimate objective.[22]

All of these examples reflect the guidance of the Generalized Theory of Distortions and Welfare, guiding Members toward choosing the policy instrument which is most directly targeted at the achievement of an objective whilst leaving the Member autonomy to choose its regulatory objectives.

There are also some instances in the WTO rules where rules may not thoroughly reflect the guidance of the Generalized Theory of Distortions and Welfare. We offer two examples.

Article 5 of the Agreement on Safeguards specifies that the objective of safeguard measures is the prevention or remedying of serious injury and the facilitation of adjustment meaning adjustment to the conditions of competition that would apply under the Members tariff bindings. This provision obliges Members to choose safeguard measures that are necessary for achieving those objectives, and further to "choose measures most suitable for the achievement of [those] objectives." This provision manifests a soft preference for price-based rather than quantity-based safeguard measures, imposing additional constraints upon the use of quantitative restrictions. A comprehensive consideration of how the domestic industry can adjust might bring to light the type and extent of changes that the domestic industry would need to implement in order to compete with imports. It is likely that subsidies contingent on specific behavioural changes might be a better way of facilitating adjustment in which case import barriers in the form of either tariffs or quotas would not be measures most suitable to achieving the objectives of preventing injury and facilitating adjustment. Indeed, the provision of any subsidy in an environment where the domestic industry must compete with imports at the bound tariff rate would generally incentivise the domestic firms to use the subsidy to become more competitive with the imports that they will have to compete with in the long run (unless they do not intend to be in business in the long run). It is apparent that Article 5 could be improved by requiring a consideration of suitable subsidies and an explanation of circumstances in which the Member considers that an import barrier would be a more suitable safeguard measure. It could also be improved by requiring, in situations where the use of subsidies is rejected, some explanation why an import tariff would not be a more suitable policy than a quantitative restriction.

A second example is the disciplines on non-prohibited subsidies. The existing regulation under the Agreement on Subsidies and Countervailing Measures (SCM Agreement) disciplines non-prohibited subsidies by exposing them to the possibility of retaliation if the subsidies are demonstrated to be specific. The retaliation may either by multilaterally authorised retaliation if they cause adverse effects or unilateral retaliation if they cause material injury to a domestic industry. Beyond those remedies, where subsidies become a major irritant to trade relations, Members have an option of engaging each other in negotiations to change the form or size of

[22]Disciplines on Domestic Regulation in the Accountancy Sector, Adopted by the Council for Trade in Services on 14 December 1998; S/L/64, 17 December 1998.

subsidies. The only aspect of the rules which directs the attention of Members to consider whether a subsidy is the optimal way of achieving a Member's regulatory objective is the requirement in Article 25.3(iii) to include in their notifications information about the "policy objective and/or purpose of a subsidy." The rules implicitly take a position that export subsidies or subsidies contingent on use of domestic goods will not be the optimal way to achieve a Member's objectives so they are prohibited leaving the Member to choose other types of subsidies. It is arguable that a Member's choice of subsidy to achieve a particular objective is further disciplined by the fact that the size of multilaterally authorised retaliation is calibrated to the size of any adverse effect and that the size of countervailing duties is calibrated to the size of the per unit subsidy and the extent of the injury to the domestic industry. However, there is nothing in the rules which make it easier to retaliate against a subsidy which is not targeted directly toward the Member's regulatory objective nor anything in the rules which insulates a subsidy targeted directly at achieving a legitimate objective from exposure to retaliatory measures. There will always be a possibility that a Member could choose the optimal policy instrument to achieve its chosen regulatory objective and still find itself subjected to retaliation. In such circumstances, the rules would be mandating welfare diminishing policy.

4.2 Selected Dispute Settlement Rulings

More often than not, it is the rulings of the WTO's Dispute Settlement Mechanism (DSM), not the WTO rules, that have been subject to considerable criticism. One of the longest-lasting and persistent criticisms has been the view that WTO tribunals, especially the Appellate Body (AB), tend to promote trade liberalization at the expense of Members' policy space in pursuing legitimate regulatory goals. Indeed, in his farewell speech, outgoing AB member Professor Van den Bossche recounted that in his nine-plus years of service as an AB member, "[t]he most challenging cases ... were those regarding the balance struck in the relevant WTO agreement between free trade and conflicting societal values".[23]

This section discusses two selected disputes involving trade and non-trade values. It shows that the AB's rulings and the outcomes of these disputes have been largely consistent with the economic recommendations derived from the Generalized Theory of Distortions and Welfare. The AB's approaches and decisions have ensured that the DSM is effective in disciplining the choice of policy instruments by Member states while not unduly impairing their capacity to pursue non-protectionist policy objectives, thereby reaching a proper balance between trade liberalization and

[23]WTO, Appellate Body, Farewell Speech of Appellate Body Member Peter Van den Bossche, (May 28, 2019), available at: https://www.wto.org/english/tratop_e/dispu_e/farwellspeech_peter_van_den_bossche_e.htm.

domestic regulatory autonomy. Accordingly, the DSM has served the underlying function of the WTO by imposing an external constraint on domestic protectionist pressure on regulatory decision-making without restraining the capacity of governments to respond to non-trade/non-protectionist interests of other domestic constituents.

4.2.1 China – Publications and Audiovisual Products (2010)

China – Publications and Audiovisual Products involved a series of Chinese measures which restricted the right to import certain cultural goods—including reading materials, audiovisual products, sound recordings, and films for theatrical release—to certain Chinese state-owned enterprises (SOEs). These restrictions were clearly incompatible with China's WTO accession commitments on the liberalization of trading rights. China did not question the findings of violations but sought to defend the measures under Article XX(a) which allows the use of WTO-illegal measures "necessary" to protect public morals. For China, the measures served to maintain an effective and efficient content review mechanism which ensures that imports do not contain content that could have negative impacts on public morals.[24] Not persuaded by China, the WTO tribunal found that some of the measures did not materially contribute to the protection of public morals and that there was a less-trade-restrictive alternative means that China could have employed to attain the objective.[25] The tribunal observed that an effective and reasonably available alternative means would have been for the Chinese government to conduct the content review of the goods imported by non-state entities. It rejected China's argument that the alternative means was too financially and administratively burdensome. While acknowledging the extra burden and costs that China may have had to undertake in switching from the chosen measure to the alternative means, the tribunal held that China failed to substantiate that these costs and burden were excessive, especially given that the Chinese government had already taken the responsibility of content review of most of the imported cultural goods. To bring the measures into WTO-consistency, China removed the restrictions on trading rights (except for the importation of films).[26]

China's objective was essentially concerned about the importation of cultural goods that contain contents contrary to China's fundamental social values. The optimal policy instrument would have been a censorship mechanism which targeted the content of imports rather than the identity of the entities that could have a right to

[24] Panel Report, China — Measures Affecting Trading Rights and Distribution Services for Certain Publications and Audiovisual Entertainment Products (China – Publications and Audiovisual Products), 7.713, WTO Doc. WT/DS363/R (adopted Jan. 19, 2010).

[25] Ibid., 7.824-911; Appellate Body Report, China — Measures Affecting Trading Rights and Distribution Services for Certain Publications and Audiovisual Entertainment Products, 269-337, WTO Doc. WT/DS363/AB/R (adopted Jan. 19, 2010).

[26] For a detailed discussion of China's implementation, see Zhou (2019), pp. 52–65.

import the relevant products. The AB's rulings had the effect of pushing China to dissociate content review from importation[27] and to liberalize trading rights. The AB did not second-guess the importance of censorship for China; nor did it ask China to reduce the desired level of censorship. This left the flexibility for China to continue to strictly enforce the censorship. The AB also considered the by-product costs associated with the use of the optimal means. However, China failed to prove that these costs would have rendered the alternative means sub-optimal. While a rigorous content review mechanism may continue to effectively limit the volume of cultural imports,[28] it no longer deprives entities (other than a handful of SOEs) of the right to import cultural goods and hence has removed the trade restrictiveness of the old mechanism and its anti-competitive effects against foreign-invested enterprises and other non-state entities vis-à-vis State import monopolies. By lifting the restriction on trading rights which arguably did not target the chosen objective directly, the new mechanism would have also become more efficient in achieving the objective.

4.2.2 EC – Seal Products (2014)

EC – Seal Products arose out of the EU ban on the importation and sale of seal products. However, this ban allowed several exceptions, with the major one being the so-called "IC Exception" granted to seal products obtained from seals hunted by Inuit or indigenous communities.[29] The EU seal regime was apparently designed with multiple objectives in mind. While the ban served to address public morality concerns about inhumane killing of seals and consumption of commercially-hunted seal products, the IC Exception sought to allow indigenous people to preserve their tradition and culture. The key weakness of the EU regime, in terms of WTO-consistency, was that it had a disparate impact on Canadian and Norwegian seal products vis-à-vis those originating in Greenland precisely due to the operation of the IC Exception. The panel found that the IC exception was made available exclusively to Greenlandic IC hunts which encompass the largest commercial hunts compared with other Inuit or indigenous communities.[30] Thus, the IC exception was not designed and applied in an even-handed manner and the discrimination had no rational connection with the objective of protecting seal welfare. Consequently, the panel ruled that the EU regime violated Article 2.1 of the TBT Agreement and

[27] Delimatsis (2011), p. 287.

[28] Conconi and Pauwelyn (2011), p. 108.

[29] For more details of the EU regime, see Panel Report, European Communities – Measures Prohibiting the Importation and Marketing of Seal Products (EC – Seal Products), 2.1-7, 7.1, 7.7-56, WTO Doc. WT/DS400/R, WT/DS401/R (adopted June 18, 2014). The other two exceptions included the MRM exception relating to seal products obtained from seals hunted for the sustainable management of marine resources, and the Travellers exception which allowed travellers to bring seal products into the EU for personal/family use.

[30] Ibid., 7.290-319.

GATT Article I:1 and did not satisfy the conditions of the Chapeau of GATT Article XX.[31]

On appeal, the AB's analysis of the justifiability of the EU regime focused on the Chapeau.[32] The AB agreed with the panel that the IC exception could not be reconciled with the moral objective and that the EU could have done something further to address seal welfare in the context of IC hunts. To implement the WTO rulings, the EU imposed an additional condition for the application of the IC exception requiring that IC hunts be "conducted with due regard to seal welfare" so that the exception would exclude IC hunts "conducted primarily for commercial reasons".[33]

This dispute involved multiple and competing policy objectives. The moral objective and the culture preservation objective were conflicting to the extent that the IC exception created "loopholes that might admit products of commercial hunts".[34] However, neither the moral objective nor the preservation objective could have explained sufficiently why the IC Exception was not applied in an even-handed manner. While the IC exception clearly reduced the effectiveness of the EU regime in fulfilling the moral objective,[35] it did not afford equal protection of the rights of indigenous communities in all the parties involved. Thus, even based on the culture preservation objective alone, the discrimination would be unjustifiable. As observed by Mavroidis, the EU regime applied different standards to the different parties to accommodate the commercial interests of EU industries.[36] This suggests that the EU regime, particularly the design and application of the IC exception, was likely compromised by protectionist interests.

The WTO rulings had the effect of compelling the EU to (1) enhance the overall welfare effects of its seal regime by "minimizing the cost to seal welfare of achieving any specified amount of Inuit culture preservation",[37] and (2) take steps to ensure that Canadian Inuit hunts eligible for the IC exception have equal access to European markets as Greenlandic Inuit hunts.[38] Accordingly, the rulings would contribute to making the regime less trade restrictive and more efficient in achieving the seal welfare goal. To the extent that the regime would now admit indigenous hunts from the other parties under the IC Exception, it would also improve the protection of the

[31]Ibid., 7.618-651.

[32]Appellate Body Report, European Communities – Measures Prohibiting the Importation and Marketing of Seal Products (EC – Seal Products), 5.8-70, 5.78-130, 5.184-290., WTO Doc. WT/DS400/AB/R, WT/DS401/AB/R (adopted June 18, 2014).

[33]Regulation (EU) 2015/1775 amending Regulation (EC) No 1007/2009 on trade in seal products and repealing Commission Regulation (EU) No 737/2010, OJ L 262/2 (October 6, 2015).

[34]Howse et al. (2014).

[35]Panel Report, European Communities – Measures Prohibiting the Importation and Marketing of Seal Products (EC – Seal Products), WTO Doc. WT/DS400/R, WT/DS401/R (adopted June 18, 2014) 7.441-461.

[36]Mavroidis (2015), pp. 391–392.

[37]Regan (2014), p. 321.

[38]Howse et al. (2014).

rights of all indigenous communities concerned. However, the revised IC Exception, which requires a consideration of seal welfare in Inuit hunts, may adversely affect the subsistence need of Greenlandic Inuit community to hunt for commercial purposes. The tribunal left the flexibility for the EU to adopt other instruments to address this subsistence need more specifically. One way would be for the EU to subsidize the community directly. In practice, this could be done under the existing EU-Greenland Partnership whereby the EU has committed to financially support Greenland in various industries including the fisheries sector.[39] Overall, the WTO decision was effective in disciplining the discriminatory and protectionist element of the EU ban while not unduly impairing the EU's capacity to pursue the multiple objectives.

4.2.3 Concluding Remarks

The case studies above have shown that the DSM has been largely effective in discouraging the use of protectionist instruments in pursuit of non-trade objectives. The approaches and decisions of the AB have arguably followed the economic guidance derived from the Generalized Theory of Distortions and Welfare and have narrowly focused on tackling the protectionist elements of a contested measure without impairing Members' capacity in pursuing any chosen non-trade objectives or desired levels of protection. By doing so, the DSM has contributed to changing domestic political dynamics in a way that disincentivizes governments from responding to protectionist demands of special interest groups but leaves the flexibility for governments to adequately accommodate non-trade interests.

5 Conclusion

External actions of States are determined by internal politics of States. Due to the political influence of import-competing producers being much greater than the influence of any other parties, a complete breakdown of the WTO may lead to the following consequences:

(1) nations would have a tendency to implement a positive level of protection in favour of import-competing producers even though doing so would impose economic welfare losses on themselves;
(2) nations would have a tendency to impose that positive level of protection by choosing policy instruments that suited the interests of import-competing producers, even though they would be the less transparent and more restrictive

[39] See generally European Commission, International Cooperation and Development: Greenland, available at: https://ec.europa.eu/europeaid/countries/greenland_en.

instruments imposing economic welfare losses larger than would be imposed by alternative available policy instruments; and

(3) protection by one country would likely lead to protection by others, and the retaliatory protection would likely have the same characteristics as the initial country's protection.

To overcome the tendency toward protectionist behaviour and avoid suffering those massive economic welfare losses, a new scheme of trade regulation would have to change the political payoffs to politicians that follow from decisions on trade measures. To do that, the critical element is to provide incentives for exporters to provide political support to politicians adopting trade liberalization to offset the opposition received from import-competing producers. A scheme of regulation which imposes stronger limits on use of more restrictive instruments and less constraint on less restrictive instruments helps exporters to have sufficient assurance that negotiated market access is reliable enough to justify them supporting trade liberalization.

Another difficulty in ensuring that there is enough political support for trade liberalization to offset opposition to it is the variety of concerns that constituents may have with retaining sovereignty and policy space. To make those concerns manageable, it is necessary that a scheme of trade regulation must strike a balance between constraining protectionism and preserving policy space to pursue non-protectionist regulatory goals. For the construction of any new treaty regulating trade, the Generalized Theory of Distortions and Welfare provides a basis for guiding the choice between policy instruments while leaving Members free to choose their own policy objectives. It does that by providing a way to rank the different policy instruments which could be utilized to achieve any given policy objective. The use of appropriately targeted instruments to achieve chosen non-protectionist policy objectives means that there will be no conflict between achieving trade liberalization and the chosen objectives. Our analysis of the "targeting rule" also revealed an appropriate legal methodology for not interfering with achievement of chosen objectives while requiring adjustments to the trade restrictiveness of measures that go beyond achieving the objectives.

The provisions of the WTO treaties did already embody to a high degree regulation of the choice of policy instrument in a manner in accordance with the guidance that can be drawn from the Generalized Theory of Distortions and Welfare. We have seen that from observing the general framework and consideration of some more specific rules (although a review of all WTO rules is beyond the feasible scope of this chapter) which respect the sovereignty of Members to choose their legitimate objectives, but require transparent specification of those chosen objectives and the matching of optimal policy instruments with objectives. Furthermore, analysis of some examples of dispute settlement cases also indicated that the dispute settlement process had abstained from interfering with Members' choices of policy objectives but had required adjustments to the choice of policy instruments in ways that accord with the theory.

Accordingly, it has become apparent that should the WTO break down, then in order to protect citizens in all countries from the economic welfare losses and possible consequent loss of political security that would flow from widespread implementation of protection, the world would need a new treaty containing rules that are very similar to the existing rules applied under the WTO, including rules similarly or better reflecting the tools for analysis provided by the Generalized Theory of Distortions and Welfare. The incorporation of the guidance provided by the theory has greatly enhanced the design of existing WTO rules and would be similarly essential to design of a good model for new architecture. We noted that the embodiment of the theory in the rules was imperfect, dwelling on two examples of safeguards and subsidies. One improvement would be for Members to clarify their objectives in negotiations so that negotiations could deal better with the choice of instruments. Similarly, the rules could be improved so that Members are always obliged to explain their objectives and therefore consultations can more effectively address the choice of instruments. In addition, there may be instances where expressing general principles is not a sufficiently effective way to guide behaviour or to provide dispute panels with adjudicable rules so more prescriptive rules may be appropriate.

Better discipline of choice of policy instruments is not a complete solution for constructing a new international order. Some other aspects of the WTO and the theoretical literature analysing international trade would also be important, in particular the questions of reciprocity, non-discrimination and the feasible degree of ambition for a single step of trade liberalization. However, in this paper, we have aimed to make the single point that appropriate choice of policy instrument is a necessary element of building a successful international economic order—even if it is not a sufficient condition. Given the space constraints for this chapter, we must leave consideration of other necessary elements for another time and later work.

Of course, instead of letting the situation deteriorate to the point that it is necessary to create a new international architecture to regulate trade, relevant actors within WTO Members could re-educate themselves about the principles of economics, public choice and game theory that are critical to the success of the WTO, and reinforce the existing rules to reflect those principles.

That would be so much better than letting the system die and then trying to rebuild it again ... "to stoop to build it up with worn-out tools".

References

Abbott KW (1985) The trading nation's dilemma: the functions of the law of international trade. Harv Int Law J 26(2):501–532

Baldwin RE (1982) The political economy of protectionism. In: Bhagwati JN (ed) Import competition and response. University of Chicago Press, Chicago, pp 263–286

Bhagwati JN (1971) The generalized theory of distortions and welfare. In: Bhagwati JN et al (eds) Trade balance of payments and growth: papers in International Economics in Honor of Charles P. Kindleberger. North-Holland Publishing Co., Amsterdam and London, pp 69–90

Bhagwati JN (2002) Free trade today. Princeton University Press, Princeton and Oxford
Buchanan JM, Tullock G (1962) The calculus of consent: logical foundations of constitutional democracy. University of Michigan Press, Ann Arbor
Conconi P, Pauwelyn J (2011) Trading cultures: appellate body report on China-Audiovisuals. World Trade Rev 10(1):95–118
Corden MW (1997) Trade policy and economic welfare, 2nd edn. Clarendon Press, Oxford, p 4
Dam KW (2005) Cordell Hull, the Reciprocal Trade Agreement Act, and the WTO. In: Petersmann EU (ed) Reforming the world trading system: legitimacy, efficiency, and democratic governance. Oxford University Press, Oxford and New York, pp 83–96
Deardorff AV, Stern RM (1987) Current issues in trade policy: an overview. In: Stern RM (ed) U.S. trade policies in a changing world economy. MIT Press, Cambridge and London, pp 15–72
Delimatsis P (2011) Protecting public morals in a digital age: revisiting the WTO rulings on US – Gambling and China – publications and audiovisual products. J Int Econ Law 14(2):257–293
Downs A (1957) An economic theory of democracy. Harper & Brothers, New York
Ethier WJ (2004) Political externalities, nondiscrimination, and a multilateral world. Rev Int Econ 12(3):303–320
Grossman GN, Helpman E (1994) Protection for sale. Am Econ Rev 84(4):833–850
Grossman GN, Helpman E (1995) Trade wars and trade talks. J Polit Econ 4:675–708
Howse R, Langille J, Sykes K (2014) Sealing the deal: the WTO's Appellate Body Report in EC – Seal Products. ASIL Insights 18(12) (4 June 2014) available at: https://www.asil.org/insights/volume/18/issue/12/sealing-deal-wto%E2%80%99s-appellate-body-report-ec-%E2%80%93-seal-products
Hudec RE (1993) Circumventing democracy: the political morality of trade negotiations. N Y Univ J Int Law Polit 25(2):311–322
Koujianou Goldberg P, Maggi G (1999) Protection for sale: an empirical investigation. Am Econ Rev 89(5):1135–1155
Kyle Bagwell K, Staiger RW (1999) An economic theory of GATT. Am Econ Rev 89(1):215–248
Mavroidis PC (2015) Sealed with a doubt: EU, Seals, and the WTO. Eur J Risk Regul 6(3):388–395
Olson M (1965) The logic of collective action: public goods and the theory of groups. Harvard University Press, Cambridge
Petersmann EU (1991) Constitutional functions and constitutional problems of international economic law. Westview Press, Fribourg, pp 95–138
Petersmann EU (1993) National constitutions and international economic law. In: Hilf M, Petersmann EU (eds) National constitutions and international economic law. Kluwer, Deventer, pp 3–52
Regan DH (2014) Measures with multiple purposes: puzzles from EC – Seal Products. AJIL Unbound 217:315
Roessler F (1985) The scope, limits and function of the GATT legal system. World Econ 8 (3):287–298
Roessler F (1993) The constitutional function of the multilateral trade order. In: Hilf M, Petersmann EU (eds) National constitutions and international economic law. Kluwer, Deventer, pp 53–62
Sykes AO (1999) Regulatory protectionism and the law of international trade. Univ Chic Law Rev 66(1):1–46
Tumlir J (1980) International economic order: rules, co-operation and sovereignty. In: Oppenheimer P (ed) Issues in international economics. Oriel Press Ltd., Stocksfield, pp 1–15
Zhou W (2019) China's implementation of the rulings of the World Trade Organization. Hart Publishing, Oxford and Portland, pp 52–65
Zhou W (2020) In defence of the WTO: why do we need a multilateral trading system. Leg Issues Econ Integr 47(1):9–42

Part III
The Post-WTO: Dispute Settlement

The EU Approach to Overcome the WTO Dispute Settlement Vacuum: Article 25 DSU Interim Appeal Arbitration as a Bridge Between Renovation and Innovation

Elisa Baroncini

Contents

1 Introduction

As it is well known, and most unfortunate, since May 2016 the United States has been blocking appointments of the members of Appellate Body (AB) of the World Trade Organization (WTO).[1] Such an approach provoked the most serious

Associate Professor of International Law, Università di Bologna.

[1]See WTO (2016) Minutes of Meeting 23 May 2016. WT/DSB/M/379, at paras 6.2–6.10 reporting why the United States could not be able to accept the reappointment of Mr. Seung Wha Chang for a second four-year term; WTO (2017) Minutes of Meeting 31 August 2017. Doc WT/DSB/M/400, where it is recorded the US position of blocking any new appointment of AB members until the Dispute Settlement Body (DSB) did not consider the serious systemic implications of former appellate judges still serving as adjudicators after their term in office ended (on the basis of Rule 15 of the Working Procedures for Appellate Review, WT/AB/WP/6); see also the US President

E. Baroncini (✉)
Università di Bologna, Alma Mater Studiorum, Bologna, Italy
e-mail: elisa.baroncini@unibo.it

M. K. Lewis et al. (eds.), *A Post-WTO International Legal Order*,
https://doi.org/10.1007/978-3-030-45428-9_7

institutional crisis of the multilateral trade system. In fact, at midnight of 10 December 2019, when the mandates of two of the three remaining judges expired,[2] what has been qualified as "the most successful appellate mechanism in international history"[3] became non-operational: the World Trade Court needs at least three members to hear cases, each appellate adjudicatory section having to be composed by three judges,[4] but now there is only one judge left, Ms. Zhao Hong (China), whose mandate will end on 30 November 2020.

The Appellate Body can no longer function until the Dispute Settlement Body (DSB) expresses its positive consensus[5] to appoint a sufficient number of new appellate adjudicators.[6] The WTO dispute settlement mechanism (DSM) thus seriously runs the risk of falling back 70 years to the GATT (General Agreements on Tariffs and Trade) 1947 system, where the unsuccessful party of a panel could impede the adoption of a report by exercising its veto power when that report was put on the agenda for approval by the GATT 1947 Council. Under the Marrakesh Agreements, characterized by the reverse consensus decision mechanism for the DSB approval of the establishment of panels, panel and Appellate Body reports, as well as the suspensions of concessions,[7] Article 16.4 of the DSU confers each disputant with the right to an appeal. Therefore, a WTO Member that loses before a panel could now impede the adoption of the panel report by appealing such report "into the void," i.e. exercising its right of appeal when the WTO Permanent Tribunal has fewer than three judges and thus cannot hear the case.

2018 Trade Policy Agenda, where the US administration finally articulated the full list of criticisms on the Appellate Body practice and case-law (Office of the United States Trade Representative, *The President's 2018 Trade Policy Agenda*, March 2018, at pp. 22–28), which were then constantly reported by the US diplomats in their official statements before the DSB (cf. e.g. WTO (2018) Minutes of Meeting 27 August 2018. WT/DSB/M/417, paras 4.2–4.17; WTO (2019) Minutes of Meeting 29 October 2018. WT/DSB/M/420, paras 4.2–4.19; WTO (2019) Minutes of Meeting 25 February 2019. WT/DSB/M/426, para 5.26).

[2]They are Mr. Ujal Singh Bhatia (India) and Mr. Thomas R. Graham (United States), who were serving as members of the Appellate Body since 11 December 2011.

[3]Statement delivered by Professor James Crawford, judge at the International Court of Justice (ICJ), in the interview given to Mizen R (2018) "Back to Square One" if WTO Appeals Body Fails: Judge James Crawford (3 August 2018) available at: https://www.afr.com/policy/economy/back-to-square-one-if-wto-appeals-body-fails-judge-james-crawford-20180802-h13hz0.

[4]See Article 17.1 of the Dispute Settlement Rules: Understanding on Rules and Procedures Governing the Settlement of Disputes, Marrakesh Agreement Establishing the World Trade Organization, Annex 2, 1869 U.N.T.S. 401, 33 I.L.M. 1226 (1994) [hereinafter DSU].

[5]Pursuant to Article 17.2 of the DSU, "[t]he DSB shall appoint persons to serve on the Appellate Body for a four-year term, and each person may be reappointed once," and has the duty to fill vacancies "as they arise." When selecting the judges of the Appellate Body, the DSB has to deliberate by positive consensus, which means that "no Member, present at the meeting of the DSB when the decision is taken, formally objects to the proposed decision" (Article 2.4 of the DSU, footnote 1).

[6]As just illustrated, the Appellate Body needs a minimum of three members to deliver its adjudicatory activity.

[7]See Articles 6.1, 16.4, 17.14, and 22.6 of the DSU.

Faced with such an unprecedented multilateral challenge, the European Union (EU) chose to be a major actor in the reform process of the international economic legal order, indicating *inter alia* that "solving the Appellate Body crisis [is] a priority" for her.[8] The EU has therefore developed an articulated strategy, based on four elements, to deal with the blocking of the World Trade Court. Firstly, at the end of 2018, the EU tabled two very interesting institutional proposals to revise the text of the DSU and provide a formal and appropriate answer to each of the critiques the US made regarding the Appellate Body's activity,[9] while guaranteeing the independence and impartiality of the World Trade Court.[10] Secondly, in order to ensure rules-based international trade in case of blockage of the WTO DSM, the EU activated the dispute settlement mechanisms of her highly important and very advanced network of free trade agreements, filing complaints with South Korea over labour commitments,[11] with Ukraine over its wood export ban,[12] and with the Southern African Customs Union (SACU) over safeguard measures affecting trade

[8]See Council of the European Union (2019) Background Brief of 22 May 2019 for the Foreign Affairs Council—Trade Issues of 27 May 2019 p. 2. Available at: https://www.consilium.europa.eu/media/39454/background-fac-trade_en.pdf.

[9]The US accuses the Appellate Body of (i) persistent overreaching, i.e. of interpreting WTO law beyond its text; (ii) delivering advisory opinions by intervening on issues not necessary to resolve a dispute; (iii) asserting that appellate reports have the value of precedent for future panels, although WTO Members did not agree on a system based on the *stare decisis* principle; (iv) reviewing panel findings of fact and considering panel findings on municipal law as legal issues rather than issues of fact, thus infringing Article 17.6 of the DSU; (v) constantly disregarding Article 17.5 of the DSU, pursuant to which appellate proceedings "[i]n no case shall . . . exceed 90 days," as the World Trade Court systematically delays the delivery of its reports; (vi) too often applying Rule 15 of the Working Procedures of Appellate Review, thus illegitimately allowing a person who has ceased to be an Appellate Body member to continue deciding appeals even if his/her term has not been extended by the DSB. On these highly important and sensitive issues see Lo et al. (2020) and Lehne (2019).

[10]Cfr. WT/GC/W/752/Rev.2 and WT/GC/W/753/Rev.1. These two communications have been highly considered by Ambassador David Walker, appointed by the General Council as facilitator of the WTO informal process on matters related to the functioning of the Appellate Body, who very recently delivered the draft for a General Council Decision aiming at gathering the positive consensus of the WTO membership to overcome the impasse: see doc. WT/GC/W/791.

[11]See *Republic of Korea – Compliance with Obligations under Chapter 13 of the EU – Korea Free Trade Agreement, Request for Consultations by the European Union*, 17 December 2018, and *Republic of Korea – Compliance with Obligations under Chapter 13 of the EU – Korea Free Trade Agreement, Request for the establishment of a Panel of Experts by the European Union*, 4 July 2019 both available at https://trade.ec.europa.eu/doclib/cfm/doclib_section.cfm?sec=130.

[12]See the *Note Verbale* of the Delegation of the European Union in Kiev presented to the Ukrainian Ministry of Foreign Affairs requesting consultations under the EU-Ukraine Association Agreement on 15 January 2019. Ref. No 005/2019; *Note Verbale* of the Delegation of the European Union in Kiev presented to the Ukrainian Ministry of Foreign Affairs requesting the establishment of an arbitration panel under the EU-Ukraine Association Agreement on 20 June 2019. Ref. Ares(2019) 3929269 - 20/06/2019.

in poultry.[13] Thirdly, in summer 2019, the EU took the lead in Geneva in establishing an interim appeal arbitration capable of guaranteeing to the Marrakesh system a dispute settlement mechanism still functioning with two levels of judgment and maintaining the use of WTO case law and procedures until the severe Appellate Body deadlock is overcome.[14] Fourthly, in December 2019, the European Commission unveiled a proposal amending the existing EU Enforcement Regulation[15] to enable the Union to adopt unilateral measures in case a WTO Member losing WTO panel proceedings just aims at escaping a negative report by not accepting the EU contingent arbitration arrangement, appealing instead the contested panel report into the void with the evident intent of condemning the dispute to remain unsettled and suspended into a legal limbo.[16]

The purpose of this chapter is to present the EU interim appeal arbitration arrangement, which is based on Article 25 of the DSU, the provision shaped during the Uruguay Round in order to make available for the WTO Members an arbitration mechanism as an alternative means of dispute settlement to facilitate the solution of certain WTO disputes. The present work will thus first provide an overview of arbitration proceedings in the history of the GATT 1947 system and under Article 25 of the DSU, also considering the only controversy where WTO Members used this alternative means of multilateral dispute settlement, the case *US — Section 110 (5) Copyright Act*.[17] Attention will then be devoted to the analysis of the EU interim appeal arbitration arrangement, for subsequently developing some considerations on the chances of the EU contingency measure being endorsed by a significant part of the WTO membership. A substantial backing of Article 25 appellate arbitration proceedings would, in fact, represent an adequate interim mechanism capable of keeping the judicial review stage in the multilateral trade system while discussions continue to successfully overcome the United States' blocking of the Appellate Body.

---

[13]See the *Note Verbale* of the Delegations of the European Union to the Kingdom of Lesotho, the Republic of Botswana, the Kingdom of Eswatini, the Republic of Namibia and the Republic of South Africa requesting consultations with the Southern African Custom Union (SACU) under the Economic Partnership Agreement between the European Union and the Southern African Development Community Member States (SADC), 14 June 2019. Ref: NV/2019.

[14]For the presentation of the EU proposal for an interim appeal arbitration as well the indications of all the relevant documents see Sect. 3 of the present work.

[15]Regulation (EU) No 654/2014, *OJEU* L 189/50 27 June 2014.

[16]See European Commission, Proposal for a Regulation of the European Parliament and of the Council concerning the exercise of the Union's rights for the application and enforcement of international trade rules, 12 December 2019, COM(2019) 623. Cf. also the Report by the European Commission on the EU Enforcement Regulation, 12 December 2019, COM(2019) 639.

[17]9 November 2011, WT/DS160/ARB25/1.

2 Arbitration Within the Multilateral Trade System: From GATT 1947 to Article 25 of the DSU

Arbitration as a peaceful means for settling disputes has a long tradition in international law. The possibility of concurring in the selection of the adjudicators as well as the definition of the applicable law, and the guarantee of a binding award for resolving the controversy, determined the success of arbitration proceedings among the disputants, because of their flexibility combined with the indispensable mandatory character of the final decision. Within the international trade law system, the Havana Charter, i.e. the never-entered-into-force treaty proposing in 1948 the creation of an International Trade Organization (ITO), contemplated the possibility for the contracting parties of resorting to arbitration.[18] However, it was only during the Uruguay Round that arbitration was formally introduced in the so called "Montreal Rules" or "Montreal Package," contemplating a provision very similar to what would become Article 25 of the DSU. In fact, paragraph E of the 1989 Improvements to the GATT Dispute Settlement Rules and Procedures established that "[e] xpeditious arbitration within GATT as an alternative means of dispute settlement can facilitate the solution of certain disputes that concern issues that are clearly defined by both parties". It continued by clarifying that resort to arbitration was to be "subject to mutual agreement of the parties which [had to] agree on the procedures to be followed," and their arrangement had to be notified to "all contracting parties sufficiently in advance of the actual commencement of the arbitration process" and consider the arbitration award as binding, while preserving the disputants' discretion on the participation of other contracting parties in their arbitration proceedings.[19]

Similarly, under Article 25 of the DSU WTO Members may employ "[e] xpeditious arbitration within the WTO as an alternative means of dispute settlement ... [to] facilitate the solution of certain disputes that concern issues that are clearly defined by both parties."[20] The arbitration proceedings require the "mutual agreement of the parties," which has to "be notified to all Members sufficiently in advance of the actual commencement of the arbitration process," a transparency obligation aimed at allowing the WTO membership to know, consider and comment on the WTO issues at the basis of the controversy, and thus also to assess whether to become party to the arbitral alternative means of dispute settlement. A questionable aspect of Article 25 proceedings is the tighter treatment of third parties by comparison to the status conferred on them in DSU panel and appellate disputes: in fact, pursuant to Article 25.3 of the DSU, "[o]ther Members may become party to an

---

[18]See Articles 93 and 94 of the Havana Charter for an International Trade Organization, Havana, 24 March 1948, UN Doc E/CONF.2/78, 3.

[19]GATT Dispute Settlement Rules and Procedures, L/6489 (12 April 1989), BISD 36S/61. On these historical aspects of arbitration within the multilateral trade system cf. Hughes (2004), pp. 75–86.

[20]Article 25.1 DSU. On arbitration proceedings under this provision see Boisson de Chazournes (2005), pp. 181–201; Jacyk (2008), pp. 235–266; Lo (2011), pp. 879–897; Malkawi (2007), pp. 173–188; Monnier (2002), pp. 481–538; Wolfrum (2006), pp. 566–571.

arbitration proceeding only upon the agreement of the parties which have agreed to have recourse to arbitration." While such a limitation to the participation of third parties may be understood on general terms, i.e. in the light of the major flexibility and discretion that DSU negotiators aimed to reserve to arbitration disputants, the multilateral and complex character of the WTO system, based on the principle of non-discrimination, demands the constant possibility of participation of any interested WTO Member to the discussion, interpretation, and litigation concerning a multilateral trade issue, an aspect fully understood by WTO adjudicators since the inception of the Marrakesh dispute settlement mechanism.[21]

Last but not least, Article 25.3 of the DSU renders the arbitral award legally binding, as "[t]he parties to the proceeding . . . [have to] agree to abide by" the latter. The arbitration award also has to be "notified to the DSB and the Council or Committee of any relevant agreement where any Member may raise any point relating thereto," thus confirming that Article 25 rulings are part of the Marrakesh case law, and about which any WTO Member has the right to comment within the DSB or any other relevant WTO body. Finally, Article 25.4 of the DSU extends to the arbitration award the power of imposing on the violator the obligation of prompt compliance, thus encompassing the procedures for the definition of the reasonable period of time for the implementation of WTO rulings, and the remedies of the suspension of concessions or other obligations enshrined in Articles 21 and 22 of the DSU.

So far, WTO Members have resorted to Article 25 arbitration only once, and only to determine the level of nullification and impairment of benefits in a situation where a breach of some TRIPs (Agreement on Trade Related Aspects of Intellectual Property Rights) obligations had already been found and the panel report adopted by the DSB.[22] In the *US — Section 110(5) Copyright Act* case, the parties asked the arbitrators to establish the damage suffered by the EU due to the breach by the US, via legislation, of copyrights of European musicians and performers.[23] In this Article 25 arbitration, the WTO adjudicators authoritatively declared the *kompetenz-kompetenz* principle, recalling the Appellate Body's finding in the *US — 1916 Act (EC)* case pursuant to which "it is a widely accepted rule that an international tribunal is entitled to consider the issue of its own jurisdiction on its own initiative."[24] In the WTO award it was consequently stated that "[i]n the absence of a multilateral control over recourse to [Article 25 of the DSU] . . . it is incumbent on the Arbitrators themselves to ensure that [such provision] is applied in accordance

[21]On the role devised for third parties in WTO litigation shaped by the case law of WTO adjudicators see Baroncini (2019), pp. 1767–1800.

[22]WTO Panel Report, United States – Section 110(5) of the US Copyright Act, 15 June 2000, WT/DS160/R.

[23]9 November 2001, WT/DS160/ARB25/1. On this award see Grossman and Mavroidis (2003), pp. 281–299.

[24]WT/DS136/AB/R, WT/DS162/AB/R, para 54.

with the rules and principles governing the WTO system,"[25] a duty including the responsibility of the WTO arbitrators to respect the obligation of Article 3.5 of the DSU, pursuant to which "[a]ll solutions" to WTO disputes "including arbitration awards . . . [have to] be consistent with [the WTO A]greements and . . . not nullify or impair benefits accruing to any Member under those agreements, nor impede the attainment of any objective of those agreements."

While recourse to arbitration under Article 25 of the DSU remained confined, within the WTO practice, to just the one reported case, the importance and value of this alternative means for settling disputes emerged in the midst of the institutional crisis caused by the US refusing to allow the appointments procedure to fill AB vacancies to proceed. Various scholars started to suggest recourse to the use of arbitration under Article 25 of the DSU "as a temporary avenue to enable appeals of panel reports."[26] The EU decided to develop and propose a model for an interim appellate review based on Article 25 of the DSU which may be easily endorsed by any willing WTO Member. Through such an approach, the EU aims at providing a prompt mechanism for dealing with the AB crisis which embodies a clear guideline and a constant method capable of guaranteeing WTO consistency and predictability in the future case law of the Article 25 appellate arbitrators. In fact, without such a model for an interim appeal arbitration arrangement, setting up of solutions on a case by case basis seems time-consuming and unlikely to result in a WTO-coherent practice when facing the blockage of the World Trade Court.

The remainder of the present work will thus be devoted to analysing the EU interim appeal arbitration, which could represent a most effective tool to temporarily overcome the impossibility for the WTO Appellate Body to adjudicate.

3 The Interim Appeal Arbitration Agreement Based on Article 25 of the DSU Proposed by the European Union

In May 2019, it was reported by the specialized press that the EU was planning to propose the use of arbitration proceedings under Article 25 of the DSU to provide a temporary solution to the AB crisis.[27] The European Commission was in fact preparing an arbitration model arrangement under Article 25 of the DSU, which would have been the basis of negotiations to be launched with other WTO Members

[25]WT/DS160/ARB25/1, para 2.1.

[26]Andersen S et al (2017) Using Arbitration under Article 25 of the DSU to Ensure the Availability of Appeals. CTEI Working Papers CTEI-2017-17, p. 1; See also Bacchus J (2018), Saving the WTO's Appeals Process, www.cato.org/blog; Hillebrand (2019), pp. 139–155.

[27]See World Trade Online, *EU Moving Forward with WTO Appellate Body Backup Plan*, 28 May 2019 available at: https://insidetrade.com/daily-news/eu-moving-forward-wto-appellate-body-backup-plan [subscription needed].

after having obtained the mandate to lead such consultations from the EU Council.[28] The latter, in the configuration "Foreign Affairs – Trade Issues," endorsed the European Commission's approach on 27 May 2019, declaring that "[a]s regards the Appellate Body crisis . . . the EU should reach out to other WTO members to work on an interim solution that preserves the binding character and the two levels of adjudication of the WTO dispute settlement system."[29]

The draft text of the joint communication containing the WTO interim appeal arbitration agreement—already leaked by the media at the beginning of June 2019[30]—was presented by the European Commission at the EU Trade Policy Committee (Deputies) in early July 2019, and then immediately brought to the attention of the EU Council, who was invited to authorise that text.[31] On 15 July 2019, the EU "Agriculture and Fisheries" Council hence "endorsed a model communication relating to interim arrangements that the EU will seek to put in place to preserve its . . . [WTO] rights pending the resolution of the blockage of appointments to the WTO Appellate Body," emphasising that "[t]hese arrangements will provide for arbitration, on the basis of Article 25 of the [DSU,] . . . to decide on appeals from panel reports if, and as long as, the Appellate Body is non-operational due to the blockage of new appointments."[32] The European Parliament finally declared to fully "[s]upport . . . [these] recent EU initiatives to conclude interim arrangements for provisional solutions with our major trade partners that would preserve the European Union's right to the resolution of trade disputes at the WTO through binding two-level, independent and impartial adjudication, while recalling that a Standing Appellate Body remains the core objective of the EU's strategy."[33]

As a first partner with which to agree on the proposed joint communication, the EU chose Canada, because of their common "strong support for the multilateral

[28]Cf. Council of the European Union (2019), Note from General Secretariat of the Council, WTO Appellate Body, 20 May 2019, 9506/19.

[29]Council of the European Union (2019) Conclusions, Foreign Affairs: Trade Issues, 27 May 2019, 9753/19, p. 3.

[30]See the post by Tom Miles, Chief Correspondent at the Reuters Geneva Bureau, dated 6 June 2019, appeared as a comment to Charnovitz S (2019) The WTO Appellate Body Crisis: A Critique of the EU's Article 25 Proposal. IELP Blog available at https://ielp.worldtradelaw.net/2019/06/the-wto-appellate-body-crisis-a-critique-of-the-eus-article-25-proposal.html.

[31]See Council of the European Union, 10905/19. The EU procedure just described in the text represents the application of the "Arrangements for Non-Binding Instruments" agreed among the Secretary Generals of the Council, the Commission and the EEAS as a follow-up to the judgment of the EU Court of Justice in case C-660/13, *Council of the European Union v European Commission*, EU:C:2016:616. See Council of the European Union (2017) Information Note, 4 December 2017, 15367/17.

[32]Council of the European Union (2019) Conclusions Agriculture and Fisheries, 15 July 2019, 11255/19, p. 11.

[33]European Parliament (2019) European Parliament resolution of 28 November 2019 on the crisis of the WTO Appellate Body, P9_TA-PROV(2019)0083, para 5.

trading system"[34] and recognition of "the indispensable role that the World Trade Organization ... plays in facilitating and safeguarding international rules-based trade."[35] At the 17th Bilateral EU-Canada Summit, held in Montreal on 17–18 July 2019, the two WTO Members therefore announced that they were "finalizing an interim appeal arbitration arrangement based on existing WTO rules which could apply until the WTO Appellate Body is able to hear new appeals again."[36] It was thus possible for the European Commission to officially present in Geneva the "Interim Appeal Arbitration Pursuant to Article 25 of the DSU," combined with its Annex on "Agreed Procedures," as an agreement with Canada, notified to the WTO Secretariat on 25 July 2019.[37] Subsequently, in September 2019, the European Commission decided to confer the Commissioner in charge for Trade with the power "to adopt, on behalf of the Commission and under its responsibility, certain measures concerning the interim appeal arbitrations at the World Trade Organization,"[38] i.e. to enter into bilateral arrangements to provisionally overcome the crisis of the blockage of the Appellate Body with any other willing WTO Member. The EU institution hence set up the necessary legal tools and framework for moving forward with the European strategy of preserving a two-tier quasi-judicial mechanism for the multilateral trade system in case the World Trade Court were stopped being operational on 11 December 2019.[39]

The EU-Canada arrangement was copy-pasted and also achieved with Norway on 21 October 2019.[40] As mentioned before, it is composed of two parts: the "Interim Appeal Arbitration pursuant to Article 25 of the DSU," and the "Agreed Procedures for Arbitration under Article 25 of the DSU in Dispute DS X," annexed to the first part of the bilateral understanding. The introductory section expresses the "utmost concern"[41] of the EU and her partner because of "the enduring absence of consensus in the Dispute Settlement Body for the proposals made to fill the vacancies"[42] of the World Trade Court, and formulates the joint political vision on which the "appeal arbitration procedure" is based, also codifying the basic principles having to characterize the interim Article 25 appeal arbitration. In the preambular part it thus "acknowledg[ed] the successful contribution of the WTO dispute settlement system

[34]Canada-EU Summit Joint Declaration, July 17–18, 2019, Montreal, para 12, available at: https://www.consilium.europa.eu/media/40403/final-2019-joint-declaration-final.pdf.

[35]Ibid.

[36]Ibid.

[37]JOB/DSB/1/Add.11, slightly modified on 21 October 2019 by the WTO document JOB/DSB/1/Add.11/Rev.1.

[38]PV(2019) 2306 final, European Commission, Minutes of the 2306th meeting of the Commission held in Brussels (Berlaymont) on Wednesday 4 September 2019 (morning), p. 10.

[39]See European Commission Adopts Mandate to Extend Interim Appeal Arbitration Arrangement, Brussels, 4 September 2019 available at: https://trade.ec.europa.eu/doclib/press/index.cfm?id=2059.

[40]JOB/DSB/1/Add.11/Suppl.1.

[41]JOB/DSB/1/Add.11/Rev.1, Interim Appeal Arbitration pursuant to Article 25 of the DSU, at p. 1.

[42]Ibid.

to the security and predictability of the multilateral trading system,"[43] and reaffirmed the commitment of the two sides "to a multilateral rules-based trading system;"[44] the "role of the Appellate Body within the WTO dispute settlement system"[45] is considered "essential,"[46] thus coherently underlining "the urgency and importance of filling the vacancies on the Appellate Body so that it can carry on its functions as envisaged by the DSU;"[47] and it is finally and consistently declared the determination of the two contracting parties "to preserve the essential principles and features of the WTO dispute settlement system which include its binding character and the two levels of adjudication through an independent and impartial appellate review of panel reports."[48] The joint communication therefore clearly states the provisional nature of the appeal arbitration procedure: the latter may be used only in the case that the Appellate Body will not be able "to hear appeals of panel reports in any future dispute between [the third country] and the European Union due to an insufficient number of its members;"[49] and the interim Article 25 arbitration has "to replicate as closely as possible all substantive and procedural aspects as well as the practice of Appellate Review pursuant to Article 17 of the DSU,"[50] foreseeing also "the provision of appropriate administrative and legal support to the arbitrators by the Appellate Body Secretariat."[51] As a guarantee that the "substantive and procedural aspects" of the WTO appellate procedures are observed in the interim Article 25 arbitration, the bilateral agreement establishes that the arbitrators of the interim procedure will be "selected by the Director General from the pool of available former members of the Appellate Body,"[52] also clearly declaring that recourse to the appeal arbitration procedure "will cease . . . as soon as the Appellate Body is again fully composed."[53]

In the Annex, the specific procedures for the interim Article 25 arbitration are considered. Once again it is clearly stated that "[t]he arbitration may only be initiated if the Appellate Body is not able to hear an appeal in [the dispute at hand] under Article 16.4 and 17 of the DSU,"[54] a situation which "is deemed to arise where, on the date of issuance of the final panel report to the parties, there are fewer than three

---

[43]Ibid.

[44]Ibid.

[45]Ibid.

[46]Ibid.

[47]Ibid.

[48]Ibid.

[49]JOB/DSB/1/Add.11/Rev.1, Interim Appeal Arbitration pursuant to Article 25 of the DSU, para 1.

[50]JOB/DSB/1/Add.11/Rev.1, Interim Appeal Arbitration pursuant to Article 25 of the DSU, para 2.

[51]Ibid.

[52]JOB/DSB/1/Add.11/Rev.1, Interim Appeal Arbitration pursuant to Article 25 of the DSU, para 3.

[53]JOB/DSB/1/Add.11/Rev.1, Interim Appeal Arbitration pursuant to Article 25 of the DSU, para 6.

[54]JOB/DSB/1/Add.11/Rev.1, Agreed Procedures for Arbitration under Article 25 of the DSU in Dispute DS X, para 2.

Appellate Body members."[55] Before the circulation of the final panel report to the WTO membership, any party may start the interim appeal arbitration procedure by requesting the panel to suspend panel proceedings for 12 months pursuant to Article 12.12 of the DSU. Therefore, "no later than 10 days after the suspension of the panel proceedings,"[56] the Notice of Appeal has to be filed with the WTO Secretariat. Such Notice of Appeal "shall include the final panel report in the official languages of the WTO,"[57] and has to be "simultaneously notified to the other party and to the third parties in the panel proceedings."[58] Furthermore, the Annex establishes that "[t]hird parties which have notified the DSB of a substantial interest in the matter before the panel pursuant to Article 10.2 of the DSU may make written submissions to, and shall be given an opportunity to be heard by, the arbitrator,"[59] applying *mutatis mutandis* Rule 24 of the Working Procedures for Appellate Review.[60] In this way, the EU interim appeal arbitration procedure overcomes the problematic aspect highlighted above on Article 25.3 of the DSU, where the latter provides that the disputants have the power to decide on the participation of other WTO Members to the arbitration proceeding: by introducing the obligation of accepting in advance the presence of third parties, the EU appeal arbitration maintains the important inclusive institutional feature of the role of third parties characterizing panel and AB adjudicatory activities.[61]

Paragraph 9 of the Agreed Procedures clarifies another fundamental aspect of the interim appeal arbitration, i.e. that such appeal, similarly to what is foreseen for the Appellate Body by Article 17.6 of the DSU, "shall be limited to issues of law covered by the panel report and legal interpretations developed by the panel,"[62] so that "[t]he arbitrators may uphold, modify or reverse the legal findings and conclusions of the panel."[63] It is established that the findings of the panel report which have not been appealed through the interim arbitration will become binding because those panel findings "shall be deemed to form an integral part of the arbitration award."[64] Of course, the Annex reiterates the immediate binding nature of the arbitration award, as the parties agree to observe the latter and consider it final, and also have

---

[55]Ibid.

[56]JOB/DSB/1/Add.11/Rev.1, Agreed Procedures for Arbitration under Article 25 of the DSU in Dispute DS X, para 5.

[57]Ibid.

[58]Ibid.

[59]JOB/DSB/1/Add.11/Rev.1, Agreed Procedures for Arbitration under Article 25 of the DSU in Dispute DS X, para 11.

[60]See WTO (2010) Appellate Body, Working Procedures for Appellate Review (16 August 2020) WT/AB/WP/6.

[61]See supra, para 2.

[62]JOB/DSB/1/Add.11/Rev.1, Agreed Procedures for Arbitration under Article 25 of the DSU in Dispute DS X, para 9.

[63]Ibid.

[64]JOB/DSB/1/Add.11/Rev.1, Agreed Procedures for Arbitration under Article 25 of the DSU in Dispute DS X, para 9.

the duty to notify it "to the DSB and to the Council or Committee of any relevant agreement,"[65] where any WTO Member has the right to deliver statements on any aspect of such award.

Most importantly, the Agreed Procedures require that awards issued under the interim appeal arbitration "be deemed to constitute Appellate Body reports adopted by the DSB for the purposes of interpretation of the covered agreements."[66] The precise qualification of the consideration to be reserved to Article 25 appellate review awards is a clear expression of the intention of the EU to establish a contingency remedy producing case law fully integrated in the WTO *acquis*, not, on the contrary, parallel jurisprudence ignoring the adopted multilateral dispute settlement reports. It is therefore a duty of the WTO Members joining the EU initiative to exercise good faith conduct in the special Article 25 appellate proceedings, and more generally in the WTO DSM, enabling the EU contingency remedy to be implemented in full harmony with the multilateral trade system, once more underlining the relevant nature of Appellate Body case law.

4 Reactions of the WTO Membership to the EU *ad hoc* Arbitration Proposal and the Strengthening of the EU Trade Toolbox for Ensuring a Rules-Based International Trade Regime

Geneva trade experts announced that the EU interim appeal arbitration proposal, beyond Canada and Norway, could be accepted by other WTO Members such as Australia, Argentina, Brazil, Chile, China, India, Japan and Turkey.[67] Those developed and developing countries share with the EU the view of the need to "continue to rely on binding dispute settlement in future,"[68] and the overall positive assessment of the Appellate Body's activity in shaping and preserving a multilateral trade system which is stable and predictable because it is rules-based and capable of issuing dispute settlement decisions that will be respected by both the disputants "as binding and final."[69] The Chinese Ambassador to the WTO, in particular, just on the eve of the Appellate Body's paralysis, declared that "Beijing is actively working to support the EU's vision of an appeal-arbitration model."[70]

[65] JOB/DSB/1/Add.11/Rev.1, Agreed Procedures for Arbitration under Article 25 of the DSU in Dispute DS X, para 10.

[66] JOB/DSB/1/Add.11/Rev.1, Agreed Procedures for Arbitration under Article 25 of the DSU in Dispute DS X, para 8.

[67] Miles (2019).

[68] Ibid.

[69] Ibid.

[70] Baschuk (2019).

The EU proposal thus seems to be gradually persuading different major actors of the multilateral trade system. Should the net of bilateral appeal arbitration arrangements start to persistently win the favour of a significant number of WTO Members, a sort of *de facto* plurilateral dispute settlement agreement could materialize. Such an important outcome could gain diplomatic space for discussions to reform the DSU and thus make the Appellate Body operational again. Furthermore, it would be smoothly achieved, avoiding all the legal difficulties of setting up a formal plurilateral agreement on dispute settlement within the WTO legal framework,[71] as well as the political and legal perplexities on the legitimate feasibility of a treaty of "The Real Friends of Dispute Settlement" outside the multilateral trade system,[72] in particular because of the principle of exclusive WTO jurisdiction for complaints concerning the Marrakesh Agreements on the basis of Article 23 of the DSU.[73] The EU choice to base her interim arbitration solution on "rules and procedures applicable to Appellate Review,"[74] including in particular the already in force WTO Working Appellate Procedures[75] and Rules of Conduct,[76] also allows avoiding the thorny issue of which procedural rules would be advisable to choose for the special Article 25 appeal arbitration to guarantee WTO compatible proceedings and awards.[77] What's more, by recalling that the interim Article 25 arbitration has "to replicate as closely as possible all substantive and procedural aspects as well as the practice of Appellate Review pursuant to Article 17 of the DSU,"[78] and expressly foreseeing that awards issued under the interim appeal arbitration procedure have to be "deemed to constitute Appellate Body reports adopted by the DSB for the

[71]On these aspects cf. Kong and Guo (2019), pp. 273–292.

[72]See Kujiper (2018), pp. 1–12, pp. 10–11.

[73]The principle of exclusive WTO jurisdiction has been interpreted as follows: "Article 23.1 ... prescribes a general duty of a dual nature. First, it imposes on all Members to 'have recourse to' the multilateral process set out in the DSU when they seek the redress of a WTO inconsistency. In these circumstances, Members have to have recourse to the DSU dispute settlement system to the exclusion of any other system, in particular a system of unilateral enforcement of WTO rights and obligations. This, what one could call 'exclusive dispute resolution clause', is an important new element of Members' rights and obligations under the DSU. Second, Article 23.1 also prescribes that Members, when they have recourse to the dispute settlement system in the DSU, have to 'abide by' the rules and procedures set out in the DSU. This second obligation under Article 23.1 is of a confirmatory nature: when having recourse to the DSU Members must abide by all DSU rules and procedures." WT/DS152/R, para 7.43.

[74]JOB/DSB/1/Add.11/Rev.1, *Agreed Procedures for Arbitration under Article 25 of the DSU in Dispute DS X*, para 8.

[75]WTO (2010) Appellate Body, Working Procedures for Appellate Review (16 August 2010) WT/AB/WP/6.

[76]WTO (1996) Rules of Conduct for the Understanding on Rules and Procedures (11 December 1996) WT/DSB/RC/1.

[77]See Hazarika and Van Vaerenbergh (2019), pp. 595–628.

[78]WTO (2019), Interim Appeal Arbitration pursuant to Article 25 of the DSU, 22 October 2019, JOB/DSB/1/Add.11/Rev.1, para 2.

purposes of interpretation of the covered agreements,"[79] the EU interim arbitration arrangement preserves and strengthens the consideration—and respect—for the most appreciated WTO case law. Overall, the legal architecture of the proposed EU contingency remedy reveals the drafters' clear intention of preventing the creation of a subspecies of WTO jurisprudence. The future appellate awards will have to be shaped in the context of the consolidated WTO practice, by WTO-experienced appellate arbitrators, with the assistance of the WTO Appellate Body Secretariat.[80] The desired jurisprudential result aims therefore at being solidly channelled in the multilateral WTO *acquis*, contributing to its harmonious and constructive development.

Realizing the significant potential of her interim appeal arbitration proposal, in mid-December 2019 the EU intensified her efforts to attract more and more WTO Members towards her contingency measure, combining plurilateral with unilateral initiatives. At the diplomatic level, the EU suggested at "a meeting of more than a dozen countries hosted"[81] in Geneva the definition of "a multi-party interim appeal arbitration arrangement," whose objective "would be to offer a stop-gap solution, pending the ... issue of appointments, by closely replicating the Appellate Body review process in the framework of Article 25 of the DSU. The stop-gap solution would apply within a group of interested members. It will preserve both the access to a binding adjudication of disputes and the right to appeal review."[82] Russia has manifested its interest in joining the EU proposal, which would be formulated in a communication to the DSB presented by all the interested WTO Members, and containing "a political commitment to apply model appeal arbitration procedures, based on Article 25 of the DSU, in disputes among themselves."[83]

Internally, the EU backed her interim appeal arbitration arrangement through a proposal to strengthen the EU Enforcement Regulation. According to amendments presented on 12 December 2019, the European Commission foresees the possibility "to expeditiously suspend obligations under international trade agreements, including regional or bilateral agreements, when effective recourse to a binding dispute settlement mechanism is not possible because the third country has rendered it impossible for the Union to do so."[84] Therefore, once the new Regulation is adopted, "if an appeal under Article 17 of the [DSU] ... cannot be completed and if the third country has not agreed to interim appeal arbitration under Article 25 of the

[79]WTO (2019), Agreed Procedures for Arbitration under Article 25 of the DSU in Dispute DS X, 22 October 2019, JOB/DSB/1/Add.11/Rev.1, para 8.

[80]WTO (2019), Interim Appeal Arbitration pursuant to Article 25 of the DSU, 22 October 2019, JOB/DSB/1/Add.11/Rev.1, paras 2–3.

[81]Cf. Kanth (2019).

[82]EU proposal reported by Kanth (2019).

[83]Kanth (2019).

[84]Seventh recital of the preamble of the EU Proposal amending the EU Enforcement Regulation, in COM(2019) 623, p. 9.

[DSU],"[85] the European Commission may adopt "appropriate commercial policy measures"[86] in order to safeguard EU interests. The same can happen "in trade disputes relating to other international trade agreements, including regional or bilateral agreements, if adjudication is not possible because the third country is not taking the steps that are necessary for a dispute settlement procedure to function,"[87] as may occur in case such country "fail[s] to appoint an arbitrator and there is no fall-back mechanism foreseen for dispute settlement to nevertheless be able to proceed."[88] In the Explanatory Memorandum introducing the proposal, the European Commission justifies the suggestion of a new option for imposing countermeasures recalling Article 52(4) of the Draft Articles on Responsibility of States for Internationally Wrongful Acts adopted by the International Law Commission (ILC) in August 2001[89] and endorsed by the UN General Assembly in December of the same year,[90] as well as ILC commentary (9) to Article 52.[91] "[W]here the responsible party fails to cooperate in good faith in the dispute settlement procedures, thereby preventing the injured party from completing such procedures,"[92] observes the EU institution, "the possibility to resort to countermeasures in accordance with the requirements of general public international law necessarily revives,"[93] and such illegitimate conduct includes the circumstance "where a State party fails to cooperate in the establishment of the relevant tribunal."[94] The just recalled situations are evidently the scenario within which the suggested EU amendments "would operate."[95]

It is, in the author's view, clear that the new penalty trade measures adoptable by the EU -in case a third country intentionally impedes the appropriate functioning of the dispute settlement mechanisms of multilateral, plurilateral and bilateral agreements of international economic law—have not been conceived by the European Commission to step back from the principles of cooperation and the rule of law when mastering the global economy, but, on the contrary, are unilateral actions aimed to

---

[85]Article 1(1)(a) of the EU Proposal amending the EU Enforcement Regulation, *ibid.*

[86]See Article 3 of the EU Enforcement Regulation.

[87]Article 1(1)(b) of the EU Proposal amending the EU Enforcement Regulation, COM(2019) 623, at p. 9.

[88]COM(2019) 623, p. 2.

[89]ILC (2001) Report of the International Law Commission on the work of its fifty-third session, 23 April–1 June and 2 July–10 August 2001, Official Records of the General Assembly, Fifty-sixth session, Supplement No.10. 2001 vol. II(2) Doc. A/56/10.

[90]UNGA Res (2002) Responsibility of States for internationally wrongful acts, A/RES/56/83.

[91]Yearbook of the ILC, 2001, vol. II, Part 2, pp. 31–143.

[92]COM(2019) 623 p. 4.

[93]Ibid.

[94]Yearbook of the ILC, 2001, vol. II, Part 2, p. 137.

[95]COM(2019) 623 final, cit., p. 4.

strengthen and "reaffirm . . . the Union's commitment to multilateralism and independent adjudication."[96]

5 Conclusions

The very delicate institutional crisis triggered by the United States over the Appellate Body composition may appear as peculiar since the World Trade Court "has over the years served as a point of reference in different academic and policy debates about efficient institutional design for international dispute resolution."[97] In such a sensitive scenario, the technical quality of the EU proposal for an interim arbitration appeal is attracting the WTO Members most committed to maintaining and strengthening the rule of law in the multilateral trade system.[98] While it seems unlikely, at least in the short time, to expect a favourable reaction from Washington to the EU initiatives, *the EU Interim Appeal Arbitration Pursuant to Article 25 of the DSU* could nevertheless provide for vital diplomatic space to fix the WTO dispute settlement mechanism, or devise *ex novo* a new multilateral legal framework, thus preserving the principle of cooperation as the central pillar of the international governance necessary for a free and fair global economy.

The US approach seems more and more characterized by the intent of disarticulating the WTO jurisdictional pillar, as most lately witnessed by the US decision to introduce drastic cuts in the WTO budget for expenses to cover the functioning of the Appellate Body.[99] Nonetheless the EU is showing the strongest determination "to preserve its rights as enshrined in the WTO Agreements, notably the right to an appeal review," and thus not to renounce "a rules based multilateral trading system," considering that such an approach is "owe[d] . . . to our citizens and our businesses, because it is them, ultimately, that benefit from the system."[100] In addition to animating the debate in Geneva, the EU has been vigilant in keeping the WTO dispute settlement mechanism at the centre of attention in the UN system,

---

[96]Ibid.

[97]Lam (2020), pp. 331–348.

[98]See the previous paragraph and Trade Promotion Council of India, WTO: Interim Arrangement for Global Trade Disputes, 16 December 2019.

[99]Originally threatening to veto the entire 2020 WTO budget, the US administration conditioned its endorsement to the latter to the acceptance by the rest of the WTO membership of drastic cuts of the Appellate Body's expenses: "[t]he deal limits annual spending for appellate body members to no more than 100,000 francs, an 87% reduction from the full allotment, and caps spending by the body's operating fund to 100,000 francs, a 95% reduction" (Baschuk B (2019) WTO Members Agree on a 2020 Budget, Averting Jan. 1 Shutdown. In Bloomberg, 5 December 2019). See also the statement of the US Ambassador Dennis Shea on Appellate Body members' compensation delivered at the DSB meeting of 22 November 2019: Statements by the United States at the Meeting of the WTO Dispute Settlement Body Delivered by Ambassador Dennis Shea, U.S. Permanent Representative to the World Trade Organization, Geneva, November 22, 2019.

[100]Statements by the European Union at the WTO General Council Meeting, 9–10 December 2019.

where the Economic and Financial Committee (Second Committee) of the UN General Assembly has recently approved, albeit with the contrary vote of the United States,[101] a draft resolution on "International trade and development" recognizing "the need to strengthen the World Trade Organization, with a view to ensuring the continued viability and effectiveness of its dispute settlement, negotiating and monitoring functions."[102] The input brought by the new European Commission to the quality and intensity of the EU participation to the discussions on overcoming the Appellate Body crisis has hence been quite significant. It is, in fact, a top EU priority "to lead the reform of the World Trade Organization, notably on the issues of subsidies, forced transfer of technologies and dispute settlement ... launch[ing] a broad initiative by the end of 2020, following the next WTO Ministerial Conference, [[103]] with a view to reaching a comprehensive agreement by 2022."[104]

The greatest attention has therefore to be reserved to the constructive initiatives proposed by the EU, as the latter is the world's largest trading block and has put forth a process of a unique political integration which, in spite of its current internal challenges,[105] could well advance a most significant contribution for governing international trade with transparent, inclusive and fair mechanisms and rules.

Acknowledgements The author is very grateful to Professors Colin Picker, Meredith Kolsky Lewis, Junji Nakagawa, Peter-Tobias Stoll and Dr. Holger Hestermeyer for having been involved in the present research project and their important comments, together with those of the other experts participating at London Workshop, on the first version of this contribution, conveyed during the King's College October 2019 meeting. The work is updated to January 1, 2020.

References

Baroncini E (2019) L'approccio inclusivo dell'Organo d'appello dell'OMC per una giurisprudenza informata, partecipata, ed aperta. In: Davì A (ed) Liber Amicorum: La vita giuridica internazionale nell'età della globalizzazione, vol III. Editoriale scientifica, pp 1767–1800

Baschuk B (2019) China may back EU's trade-dispute 'Plan B' as Trump Hobbles WTO. Bloomberg, 10 December 2019

[101]See UNGA (26 November 2019) GA/EF/3528.

[102]UNGA (20 November 2019) A/C.2/74/L.15/Rev.1, where it is stated *inter alia* that the EU "attach the greatest importance to the development and strengthening of a multilateral trading system centered around the WTO that is open, transparent, universal and rules-based," and that "[a]s a matter of urgency, the WTO two-step dispute settlement mechanism needs to be restored and Appellate Body nominations need to resume without delay."

[103]The Twelfth WTO Ministerial Conference (MC12) will take place from 8 to 11 June 2020 in Nur-Sultan, Kazakhstan.

[104]See Ursula von der Leyen, President-elect of the European Commission, Mission Letter to Phin Hogan, Commissioner-designate for Trade, Brussels, 10 September 2019, p. 4.

[105]Challenges to the EU integration process range from the thorny saga of Brexit to the highly unsatisfactory approach on migration policies.

Boisson de Chazournes L (2005) Arbitration at the WTO: a terra incognita to be further explored. In: Charnovitz S, Steger D, Van den Bossche P (eds) Law in the service of human dignity: essays in honour of Florentino Feliciano. Cambridge University Press, Cambridge, pp 181–201
Grossman G, Mavroidis P (2003) US – Section 110(5) copyright act United States – Section 110 (5) of the US copyright act, recourse to arbitration under Article 25 of the DSU: would've or should've? Impaired benefits due to copyright infringement. World Trade Rev 2(2):281–299
Hazarika A, Van Vaerenbergh P (2019) "One Rule to Rule Them All": rules for Article 25 DSU arbitration. J Int Arbitr 36(5):595–628
Hillebrand P (2019) Blueprint for a plurilateral WTO arbitration agreement under Article 25 of the dispute settlement understanding. In: Prévost D, Alexovičocá I, Hillebrand Pohl J (eds) Restoring trust in trade, Liber Amicorum in Honour of Peter Van den Bossche. Hart, Oxford, pp 139–155
Hughes V (2004) Arbitration within the WTO. In: Ortino F, Petersmann EU (eds) The WTO dispute settlement system 1995–2003. Kluwer Law International, The Hague, pp 75–86
Jacyk D (2008) The integration of Article 25 arbitration in WTO dispute settlement: the past, present and future. Aust Int Law J 15(1):235–266
Kanth R (2019) WTO: interim arrangement to resolve global trade disputes in the works. The Hindu Business Line (15 December 2019) Available at: https://www.thehindubusinessline.com/economy/wto-interim-arrangement-to-resolve-global-trade-disputes-in-the-works/article30313045.ece#
Kong Q, Guo S (2019) Towards a mega-plurilateral dispute settlement mechanism for the WTO? J World Trade 53(2):273–292
Kujiper P (2018) From the board: the US attack on the WTO Appellate Body. Legal Issues Econ Integr 45(1):1–12, 10–11
Lam J (2020) WTO AB as a model for other adjudicatory bodies – the case of EU's investment court system. In: Lo C, Nakagawa J, Chen T (eds) The Appellate Body of the WTO and its reform. Springer, Heidelberg, pp 331–348
Lehne J (2019) Crisis at the WTO: is the blocking of appointments to the WTO Appellate Body by the United States legally justified? Carl Grossman Verlag, Berlin
Lo C (2011) The shrinking role of Article 25 arbitration in DSU: a proper understanding of "clearly defined" issues to enhance efficiency of WTO dispute settlement procedure. US-China Law Rev 8(10):879–897
Lo C, Nakagawa J, Chen T (eds) (2020) The Appellate Body of the WTO and its reform. Springer, Heidelberg
Malkawi B (2007) Arbitration and the World Trade Organization – the forgotten provisions of Article 25 of the dispute settlement understanding. J Int Arbitr 24(2):173–188
Miles T (2019) EU, Canada agree first workaround to avoid U.S. Block on WTO Judges. Reuters Business News
Monnier P (2002) Working procedures before panels, the Appellate Body and other adjudicating bodies of the WTO. Law Pract Int Courts Tribunals 1(1):481–538
Wolfrum R (2006) Article 25 DSU – arbitration. In: Wolfrum R, Stoll P-T, Kaiser K (eds) WTO - institutions and dispute settlement. Martinus Nijhoff, Leiden, pp 566–571

Like a Rolling Stone: Exploring Viable Options for the WTO Dispute Settlement Mechanism to Evolve Forward in the Post-WTO Era

Tomohiko Kobayashi and Yuka Fukunaga

Contents

You used to ride on the chrome horse with your diplomat

Who carried on his shoulder a Siamese cat

Ain't it hard when you discover that

He really wasn't where it's at

After he took from you everything he could steal

This research is supported by a grant-in-aid from the Zengin Foundation for Studies on Economics and Finance.

Respectively a Professor of International Economic Law at Otaru University of Commerce, and a Professor of International Economic Law at Waseda University.

T. Kobayashi (✉)
Otaru University of Commerce, Otaru, Japan
e-mail: kobayashi@otaru-uc.ac.jp

Y. Fukunaga
Waseda University, Tokyo, Japan
e-mail: yuka-fukunaga@waseda.jp

M. K. Lewis et al. (eds.), *A Post-WTO International Legal Order*,
https://doi.org/10.1007/978-3-030-45428-9_8

Bob Dylan, Like a Rolling Stone (1965)

1 Introduction

The World Trade Organization is on the brink of demise or, at least, irrelevance. WTO Members' distrust towards the organization is rampant; for some, the core of their concerns focuses on the WTO's dispute settlement mechanism. Several proposals to fix the WTO DSM have been presented and discussed among the Members, but to no avail. The distrust is so profound that WTO Members have been struggling to reach a consensus.

The direct cause of the current crisis regarding the WTO dispute settlement mechanism is the United States' blocking of the appointment of AB members. However, it is inaccurate to think that the United States alone is critical of the DSM, which was once praised as the crown jewel of the WTO. Instead, the United States merely highlights, in a brutal but effective way, some longstanding concerns. Beneath the unquestionable success of the DSM, problems have been creeping in from both inside and outside the WTO.

First, this chapter briefly reviews the problems with the current WTO DSM, and then, it envisions two new trade dispute settlement mechanisms. The objective of the paper is not to propose short-term solutions but to provide a conceptual basis for the new trade dispute settlement mechanisms—usable within the current WTO or in a successor regime.

2 Problems with the Current WTO Dispute Settlement Mechanism

The United States has repeatedly highlighted problems with the current WTO DSM, which include procedural[1] and systemic[2] concerns. These concerns relate to the scope and nature of the authority of the AB under the Understanding on Rules and

[1]United States' statements concerning former Appellate Body member continuing to serve on appeals, Statements by the United States at the Meeting of the WTO Dispute Settlement Body, Geneva, February 28, 2018, pp. 10–14. https://geneva.usmission.gov/wp-content/uploads/sites/290/Feb28.DSB_.Stmt_.as-delivered.fin_.public-1.pdf. United States' statements concerning the repeated issuance of Appellate Body reports beyond the 90-day deadline, Statements by the United States at the Meeting of the WTO Dispute Settlement Body, Geneva, June 22, 2018, pp. 9–21. https://geneva.usmission.gov/wp-content/uploads/sites/290/Jun22.DSB_.Stmt_.as-delivered.fin_.public.rev_.pdf.

[2]United States' statements concerning the appellate review of panel findings of fact, Statements by the United States at the Meeting of the WTO Dispute Settlement Body, Geneva, August 27, 2018, pp. 10–31. https://geneva.usmission.gov/wp-content/uploads/sites/290/Aug27.DSB_.Stmt_.as-delivered.fin_.rev_.public.pdf. United States' statements concerning the issuance of advisory

Procedures Governing the Settlement of Disputes (DSU). In the view of the United States, the AB has been exercising power beyond what is conferred to it under Article 17 of the DSU and adding to or diminishing the rights and obligations of Members in contravention of Article 3.2 of the DSU. The US concern reflects the unquestionable fact that the AB's *de facto* authority to make pronouncements on significant interpretative questions has been growing in the absence of tools for Members to counterbalance such authority.

The US's concerns are shared by other Members to some extent as indicated by subsequent discussions on improvements of the work of the AB. Many of the fixes proposed by other Members seek to re-establish a proper balance between the AB and WTO Members, for example, by enhancing the involvement of the disputing parties in decisions of procedural matters during dispute settlement proceedings[3] or facilitating dialogue between Members and the AB.[4] However, the United States has categorically rejected these proposals, stating that "the proposals would not effectively address the concerns."[5] Apparently, more robust improvements would be needed to satisfy the demands of the United States. Or, perhaps it is the case that there are no improvements which would be sufficient given the profoundness of its concerns with the existing dispute settlement mechanism. If so, new ideas would be needed to break the current impasse.

Since December 2019, the AB has ceased to function due to the shortage of its membership. Article 17.1 requires at least three members to hear individual cases: "[i]t shall be composed of seven persons, *three* of whom shall serve on *any one case*" (emphases added). This disfunction is not limited to the appeal phase, but may nullify the entire dispute settlement mechanism. Article 16.4 of the DSU provides disputing parties the "right" to appeal to the AB, and "[i]f a party has notified its decision to appeal, the report by the panel *shall not* be considered for adoption by the DSB *until after* completion of the appeal" (emphases added). It means any disputing party that is unsatisfied with its panel's findings can block adoption of the entire panel report just by filing an appeal, preventing the DSB from making decisions.

Proposals that pursue alternative means to account for the loss of the current AB stage include: (1) the use of *ad hoc* arbitration under Article 25 DSU, (2) authoritative

---

opinions, Statements by the United States at the Meeting of the WTO Dispute Settlement Body, Geneva, October 29, 2018, pp. 10–26. https://geneva.usmission.gov/wp-content/uploads/sites/290/Oct29.DSB_.Stmt_.as-delivered.fin_.rev_.public.pdf. United States' statements concerning the precedential value of panel or Appellate Body reports, Statements by the United States at the Meeting of the WTO Dispute Settlement Body, Geneva, December 18, 2018,pp. 9–35. https://geneva.usmission.gov/wp-content/uploads/sites/290/Dec18.DSB_.Stmt_.as-deliv.fin_.public.pdf.

[3]Communication from the European Union, China, Canada, India, Norway, New Zealand, Switzerland, Australia, Republic of Korea, Iceland, Singapore, Mexico, Costa Rica and Montenegro to the General Council: Revision. WT/GC/W/752/Rev.2 (11 December 2018), pp. 1–2 and 4.

[4]Ibid., Another proposal has been made to streamline the selection process of Appellate Body members. Communication from the European Union, China, India and Montenegro to the General Council: Revision, 11 December 2018, WT/GC/W/753/Rev.1.

[5]US Statements of December 2018, *supra* note 2, at 44.

interpretations under Article X:2 of the Marrakesh Agreement Establishing the World Trade Organization, (3) a waiver under Article X:3 thereof, or (4) agreements not to appeal. However, most of these options are legally untenable.[6] First, there are serious concerns regarding the recourse to Article 25 arbitrations, which include (i) a lack of transparency and predictability; (ii) a lack of technical and financial support by the Secretariat; and (iii) insufficient third-party rights, because the disputing parties have wide discretion on the procedures (paragraphs 2 and 3 of Article 25 DSU). Secondly, seeking a waiver by voting under Article X:3 of the Marrakesh Agreement is not available in this context because a waiver can free Members from the "obligation," but it cannot deprive Members of a positive "right" to appeal. Also, the DSB may indeed adopt an internal law, like bylaws of a partnership or corporation, to establish technical rules and procedures governing the appointment of AB members that are separate from the DSU itself. However, the "decision" to adopt such bylaws or subsidiary rules must be made by consensus, which does not exist in this context. Thirdly, reaching an agreement not to appeal before the panel process is possible, but it would significantly undermine the sense of trust in the WTO dispute settlement mechanism. Also, its enforceability would be set aside once a disputing party violated the agreement and filed a notice of appeal as of right under Article 16.4 DSU.

With hope that the existing dispute settlement mechanism will survive the ongoing crisis, this chapter envisions two new schemes for overcoming the challenges faced by the WTO dispute settlement mechanism, but which also may be employed as either primary or backup processes in any successor regime, should the WTO fail to weather the current storm. These mechanisms are not meant to replace the existing dispute settlement mechanism but to supplement it, either in an extant WTO or in a successor regime. Both options (described in detail below) are expected to remove the burden of panels and the AB by allocating the power to settle trade disputes through multiple mechanisms. This would reestablish a healthy balance between Members and the WTO organs or between members and future successor regime bodies.

3 Transplanting the Appeal Mechanism Into the Panel Process

This section explores the possibility of salvaging a substantial part of the appeal mechanism by incorporating it into the panel phase.[7] Even if the dysfunction of the AB has a significant impact on the WTO, it does not terminate the WTO dispute settlement mechanism. In other words, we should not throw the entire crown away even though the largest gem on top may be lost. Similarly, in some future successor

[6]See also Payosova et al. (2018), p. 10.

[7]As an early version of this section, see also Kobayashi (2019), pp. 207–209.

regime, the idea underlying the WTO's AB system could still be recovered, albeit within the panel process.

3.1 Reviewing the Role of the Panel Process

Why do scholars and practitioners take the role of the AB so seriously, but pay significantly less attention to the panel stage when discussing the fate of the WTO dispute settlement mechanism? Not only is the frequency of appeals remarkable, but the robustness of the AB's jurisprudence during the first two decades has also been outstanding. Moreover, the AB has a well-staffed standing Secretariat. However, we should not disregard the role of the panel process. The panel process, which was established under the General Agreement on Tariffs and Trade (GATT) (1947), has established rules and practices for appointing panelists, holding hearings, and drafting reports since 1970s.

First of all, fact-finding is within the exclusive jurisdiction of panels rather than the AB. For elaborating legal reasonings, the Legal Affairs Division and the Rules Division for trade remedies disputes of the WTO Secretariat have institutional capacities to support panels. It helps to ensure that their reports maintain adequate quality, especially as some panelists have neither expertise in administering proceedings similar to lawsuits nor professional knowledge of law.

Second, the process's flexibility is another benefit of the panel stage. When in agreement, disputing parties can select panelists by agreement. It is true that, in reality, disputing parties sometimes fail to agree on the composition of the panel and that this results in requests to the Director-General to choose the panelists *ex officio*. Still, the disputing parties' inherent discretion of selecting panelists is the fundamental feature of the WTO dispute settlement mechanism. In addition, in practice, the time constraints are less stringent than those for the AB. A popular criticism of the AB is that it often fails to meet its ninety-day deadline.[8] A panel's failure to meet the maximum nine-month period of panel deliberation (Article 12.9 DSU) is not seen as problematic. This is partly because of the different natures of the panel and AB regarding the strictness of their deadlines.[9]

In this context, how can we utilize the panel stage to save the entire WTO dispute settlement mechanism when the AB's function is extremely restricted? Or how can we help to create a future sufficiently robust panel process in a successor regime,

---

[8]See e.g., Statements Delivered to the General Council by Ambassador Dennis Shea, U.S. Permanent Representative to the World Trade Organization, Geneva, October 15, 2019, https://geneva.usmission.gov/2019/10/15/statements-by-the-united-states-at-the-wto-general-council-meeting/.

[9]Article 12.9 DSU reads "In no case *should* the period from the establishment of the panel to the circulation of the report to the Members exceed nine months" (emphasis added) for the duration of panels; Article 17.5 DSU reads "In no case *shall* the proceedings exceed 90 days" (emphasis added) for duration of the AB's proceedings.

even in the absence of an appellate structure. In the current WTO context, at least, having an agreement not to appeal is an indispensable requirement for keeping the decision-making process active; in a way, this is similar to the spontaneous practice of "sequencing" agreements to solve conflicting procedures under Article 21.5 and Article 22 DSU.[10] However, maintaining a panel phase without an appeal mechanism would only serve to reduce trust in the system. What other options do we have so that we may rescue the organizational knowledge of the WTO dispute settlement mechanism and effectively solve serious trade disputes?

Hiring more qualified and reliable panelists, such as former AB members, will not solve this problem. It is true that the DSB can create non-binding rosters without amending the DSU at any time, and there have been proposals to establish rosters of chairpersons, thus adding to the indicative list of non-governmental panelists under Article 8.4 DSU. However, the existing indicative lists of panelists created under the DSU and the Agreement on Subsidies and Countervailing Measures (SCM Agreement) have had a limited impact in practice. Assuming that the panel's findings would become decisive and the appeal mechanism would not be available, the battle to select panelists would become much more intense between disputing parties, which would make a pre-fixed list of candidates far less meaningful.

Even under different scenarios for the panel compositions, the result would be the same. For example, once the AB phase ceases to function, WTO members likely would take the panel phase more seriously and shift to selecting panelists from a smaller cohort of reliable, respected, established experts, or a notable person such as a former AB member. Obviously, this would help to maintain integrity with regard to the findings. However, it would also place more burdens on these experts compared to what they experienced as AB members, since the panel phase involves detailed fact-finding examinations that would require extended periods of time far longer than anticipated under the DSU. The smaller the size of a panel roster, the heavier the burden placed on each roster member. The larger the roster becomes, the more difficult it is to maintain the consistency of legal interpretations and the collegiality within the roster.

Furthermore, this practice would not be sustainable. If there were only a limited number of experts appointed as panelists for an extended period of time, then no one else would be able to enter the market and develop their expertise. Eventually, those distinguished figures would have to retire, after all. Sooner or later, it will lead to the politicization of the appointment process for the next-generation members. If consensus is required to appoint a roster member, any member state can block the appointment process in a way similar to the blocking of AB members' appointments.

Finally, given the likelihood that WTO member states will not reach an agreement to create another appeal mechanism to take the place of the AB, it could be said that the panel phase will be the only asset available. If a dispute settlement process were to be part of a successor regime, figuring out how to do so without an appellate process would be critical. However, even assuming that the negative consensus

[10] WTO (2017), p. 151.

mechanism will remain intact in a successor regime, simply maintaining the panel phase is not sufficient for maintaining and developing reliable case law to handle a growing number of hard cases. We need a new approach to revitalize the role of the panel process in order to rescue the post-WTO dispute settlement mechanism.

3.2 "Expert Review Groups" as a Potential Vehicle to Incorporate the Appellate Function

Using "expert review groups" ("ERG"), as stated in Article 13.2 and Appendix 4 of the DSU, can be one option for transplanting the appellate function into the panel phase. Paragraph 2 of Article 13 DSU (Right to seek information) reads as follows:

> Panels may seek information from any relevant source and may consult experts to obtain their opinion on certain aspects of the matter. *With respect to a factual issue concerning* a scientific or *other technical matter* raised by a party to a dispute, a *panel may request an advisory report* in writing from an expert review group. Rules for the establishment of such a group and its procedures are set forth in Appendix 4. (Emphases added.)

It is a general perception that an ERG is supposed to handle only "a factual issue concerning a scientific or other technical matter," excluding legal analysis from ERG's mandate. However, panels are not prohibited from asking the ERGs to report their legal and factual analyses to the extent that they involve issues "with regard to" factual issues concerning scientific or other technical matters. In addition, the ERG can extend its mandate to review legal reasonings made by the panel in order to evaluate if the panel fully covers all the necessary facts to be analyzed. This interpretation of the DSU is similar to the one employed by the AB in conducting factual findings to "complete the analysis,"[11] although the AB's mandate is, on its face, limited only to the issue of law.[12]

Among the several practical advantages of using ERGs, the most prominent advantage is that an ERG is a panel's subsidiary. Therefore, it is "under the panel's authority" and "shall report to the panel" in accordance with paragraph 1 of Appendix 4 (Expert Review Groups) DSU. Reversing the relationship between the panels and the AB would alleviate Members' concerns about the ERG's power. In addition, members of the ERG should be experts with "professional standing and experience in the field in question" (paragraph 2 of Appendix 4 DSU). In contrast to the non-citizenship requirement for selecting the panelists, the panel has wide discretion over the ERG's composition regardless of its members' citizenship. Finally, an ERG can hear opinions from both parties as potential appellant and appellee in accordance with its power to "seek information [...] from any source" (paragraph 4 of Appendix 4 DSU). This confidential information is protected under paragraph 5 of Appendix

[11]See e.g. Appellate Body Report (1996), *United States – Standards for reformulated and conventional gasoline*. WT/DS2/AB/R (20 May 1996), p. 19.

[12]DSU, Art. 17.6.

5, thus allowing the ERGs to access confidential information to the same extent that panels and, formerly, the AB could.

Finally, the ERG submits a final "advisory report" (Article 13.2 DSU) to the panel, which "shall be advisory only" (paragraph 6 of Appendix 4 DSU). Therefore, the ERG's institutional subordination to panels and the non-binding nature of ERG reports would alleviate Members' concerns about abusive exercises of the ERG's authority and enable disputing parties to agree not to appeal the panel report. On the other hand, ERGs can exercise similar "review" functions to those of the AB in terms of legal analysis, along with the inherent power to review the panel's fact finding. The final advisory report may contain conflicting views within the ERG, who still bring new insights for the panel to consider while finalizing its report.

Ideally, the DSB can form a roster of ERG members from a small group of experts at its discretion,[13] as an exclusive list of qualified individuals suitable for serving as ERG members. Arguably, this action can be considered to fall outside of the "decision" under Article 2.4 DSU, which can be made by voting rather than consensus. If it is the case, the DSB can agree to select such experts through majority voting, or supermajority voting to ensure the legitimacy of the cohort. Even if the consensus is required under Article 2.4 DSU, the member states would be less inclined to block the appointment process (compared to appointing a specific person as an AB member) because, after all, it is each panel's discretion to select the ERG members for individual cases. In any case, the key component of this proposal is to remove the risk of a procedural stalemate,[14] while incorporating the essence of an appellate mechanism with fewer political concerns over the abuse of power. As a good practice, panels can agree on working procedures to incorporate the ERG's findings through a negative consensus—that is, the ERG report is almost automatically incorporated into the panel report unless the DSB reaches a consensus not to do so. The DSB may also create a standard template for ERG's working procedures, which does not force all panels to adopt it for individual cases.

It is understandable that, until now, no panels have ever used ERGs because they have been reluctant to create a "tribunal within a tribunal."[15] However, in a successor regime without an appellate process, there needs to be a second opinion, or friendly competition, that has already been established to ensure the reliability of the panel process. Needless to say, panels would still have the formal power to disregard the ERG's observations, even though they may be influential in future proceedings. In this context, WTO lawyers can learn from the role taken on by Advocates General in the development of case law in the Court of Justice of the European Union (CJEU).[16] Therefore, utilizing a review mechanism within the panel process—and not above

[13]DSU, Art. 2.1.

[14]DSU, Art. 16.4.

[15]Pauwelyn (2002), p. 328.

[16]For the brief overview of the role of Advocates General in the EU court system, see European Parliament website. https://www.europarl.europa.eu/thinktank/en/document.html?reference=EPRS_BRI(2019)642237.

it—would be a valuable safeguard to ensure the trustworthiness of panel reports and a political safety valve that disputing parties can utilize to justify waiving the right to appeal.

4 Trade Dispute Settlement Mechanism Accessible by Private Parties

This section explores the possibility of establishing a new trade dispute settlement mechanism that could be used by private parties—which could be of use within the existing WTO or could be considered as part of any successor regime. For that purpose, this section draws insights from investor-state arbitration and individual communications under optional protocols to human rights treaties, both of which are primarily used by private parties. It examines whether a similar mechanism could be created under the WTO agreements. This section's approach resonates with that of Canada's discussion paper, which suggests diverting certain disputes from the existing dispute settlement mechanism[17] and developing alternative procedures tailored to specific kinds of disputes.[18] More specifically, it asks the following two questions: First, can private parties be given the right to have recourse to a trade dispute settlement mechanism under the WTO agreements? Second, if the answer to the first question is yes, how should violations be redressed in the new mechanism?

4.1 Standing: Can Private Parties Be Entitled to Have Recourse to Trade Dispute Settlement?

Investment agreements often provide that an investor of a contracting state to the agreement may submit a claim to investor-state arbitration when it has incurred loss or damage as a result of a breach of an obligation under the agreement by another contracting state.[19] As the contracting states have given prior consent to arbitration in the agreement, they cannot refuse the claim. Similarly, optional protocols to some human rights treaties provide that individuals who claim that any of their rights enumerated in the treaty have been violated by a contracting state may submit a communication to a committee established under the treaty if the state has ratified the protocol.[20] The committee considers the communication and forwards its views to

[17]Strengthening and Modernizing the WTO: Discussion Paper Communication from Canada, JOB/GC/201 (24 September 2018), p. 3.

[18]Ibid.

[19]See e.g. Treaty Between United States of America and the Argentine Republic Concerning the Reciprocal Encouragement and Protection of Investment, Art.7.

[20]See e.g. Optional Protocol to the International Covenant on Civil and Political Rights.

the state and the individuals involved. Thus, investors and individuals have recourse to international dispute settlement mechanisms under some international agreements. As private parties do not have standing in international dispute settlement mechanisms under general international law, this right is specifically conferred to them by investment agreements and protocols to human rights treaties.

Investment agreements and optional protocols to human rights treaties confer private parties the right to have recourse to international dispute settlement mechanisms primarily for two reasons. First, the substantive rights protected under these treaties are the rights of private parties rather than those of the contracting states. For example, the fair and equitable treatment obligation under an investment agreement protects private investors and their investments from arbitrary and unreasonable treatments by the host state. An investment agreement also requires the host state to ensure that investors are not deprived of their investments without compensation by illegal expropriation. Similarly, the principal objective of a human rights treaty is to protect the rights of private parties. For example, the preamble of the International Covenant on Civil and Political Rights (ICCPR) states that the Covenant is agreed upon in the recognition that "the inherent dignity and ... the equal and inalienable rights of all members of the human family is the foundation of freedom, justice and peace in the world."

The second reason is that private parties would encounter difficulties in obtaining redress if they did not have access to international dispute settlement mechanisms. For example, while private parties claiming that their rights have been violated by a contracting state are required by human rights treaties to first seek domestic remedies in that state, their claims may face reluctance from the state's competent authority, such as the judicial branch, to find violations by another authority of the state. The limited application of human rights treaties by domestic courts also makes it difficult for private parties to claim violations of human rights treaties. The difficulty is even more evident in the case of investment agreement violations. If investor-state arbitration were not available, an investor would have to bring its claim to the domestic procedures in the foreign host state that has allegedly breached its rights. Likely the authority of the host state reviewing the claim would be sympathetic to the host state rather than the foreign investor. Diplomatic protection may cover private parties' claims of human rights violations or investment agreement violations that have not been remedied through domestic procedures under certain circumstances, but only if their home states are willing to espouse their claims. Given these difficulties, investor-state arbitration and individual communications are essential mechanisms for private parties to obtain secure and effective remedies for violations of their rights.

Under trade agreements, the benefits of States (or separate customs territories) are traditionally protected. For example, the most favoured nation principle and the national treatment principle under the GATT prohibit discrimination based on the national origin of products. A discriminatory measure against a single exporter from a certain WTO Member does not necessarily constitute a violation of these principles unless it amounts to discrimination against products from that Member. In addition, as repeatedly confirmed in past WTO disputes, the rules under the WTO agreements reflect a negotiated balance of rights and obligations among the WTO Members. In other words, the rights to trade of individual exporters and producers are not reflected in the WTO agreements. As a corollary, the principal function of the WTO dispute settlement mechanism is "to preserve the rights and obligations of Members" under the WTO agreements.[21] Thus, the WTO dispute settlement mechanism may only be used by a Member when it "considers that any benefits accruing to it directly or indirectly under the covered agreements are being impaired by measures taken by another Member."[22]

It is undeniable, however, that certain WTO agreements are inextricably intertwined with the protection of private parties' benefits and that some trade disputes are directly concerned with these benefits.

Trade remedies, such as anti-dumping, countervailing duties, and safeguard measures, are imposed on imports from individual exporters and producers. Decisions as to whether anti-dumping measures should be imposed or what level of anti-dumping duties should be imposed are made based on the conduct of each exporter or producer regardless of the conduct of their home country. Moreover, although the WTO agreements concerning trade remedies do not explicitly provide private parties' rights, many of its rules, at least indirectly, protect their benefits. For example, Articles 6 and 12 of the Agreement on Implementation of Article VI of the General Agreement on Tariffs and Trade 1994 (Anti-Dumping Agreement) require that exporters, producers, and importers shall be properly notified of the relevant information and be given ample opportunity to present their case during an anti-dumping investigation. Article 9 of the Anti-Dumping Agreement, which requires that the amount of an anti-dumping duty imposed on an exporter or producer not exceed the margin of dumping, ensures that neither would not be subject to an excessive anti-dumping duty. Thus, it is primarily the individual exporters and producers that incur loss or damage in the case of violations of the Anti-Dumping Agreement.

In addition to trade remedies, intellectual property rights are directly concerned with the rights of private parties. The preamble of the Agreement on Trade-Related Aspects of Intellectual Property Rights (TRIPS Agreement) explicitly recognizes that intellectual property rights are private rights and Article 1.3 of the TRIPS Agreement provides that Members shall accord the treatment provided for in the Agreement to the nationals of other Members. In addition, Part II of the TRIPS Agreement sets minimum standards of intellectual property protection that have to be provided to the nationals of other Members. The rules under the TRIPS Agreement are normally implemented through the domestic law of WTO Members and private parties' intellectual property rights are primarily protected under domestic law. Nevertheless, a breach of private parties' intellectual property rights under domestic law could result in a breach of the minimum standards requirements under the TRIPS Agreement.

---

[21] DSU, Art.3.2.

[22] DSU, Art.3.3.

Even though the benefits of private parties are protected by the WTO agreements, this does not necessarily mean that private parties should be given the right to have recourse to the WTO dispute settlement mechanism. In fact, the WTO agreements assume that private parties claiming that they have suffered loss or damage as a result of violations of the WTO agreements should seek domestic remedies within the jurisdiction of WTO Members. For example, Article 13 of the Anti-Dumping Agreement requires Members to maintain judicial review procedures to which a private party may have recourse if it considers that it is subject to an illegally imposed antidumping duty. Similarly, Part III of the TRIPS Agreement requires Members to provide enforcement procedures under their domestic law that allow private parties to take effective action against any act that infringes on intellectual property rights protected by the TRIPS Agreement.

It should be pointed out that private parties may encounter difficulties when they seek to obtain domestic remedies for violations of the WTO agreements as in the case of violations of human rights treaties or investment agreements. If exporters and producers claim that they have been subject to illegal anti-dumping measures, they may find themselves in a similar position to a foreign investor seeking to obtain domestic remedies in that they would have to make their case before a domestic court which is likely to be sympathetic to the other disputing party, i.e., the authority of its own country, rather than foreign exporters and producers. In case they fail to obtain domestic remedies, private parties may request that their own government commence WTO dispute settlement proceedings on their behalf. However, leaving aside the costs of WTO proceedings, the government may hesitate if its interests differ from private parties' interests or if private parties' interests are conflicting with each other within that country.

Given these difficulties, it would be justifiable to create a new trade dispute settlement mechanism in the WTO that could be directly used by private parties when they have suffered loss or damage due to violations of the WTO agreements. In particular, given the exceptionally large number of anti-dumping disputes that have been referred to the existing WTO dispute settlement mechanism,[23] creating a supplemental dispute settlement mechanism for anti-dumping disputes could be beneficial because it would lessen the burden on panels and the AB in the existing mechanism.

4.2 Remedies: How Should Violations Be Redressed?

If a new trade dispute settlement mechanism were established in the WTO or in a successor regime to allow private parties to directly obtain remedies when they have

[23]The Anti-Dumping Agreement was cited in the request for consultations in 133 cases out of the total 593 cases brought to the DSM. WTO, Disputes by agreement, https://www.wto.org/english/tratop_e/dispu_e/dispu_agreements_index_e.htm.

suffered loss or damage caused by, for example, violations of the Anti-Dumping Agreement [*hereinafter* the special anti-dumping dispute settlement mechanism], how should the violations be redressed in this mechanism?

In the existing WTO dispute settlement mechanism, panels and the AB review complaints brought by a WTO Member claiming that measures taken by another Member have violated the WTO agreements. If they affirmatively conclude that there are violations, the DSB recommends that the Member concerned bring the measures into conformity with the agreements.[24] Continuing with the example using the Anti-Dumping Agreement, in many of the anti-dumping disputes, DSB recommendations request the Member concerned to either withdraw or modify the anti-dumping measures at issue. In cases where panels and the AB find that the anti-dumping law "as such" violates the Anti-Dumping Agreement,[25] the respondent Member may have to amend the law itself in order to implement a DSB recommendation. The remedies provided by DSB recommendations are consistent with the objective of the WTO dispute settlement mechanism to secure compliance of the measures at issue with the relevant WTO agreements in a prospective manner.

In contrast, the objective of investor-state arbitration under investment agreements and individual communications under human rights treaties is to redress loss or damage that private parties have already incurred. In investor-state arbitration, remedies are almost always given in the form of monetary compensation and damages. While specific performance is occasionally requested, it is rarely granted. Regarding individual communications, remedies can either be specifically addressed to the authors of the communications or they can have more general implications, but the most common remedies are compensation that is specifically addressed to the authors. Remedies addressed to specific private parties may fall short of promoting general compliance with the relevant rules of international law, but they could remedy the specific loss or damage of private parties more promptly and effectively. Moreover, specifically addressed remedies would be less intrusive to the regulatory autonomy of the respondent state compared to more general remedies.

The structure of the special anti-dumping dispute settlement mechanism, proffered as an example here, should adopt the approach of investor-state arbitration and individual communications in terms of remedies while also incorporating some of the existing WTO dispute settlement procedures.

First, an exporter or producer should only be allowed to bring claims to the new mechanism when it has been subject to the anti-dumping measure at issue. Its claims should be directly related to a specific application of the anti-dumping law to it. In other words, claims concerning the anti-dumping law "as such" should not be allowed. In light of the potentially large number of exporters and producers that

[24]DSU, Art.19.1.

[25]In the DSM, a Member may challenge another Member's legislation, independently from the application of that legislation in specific instances. See, e.g., Appellate Body Report (2000), *United States – Anti-Dumping Act of 1916* WT/DS136/AB/R, WT/DS162/AB/R (28 August 2000), paras 55–83.

are involved in a single anti-dumping measure, the possibility of class action should be explored. In addition, it is desirable to allocate the costs of dispute settlement proceedings between exporters and producers bringing claims and WTO Member governments.

Second, claims would be reviewed by a panel that is constituted in accordance with the existing rules of the DSU. The applicable law should be limited to the Anti-Dumping Agreement as well as Article VI of the GATT (or their equivalent in any successor regime) to enable a panel to focus on issues that are directly related to the claimant. In order to avoid overburdening the AB, or if there is no extant appellate mechanism, no appeal should be allowed in this mechanism. The jurisprudence developed by the DSM should be applied to ensure consistency in the interpretation of the relevant agreements resolved through WTO dispute settlement and through the new mechanism. Although panels are constituted on an *ad hoc* basis and are independent from each other, they should endeavor to ensure coherence and consistency in their decisions.

Third, the objective of remedies in the special anti-dumping dispute settlement mechanism should be limited to compensating for the loss or damage that has been incurred by the claimant. Thus, if a panel finds that the anti-dumping measure to which the claimant has been subject violates obligations of the Anti-Dumping Agreement, the DSB should recommend that the Member concerned either modify or withdraw the measure at issue as applied to the claimant. When it is possible, the claimant should be entitled to a refund of the illegal duty that was paid.

Finally, the new mechanism could be established by adopting a new agreement for the settlement of anti-dumping disputes between private parties and a Member [*hereinafter* the "New Agreement"] as a plurilateral trade agreement in the WTO or as part of the dispute settlement mechanism of a successor regime. With respect to the WTO, as provided for in Article II:2 of the Marrakesh Agreement, the New Agreement would be binding only for Members that have accepted it, and it would not create either obligations or rights for Members that have not accepted it. Thus, only the private parties of WTO Members that have accepted the New Agreement would be entitled to have recourse to the new mechanism, and only the WTO Members that have accepted the New Agreement could be respondents. The New Agreement may be able to encourage more WTO Members, particularly frequent anti-dumping user Members, to accept the Agreement by restricting the submission of anti-dumping disputes to the DSM.

5 Conclusion

There is a common motive in the ambitious proposals described above (Sections III and IV), as the authors are all deeply concerned about the fate of the WTO dispute settlement mechanism. It is not only the AB that is vulnerable to political turmoil. Without an effective dispute settlement mechanism, most of the detailed substantive rules under the WTO would be meaningless. It is unclear whether free trade agreements (FTAs) would be able to take on the role played by WTO dispute settlement mechanisms. In addition, it is not solely a US President who is to blame, even though the current one opened a Pandora's Box by ransoming the functioning of the then "crown jewel" of the WTO system.

We need to think outside the box and pursue new ideas to overcome the largest existential challenges that the WTO has ever faced and to prepare for the possibility of the need for a successor regime. Although the use of ERGs may not save all of the AB's functions, it could still address many existing concerns. Allowing the involvement of private parties may be considered as having only a slight chance of success, but it could also provide a straightforward means for solving the anti-dumping disputes, which have endured as the most frequently contested area of WTO law. These two ideas may stand separately, but they may also be adopted simultaneously. It is necessary to have as many new ideas as possible to securely save the assets of the WTO DSM from the risk of impending collapse; in order to accommodate situational changes as they occur, it must become like a rolling stone.

References

Kobayashi T (2019) The use of panel process to improve the function of the Appellate Body. In: Lo C, Nakagawa J, Chen TF (eds) The Appellate Body of the WTO and its reform. Springer, Singapore, pp 207–209

Pauwelyn J (2002) The use of experts in WTO dispute settlement. Int Comp Law Q 51(2):325–364

Payosova T, Hufbauer GC, Schott JJ (2018) The dispute settlement crisis in the World Trade Organization: causes and cures. PIIE Policy Brief, p 10

WTO (2017) A handbook on the WTO dispute settlement system, 3rd edn. Cambridge University Press, Cambridge, p 151

What Can We Learn from Our Struggling Cousin?: Recent Discussions on Reform of International Investment Law and Investment Dispute Settlement Proceedings

Jaemin Lee

Contents

1 Multilateralism at a Critical Crossroad

The global trading regime is now facing an unprecedentedly perilous situation, to say the least. Sadly, multilateralism has been gradually losing its stature and authority, and protectionism of various sorts and types has been on the rise. Indeed, the year 2019 made us realize the aggravating situation and the resulting negative

Professor of Law at School of Law, Seoul National University in Seoul, Korea.

J. Lee (✉)
School of Law, Seoul National University, Seoul, Korea
e-mail: jaemin@snu.ac.kr

M. K. Lewis et al. (eds.), *A Post-WTO International Legal Order*,
https://doi.org/10.1007/978-3-030-45428-9_9

consequences for all states. And yet, neither a breakthrough nor a grand settlement is in sight. Chances are, 2020 (and the following years) will see more instances of protectionism together with escalating tensions and confrontations.[1] States are not only criticizing each other, but also taking pre-emptive measures, retaliatory measures and countermeasures to protect their own domestic industries and to cater to domestic demands.[2]

Trusted leadership and a sense of togetherness can guide states away from these self-interested, short-sighted, and domestic-focused measures. Critically, both are missing at the moment, and there is no tangible sign that we will get them back any time soon. Moreover, the key states that are supposed to show such leadership are engaged in their own direct confrontation, making the situation even worse.[3] An increasing trend is for many states to portray international trade as a 'zero-sum' game in their domestic politics. In the absence of the two missing elements (i.e., leadership and sense of togetherness), we are bound to be stuck in a downward spiral. We all hope that the global community realizes the grave peril that lies ahead and makes 'serious' efforts to change the current course of events. But unfortunately, it seems that the global trade landscape has now dramatically changed for the worse.[4] Hopes may not materialize any time soon.

At this juncture, we might want to look at our situation from a more objective perspective and assess how we would look through the eyes of other global institutions and regimes. We could turn to various barometers, one of which is probably the investment law regime. Recent discussions on international investment law and arbitration reform provide a useful example of such outside observations. Since 2015, states and institutions have presented a variety of proposals and suggestions to reform international investment law, and particularly its dispute settlement system.[5] Concrete actions and new negotiations have since followed.[6] In several years' time a new regime will likely be adopted in the field. Interestingly and notably, these proposals in the investment law field often look to the World Trade Organization

[1]Pressman and Chandler (2019), Ciuriak (2018).

[2]Levi (2018), Nicita et al. (2018).

[3]Bacchus (2018a), Brown and Kolb (2018).

[4]Lei (2017).

[5]For example, in 2015, the EU proposed to reform international investment agreements and investor-state dispute settlement proceedings (ISDS proceedings). Cf. European Commission (2015) Commission Proposes New Investment Court System for TTIP and Other EU Trade and Investment Negotiations. Press Release, 16 September 2015, http://trade.ec.europa.eu/doclib/press/index.cfm?id=1364. Woods (2019).

[6]Sornarajah (2016).

("WTO") and its dispute settlement system as a viable alternative for their own future.[7] Considering the WTO's present struggles and the fast erosion of multilateralism on the trade front, the investment regime's effort to rely on the WTO as its future guidance is rather ironic and telling. It indicates how precious an asset we are about to lose in the global trading regime.

While the investment arbitration reformists are looking at us as the best example for their future, we seem to be losing our original strength and taking steps backwards. In a sense, we are heading back in the direction from which the investment law reformists are striving to turn away. And remarkably, on the trade front we are moving back to the 'old' regime faster and faster. If we continue to stay on the current path, we might end up encountering a much more dangerous and treacherous trade landscape than now. Given the gravity and expanse of trade issues, the consequences here would be much wider and deeper than in other areas such as the international investment law.

In short, the recent discussions in the investment law and arbitration reform context provides important food for thought concerning the current situation of the international trade regime. It offers a rough silhouette of the landscape that we will see in the near future unless the current tide is turned. It is unfortunate that we are losing the leadership and sense of togetherness to turn this tide.

2 Recent Phenomena in Investment Agreements and Arbitration

Robust efforts of these days to reform international investment agreements and arbitration can be summarized a collective endeavour to introduce 'multilateralism' and 'institutionalization' reflecting 53 years of experience since 1966. In the absence of a multilateral umbrella, there are now over 3300 international investment agreements,[8] almost all of which have their own separate dispute settlement mechanisms. This 'fragmented' system has turned out to be one of the main problems for the current international investment agreements and their dispute settlement systems.[9] It

[7]UNGA Future Work in the Field of Dispute Settlement: Reforms of Investor-State Dispute Settlement (ISDS). UN Doc. A/CN.9/917 (20 April 2017), https://documents-dds-ny.un.org/doc/UNDOC/GEN/V17/023/69/PDF/V1702369.pdf?OpenElement. paras 63–66; Leventhal AG (2018) The 2018 Proposals for Amendments of the ICSID Rules: ICSIC Enters the Era of Trump, Populism, and State Sovereignty Am S In L 22(15)The UNCITRAL's Working Group III completed its most recent discussion in October 2019. Cf. UN Information Service (2019) Successful conclusion of the UNCITRAL meeting in Vienna on the reform of investor-State dispute settlement (ISDS). UNIS/L/285 (21 October 2019), http://www.unis.unvienna.org/unis/en/pressrels/2019/unisl285.html.

[8]United Nations Conference on Trade and Development (2017), p. 6.

[9]Schill (2011), p. 1093; United Nations Conference on Trade and Development (2018), pp. 68, 71, 76, 82–83; Sauvant and Ortino F (2013), pp. 27–32.

is said that stronger institutionalization, in particular equipped with a standing entity for dispute settlement, is in great demand.[10] At this point, investment regime reformists are encouraged and incentivized to turn to the WTO regime for a multilateralism benchmark.

Consider the circumstances of international investment agreements and dispute settlement proceedings that are being criticized at the moment. Remarkably, these circumstances are precisely those that we ourselves are increasingly encountering in the global trade regime.

2.1 *Fragmentation*

First of all, fragmentation is said to be one of the most critical problems in the current global investment law regime. With more than 3300 international investment agreements containing non-identical provisions and independent dispute settlement proceedings, in the absence of a central entity overseeing and coordinating these numerous agreements, development of coherent and consistent jurisprudence has been elusive in a way that is now arguably threatening the principle of rule of law.[11] Thus, the crux of the present reform proposals aims to overcome this problem of fragmentation through 'multilateralization' of investment agreements and/or dispute settlement systems. These proposals, while containing diverse ideas and schemes, view the WTO regime as a viable example and a proven path.[12]

Ironically, the trade regime is facing a surge of 'fragmentation' of its own with the increasing number of free trade agreements ("FTAs") and even mega-regionals such as the *Comprehensive and Progressive Agreement for Trans-Pacific Partnership* ("CPTPP").[13] Of course, FTAs and regional trade agreements still remain subject to the WTO review under Article XXIV of the *General Agreement on Tariffs and*

---

[10]Howard (2018), pp. 15–43.

[11]Yannaca-Small C (2006) Improving the System of Investor-State Dispute Settlement: An Overview, OECD Working Papers on International Investment No. 2006/1 https://www.oecd.org/investment/internationalinvestmentagreements/40079647.pdf. pp. 185–186.

[12]Pauwelyn (2014), p. 378. Pauwelyn stated "first, unlike, for example, UN, WTO or EU law, FIL is *not* organized around a single multilateral treaty or central international organization. Instead, FIL is heavily decentralized and composed of a multitude of bilateral, regional and multilateral treaties (BITs, North American Free Trade Agreement (NAFTA), FTAs, the European Energy Charter Treaty (ECT) etc.) . . . and a diversity of arbitral institutions . . . and domestic courts and investment agencies, *without* central authority."

[13]Zang (2018), pp. 33–61.

Trade ("GATT 1994") and other related provisions. However, the rigor and completeness of the review is questionable.[14] As a matter of fact, as the WTO regime fails to deliver, Member states are turning to FTAs and regional trade agreements more frequently and more expansively. As the WTO's authority weakens, the centrifugal force is intensifying. Recent FTAs do not just include tariff eliminations but increasingly experiment with various new norms and schemes that could (or perhaps should) otherwise be taken up by the WTO.[15]

Noting the struggles and discussions in the international investment regime, this recent tendency of widening and deepening fragmentation in the trade sector is indeed worrisome. What has happened in the investment sector is likely to occur in the trade sector. Consider the continuous spread of the FTAs including so-called mega-FTAs such as the CPTPP[16] and the *United States-Mexico-Canada Agreement* ("USMCA")[17] in tandem with the weakening centrifugal force of the WTO, most notably the breakdown of the Appellate Body as of December 11, 2019. States are now more prone (or forced) to settle their disputes bilaterally, either through FTA dispute settlement proceedings or other FTA consultation mechanisms, or unilaterally, through threats and imposition of trade restrictions.

2.2 *Challenges to Legitimacy and Spreading Mistrust*

The present global drive to reform the investment agreements and arbitration has been triggered by the eroding authority of the regime and increasing challenges to the legitimacy of the entire system. Mistrust of stakeholders—in particular sovereign states and the general public—has deepened over the years, based on the perception that governments' regulatory authority has been either undermined or insufficiently protected under the present investment agreements. Perhaps, this is the other side of the same coin as the fragmentation problem. A fragmented system inevitably involves inconsistent norms and conflicting interpretations. As a consequence, stakeholders and interested groups are unsure whether a particular interpretation is accurate or a decision reliable. A multilateral system with a standing entity (or

[14]Bown CP (2016) Mega-Regional Trade Agreements and the Future of the WTO. Council on Foreign Relations Part of Discussion Paper Series on Global and Regional Governance, 26 September 2016, https://www.cfr.org/report/global-order-and-new-regionalism. p. 5: Bown stated "Unfortunately, while the WTO membership appears to increasingly recognize that some problems associated with RTAs will plague the multilateral system, the WTO has taken few concrete steps thus far to address the competition introduced by RTAs."

[15]Goldstein (2017), pp. 545–564; Bacchus (2018b).

[16]New Zealand Foreign Affairs & Trade, Comprehensive and Progressive Agreement for Trans-Pacific Partnership, https://www.mfat.govt.nz/en/trade/free-trade-agreements/agreements-under-negotiation/cptpp-2/.

[17]United States Trade Representative, United States-Mexico-Canada Agreement, https://ustr.gov/trade-agreements/free-trade-agreements/united-states-mexico-canada-agreement.

something akin to it) is believed to cure or at least alleviate the problem, and, again, the WTO is seen as a reliable benchmark.[18]

Until recently, it was almost unthinkable to challenge the legitimacy of the multilateral trading regime enshrined in the WTO system. Changes are being felt, however. Voices of criticism existed even in the early days of the WTO,[19] but they are getting louder these days. More importantly, those voices are getting politically popular. The fundamental restructuring or even the collapse of the multilateral trading regime is now being talked about as a possibility, even if as a remote one.[20] This is a significant change from situations just several years ago. If the current circumstances persist, we may soon be facing increasing challenges against the authority and legitimacy of the WTO system. We might find ourselves in a similar situation that has triggered the whole debates on the investment agreements and arbitration reform. Regrettably, the trading regime seems to be moving in that direction.

2.3 Absence of an Institutional Framework

The absence of an institutional framework also stands out as a central issue in the present discussion on the reform of the investment agreements and arbitration. In particular, the absence of a standing entity that can resolve investment disputes in a systematic and consistent fashion has been the core topic of the reform negotiation. What is now proposed by a certain group of states is to introduce a standing court equipped with an appellate mechanism. Thus, the WTO's Secretariat and Appellate Body have been analyzed by the proponents with a great deal of interest and enthusiasm in this regard.[21] To them, the present WTO system and its Appellate Body are veiwed as success stories.

However, the WTO's Secretariat and the Appellate Body have been struggling recently. The Secretariat is suffering from deficient resources and inefficient decision-making processes of the Members. The Appellate Body, more critically, stands now on the verge of a paralysis due to the continuous blockage of a new

[18] Cf. Howard (2018), pp. 36–38.

[19] Wolff (2001), pp. 417–426.

[20] Bacchus (2018b).

[21] For instance, the EU's proposal to reform the international investment system includes many aspects from the WTO system. Cf. European Commission (2016) Transatlantic Trade and Investment Partnership: Trade in Services, Investment and E-Commerce, Chapter II – Investment. Commission draft text TTIP – investment, 12 November 2016, http://trade.ec.europa.eu/doclib/docs/2015/september/tradoc_153807.pdf. Article 9(12) and 10(12).

Appellate Body member appointment. As of December 11, 2019, the Appellate Body has ceased to function due to the failure to resolve the current impasse.[22] Some fear that even if the current stalemate is somehow resolved in the near future, the scar has been so deep that a future Appellate Body will never be the same or as active as before. Despite the praise and respect from investment reform proponents, we are moving backwards rapidly on this score. The WTO's cherished institutional infrastructure is losing its stellar status.

2.4 *Lack of Leadership*

It is hard to find a state or a group of states that exercises leadership in the international investment regime. In a highly fragmented system, there is simply no vehicle for any meaningful leadership to take hold. Each state aims to contemplate its own gains and maximize own interest. Few, if any, realize the importance of a reliable system in general or observe the problems from a systemic point of view. Agreements and dispute settlement proceedings are all individualized and compartmentalized, so that there is no room for systemic consideration or long-term contemplation with global 'rule of law' in mind. The current struggles and the resulting reform discussions in the investment regime context are largely the outcome of such a lack of leadership.[23] Critics tend to look at the WTO and its decision-making process as a viable alternative, where as many as 164 states strive to act and decide together.

Unfortunately, however, a similar lack of leadership is also harming the global trading regime and the WTO as well. The two most influential Members, the United States and China, are engaged in direct confrontation and escalating retaliation.[24] With varying degrees, other major countries are also taking measures of a dubious legal nature.[25] The "broken window" phenomenon is spreading fast among the Members. Not surprisingly, many participants are losing faith and trust in the system itself. Unless the current tide is reversed immediately, the speed of loss of faith and

[22]Cf. Bacchus J (2018) Might Unmakes Right – The American Assault on the Rule of Law in World Trade. CIJI Papers No. 173, May 2018, https://www.cigionline.org/sites/default/files/documents/Paper%20no.173.pdf. pp. 8–13.

[23]Malmström C (2015) Proposing and Investment Court System. Commission and Its Priorities Blog Post, 16 September 2015, https://ec.europa.eu/commission/2014-2019/malmstrom/blog/proposing-investment-court-system_en. The European Trade Commissioner, Ceclia Malmstrõm, proposed that the EU takes on the leadership of developing a more concrete system: "What has clearly come out of the debate is that the old, traditional form of dispute resolution suffers from a fundamental lack of trust. However, EU investors are the most frequent users of the existing model, which individual EU countries have developed over time. This means that Europe must take the responsibility to reform and modernise it. We must take the global lead on the path to reform."

[24]Brown and Kolb (2018).

[25]Durusoy et al. (2015), pp. 57–68.

trust will accelerate even further. Indeed, the WTO's recent trouble reflects the same concerns of the investment regime reformists. While the investment regime is trying to overcome its problems through various means and diverse proposals, the international trade regime is failing to respond to the snowballing crisis swiftly and effectively, and allowing the situation to further deteriorate. In the meantime, key states are eager to protect their own short-term interests first, thereby actually facilitating the leadership dearth.

2.5 Increasing Gaps Between Reality and Norms

The investment regime reformists point to the widening gap between the fast-changing business realities and outdated norms. Provisions and systems in the conventional investment agreements have been criticized for lagging behind the developmets in the markets and businesses.[26] In fact, the current international investment regime was introduced in 1966. Almost six decades later, the need to update the regime has become ever more acute. As legal norms dealing with international business activities and investment flows, investment agreements' apparently increasing detachment from the fast-changing fields and practices has only stoked, among the interested groups and stakeholders, concerns over and mistrust for the appropriateness and persuasiveness of the norms therein. The legal bounds imposed by the general rules of treaty interpretation contained in Article 31 of the *Vienna Convention on the Law of Treaties*, placing an emphasis on the texts, have effectively tied the hands of contracting parties and adjudicators in adopting interpretations unless the treaty texts are amended. So, they have to deal with various complex issues being unfolded these days within the strict confinement of texts. However, the texts are sometimes decades old and cannot easily accommodate present business models and investment activities. Old texts are also unable to reflect sometimes legitimate concerns of governments regulating foreign investment. This norm-reality mismatch has been one of the major driving forces for the present reform efforts for the international investment regime.

Not surprisingly, the WTO regime is also struggling with this increasing gap between business realities and legal norms. The GATT norms were adopted as long ago as in 1947. Other covered agreements of the WTO were adopted in 1994 as a result of negotiations between 1986 and 1994. Given the drastic changes during the past three decades, the norms contained in the present WTO Agreements are arguably outdated and fail to provide reliable legal guidance for states and business entities. The efforts of the WTO Members to amend the agreements have failed to

[26]Zhan (2017), p. xii. Zhan stated "Old treaties abound: more than 2,500 IIAs (International Investment Agreements) in force today (95 per cent of all treaties in force) were concluded before 2010. Old treaties "bite": as of end-2016, virtually all known ISDS cases were based on those treaties. And old treaties perpetuate inconsistencies: their continued existence creates overlaps and fragmentation in treaty relationships and poses interaction challenges."

deliver as the Doha Development Agenda ("DDA") has faltered.[27] There were some achievements, such as the Trade Facilitation Agreement, but they were well short of DDA's intended goals. Widening gaps between reality and norm have further made the Members lose faith and trust in the present trading regime. But a major overhaul of the WTO Agreements in the near future does not seem likely. Unfortunately, the global trading regime will encounter more and more difficult challenges as time goes by. For these issues, time is apparently not on our side. If the present efforts in the investment sector materialize, the investment regime will overtake and surpass the trade regime sometime soon.

3 What Can Be Done to Disprove a Dystopia?

It is indeed unfortunate that the WTO regime is now losing its original vitality and, more importantly, its momentum for establishing, buttressing and spreading the rule of law in the global community.[28] As it currently stands, no visible sign is palpable to change the current course of events in the near future.[29] The cessation of operation of the Appellate Body as of December 11, 2019 is touted as a symbolic incident showing the increasing irrelevance of the WTO as a key international organization handling trade matters. It appears that we are locked in a downward spiral. By all accounts, the situation will become even worse over the next several years.

Suppose the global community fails to take adequate action soon. The international trade regime will then regress into the very circumstances the global investment regime is currently confronted with—the one lacking a multilateral agreement but filled with numerous fragmented agreements scattered all over the world. It is ironic that states are trying to break away from the old circumstances in the investment regime while they are moving back to the very circumstances in the trade sector. This situation may lead to a gradual (if not fast) erosion of multilateralism and a possible demise of the WTO. Before we realize, we may backslide into a myriad of bilateral and regional networks with fragmented norms and competing regimes without a multilateral centric force that binds us together under one umbrella—the very situation that the investment regime is striving so hard to overcome. Of course, we have seen many disputes between and among states since the inception of the WTO. And yet, all these disputes have been raised,

[27]Bacchus (2018b), p. 10. Bacchus stated "Absent progress within the WTO system, the alternatives are more bilateral, regional, and mega-agreements on trade made outside the sheltering legal framework of the WTO among the more ambitious members. Already, hundreds of trade agreements have been concluded outside the WTO—the vast majority of them since the start of the deadlock in the Doha Development Round."

[28]Baldwin (2016), p. 95; Winters LA (2015) The WTO and Regional Trading Agreements: Is it all for Multilateralism? EUI Working Papers No. 94, 23 December 2015, https://cadmus.eui.eu/bitstream/handle/1814/38266/RSCAS_2015_94.pdf?sequence=1&isAllowed=y.

[29]Wagner (2020), pp. 67–90; Pauwelyn (2019), pp. 297–321.

heard and dealt with under a single instrument and under the WTO's roof. Unfortunately, the instrument has become outdated and the roof has now been half blown away with the house's structure shaking at its core.

Unfortunately, a major breakthrough in the near future seems unlikely. It is worrisome that the current impasse will continue for some time given the structural nature of the problems, and over time the trade regime will be further fragmented, weakened and ultimately marginalized. Thus, in the absence of determined and swift action, we are probably doomed to head towards a dark and gloomy terrain. It is embarrassing that while the investment regime reformists look to the WTO and its dispute settlement system as a guiding light for their future, the WTO system itself is now faltering and struggling, with the dispute settlement system losing its stellar status.[30] The situation at hand is not merely about trade friction. Nor is it entirely stemming from certain countries' absurd demands. Nor can it be ascribed to the intensifying Sino-U.S. confrontation. The very fundamentals of the post-World War II trade regime are shaking at the core. It is critical for the global community to have a sense of urgency. Complaints abound and worries arise. But a true sense of 'urgency' is not palpable yet. Indeed, some states may be more to blame for the current situation. Nevertheless, to the extent the current trade regime failed to keep up with the fast-changing business activities and diversifying interests of states,[31] it is the global community generally that is responsible for todays plight. The failure to wrap up the DDA and thus to upgrade covered agreements in a timely manner is a collective misjudgment. In retrospect, all Members should have engaged in the DDA negotiations more actively and tightly. The WTO Secretariat should have taken the whole situation more seriously when the negotiations faltered. Missed opportunities have bred mistrust, and such mistrust has snowballed into antagonism fueled by domestic political winds for populism.

Bearing this in mind, states need to consider what can be done immediately. They need to find and focus on something practical and doable as opposed to something abstract or theoretical. We need a momentum to turn the tide around. Given where we stand at present, this task will be anything but easy. But, still, we will have to do what we can, hoping for the best. The following can be considered in this regard.

3.1 Revive Belief in Multilateralism

Firstly, it is essential that the states (*i.e.*, WTO Members) revive their belief in multilateralism. Most (if not all) of them praise multilateralism, lament its retreat, and dread its demise.[32] Many, however, seem to accept the retreat and possible

[30]Brewster (2019), pp. 61–66.

[31]Ahmed et al. (2016), p. 657.

[32]Menon V (2019), 74th UNGA Debate: Nationalism or Multilateralism? RSIS Commentary No. 217, 30 October 2019, https://dr.ntu.edu.sg/bitstream/10356/136617/2/CO19217.pdf.

collapse as something unchangeable and unstoppable.[33] This sort of pessimism would not be of great help. A sense of defeat would only accelerate the weakening of multilateralism. Instead, states would have to reaffirm their commitment to multilateralism in a serious manner. Revival of multilateralism has been in oversupply as political rhetoric; serious talks among states' leaders, however, have yet to take place. The first thing now is to begin a real discussion, so that the states and their leaders could realize that (i) multilateralism is still the best option to ensure long-term success for all, (ii) that some gains from unilateralism and regionalism are illusory and short-lived, and (iii) that spreading protectionism is only to be curbed by multilateralism. The trade regime is not and does not have to be a zero-sum game. It is something more than mere tariff imposition or elimination. It is about establishing the global regulatory system where all of us can prosper together.

The first step toward initiating such a serious discussion is to dispel 'mistrust' and 'suspicion' against each other.[34] At this time, many states view the WTO regime and its multilateralism as a sort of a zero-sum game, as opposed to a framework promising long-term mutual prosperity.[35] A community spirit and a sense of togetherness in the global economy in this era of hyper-connectivity and digital technologies must settle in. The WTO should plan gatherings, events and projects for this objective. The WTO (more precisely, its Members) should place priority on this endeavor. Negotiations on specific topics and technical issues are always important and they should continue, but an immediate priority for now should be to break the chain of mistrust and foster a spirit of togetherness and collectivism. Negotiations on specific items should be aligned to achieve (not undermine) this objective. One possible option available to dispel mistrust and bring back mutual trust in this regard might be a global agreement, sponsored and brokered by the WTO, for a standstill—a covenant for a moratorium not to worsen the current situation or to introduce new restrictive measures. Such an agreement doesn't have to be a treaty: if a treaty is impractical, it could come as a declaration, joint statement, or promise.

The success of the GATT/WTO regime and its dispute settlement system is largely due to the strong belief in multilateralism stemming from the bitter experience that led to the World War II. A fix for the struggling WTO should be found from contemplating how to resurrect such a belief in multilateralism. This is more important than new norms, package deals, the Appellate Body, or Ministerial Conferences.

[33]Tocci (2018), p. 1.

[34]Linn (2018), pp. 86–113.

[35]Haley JA (2017) How the WTO Can Stand Up to Nationalism. CIGI Articles, 14 December 2017, https://www.cigionline.org/articles/how-wto-can-stand-nationalism.

3.2 Lower Expectations

At the same time, states are also advised to lower their expectations. Given the gravity of the situation, a high ambition or expectation seems unrealistic, if not entirely impossible, at this point. A WTO with the authority and leadership of the early days may not be feasible, at least in the foreseeable future. Quite sadly, its dispute settlement system will have to lessen its judicial grip and accommodate a political compromise. The Members might want to reconsider such principles as the "single undertaking," which is ideal but arguably no longer practical.[36] These measures are unquestionably regressive steps along the scale of rule of law, but they may turn out to be necessary to prevent the trade regime from imploding. Unfortunately, it is time for a Plan B or even a Plan C. The best should not be the enemy of the good. Even if there are loopholes and weaknesses, having a system would be a better option than having nothing. Viewed from this perspective, it would not be wise to simply lament the present situation and miss the heyday of the WTO.

Going forward, states will have to be realistic. Any proposal should be doable and achievable. The WTO should be practical. Saving the system is more important than exploring a perfect model and leaving the WTO regime to disintegrate. Once the global community succeeds in riding out the current storm, time will then come to upgrade and improve the system.

3.3 Focus on (Small) Tangible Outcomes

Related to the previous point, once the expectation levels are lowered, states would then need to focus on smaller and more tangible outcomes that they could achieve easily and quickly. Important but difficult topics should be set aside for the future. Such topics, while important, may only aggravate the situation. They may help some states find easy scapegoats to let multilateralism wither and crumble. Furthermore, as noted above, time is of the essence now. States should find and focus on (relatively) non-controversial and easy issues in order to keep the system afloat. The recent Trade Facilitation Agreement demonstrates that a narrower focus can facilitate the negotiation process and allow states to actually achieve something tangible.[37] Small

[36]Hoekman B, Bluth C, Esche A (2018) Revitalizing Multilateral Governance at the World Trade Organization/ Council for Global Problem-Solving, October 2018, https://www.cgp-council.org/wp-content/uploads/2018/10/Revitalizing-Multilateral-Governance-at-the-World-Trade-Organization.pdf.

[37]Beverelli C, Neumüller S, The R (2015) Export Diversification Effects of the WTO Trade Facilitation Agreement", FIW Working Paper No. 137, https://www.econstor.eu/bitstream/10419/121140/1/N_137.pdf.; International Centre for Trade and Sustainable Development (2017) WTO's Trade Facilitation Agreement Takes Effect. Bridges, 23 February 2017, http://www.ictsd.org/bridges-news/bridges/news/wtos-trade-facilitation-agreement-takes-effect.

yet tangible outcomes could provide a morale boost for the Members so that they could at least stay together under the big umbrella of the WTO regime.

So, states would have to find some low-hanging fruits that many states could easily agree upon, and then go from there. Perhaps not merely low-hanging but lowest-hanging ones should become the targets at this juncture. Introduction of new fisheries subsidies norms and notification of industrial subsidies are good examples for these exercises. There is a long way to go even for these easy subjects to achieve their final objectives. However, small steps with compromise packages may help restore the trust, save the system and lay the groundwork for further difficult discussions afterwards. Likewise, if necessary, a simple agreement to maintain the status quo may also be an option. In other words, if we are not able to move forward, at least for the time being we should try to manage the current situation so as not to exacerbate it. A moratorium on new trade measures for the next 12–24 months could be an example. Non-referral of trade disputes to the dispute settlement proceeding for a certain period of time could be another easy option. While such a moratorium cannot solve the problem, it can at least give the states time to pause and ponder.

3.4 Facilitate Monitoring and Advisory Roles

Traditionally, the WTO's monitoring and advisory roles have not been regarded as central or major functions of the organization. In an effort to engage all Members in a non-contentious manner and to strengthen the spirit of cooperation and togetherness, intensifying the monitoring and advisory roles of the WTO would be another viable starting point. Collecting information on exactly what is happening in the global markets and sharing it among the Members will be the first step for the WTO to discuss what to do now. Such monitoring will also have the effect of naming and shaming, and may ultimately guide the Members in certain directions in compliance with the obligations of the WTO Agreements.

The Trade Policy Review Mechanism ("TPRM") has been largely effective,[38] and states could consider elaborating upon and expanding this mechanism within the existing regime of the WTO.[39] Through enhanced transparency and a soft-toned approach towards implementation of the WTO Agreements, the WTO regime may have a better chance of surviving the current storm.[40] For this, the TPRM merits more attention. Likewise, enhancing the advisory roles of the WTO is another option

[38]Lu (2015), p. 83.

[39]Ghosh (2010), pp. 419–455; Francois JF (1999) Maximizing the Benefits of the Trade Policy Review Mechanism for Developing Countries: prepared for the World Bank Institute, February 1999, http://citeseerx.ist.psu.edu/viewdoc/download?doi=10.1.1.202.3877&rep=rep1&type=pdf.

[40]Francois (2002), p. 312.

that we can consider. Projects such as the Advisory Center for WTO Law ("ACWL") should be further strengthened.[41] Developing Members and the least developed Members will benefit from this, which may restore their belief and trust in the entire system.[42]

3.5 Facilitate Non-Binding Dispute Settlement Proceedings

While its dispute settlement mechanism is arguably the WTO's most praised achievement,[43] sometimes the legally binding mechanism could become too contentious and controversial.[44] Some recent disputes have become too confrontational. At the same time, the proceedings take a lengthy amount of time, and the final decisions are only prospective in nature.[45] These inherent traits have frustrated disputing parties and business entities.[46] In this respect, states could also consider facilitating non-binding dispute settlement proceedings to deal with trade disputes.[47] The use of non-binding dispute settlement mechanisms could contribute to soothing the present concerns and frustration of the Member states.[48] Perhaps non-prevailing Members may feel less intrusion into their sovereignty. Such a mechanism may also help ease the tension between trading partners. The *Understanding on Rules and Procedures Governing the Settlement of Disputes* ("DSU") has a provision setting forth a non-binding dispute settlement mechanism.[49] Most notably, the provision contains mediation as well.[50] However, the provision merely offers parties a

[41]Meagher N (2018) Representing Developing Countries before the WTO: the Role of the Advisory Centre on WTO Law (ACWL) (May 2015) Robert Schuman Centre for Advanced Studies Research Paper No. RSCAS PP2015/02; Bown and McCulloch (2010), pp. 58–59.

[42]Nottage H (2009) Developing Countries in the WTO Dispute Settlement System. GEG Working Paper No. 2009/47, January 2009, https://www.econstor.eu/bitstream/10419/196308/1/GEG-WP-047.pdf. Rockfall Lekgowe G (2012) The WTO Dispute Settlement System: Why it doesn't Work for Developing Countries? 24 April 2012, https://papers.ssrn.com/sol3/papers.cfm?abstract_id=2045470.

[43]Jackson et al. (2000), pp. 179–180; Schoenbaum (1998), p. 647.

[44]Wolff (2001), McRae (2004), pp. 4–5; Garrett G, Smith JM (2002), The Politics of WTO Dispute Settlement UCLA Occasional Paper Series, 31 July 2012, https://escholarship.org/content/qt4t4952d7/qt4t4952d7.pdf.

[45]Johannesson (2018).

[46]White & Case LLP (2014).

[47]Hudec (2000), p. 345.

[48]Torres RA (2012) Use of the WTO Trade Dispute Settlement Mechanism by the Latin American Countries – Dispelling Myths and Breaking Down Barriers. Staff Working Paper ERSD-2012-03, February 2012, https://www.wto.org/english/res_e/reser_e/ersd201203_e.pdf., pp. 14–16; Wolff (2001), p. 423.

[49]World Trade Organization, Understanding on Rules and Procedures Governing the Settlement of Disputes, https://www.wto.org/english/docs_e/legal_e/28-dsu_e.htm. Article 5.

[50]Ibid.

possibility to explore these alternative dispute settlement options in an abstract and passing manner. It does not stipulate a structure or build a system that can facilitate actual utilization of such alternatives. The absence of precedents relying on the provision compared to the high number of disputes lodged to the binding dispute settlement mechanism of the DSU arguably reflects that the current provision is not sufficient or detailed enough in this regard. As such states' renewed effort at the moment should explore an option of more systematized and structured mechanism on this issue, in particular on mediation.

This suggestion is not to replace the current dispute settlement system with non-binding proceedings; if anything, the current dispute settlement system should be maintained and emphasized as a key pillar of the present and future WTO regime. The use of non-binding dispute settlement proceedings could be designed just to complement the existing one. Some highly sensitive disputes could be better handled by these alternative non-binding proceedings.

As a matter of fact, states have already started experimenting with non-binding dispute settlement mechanisms outside the WTO.[51] This effort could be replicated in the WTO regime, so that the Members could have additional options between a direct negotiation and the binding dispute settlement mechanism. At present, states seem to have only two black-or-white options—direct negotiations between the parties or high-profile panel proceedings.

4 Conclusion

By any account, the multilateral trading system is faltering. The WTO's leadership is at its lowest point since its inception. Many states are not bothering to hide their suspicion toward the WTO as the sole guardian of their trade interests. More sadly, the WTO dispute settlement system has also lost its premium status and ambience as its Appellate Body ceased to function in December 2019. And yet, there is no visible sign as of April 2020 that this global hemorrhage will stop any time soon.

What is all the more embarrassing, at this very juncture, is that the global investment law reformers, in their effort to multilateralize the investment regime, are turning to the WTO and its dispute settlement mechanism as an important benchmark. In their eyes, the multilateralism enshrined in the WTO is regarded as the right direction that the investment regime should also follow, after their six decades of experience of 'non-multilateralism'. So they stand watchful of the evolution of events in the trade sector. Failure of the WTO will negatively affect the contemporary efforts on the international investment front. A possible demise of

[51]Free Trade Agreement between the Republic of Korea, of the one part and the European Union and its Member States, of the other part (entered into force on 1 July 2011), Annex 14-A; Free Trade Agreement between the Government of the Republic of Korea and the Government of the People's Republic of China (entered into force on 20 Dec 2015), Article 20.5, para 4.

the multilateral trading system may deliver a fatal blow to their current efforts to initiate a similar endeavor in the international investment sector. In the alternative, more ironically, the investment regime may successfully transplant multilateralism, while we ourselves are losing it.

Consequences will not just be confined to investment. Other sectors considering a multilateral approach, such as global competition regulation, may be affected as well. Newly emerging areas such as artificial intelligence and digital economy may also find it difficult to pursue a new global regime, having seen the fall of a once-dominant global multilateral regime on trade. In a sense, the global rule of law may fade and lose its relevance gradually.

As a beacon of multilateralism, the WTO should realize its mandate on the global plane as such. So should states and governments. The WTO and its Members should be aware that what is at stake is not simply trade liberalization and tariff increases. It is the 73-year accumulation of global efforts (since the GATT era) to establish a truly multilateral system.

The global trade regime with its multilateral structure is a vital asset of the global community. The recent phenomena of shaking and undermining the regime should be ceased as soon as possible. More efforts need to be mobilized to counter the current development. It is indeed important to stop the spread of protectionism and restore the commitment to free and fair trade. It is all the more important for the permeation of multilateralism and rule of law in many different sectors of the global community. What is at stake is not merely goods or services trade; it is about maintaining and developing the global governance based on rule of law.

References

Ahmed G, Tellez Gaytan JC, Lee C (2016) Two decades of WTO: governance, innovation and prospects. Proceedings of the 14th International Conference of the SGBED. https://www.researchgate.net/profile/Arshad_Mahmood13/publication/305688429_Beyond_Wit_and_Grit_Spiritual_Quotient_the_key_to_Organisational_Development/links/5799db3308aeb0ffcd0fa2a3.pdf#page=670

Bacchus J (2018a) Might unmakes right – the American assault on the rule of law in world trade. CIJI Papers No. 173. https://www.cigionline.org/sites/default/files/documents/Paper%20no.173.pdf

Bacchus J (2018b) Was Buenos Aires the beginning of the end or the end of the beginning? The future of the World Trade Organization. CATO Institute Policy Analysis No. 841. https://www.cato.org/publications/policy-analysis/was-buenosaires-beginning-end-or-end-beginning-future-world-trade#full

Baldwin R (2016) The World Trade Organization and the future of multilateralism. J Econ Perspect 30(1):95–116

Bown CP, McCulloch R (2010) Developing countries, dispute settlement, and the advisory centre on WTO law. J Int Trade Econ Dev 19(1):33–63

Brewster R (2019) WTO dispute settlement: can we go back again? AJIL Unbound 113:61–66

Brown CP, Kolb M (2018) Trump's Trade War timeline: an up-to-date guide. Peterson Institute for International Economics, https://piie.com/blogs/trade-investment-policy-watch/trump-trade-war-china-date-guide

Ciuriak D (2018) The March into Trade Wars: US policy aims and the implications for reconciliation. C.D. Howe Institute, https://www.cdhowe.org/print/6751?utm_source=C.D.%20Howe%20Institute%20Mailing%20List&utm_campaign=c6c410fca0-Verbatim_Long%20Peace%20Over_RN__&utm_medium=email&utm_term=0_27c04c9c54-c6c410fca0-270531669

Durusoy S, Sica E, Beyhan Z (2015) Economic crisis and protectionism policies: the case of the EU countries Int J Human Soc Sci Res 5(6(1)):57–68

Francois JF (2002) Trade policy transparency and investor confidence: some implications for an effective trade policy review mechanism. Rev Int Econ 9(2):303–316

Ghosh A (2010) Developing countries in the WTO trade policy review mechanism. World Trade Rev 9(3):419–455

Goldstein J (2017) Trading in the twenty-first century: is there a role for the World Trade Organization? Annu Rev Polit Sci 20:545–564

Howard DM (2018) The need for a supranational organization in foreign investment. Notre Dame J Int Comp Law 8(2):15–43

Hudec R (2000) Broadening the scope of remedies in WTO dispute settlement. In: Weiss F, Wiers J (eds) Improving WTO dispute settlement procedures. Cameron May Publishers, London, pp 345–376

Jackson J, Hudec R, Davis D (2000) The role and effectiveness of the WTO dispute settlement mechanism [with comments and discussion]. Brookings Institution Press, Washington, DC, pp 179–180

Johannesson L (2018) Efficiency gains and time-savings of permanent panels in the WTO dispute settlement. IFN Working Paper No. 1219. http://www.ifn.se/wfiles/wp/wp1219.pdf

Lei X (2017) Changes in global trade and investment and implications for China-U.S. economic relations. Center for Strategic & International Studies, https://www.csis.org/changes-global-trade-and-investment-and-implications-china-us-economic-relations

Linn J (2018) Recent threats to multilateralism. Glob J Emerg Mark Econ 9(1–3):86–113

Levi L (2018) Governing globalization. The challenge of protectionism to multilateralism. The Federalist Debate. https://www.degruyter.com/downloadpdf/j/tfd.2018.31.issue-3/tfd-2018-0025/tfd-2018-0025.pdf

Lu X (2015) Reflections and recommendations on the WTO's trade policy review mechanism. J WTO China 5(4):81–92

McRae D (2004) What is the future of WTO dispute settlement? J Int Econ Law 7(1):3–21

Nicita A, Olarreaga M, da Silva P (2018) A trade war will increase average tariffs by 32 percentage points. Vox, 5. https://voxeu.org/article/trade-war-will-increase-average-tariffs-32-percentage-points

Pauwelyn J (2014) At the Edge of Chaos? Foreign investment law as a complex adaptive system, how it emerged and how it can be reformed. ICSID Rev Foreign Invest Law J 29(2):372–418

Pauwelyn J (2019) WTO dispute settlement post 2019: what to expect? J Int Econ Law 22 (3):297–321

Pressman A, Chandler C (2019) 8 Predictions for U.S.-China economic relations in 2019. Fortune Data Sheet. http://fortune.com/2019/01/04/data-sheet-china-predictions-trade-war/

Sauvant KP, Ortino F (2013) Improving on the international investment law and policy regime: options for the future. Ministry of Foreign Affairs of Finland. http://ccsi.columbia.edu/files/2014/03/Improving-The-International-Investment-Law-and-Policy-Regime-Options-for-the-Future-Sept-2013.pdf

Schill SW (2011) System-building in investment treaty arbitration and lawmaking. German Law J 12(5):1083–1110

Schoenbaum T (1998) WTO dispute settlement: praise and suggestions for reform. Int Comp Law Q 47(3):647–658

Sornarajah M (2016) An International Investment Court: panacea or purgatory? Columbia FDI perspectives: perspectives on topical foreign direct investment issues No. 180. http://ccsi.columbia.edu/files/2013/10/No-180-Sornarajah-FINAL.pdf

Tocci N (2018) The demise of the international liberal order and the future of the European project. IAI Comment 18(63):1–6

United Nations Conference on Trade and Development (2017) Investment policy monitor. UNCTAD, p 6. https://unctad.org/en/PublicationsLibrary/webdiaepcb2017d9_en.pdf

United Nations Conference on Trade and Development (2018) UNCTAD's reform package for international investment regime. https://investmentpolicy.unctad.org/uploaded-files/document/UNCTAD_Reform_Package_2018.pdf

Wagner M (2020) The Appellate Body of the WTO and its reform. In: The Appellate Body of the WTO and its reform. Springer, Singapore, pp 67–90

White & Case LLP (2014) WTO dispute settlement – long delay hit the system. Lexology. https://www.lexology.com/library/detail.aspx?g=13fe0fa8-2e4c-45ca-b619-c4609ae96797

Wolff AW (2001) Problems with WTO dispute settlement. Chic J Int Law 2(2):417–426

Woods L (2019) Fit for purposes? The EU's investment court system. Kluwer Arbitration Blog, http://kluwerarbitrationblog.com/2016/03/23/to-be-decided/

Zang MQ (2018) When the multilateral meets the regionals: regional trade agreements at WTO dispute settlement. World Trade Rev 18(1):33–61

Zhan J (2017) World investment report. United Nations Publication, Geneva, p xii

Reaching for Utopia, Geneva as Inspiration for Investment Disputes?

Chin Leng Lim

Contents

Choh-ming Li Professor of Law at The Chinese University of Hong Kong, and a barrister at Keating Chambers, London.
A version of this paper was delivered at the 2019 AWRN retreat in Tokyo and the AAIL Side Event, 39th Sess. UNCITRAL Working Group III. This chapter also reflects remarks made at Dutch Arbitration Day 2019.

C. L. Lim (✉)
Faculty of Law, The Chinese University of Hong Kong, Sha Tin, Hong Kong SAR, China
e-mail: chin.leng.lim@cuhk.edu.hk

M. K. Lewis et al. (eds.), *A Post-WTO International Legal Order*,
https://doi.org/10.1007/978-3-030-45428-9_10

1 Introduction

Imagine four periods,[1] in the recent post-globalization history of international economic regulation. By post-globalization I mean that era after the fall of the Berlin Wall during the winter of 1989, the same year the term "Washington Consensus" was coined by John Williamson. In Phase One there emerged a backlash against economic globalization which manifested itself during the late 1990s in the collapse of the Multilateral Agreement on Investment (MAI) and the WTO protests in Seattle and subsequently in Cancun in 2003. During Phase Two, the WTO was able to launch the now long-dormant Doha Development Round of trade negotiations in 2001 while, in the investment treaty policy sphere, the United States (US) and Canada had, by 2004, produced rebalanced model bilateral investment treaties (BITs). It was not until 2007 however, when the South American backlash against the International Centre for the Settlement of Investment Disputes (ICSID) began, that a Third Phase, accompanied by the Global Economic Crisis,[2] commenced. With this, BITs and investment treaty arbitration came under immense pressure.[3] During this third phase the Doha Round lingered on while the US complained about WTO Appellate Body overreach.[4] It was not until the Trump Administration entered the White House that events now led, in a Fourth Phase, to the current effort to reform the WTO DSS. By now, there was also a parallel attempt in the investment arbitration sphere to borrow the idea of an Appellate Mechanism from trade law as a way of addressing the investment law backlash—and it is this last with which this chapter is concerned.

This chapter is about a utopian vision. It concerns an attempt to adapt lessons learnt from the WTO DSS in midst of an on-going backlash against the investor-State dispute settlement system, and the fact that by December 2019 the WTO Appellate Body had come to a stand-still as a new decade was about to begin. The prevention of further Appellate Body appointments[5] has meant that any appeal now plunges a dispute process into a procedural blackhole. Under Article 16.4 of the WTO Dispute Settlement Understanding (DSU), any appeal effectively blocks a panel report and recommendations from being adopted. Lack of a quorum to hear the appeal in turn prevents the appeal from being heard and the dispute from being resolved. There is no way out short of an amendment to the WTO DSU for the

[1]For earlier discussions of these phases or periods, see Lim (2016), pp. 23–33, pp. 444–445; Lim (2018), pp. 551–554.

[2]Lim and Mercurio (2015), Chap. 1, making no deeper claim about the effect of the crisis on international economic regulation than the persistent fragmentation of the discipline.

[3]See e.g. Lim (2016), Chap. 16.

[4]Statements by the United States at the meeting of the WTO dispute settlement body, Geneva, 18 Dec 2018, p. 9 ("US December 2018 Statement").

[5]Peker E (2019) "The WTO is in crisis": Dispute puts global trade regulator at risk. https://www.wsj.com/articles/the-wto-is-in-crisis-dispute-puts-global-trade-regulator-at-risk-11575889201.

quorum rule is written into Article 17.1 of the DSU, which specifies a Division of three Appellate Body Members to hear the appeal.[6]

What the European Union (EU) seeks to address—in, as we shall see, two separate reform proposals respectively in the trade and investment law spheres—are certain specific criticisms, which are very different, about how we resolve disputes under WTO law and BITs, and the EU does this by doubling down on the WTO model.

Section 1 of the current chapter describes present-day events. Section 2 describes the proposal for an Appellate Mechanism for investment treaty disputes. The proposal includes—but is not necessarily limited to—the EU's narrower proposal for a two-tier multilateral investment court (MIC), one which takes inspiration from the WTO panel and Appellate Body system. It is not limited to that model alone for the EU position would also allow a free-standing Appellate Mechanism for investment disputes. Section 3 of this chapter then introduces the EU's proposal for a full-blown two-tier MIC. Section 4 goes on to list some common questions about having any Appellate Mechanism in both the trade and investment law spheres. Then, Sect. 5 discusses how the two sets of current reform proposals—for investment and trade dispute settlement—interact.

What makes the European proposal—or proposals—utopian is discussed in the concluding part, Sect. 6; namely, to adapt a broken system—for that at the time of writing is what the WTO DSS has become—to other purposes is simply remarkable. Is it realistic? Is it not idealistic? These however are different but related senses of utopianism. A utopian proposal or project may be idealistic while still being achievable in practice. Or is it not simply a rebuke directed at the present conditions in international economic law? Utopian imaginings are political projects after all, and "in Europe, you cannot swing anything around without hitting an institution."[7]

2 The Backlash Against Investment Treaties and Investment Arbitration, and the Proposals for an Appellate Mechanism in a Two-Tier Multilateral Investment Court (MIC)

The conditions which led to the EU proposal in the investment dispute resolution sphere are different from those which led to the creation of a two-tier WTO DSS. The EU and Japan, weary of US unilateralism in international trade, pushed for what became nearly a compulsory dispute resolution system, one which resembles in some senses adjudication before an international court. What made the system

[6]See further, for discussion of the proposal to substitute the Appellate Body function with arbitration, Charnovitz (2019).

[7]I am grateful to Martins Paparinskis for this; and for organising "A Fireside Chat with Elias and Lim", University College London, 28 January 2020.

different from a court was the need for the WTO Dispute Settlement Body's (DSB) political approval of reports and recommendations by panels and, if there had been an appeal, by the Appellate Body. What made this system nonetheless similar to compulsory adjudication was the fact that by virtue of the negative consensus rule, used in the DSB for such approval, a report and its recommendations will in practice be adopted unless the winning party itself agreed to its disapproval.[8] What however made it a system of adjudication was the fact that panels and the Appellate Body apply trade law—in the form of the WTO covered agreements—through legal reasoning.[9] It is a "near-compulsory, near-adjudicative" system. The conditions which have led to the current EU proposal for a two-tier MIC for investment disputes has, however, different roots.

The contemporary backlash against investment treaties and investment arbitration has its origins elsewhere. It began, in large part, with Bolivia's denunciation of the ICSID Convention which took effect in November 2007, under Article 71 of the Convention.[10] This was followed by similar denunciations by Ecuador, which came into effect in January 2010, and Venezuela whose own denunciation of the ICSID Convention came into effect in July 2012.[11] These Latin American withdrawals from the ICSID Convention were significant principally because criticism of investor-State dispute settlement (ISDS) had hitherto been the province not of national governments mainly, but of non-governmental organisations. At the time, they were seen to be events limited to the South American Continent. That perception was however to change. In a new phase, South Africa in November 2012 started to terminate its BITs with successive European countries.[12] The backlash had widened geographically. At the same time, calls for both procedural as well as substantive reform of international investment law and arbitration began to coalesce. Such calls now extended beyond withdrawals from the ICSID Convention and had begun to include disaffection with BIT substantive protections. All of this mirrored what international economic lawyers have called the "death of treaties" phenomenon.[13] In early 2014 Indonesia was to announce that it intended to terminate its BIT with the Netherlands. By March of 2015, India had released its new Draft Model BIT together with the announcement of a programme to replace Indian BITs with new treaties based on the new Model BIT. By March of 2017 India had sent notices of termination to 58 treaty partners.[14] Indonesia had by now engaged in several

[8]Cf. DSU, arts. 16(4), 17 (14). The literature is voluminous. For this author's views, see Lim (2002), pp. 436–497.

[9]For this meaning of international adjudication, see Moore (1929), pp. xxxvi–xci.

[10]For the law, see Schreuer (2010), p. 353.

[11]Bland and Donnan (2014) and Ripinsky (2012).

[12]Discussed in Schneiderman (2016), p. 131, pp. 142–143.

[13]Trachtman (2014), pp. 36–40.

[14]Ranjan (2017).

terminations.[15] Thus began a new thread—a growing policy of replacing existing BITs with rebalanced treaties.

In 2015, in the context of the Trans-Atlantic Trade and Investment Partnership negotiations between the US and Europe, the EU proposed a bespoke investment adjudication system as a wholesale alternative to investor-state arbitration.[16] It did so against the backdrop of a longer standing proposal; namely the creation of an Appellate Mechanisms for investment treaty arbitration. It is this last with which the current short paper is concerned, and within it the European proposal for a two-tier MIC. As of July 2017, debate on ISDS reform has focused on the work being done in UNCITRAL Working Group III (WGIII).[17]

3 The Proposal for Appellate Review of Investment Arbitration

We might begin then with the more limited proposal for an investment Appellate mechanism. This had been raised earlier, in ICSID's 2011 annual report,[18] a key argument being the need to ensure stability and consistency in arbitral awards, and the absence of a framework for handling parallel proceedings. At the same time, there had been vocal criticism of investment arbitration for lacking impartiality and independence on the part of the arbitrators; this last having to do with "double-hatting" (serving as counsel and arbitrator), and repeat appointments due to a small pool of well-remunerated arbitrators.[19] The problem unlike in the trade sphere was not that there was an inability to bring disputes to a semblance of adjudication, but that the system of international adjudication represented by investment treaty arbitration has gone out of control and now requires oversight.

The proposal for an Appellate Mechanism differs in truth from the ICSID regime as it was always conceived. First, ICSID's framers had accepted inconsistency in arbitral awards as a fact. They saw the underlying issue as one involving a need to

[15] Lingard and Menish (2017); See also GAR live Hong Kong lookback: Asia's overlapping investment treaties, chaos or cohesion?, GAR, 15 Aug. 2018.

[16] See European Commission (2016). Lim et al. (2019), p. 504.

[17] For a summary, see Roberts (2018).

[18] ICSID Annual Report (2011), p. 39; Ngangjoh-Hodu and Ajibo (2015), p. 308, pp. 314–315 and the works cited therein.

[19] See e.g. Lai (2019), p. 419. ("Mapping the way forward") There are consequences for when constituting a tribunal. Challenges to proposed appointments are now not infrequent, and the need for greater transparency has led ICSID to seek to reform its practice and to publish decisions on such challenges. I am grateful to Professor Wenhua Shan for raising these points during a recent debate which this author had the privilege of chairing; ibid., p. 220, p. 222.

ensure the independence and impartiality of arbitrators instead[20]—i.e. under the criteria listed now under Article 14 of the ICSID Convention as well as that Convention's provision on arbitrator challenges, Article 57. The legendary Aaron Broches at the World Bank had taken the view one would ordinarily express to any client—arbitration brings risks. The Working Party on the Draft ICSID Convention concluded eventually that a five-member panel would serve to ensure such impartiality.[21] So today Article 52 precludes review for any substantive legal error. Secondly, the ICSID Convention is therefore concerned only with a narrow legitimacy—of the decision-making process which arbitration represents. Thirdly, ICSID Arbitration is widely seen to be delocalized, there is no—or usually not[22]—any scope for annulment by national courts. ICSID would have national courts become passive debt collectors.[23] In contrast, even review for substantive legal error may be available in the case of non-ICSID arbitration, where the law of the seat permits it.[24]

4 The EU's Full-Blown "Two-Tier MIC" Proposal

Here enters the EU's full proposal for a two-tier MIC. Inspired by the WTO's example,[25] such an upper court would uphold, modify or reverse the decision of a first instance tribunal.[26] It is not the only option within the realm of possibilities. The idea of an Appeals Mechanism which could exist independently is envisaged in non-EU treaties.[27] The EU position appears pragmatic. For the EU, there in fact are three options in the current diplomatic discussions taking place in UNCITRAL Working Group III—(1) Option A, having a two-tier MIC, (2) Option B, having a free-standing Appeals Mechanism, and (3) Option C, the EU "Open Architecture" so-called envisages that States which do not accept the MIC could "opt in" not to a free-standing Appeals Mechanism as such but to the appellate body which is a part of the MIC.[28]

[20]Thomas (2016).

[21]On the basis that the parties would each only be entitled to appoint one arbitrator out of a college of five.

[22]Article 26 of the ICSID Convention states that consent to ICSID arbitration shall, one might wish to add "only", in the absence of express party choice be deemed consent to exclude any other remedy. In other words, the parties can choose to "localize" ICSID arbitration. See Schreuer et al. (2009), p. 351; for a possible example of such a clause, see Lim (2019), pp. 313–334.

[23]ICSID Convention, Art. 53.

[24]For example, under s. 69 of the UK Arbitration Act 1996.

[25]DSU, Art. 17.13.

[26]CETA, Art. 8.28(2). See also the EU's FTAs with Vietnam, Singapore and Mexico and the TTIP Draft Investment Chapter, below.

[27]See CPTPP, Art. 9.23(11); China-Australia FTA, Art. 9.23; US-Singapore FTA, Art. 15.19(10).

[28]UN Doc. A/CN.9/WG.III/WP.159, add. 1, para 3.16.

Coming back, however, to the proposal for a full-blown MIC, it is said to address three criticisms in particular. First, that ethical questions have arisen about the behaviour or conduct of arbitrators—as mentioned earlier, double-hatting for example, and repeat appointments. Secondly, that this in part is due to the existence of only a small pool of arbitrators. Thirdly, the inconsistency of investment tribunal awards has led to an incoherent jurisprudence.

There are answers to all three criticisms. Firstly, that concerns with conflicts of interest may be addressed without so radical a proposal as the replacement, or attempted replacement, of an investment arbitration system with a court. New BITs and investment chapters in FTAs such as the TPP/CPTPP already envisage a code of conduct for arbitrators. Secondly, would fifteen judges accepting 100% of disputes be better than a small pool of 40 arbitrators hearing 50% of disputes? Or in the case of repeat appointments, should we not consider that in one year the ICSID statistics show that in 147 disputes there were only 7 respondents? Are these respondents to seek different arbitrators each time? Finally, as we shall see below in Sect. 5 of this chapter, it is precisely the US criticism of the Appellate Body that it has sought to develop some form of *jurisprudence constante* which on some points it is—at least according to the US view-point—consistently wrong.[29]

Some might also choose to distinguish between the EU's systemic reform proposal, envisaging an MIC, and other more incrementalist proposals.[30] Current attempts at procedural and substantive reform may also be seen as a response to the EU proposal in an attempt at rollback where the focus has been placed more firmly—rightly or otherwise—on substantive rather than procedural reform.[31] For example, the Trans-Pacific Partnership—and the Comprehensive and Progressive Agreement for Trans-Pacific Partnership—only acknowledge the possibility of an Appellate Mechanism.[32]

[29]I am grateful to Professor Bridgitte Stern of the Université Pantheon-Sorbonne for these points; ICSID Convention (2011) ICSID annual report 2011. http://documents.worldbank.org/curated/en/219201468331759365/ICSID-annual-report-2011. "Mapping the way forward". https://www.aail.org/ufiles/ckeditor/files/Proceedings_of_ISDS_Reform_Conference_2019.pdf.

[30]Roberts (2018).

[31]Describing the TPP's/CPTPP's framers' attempt as one of embedding investment rules in the various domestic social purposes that signatories have considered important, see Lim (2018), For the view that the procedural reform issue is more significant for that is where the real need lies—e.g. in saving time and costs for host States and indeed claimants, see Matthew Hodgson's (Allen & Overy) intervention at "Gar live Hong Kong lookback" (2018).

[32]TPP, Art. 9.23(11). See further, on the TPP/CPTPP, Lim (2018).

5 Questions Surrounding the Broader Proposal

Let us turn now to the idea that there should be a right to an appeal and in the course of so doing turn also to questions about the scope and mechanism for such a right, and to questions about the applicable law as well as the enforcement of Appellate Tribunal rulings. Other questions—such as the institutional architecture of a permanent body and the appointment of Appellate Mechanism members/judges will be left to the subsequent part—Sect. 5—where we draw a comparison with the current process of WTO Appellate Body reform.

5.1 A Right to Appellate Review?

Take, for example, the current European conception of an Appeals Mechanism such as that envisaged in the EU-Canada Comprehensive Economic and Trade Agreement (CETA), the Draft Investment Chapter of the Transatlantic Trade and Investment Partnership (TTIP), and in other recent EU treaties. That model derives from the WTO Appellate Body.[33] It is therefore tied to a particular institutional architecture which is—and is meant to—resemble the function of the WTO's Appellate Body.

Going by the WTO's experience then, we might find an 80% rate of findings of legal error of some kind in connection with appealed panel reports.[34] As for the rates of appeals, which are effectively as of right,[35] these have ranged between 1999 and 2015 from the appeal of 40% of panel reports in 2010, to 100% of all panel reports in 1999. The upshot is that an Appeals Mechanism prolongs disputes and increases costs.

Being mindful of the finality of awards, as well as of time and cost as factors, might we not imagine instead a mechanism where appeal is only by leave of the appellate tribunal or by the agreement of the parties, but not as of right? Rather than the WTO model, might not s. 69 of the UK Arbitration Act 1996 present another model?[36] Something more needs to be said about this option, for the benefit of certain readers. The UK Act stands out today in a sea of arbitration friendly regimes wherein the right to appeal a substantive point of law has diminished significantly. Jurisdictions which have followed the UK approach have slowly begun to abandon it—including places in the Commonwealth such as Malaysia, for example, or Hong Kong. Still, this should not cloud how restrictive the possibility of an appeal on a substantive point of law is in practice under s. 69 or what once was known as the "Nema" principles under English law. The alternative therefore, if only to make the

---

[33]Baetens (2017), p. 438.

[34]Baetens (2017).

[35]DSU, Art. 16.3, subject to the negative consensus rule.

[36]UK Arbitration Act 1996, s. 69(2). Discussed further, below.

comparison clear by making it as stark as possible, is to have not a right of appeal but the possibility of appeal on a substantive point of law where the conditions to be met for obtaining leave to appeal are stringent, indeed so stringent that it has attracted complaint in England that the balance tilts too much in favour of commercial arbitration at the expense of the role—the very important role—of the courts in contributing to the development of commercial law. The parallels with the debate on the reform of investor-State dispute settlement are clear—it is a lack of coherence and consistency, supposedly in investment arbitration awards which has led to the proposal for an appellate function. But as we shall see in the next section—Sect. 5, below—it is the opposite complaint that has become the undoing of the WTO Appellate Body; namely, the complaint that in the case of the WTO the Appellate Body has developed consistently wrong lines of jurisprudence and that legal errors have become entrenched.

The counterargument to all this may be that if, truly, we are concerned with time and costs then an ICSID annulment procedure with similar cost and time implications already exists. However, that only suggests—as some have suggested—avoidance of ICSID arbitration in favour of say *ad hoc* or other institutional arbitration,[37] perhaps based on the UNCITRAL Rules. The argument that because ICSID arbitration already leads to frequent annulments an investment disputes Appellate Mechanism becomes justified is, in that sense, specious.

5.2 *Scope of Review*

It is precisely because review for substantive legal error is precluded in the case of ICSID—under article 52[38]—that there have been calls for a body that can ensure the stability and predictability of investment awards. Regarding the scope of review, the EU approach is to extend that to[39]:

- Errors in the interpretation of applicable law,
- Cases where the tribunal has manifestly erred in the appreciation of facts, including in the appreciation of domestic law, or

[37]See e.g. Burgstaller and Rosenberg (2011), pp. 91–108.

[38]The distinction between substantive and procedural review can, however, be overplayed. In practice, losing parties seek to disguise arguments for substantive law review with claims to manifest excess of jurisdiction. See ICISD Convention, Art. 52(1)(b). See further Baetens (2017), p. 444. So too can consistency may be overplayed, it has been observed that it is not the same thing as correctness. This is an issue which should be discussed in the next section. Suffice to point out that, similar to the "trade and..." debate in trade law debates, there is a similarly complex issue of the systemic integration of international investment law within the hierarchy of public international law norms—e.g. human rights norms, including the right to development. Consistency is not correctness, and it is not necessarily coherence. See Lim (2016), p. 94, p. 102.

[39]See e.g. CETA, Art. 8.28; TTIP Draft, Art. 29(1).

- The grounds under Article 52 of the ICSID Convention insofar as they are not covered by the above.[40]

In contrast, the WTO Appellate Body as is well-known is limited to "issues of law covered in the panel report and legal interpretations developed by the panel".[41] Indeed, during consultations the EU had not previously envisaged appeals on questions of fact and this was only to appear subsequently.[42]

What then happens following review? According to the EU two-tier MIC model,[43] the position would be similar to that in the case of the WTO Appellate Body which has the power to uphold, modify or reverse a panel report.[44] And if it should modify or reverse then this is where another significant difference emerges. The WTO Appellate Body has no remand authority.[45] The EU's MIC Appellate Mechanism however does.[46]

5.3 Applicable Law

This brings us to the issue of the applicable law. In the case of ICSID annulment that law is procedural. However, if review for substantive legal error were allowed this procedural reform would merge with what in essence is a question of substantive reform. The latter is precisely what the rewriting of regulatory expropriation and fair and equitable treatment clauses has been about in recent years in an attempt to rebalance substantive BIT protections.[47] Ultimately, the applicable law question will be determined by the underlying BIT or FTA investment chapter treaty protections, interpreted according to customary principles as codified in the Vienna Convention on the Law of Treaties and other rules of international law applicable between the Parties.[48] But does it end there? As events in Geneva relating to WTO Appellate Body reform show, oversight may be needed to counter risks associated with excessive institutional independence—in Geneva's case where the current US

[40]In other words where the tribunal was not properly constituted, has manifestly exceeded its powers, there was corruption on the part of a Tribunal member or a serious departure from a fundamental rule of procedure, or the award has failed to state the reasons.

[41]DSU, Art. 17.6, and this involves also the debate about the wisdom of amending the DSU to include a remand function.

[42]Baetens (2017), p. 444.

[43]CETA, Art. 8.28(2), TTIP Draft, Art. 29(2).

[44]DSU, Art. 17.13.

[45]Palmeter and Mavroidis (2012), p. 227.

[46]CETA, Art. 8.28(7); TTIP Draft, Art. 28(6).

[47]For this author's views, see further, Lim CL, Reports of TPP's death have been greatly exaggerated. In: Mohan M, Brown C (eds) The Asian turn in investment arbitration. CUP, Cambridge (in press).

[48]CETA, Art. 8.31; TTIP Draft, Art. 13.

complaint is well-known, having to do with the US perception and criticism of excessive WTO Appellate Body independence.[49] One particularly thorny issue has concerned the way the WTO Appellate Body has approached the interpretation of domestic law. In this regard, the EU treaties which contain provisions for a two-tier MIC state that the applicable law does not include the "power to interpret and apply domestic law".[50] As we will see below, this fits then, neatly, with current proposals about reform of the WTO Appellate Body. It is apparent that the EU reform proposal for investment arbitration is intended to construct two parallel and similar regimes and approaches towards both trade and investment dispute settlement.

5.4 *Enforcement*

I do not wish to dwell on enforcement. ICSID requires Contracting States to enforce awards,[51] whereas non-ICSID awards may be enforced by relying on the 1958 Convention on the Recognition and Enforcement of Foreign Arbitral Awards (the New York Convention) where the award is issued by a tribunal seated in a New York Convention Contracting State. However, a free-standing investment appeal body, or even one called a court as a part of the architecture of the two-tier MIC, and which accepts appeals from tribunal awards, may find itself not unlike any national court which has refused to enforce an award. Imagine if the appellate function is exercised in the context of a two-tier court. The award purportedly has been modified or reversed. Still, the appellate body may find itself in a position where the original tribunal award may still be sought to be enforced by the winning party elsewhere, by another national court. It is this which now brings the European proposal for a two-tier court fully into focus.

6 The Geneva Lesson and the Vienna Initiative

Let me now also attempt to touch upon the principal themes of this book—about the kinds of utopian and dystopian stories we might tell. There are at least two ways to tell the story of a particular allegation. It need hardly be said that it involves no claim whatsoever of such allegations being true or indeed false. What I would suggest is

[49]See below.

[50]The EU treaties do not specify the law to be applied by the Appeals Tribunal expressly. Rather they specify the applicable law to be applied by the Tribunal of First Instance. The Tribunal should follow the interpretation of national courts or authorities; CETA, Art. 8.31(1); TTIP Draft, Art. 13 (3). They have no jurisdiction to bind domestic courts in the interpretation of domestic law or to call into question the legality of a domestic measure under domestic law; CETA, Art. 8.31(2); TTIP Draft, Art. 13(4).

[51]See ICSID Convention, Art. 54 and also 55.

that, anecdotally speaking, it is an allegation which is heard. According to one telling, WTO dispute resolution is assisted by a secretariat which has been responsible for creating the WTO Analytical Index. Secretariat lawyers assisting panels and the Appellate Body cut and paste from the index, then move through a revolving door to law firms after a few years where in their pleadings in WTO disputes they continue to do the same thing. There is, in short, an in-built rigidity to the approach taken towards interpreting WTO law because of the way WTO law is practised.[52] Friends in the Secretariat may mutter that this is a tall tale and is in any case extremely unfair. Appellate Body members will tell you that their reports and recommendations are theirs at the end of the day. Rightly so, but I mention it because the current US complaint is made more easily understood.

According to a December 2018 statement, the US has for 15 years sought to advance the case for WTO Appellate Body reform on the basis that the Appellate Body has exceeded its authority. More recently there have been other complaints too,[53] but let us just focus on this allegation of Appellate Body "mission creep". In this specific regard, the US complains that[54]:

- The WTO Appellate Body is usurping the power of the WTO's Ministerial Conference and General Council to adopt authoritative interpretations, whereas the Appellate Body should concern itself with the application of the rules of public international law in construing a Member's commitments under the WTO covered agreements.
- Specifically, the Appellate Body has required panels to comply with its rulings absent "cogent reasons". It assumes that its interpretations are "correct" and "the best" under this cogent reasons doctrine.
- The Appellate Body's position "diminishes" therefore the full, true or original function of WTO panels which, as with the Appellate Body itself, is to resolve disputes rather than to "make law".

In sum, the allegation is that the Appellate Body suffers from mission creep. It has not confined itself to resolving disputes but is behaving as if it were a Supreme Court capable of issuing binding precedents. In addition, the Appellate Body is taking too long to do its work. These US concerns are at present addressed in a recent Appellate Body reform proposal ("2018 AB Reform Proposal") by the EU, Chinese, Canadian,

[52]See for background, Pauwelyn and Pelc (2019).

[53]Namely, (1) the retention of Appellate Body Members beyond their term of service, (2) the Appellate Body failing to meet the 60-day/90-day rule and issuing reports beyond the 90-day deadline, (3) the Appellate Body reviewing panel fact-finding, including determining the meaning of WTO Members' municipal law where it lacks the authority to do so, and (4) the Appellate Body making advisory opinions. See US December 2018 Statement, p. 9.

[54]See US December 2018 Statement, p. 19 et seq and the references cited therein.

Indian, Norwegian, New Zealand, Swiss, Australian, Korean, Icelandic, Singaporean and Mexican delegations.[55] This multinational proposal closely mirrors the EU's own views about the functioning of an MIC Appellate Tribunal, or we could say that in truth it may be the other way round since the EU's idea of a two-tier MIC is derived from the WTO Appellate Body in the first place.

However, there are fundamental questions about the relationship between the current process of WTO Appellate Body reform and the European proposal for a two-tier MIC arises, as well as in respect of other related proposals:

- How one might address the US complaint that the WTO Appellate Body has overstepped the mark by laying down precedents. After all, it is precisely the ability of a two-tier MIC, indeed of any Appellate Mechanism, to lay down precedents which brings value, i.e. to achieve consistency in investment law. There are other related questions, and I would list them in the following way.
- If instead of having the European two-tier MIC, there were, instead, to be a different Appellate Mechanism, should there be a single, global Appellate Tribunal or multiple appeals tribunals that are as scattered and fragmented as there are BITs and other investment treaties. The EU's "open architectural" proposal is that there should, ideally, be one Appellate Body which shall rule them all, one that functions as a part of a two-tier court system while farming out its services as an appeals body for tribunals constituted under various other treaty arrangements.[56]
- What is the inter-relationship, if any, with ICSID reform? What happens if an Appellate Tribunal ruling conflicts with an ICSID Annulment Award?[57]
- What about the number, selection and qualifications of appellate body members or judges? In terms of the number of appellate body members or judges, in the sporadic treaties which serve in effect as bilateral building-blocks to an eventual MIC,[58] Chapter Eight of the text of the CETA between the EU and Canada envisages fifteen members of the first instance Tribunal leaving a decision to be taken on the number of Appellate Tribunal members, and as for the first instance Tribunal five will be Canadian, five EU nationals and the other five will be from third countries, sitting in divisions of three[59] although the parties may choose instead to have a sole member.[60] Chapter Three of the EU-Vietnam Investment

[55]In communications dated 23 Nov 2018.

[56]For a similar proposal about farming out the WTO Appellate Body for FTA disputes, see Gao and Lim (2008), pp. 899–925.

[57]Baetens (2017), p. 444.

[58]In each of the EU treaties I mention below, a separate clause envisages the day when the bilateral investment dispute settlement system could be merged with an eventual MIC or "Multilateral Investment Tribunal", see e.g. EU-Canada CETA, Art. 8.29, compared to the bilateral system under arts. 8.27 and 8.28.

[59]This is the same number as for an ICSID Annulment Committee and for WTO Appellate Body Divisions.

[60]EU-Canada CETA, Art. 8.27.

Protection Agreement envisages nine first instance Tribunal members along the same lines,[61] and stipulates that there shall be six Appellate Tribunal members.[62] Chapter Three of the EU-Singapore Investment Protection Agreement stipulates six members of a "Tribunal of First Instance",[63] again along similar lines and, as with the EU-Vietnam treaty, it stipulates that there shall be three Appellate Body Members.[64] The EU negotiating text for TTIP has similar provisions, and proposes fifteen Tribunal of First Instance members and six Appellate Tribunal Members.[65] In terms of qualifications, the requirements are again fairly similar across the various EU texts. Taking CETA as an example, they shall have the qualifications required for national judicial office or be "jurists of recognized competence" and "shall have demonstrated expertise in public international law" whereas it is "desirable that they have expertise in particular, in international investment law, in international trade law and the resolution of disputes arising under international investment or international trade agreements."[66]

- Most importantly perhaps we might ask whether the "trade law model"—where appeal is nearly as of right under the negative consensus rule—presents the best way forward. Even if one accepts review for substantive legal error, there are other models. One comparison which has been mentioned would be with the "*Nema*" principles under English law,[67] now codified in s. 69 of the UK Arbitration Act. Under this "Section 69" model, let us just call it that, the parties may contract out of such appeals. If the parties have not contracted out, they may either agree to appeal or absent agreement leave to appeal may be obtained by one party. Leave when applied for is granted however only if certain conditions are met. These are (1) only if there is a question of law, (2)which substantially affects one or more of the parties' rights and (3) which the arbitral tribunal was asked to determine, and (4) on which the tribunal's decision was either obviously wrong or which, being a question of general public importance, was at least open to serious doubt, and—finally—(5) it must be just and proper for the English Court to determine that question.[68] This allows the parties to "opt in" to or to "opt out" of the possibility for appeal.[69] These other kinds of possibilities do also address the

[61]EU-Vietnam IPA, Art. 3.38.

[62]EU-Vietnam IPA, Art. 3.39.

[63]EU-Singapore IPA, Art. 3.9.

[64]EU-Singapore IPA, Art. 3.10.

[65]TTIP negotiating text tabled in 2015, Chap. 3, Sect. 3, Art. 9 and 10.

[66]EU-Canada CETA, Art. 8.27; cf. EU-Vietnam IPA, Art. 3.38 (First Instance), 3.39 (Appellate Tribunal); EU-Singapore IPA, Art. 3.9 (First Instance), 3.10 (Appellate Tribunal); TTIP negotiating text, Chapter 3, Section 3, arts. 9 (First Instance) and 10 (Appellate Tribunal).

[67]See e.g. Lord Justice Gross (2018). See further, the 2001 Companion to Mustill and Boyd (1989), p. 357.

[68]Gross (2018); See further, the 2001 Companion to Mustill, Boyd (1989), p. 355 et seq.

[69]See also section 23 of the previous Arbitration Ordinance in Hong Kong.

US criticism; while admitting at the same time that stability and certainty has important benefits.[70] In the absence of a system of binding precedent the current fear is that a tribunal may yet accept an argument rejected by ten other tribunals previously.[71]

7 Conclusion

> Actual happiness always looks pretty squalid in comparison with the overcompensation for misery. . .Happiness is never grand.[72]

The convergence in the proposals for trade and investment dispute settlement reform may, in essence, be viewed as a conjunction of the EU's MIC and AB Reform proposals. Observers have asked if either or both are practicable perhaps recalling the collapse of the MAI and the desultory state of the Doha Round. Can the WTO Member States save the WTO, let alone have their efforts mimicked in investment dispute settlement? After all, there is a larger threat from the Trump Administration's policies on trade.[73] Current Section 301 (and to an extent also Section 232) action threatens to undermine the entire premise of a WTO DSS whose Appellate Body function has also ground to a halt on account of the blocking of appointments to that body. The system in place that disputes should first go to dispute settlement, and that thereafter the losing Party has the choice of complying, compensating or stonewalling,[74] is for now in a coma despite much hope that the patient may yet revive. But under that system which had lasted until December 2019, if the losing party stonewalls then this may be met with retaliatory tariffs. Trump tariffs however put the cart before the horse. They idealise a past in which unilateral trade retaliation had been the norm. Such a past has no place for the WTO DSS.

Might we have a MIC based on the WTO's own two-tier structure where a principal US criticism of that structure is that the WTO Appellate Body has assumed its interpretations of WTO law to be the correct and best interpretations? It is this reason which provides some semblance of principle to Washington's current efforts to prevent new appointments to the Appellate Body, thereby bringing the functioning of that body to a standstill.[75] Fundamentally, does the world need certainty in

---

[70]Such as the fact that future investment dispute pleadings would not have to "leave no stone unturned", with the attendant cost consequences, which presently is the case since investment arbitration tribunals are not bound by precedent, and that therefore even a long existing line of tribunal awards pointing in a particular direction may be rejected by the instant tribunal.

[71]Emmanuel Jacomy, debate in ISDS Reform Conference (2019), p. 235, p. 238.

[72]Huxley (2005).

[73]See this author's previous views in Stewart (2018).

[74]Bello (1996), pp. 416–418; Jackson (1997), pp. 60–64.

[75]The EU has since proposed an Interim Appeal Arbitration Agreement based on Article 25 of the DSU. This idea is to employ arbitration for appeals from panel reports and recommendations.

trade and investment law, or simply that there should be some form of dispute resolution?

Be that all as it may, Geneva still inspires. The EU has doubled down in the Age of Trump. There may be no better example of a utopian vision of the future of trade dispute settlement than to attempt to mimic it in the fraught atmosphere of investor-State dispute settlement reform. Utopian projects are imaginary and the dream in this instance is that:

- The age of multilateral treaties is not dead; that we can not only reform but rebuild and improve the international economic system;
- There is a future in which trade and investment dispute settlement may become aligned using the same model for both;
- Even with thousands of BITs, the EU's open architecture model might see central global institutions exercise a supervisory appellate function over not only WTO panel reports and recommendations and a first instance multilateral investment court's decisions, but over, at least potentially, all—A-L-L, all—investment dispute settlement, including investment arbitration that may exist alongside a MIC; and
- That, going further than what has been proposed but adopting that same vision, we can even imagine a WTO Appellate Body—revived, restored and flourishing—which could serve as an "opt in" device for FTA dispute settlement[76]; and
- That, if we shut our eyes and imagined harder, the two dispute settlement systems—for trade and investment—could even be unified into a single, two-tier International Economic Court,[77] bringing us so much closer to the idea of a true "World Court", could we not?

All this takes place against the fact that the WTO system is collapsing or has already collapsed. That is what makes the EU proposal utopian. It seeks to use what in effect is a failure as a model for reform. Among some other oppositional relations we might think of,[78] aside from utopian versus dystopian views, is that between utopianism and realism. Those who proclaim the death of treaties,[79] or a WTO crisis are—in this vein—realists.

It is only when we turn to a different kind of opposite—of extremes—that we find dystopianism, taking the form of the current narrative that not only has the WTO system been brought to its knees, but that we are now brought back to the pre-1995 trading era.[80] When Section 301 measures were commonplace and a near

---

[76]See Gao and Lim (2008).

[77]For the fragmented nature of international economic law, see Lim and Mercurio (2015).

[78]See Halpin (1985), p. 440 et seq, drawing—as any student of John Mitchell Finnis would—on Aristotle. Koskenniemi introduces another well-known oppositional relation—utopianism versus apology; see Koskenniemi (1989).

[79]Contra Trachtman (2014).

[80]See this author's remarks in Stewart (2018).

compulsory, near adjudicative WTO DSS was but a dream. This brings out another sense of utopianism—idealism. But if the WTO DSS has been itself a kind of "periodic utopianism", one realized for a short time, expanding it to other spheres of international economic law—spheres which in fact might bear no similarity in their underlying conditions—may not only be idealistic but serves as a kind of European exaggeration. The EU proposal's ultimate usefulness may not lie in successful reform but could operate as a moral indictment instead[81] of the condition of our institutions of global trade and investment dispute resolution.

In other words, the proposal's true significance may be as a political statement. As such, we might also wish to keep in mind that utopias differ according to the beholder.[82] In the EU's case it is a part of a teleological viewpoint, a "European Benchmark" as I have called it,[83] which would have for the rule of law in international economic affairs an equivalent of the European Court of Justice.[84] That reflects a deeper European intellectual thread.[85] But are courts better than arbitration?[86] The WTO disputes system fills a need for the "international adjudication" of trade disputes. In the investment sphere, however imperfectly, that gap in international law—bringing States to binding dispute settlement[87]—is at least filled, by arbitration.

Even if it fails to establish a MIC for investor-State dispute settlement, the EU proposal would now serve as an expression of political defiance. Narcissistic or otherwise it now draws attention to the crisis in Geneva, even if at the beginning the proposal did not start out as such. Ultimately, in the Empire of Ideas—and of ideals—nothing fades. Calling the EU's proposal "utopian" is arguably important in a practical respect, for it is precisely that given sense of futility which often gives great energy and lastingness to utopian thought.

Acknowledgements The author is grateful to Ms. Xueji Su.

References

Baetens F (2017) Judicial review of international adjudicatory decisions: a cross-regime comparison of annulment and appellate mechanisms. J Int Dispute Settlement 8(3):432–495

Bello JH (1996) The WTO dispute settlement understanding: less is more. Am J Int Law 90 (3):416–418

[81] See Kateb (2006), p. 616, discussing the varieties and uses of utopianism.

[82] Kateb (2006), p. 621.

[83] Lim (2011), p. 25, p. 41.

[84] Bown (2019).

[85] Weiler (2000), pp. 201–202; Lim (2011), pp. 41–48.

[86] See Lim CL, The Cambridge Companion to International Arbitration. Forthcoming.

[87] Moore (1929), Preface, p. l.

Bland B, Donnan S (2014) Indonesia to terminate more than 60 bilateral investment treaties. Financial Times 26
Bown CP (2019) Can we save the WTO Appellate Body? www.piie.com
Burgstaller M, Rosenberg CB (2011) Challenging international arbitral awards: to ICSID or not to ICSID? Arbitr Int 27(1):91–108
Charnovitz S (2019) The WTO Appellate Body crisis: a critique of the EU's article 25 proposal. International Economic Law and Policy Blog. www.worldtradelaw.net
European Commission (2016) Inception impact assessment: Establishment of a multilateral investment court for investment dispute resolution. European Commission. https://ec.europa.eu/smart-regulation/roadmaps/docs/2016trade024courtoninvestmenten.pdf
Gao H, Lim CL (2008) Saving the WTO from the risk of irrelevance: the WTO dispute settlement mechanism as a "common good" for RTA disputes. J Int Econ Law 11(4):899–925
Gross PH (2018) Courts and arbitration. The Jonathan Hirst QC Commercial Law Lecture, 1 May 2018. www.judiciary.uk
Halpin AK (1985) Hohfeld's conceptions: from eight to two. Cambridge Law J 44(3):435–457
Huxley A (2005) Brave new world. Harper Collins, New York
Jackson JH (1997) The WTO dispute settlement understanding-misunderstandings on the nature of legal obligation. Am J Int Law 91(1):60–64
Kateb G (2006) Utopias and utopianism. In: Borchert DM (ed) Encyclopedia of philosophy. Macmillan, p 616
Koskenniemi M (1989) From apology to utopia: the structure of international legal argument. Finnish Lawyers' Publishing Company, Helsinki
Lai A (2019) ISDS reform conference: mapping the way forward discussion paper for the session on appointment of arbitrators and related issues. Paper presented at: ISDS reform conference - mapping the way forward, Hong Kong SAR, 13 February 2019, p. 419
Lim CL (2002) Law and diplomacy in world trade disputes. Sing J Int Comp Law 6:436–497
Lim CL (2011) Who's afraid of Asian trade regionalism, and why? In: Buckley RP, Hu RW, Arner DW (eds) East Asian economic integration: law, trade and finance. Elgar, Cheltenham, pp 25, 41
Lim CL (2016) Alternative visions of the international law on foreign investment: essays in honour of Muthucumaraswamy Sornarajah. CUP, Cambridge, pp 23–33, 444–445
Lim CL (2018) Finding a workable balance between investor protection and the public interest. In: Kingsbury B et al (eds) Mega regulation contested: global economic ordering after TPP. OUP, Oxford, pp 551–554
Lim CL (2019) The function of the transnational Chinese contract. J World Invest Trade 20 (2–3):313–334
Lim CL, Mercurio B (2015) International economic law after the global crisis. CUP, Cambridge
Lim CL, Ho J, Paparinskis M (2019) International investment law and arbitration. CUP, Cambridge, p 504
Lingard N, Menish L (2017) Indonesia's BIT terminations: not the end of the story. GaR
Moore JB (1929) International adjudications, ancient and modern, history and documents: modern series. OUP, Oxford, pp xxxvi–xci
Mustill L, Boyd SC (1989) Commercial arbitration, 2nd edn. Butterworths, London, p 357
Ngangjoh-Hodu Y, Ajibo CC (2015) ICSID annulment procedure and the WTO appellate system: the case for an appellate system for investment arbitration. J Int Dispute Settlement 6 (2):308–333
Palmeter D, Mavroidis PC (2012) Dispute settlement in the World Trade Organization. CUP, Cambridge, p 227
Pauwelyn J, Pelc KJ (2019) Who writes the rulings of the World Trade Organization? A critical assessment of the role of the secretariat in WTO dispute settlement. SSRN Electron for instance. https://papers.ssrn.com/sol3/papers.cfm?abstract_id=3458872
Ranjan P (2017) As India's new bilateral investment strategy sputters out, the secrecy and opaqueness must go. The Wire. https://thewire.in/130524/bits-investment-strategyfailure

Ripinsky S (2012) Venezuela's withdrawal from ICSID: what it does and does not achieve. Investment Treaty News 13
Roberts A (2018) Incremental, systemic, and paradigmatic reform of investor-state arbitration. https://doi.org/10.2139/ssrn.3189984
Schneiderman D (2016) The paranoid style of investment lawyers and arbitrators: investment law norm entrepreneurs and their critics. In: Lim CL (ed) Alternative visions of the international law on foreign investment. Cambridge University Press, Cambridge, pp 131, 142–143
Schreuer C (2010) Denunciation of the ICSID Convention and consent to arbitration. In: Waibel M et al (eds) The backlash against investment arbitration. Kluwer, Hague, p 353
Schreuer CH, Malintoppi L, Reinisch A, Sinclair A (2009) The ICSID Convention: a commentary. CUP, Cambridge, p 351
Stewart E (2018) Can the US-China trade war be stopped? 11 experts weigh in. VOX. https://www.vox.com/policy-and-politics/2018/7/8/17544460/trump-china-tariffs-trade-war
Thomas C (2016) An appellate mechanism for investment treaty disputes? UN Web TV
Trachtman JP (2014) Reports of the death of treaty are premature, but customary international law may have outlived its usefulness. AJIL Unbound 108:36–40
Weiler JHH (2000) Epilogue: towards a common law of international trade. In: Weiler JHH (ed) The EU, the WTO, and the NAFTA: towards a common law of international trade. OUP, Oxford, pp 201–202

A Possible Hierarchy of Dispute Settlement Systems?

Engela C. Schlemmer

Contents

> We cherish our democracy and national sovereignty, and yet we sign one trade agreement after another and treat free capital flows as the natural order of things. This unstable and incoherent state of affairs is a recipe for disaster.[1]

1 Introduction

In a post WTO-era, where the WTO dispute settlement system as we currently know it will no longer be functioning, there will still be a need to settle trade-related disputes albeit not mainly at the level of an overarching international trade dispute

Professor of Law and Assistant Dean for Academic Planning and Strategy at the Faculty of Commerce, Law and Management at the University of the Witwatersrand, Johannesburg.

[1]Rodrik (2011), p. 158; Parts of this contribution is based on Schlemmer (2019), pp. 226–251.

E. C. Schlemmer (✉)
School of Law, University of the Witwatersrand, Johannesburg, South Africa
e-mail: engelac.schlemmer@wits.ac.za

M. K. Lewis et al. (eds.), *A Post-WTO International Legal Order*,
https://doi.org/10.1007/978-3-030-45428-9_11

settlement body. It can be foreseen that the regional organisations' new (and sometimes not so new) dispute settlement mechanisms could be used and developed to ensure that trade-related disputes can be resolved using the international trade law principles created by the WTO, but applied by the different regional bodies. This chapter thus argues that in a post-WTO world WTO-created law should continue to be used in dispute settlement mechanisms created by regional trade agreements and should continue to be developed further in order to ensure consistency in the legal pathway created by the WTO's dispute settlement body, where there has been to date legal certainty regarding the meaning and interpretation of common trade terms and concepts. Hence, in a dystopian future where the WTO no longer exists, the remaining trade agreements' dispute settlement bodies would continue to use and expand on WTO-developed legal principles.

2 Sovereignty and Governance

It has become clear that sovereignty and governance (through the WTO's dispute settlement body) are at odds and that is partly the reason why we are seeing the decline of the WTO and multilateral level approaches. While at the same time we are seeing a more inward-looking tendency in many states, which can be linked to a rise in nationalism, bringing the system one closer to the Westphalian concept of sovereignty.

Apart from the growth in nationalism and a stronger focus on sovereignty, there is also a growth of regional trade agreements (in direct contrast to the focus on and claims of the inroads on sovereignty) and in particular we are seeing a growth in mega regional trade agreements or at least in the negotiations towards forming them: the Trans-Pacific Partnership (TPP), the Transatlantic Trade and Investment Partnership (TTIP), Trade in Services Agreement (TiSA) and the Regional Comprehensive Economic Partnership (RCEP) come to mind.[2] Similarly the development in the African Union with the coming into operation of the African Continental Free Trade Area should also be mentioned.[3]

Taking the foregoing comments into account, the move to regionalism does not make much sense in light of the continuing limitations on a state's sovereignty. What it does show, however, is that perhaps the broader globalisation brought about by the World Trade Organisation (WTO), does not appear to cater for all the needs of a region and also that the notion of sovereignty as understood in terms of the Westphalian concept no longer applies but has undergone changes.

[2]For an analysis of the agreements (apart from TTIP), see Juutinen M (2016) Regional trade agreements: a strike at multilateralism? Observer Research Foundation Occasional Paper 93.

[3]African Continental Free Trade Area (AfCFTA) https://au.int/en/cfta.

Furthermore, the failure of the WTO to adopt any meaningful new agreements[4] since its inception, as well as the growing competition between major trading blocs, might also have prompted the turn towards plurilateralism and thus creating (new) forms of economic governance, seemingly separate from the multilateral WTO.

The proliferation of preferential agreements seems to support the idea that states are more inclined to accept limitations placed on their sovereignty when their immediate regional partners are involved, rather than in instances where the benefit of the multilateral "community of all" is at stake. The PTAs are seemingly replacing the WTO and are not acting as stumbling blocks[5] but seem to be forming a new foundation for an international trading system structured according to a different architecture. All this being said, the foundation that had been laid by the WTO should also not just be discarded in any post WTO-era—despite an apparent triumph of sovereignty over multilateralism.

In the section that follows it will be argued that since there is such a proliferation of regional agreements with many, if not most, containing their own dispute settlement mechanisms, thought should be given to the role of WTO law (i.e. international trade law principles) in trade disputes in those and other fora in a post-WTO era. Thus, not only in the current threatened WTO system but also within other (regional) international trade dispute settlement systems which would survive the end of the WTO. If one is to focus only on the proliferation of dispute settlement mechanisms which has been brought about by the rise in regionalism or plurilateralism, an interesting picture can be painted of that post-WTO world. As an introduction to the discussion, the focus first falls on the development of international trade law principles within the WTO system that, this chapter will afterwards argue, would be of direct relevance to those regional or plurilateral systems in a post-WTO world.

3 Governance Through Dispute Settlement Mechanisms in Trade Agreements

From an international relations perspective, the developments in regional organisations or through plurilateral agreements are not in competition, but rather complementary to each other.[6] Thus, if multilateralism is looked at as being part of globalisation, then perhaps plurilateralism (or regionalism) should not have been seen as providing a threat to the future of the WTO but rather as having been

---

[4]Apart from the Information Technology Agreement (ITA) 1996 and 2015 and the Trade Facilitation Agreement (TFA) 2017.

[5]See Matshushita et al. (2015), p. 510 and the sources referred to.

[6]Rüland J (2002) The European Union as an inter- and transregional actor: lessons for global governance from Europe's relations with Asia. Paper presented at The European Union in International Affairs Conference, Australian National University, 3–4 July, 2002: 'globalization and regionalization are complementary to each other'. https://openresearch-repository.anu.edu.au/bitstream/1885/41658/3/ruland.pdf.

supportive of the system. Considering that some of the problems encountered in the multilateral system are being addressed by and in plurilateral agreements and fora,[7] it makes sense to look at the two approaches as complementary rather than competing with one another but whether this will hold true throughout will have to be seen.

The number of plurilateral agreements concluded since the coming into existence of the WTO has proliferated.[8] It is obvious too that many of the states who are negotiating these agreements are, on the face of it, taking their WTO obligations seriously since these newly negotiated agreements or draft agreements[9] at least, contain provisions which refer to the WTO agreements and their obligations in terms of it. However, very few, if any of these agreements have been notified to the WTO which creates the impression that the WTO is not seen as creating the 'world trade constitution' which everyone adheres to, quite to the contrary.

The proliferation of plurilateralism has also brought about a proliferation of dispute settlement mechanisms.[10] In a post-WTO world, a number of issues need to be considered which arises as a result of this proliferation, namely the potential need of a hierarchy of tribunals, issues of forum shopping, applicable law, legal certainty, predictability and legitimacy, to mention a few. All these aspects play an important role in a discussion relating to the future of the globalised trade world post WTO.

The legitimacy of dispute settlement systems is an important element ensuring that their governance role is effective. This can only be achieved when the outcomes of the disputes, when they relate to similar provisions and principles, are predictable and certain. To ensure that this happens, one needs to be certain that the interpretation of similar provisions in similar treaties are consistent, coherent and predictable

[7]It is for instance easier to reach consensus on issues in smaller groupings than in multilateral settings. And being part of a group also gives smaller states a bigger voice in larger fora. See also Siziba C (2016) Trade Dispute Settlement in the Tripartite Free Trade Area. SECO/WTI Academic Cooperation Project Working Paper 02/2016: 6.

[8]See also Batchkova T (2013) Die Lissabon- und die Europa 2020-Strategie – Antwort der Europäischen Union auf die Globalisierung? Thesis, Halle-Wittenberg: p. 62 et seq p. 66 et seq 'Durch die Globalisierung herbeigeführten staatlichen Steuerungsdefizite können durch Integration und Regionalisierung aufgefangen werden. Die explosionsartig angestiegene Neugründung regionaler Organisationen in den letzten Dekaden beweist, dass der politische Regionalismus generell als Antwort auf die Globalisierung verstanden werden kann' (69); and Rüland (2002): 'there is good reason to argue that globalization has facilitated the emergence of a multilayered system of global governance which is built on regional organizations. Regionalism is a response of nation states to the manyfold challenges posed by globalization' (2); Messner (2005), pp. 27–54; and in general Matshushita et al. (2015), p. 510; Koskenniemi M (2006) Fragmentation of international law: difficulties arising from the diversification and expansion of international law – report of the study group of the international law commission. UN Doc A/CN.4/L.682.

[9]This contribution's focus is agreements with the southern Africa region.

[10]See for the southern African region, Schlemmer (2019), pp. 243–251.

and this can only be achieved when the rules that are applied, are applied consistently and in a uniform manner.[11]

The starting point until now has been the nature of the law of the WTO as the guiding rules of trade governance, and in accepting that the WTO was creating an international institutional (and legal) framework within which trade takes place, thus setting the scene for the development of international trade law and indeed developing international trade law through its dispute settlement body. Even if one were to consider that the WTO dispute settlement body is close to its death, the future role of the trade law principles that had been developed in this forum cannot be discarded.

The following discussion focuses on the international trade law principles that were developed by the WTO's dispute settlement body in order to determine the validity of the assumption in this contribution that there is a new kind of 'customary law' of international trade developing that will or should survive the death or decline of the WTO and that tribunals dealing with the same or similar international trade law principles, should be applying the principles in the same manner and that the respective tribunals should be looking at the decisions of each other on the application and development of international trade law concepts and principles to ensure cohesion and uniform application of principles and interpretations. If this is not the case then, in the absence of a hierarchy of tribunals, the tribunals should be limited to their own treaties[12] and customary rules of interpretation of international law and general principles of international law in order to prevent a fragmentation of the law that would be even more acute in a post-WTO world.

3.1 The Development of the Law of the World Trade Organisation

The position of the law of the WTO in the international law context has been discussed by a number of authors[13] who either argue that it is a closed system,[14] or who argue the opposite.[15] The Appellate Body has rejected the closed-system approach and stated that WTO agreements should not be read 'in clinical isolation from public international law'.[16]

---

[11]See some of the US criticism on the functioning of the WTO dispute settlement mechanism, whether valid or not—Lester and Bacchus (2019), pp. 1–6.

[12]I.e. the treaties that established them.

[13]See Van den Bossche and Zdouc (2013), p. 96 ff referring to Donald McRae and other sources.

[14]Ibid., p. 97.

[15]For e.g. Hu (2004), pp. 143–167; see also Pauwelyn (2001), pp. 535–538. See also generally McRae (2000), pp. 27–41.

[16]*United States — Standards of Reformulated and Conventional Gasoline* WT/DS2/AB/R (20 May 1996), p. 17.

When one looks at the dispute settlement system of the WTO, it is clear that apart from resolving individual disputes, it also provides the basis for developing a wider international trade law through judicial decision-making. The application and refinement of concepts and doctrines of international law is dealt with in such a way that one can consider the 'interpretation of the WTO agreements [as] an active, law-creating process'.[17]

It is accepted that the interpretation of the WTO agreements by panels and the Appellate Body is to be distinguished from an 'authoritative interpretation' in terms of article IX:2 of the WTO Agreement. In terms of this provision the 'exclusive authority to adopt interpretations' of the WTO Agreement lie with the Ministerial Conference and the General Council of the WTO. Whereas the 'authoritative interpretations' are binding on all the members of the WTO, interpretations by panels and the Appellate Body only bind the parties to a dispute upon adoption of the relevant report.[18]

The question that thus arises is whether and to what extent the Dispute Settlement Body of the WTO is then 'developing' international law—or international trade law for that matter—because if it is indeed developing international trade law, there is all the more reason for other tribunals, outside of the WTO, to take note of these developments and to apply them, even in a post-WTO world, in their own decisions to ensure that universal cognisance is taken of these developments.

Under article 3 of the Dispute Settlement Understanding, the WTO agreements must be interpreted and applied 'in accordance with the customary rules of interpretation of public international law'.[19] However, due to the fact that the Vienna Convention on the Law of Treaties (VCLT) is to a significant degree considered to be a codification of customary international law, the Appellate Body has been using the VCLT in the interpretation of the WTO agreements and as a result has created a 'rich source for the development of *that body of law*'.[20] This is especially so in relation to the application of article 31 of the VCLT. Apart from relying on and applying customary international law principles in relation to the interpretation of treaties, the Appellate Body has also applied 'relevant rules of international law' in general in interpreting these agreements.[21] According to Mitchell and Heaton this is

[17]McRae (2000), p. 30.

[18]WTO Secretariat (2017), p. 12.

[19]This makes allowance for those states who are not party to the Vienna Convention on the Law of Treaties (VCLT) 3 May 1969 1155 UNTS 331.

[20]McRae (2000), p. 36 emphasis added.

[21]'"Rules of international law" in the sense of Article 31(3)(*c*) of the VCLT corresponds to the sources of international law in Article 38(1) of the Statute of the ICJ, and thus includes treaty law, as well as customary rules of international law and general principles of law'—WTO Secretariat (2017), p. 11 with reference to the Appellate Body Report *United States – Definitive Anti-Dumping and Countervailing Duties on Certain Products from China* WT/DS379/AB/R (adopted 25 Mar 2011) par 308, that said the following: 'First, the reference to "rules of international law" corresponds to the sources of international law in Article 38(1) of the Statute of the International Court of Justice and thus includes customary rules of international law as well as general principles of law.

as a result of the inherent jurisdiction of the WTO tribunals.[22] They argue that although WTO tribunals have inherent jurisdiction, it does not allow them to resolve WTO disputes by employing any international law principles. According to them, the WTO tribunals are permitted to apply only international law rules if (i) it is necessary for the WTO tribunal for the proper exercise of its adjudicatory function; (ii) the rule in question does not have any 'substantive content of its own'; and (iii) the application of the rule is not inconsistent with the covered agreements.[23] It seems important to note though that the application of 'rules of international law' is for purposes of resolving a dispute and not for purposes of interpretation under article 31 (3)(*c*) of the VCLT.[24]

When one looks at dispute settlement, the starting point is articles 3(2) and 19 (2) of the Dispute Settlement Understanding which provides that through dispute settlement the rights and obligations of members under the covered agreements should be preserved. Koskenniemi indicates that some have interpreted this to mean that law other than the law of the WTO cannot be used in any way to effect whatever 'rights and obligations' are provided under the law of the WTO. He shows that this is clearly not the case when cognisance is taken of the further language of article 3(2) of the Dispute Settlement Understanding which requires panels and the Appellate Body to apply the 'customary rules of interpretation of public international law'. In terms of articles 31 and 32 of the VCLT, an interpretation should also take into account 'any relevant rules of international law applicable in the relations between the parties'.[25] This provides a clear indication that not only the rules of WTO law, but also customary international law rules and also other relevant rules of international law (including plurilateral treaties relating to international trade) applicable in the relations between the parties, should be taken into account.

Second, in order to be relevant, such rules must concern the same subject matter as the treaty terms being interpreted. To the extent that Articles 4, 5, and 8 of the ILC Articles concern the same subject matter as Article 1.1(a)(1) of the *SCM Agreement*, they would be "relevant" in the sense of Article 31(3)(c) of the *Vienna Convention*. With respect to the third requirement, the question is whether the ILC Articles are "applicable in the relations between the parties". We observe that Articles 4, 5, and 8 of the ILC Articles are not binding *by virtue of* being part of an international treaty. However, insofar as they reflect customary international law or general principles of law, these Articles are applicable in the relations between the parties.' Footnotes omitted. See also Appellate Body Report *Canada – Continued Suspension of Obligations in the EC – Hormones Dispute*, WT/DS321/AB/R (adopted 14 Nov 2008) par 382; Panel Report *United States – Measures Affecting the Cross-Border Supply of Gambling and Betting Services* WT/DS285/R (adopted 20 Apr 2005) para 6.128.

[22] See Mitchell and Heaton (2010), pp. 561–621.

[23] Ibid., p. 563.

[24] Ibid., p. 566; On inherent jurisdiction see also Pauwelyn (2003), p. 447 ff; Appellate Body Report *United States—Anti-Dumping Act of 1916* WT/DS136/AB/R WT/DS162/AB/R (adopted 26 Sep 2000); Appellate Body Report *Mexico—Tax Measures on Soft Drinks and Other Beverages* WT/DS308/AB/R (adopted 6 Mar 2006); Pauwelyn (2001), p. 555.

[25] Koskenniemi (2006) para 167 (footnotes omitted).

The Appellate Body of the WTO has long recognised that articles 31 and 32 of the VCLT are customary international law.[26] The conclusion concerning the applicable law in the WTO is thus that there are basically two approaches: one holds the WTO as 'part of international law, operating within the general system of international law rules and principles' and the second 'focuses on the provisions in the DSU that require that the panels and the AB neither add to nor diminish the obligations under the covered treaties'.[27] And since Koskenniemi found that these two positions or approaches can easily be reconciled there is little reason to deviate from the view 'that general international law supplements WTO law unless it has been specifically excluded and that so do other treaties which should, preferably, be read in harmony with the WTO covered treaties'.[28] It seems that one could thus argue that when tribunals *outside* of the WTO adjudicate a matter—they should also take these sources into account.

3.2 International Economic or Trade Law as a Special International Law Regime

If one argues that the same principles applied in the WTO's dispute settlement body should also be applied in regional or plurilateral institutions, one may even argue that international economic law is a self-contained regime—or rather a *lex specialis* regime under article 55 of the Articles on State Responsibility. As such, the interpretation of all international trade agreements that contain similar provisions should be able to influence the interpretation of another similar provision before a different international tribunal. If this is to happen, it will mean that certain provisions or concepts that are well-known and perhaps only (or mostly) used within the context of international economic law can develop to the status of customary international (economic) law concepts and as such be used in the interpretation of treaties and in the resolution of disputes. Thus, if there are multiple tribunals that could potentially have jurisdiction over a particular matter, the tribunal that hears the dispute should be entitled, perhaps even obliged, to take other international economic (trade) treaty interpretations into account to ensure that there is legal certainty, consistency and coherence also at this level of treaty interpretation.

Koskenniemi, when discussing article 31(3)(*c*) of the VCLT in relation to treaty interpretation, states that:

> According to paragraph 3, three matters, not ranked in any particular order of priority, should be taken into account in treaty interpretation in addition to the context. The third of them are

[26]See *US — Gasoline* (n 16), p. 17 with reference to *inter alia Territorial Dispute Case (Libyan Arab Jamahiriya v Chad)* 1994 ICJ Reports 6 (International Court of Justice); See also Koskenniemi (2006) para 168.

[27]Koskenniemi (2006) para 169.

[28]Ibid.; referring to Pauwelyn (2003).

> "any *relevant rules of international law applicable in the relations between the parties*"[29]. The provisions are *a mandatory part of the interpretation process*. Unlike the provision of article 32 on *travaux préparatoires* as a "supplementary means of interpretation" they are to be referred [to] where the meaning of treaty terms is ambiguous, obscure, absurd or unreasonable.[30]

The argument above can be extended to the relations between states that are for example members of the WTO as well as other regional organisations or preferential trade areas: all those international economic (trade) law concepts and treaties applicable to the respective parties, are 'any relevant rules of international law applicable in the relations between the parties' which must be taken into account in the interpretation process, both of the WTO agreement, as well as, one could contend, the interpretation of other plurilateral agreements.

International law encompasses all international treaties including regional and plurilateral agreements which cannot, should not, be ignored when dealing with WTO-related matters. The same should apply when issues of international trade law arise in other fora which need interpretation—WTO law is part of international law and needs to be considered in the same fashion by those tribunals.

If one considers the WTO to be providing the constitutional (or merely institutional) framework for international trade, it is advisable that in dealing with preferential trade agreements and customs unions especially those formed after the coming into operation of the WTO, even after the death of the WTO (were that to happen), that there is compliance with the WTO-developed principles.[31] In the light of the sensitive political balances that are always at stake, it is doubtful whether this will in fact ever take place, casting a shadow on the idea of a real multilateral constitutional framework. The potential death of the WTO bears testimony to this and makes it all the more important to not disregard the WTO-developed international trade law principles which currently form the basis of many of the trade-related treaties negotiated in the regional groupings.

The existing and developing plurilateral systems of trade governance[32] can play an important role in the development of international economic (trade) law and if the interpretation of treaty provisions is to be done in accordance to the existing international trade law (including the law developed by the WTO), legitimacy issues (at least at the level of the application of the law and legal principles) should not arise.

[29]'The formulation refers to rules of international law in general. The words cover all the sources of international law, including custom, general principles, and, where applicable, other treaties' (Koskenniemi (2006) para 426(b)).

[30]Koskenniemi (2006) para 425 emphasis added.

[31]See Cottier T (2004) The legal framework for free trade areas & customs unions in WTO Law. Paper presented at Multilateralism and Bilateralism after Cancún – Challenges and Opportunities of Regionalism Workshop. Berne 15 April 2004. See also Mavroidis (2005), p. 230 ff; Erasmus (2009), p. 374 ff.

[32]Similar to those that are discussed in Schlemmer (2019).

4 Hierarchy of Treaties

4.1 Introduction

During the existence of the WTO (assuming that it will cease to exist), there had been discussions relating to the status of the WTO-developed or -related legal principles in relation to legal principles developed at the national and regional level and which of these regimes should take preference. Having the WTO as the most comprehensive system has caused legal scholars to argue that if there is a potential conflict, that the international trade law rules developed by the WTO should prevail over national and regional rules.[33] However, there is no universal established hierarchy of treaties amongst the plurilateral agreements at the regional level, for example in Southern Africa, neither is there a universal hierarchy of courts.[34] The same applies in relation to the WTO Agreement. Furthermore, there is not always clarity on the ideal choice of forum when there are overlapping jurisdictions.[35]

The interpretation of international trade law principles in a coherent and predictable way is crucial for the legitimacy of the dispute settlement mechanisms (also acting as governance institutions) in the relations among states. Cottier and Schefer thus caution against ignoring the consistency of the law of the WTO which can easily follow if regional and national courts embark on giving autonomous interpretations of WTO rules.[36] This should apply equally in relation to the consistency of international trade law principles in general where interpretations are given by different tribunals under different treaties, and even by the dispute settlement body of the WTO. Should the WTO continue, similar issues may arise in a context where there is no hierarchy of courts which includes international courts or tribunals in instances where some or all of these tribunals may have jurisdiction to decide matters that may also fall within the ambit of the WTO rules. Petersmann summarises the situation aptly by stating that outside of Europe there are hardly any 'constitutional theories of international conflict resolution among states'. Neither are there transnational dispute settlement procedures which neglect the dispute settlement function of international courts as 'part of a broader "constitutional function" to settle "disputes concerning treaties, like other international disputes, … in conformity with the

---

[33]See Cottier and Schefer (1998), p. 85.

[34]Apart from perhaps in the Common Market for Eastern and Southern Africa, although this too has not yet played any significant role and there is very little if any jurisprudence from the court.

[35]See Schlemmer (2019) § 8.2 ff; and for discussions concerning Europe, see Cottier and Schefer (1998), p. 83 ff; Petersmann (2008), p. 834; see also Palmeter and Mavroidis (1998), p. 402 and the sources they refer to.

[36]Regional courts refer to courts similar to the European Court of Justice in relation to its jurisdiction and status and not merely a court or tribunal like the now defunct tribunal of the Southern African Development Community.

principles of justice and international law" and human rights'.[37] This will become more pertinent when one is confronted with a world without the WTO.

The Appellate Body stated in its report in *US – Final Anti-Dumping Measures on Stainless Steel from Mexico* that '[e]nsuring "security and predictability" in the dispute settlement system, as contemplated in Article 3.2 DSU, implies that, absent cogent reasons, an adjudicatory body will resolve the same legal question in the same way in a subsequent case'.[38] The same reasoning should also be applied in other dispute settlement mechanisms whether there is a choice of forum involved, or not—if the dispute is international trade law-related, regard should be given to other tribunals' handling of the same legal question.

If this were to be applied consistently by international tribunals, the judges will be required to 'review their traditionally state-centred conceptions of public international law, for example by judicial "balancing" among competing principles, rights and other rules of law.'[39] Security and predictability of the international trading system is non-negotiable, even without the WTO.

For example, if this is taken into account in the practice of the dispute settlement mechanisms in the African Union and the southern African region, it means that the tribunals and panels that may be established for trade-related disputes, should take note of the decisions of the WTO's Dispute Settlement Body and also other tribunals that deal with substantially similar treaty provisions and treaty obligations in order to ensure that predictability and coherence in the international trade law sphere is not undermined.[40]

With the proliferation of trade agreements in the southern African region, the hierarchy of the agreements (including the role of the WTO agreement and covered agreements) and choice of forum are becoming more and more important. Unless an agreement specifically stipulates what is to happen confronted with conflicting provisions in other agreements, the normal rules of international law concerning the interpretation of treaties will apply.[41] The Tripartite Free Trade Area[42] is the only

[37]Petersmann (2008), p. 834; see also Palmeter and Mavroidis (1998), p. 402.

[38]WT/DS344/AB/R (30 Apr 2008) para 160; Petersmann (2008), p. 841.

[39]Petersmann (2008), p. 838. '[The] Panel's failure to follow previously adopted Appellate Body reports addressing the same issues *undermines the development of a coherent and predictable body of jurisprudence* clarifying Members' rights and obligations under the covered agreements as contemplated under the DSU' (*US – Final Anti-Dumping Measures on Stainless Steel from Mexico* (ibid) paras 160–161)—this would also be true for other tribunals in other treaty regimes that deal with similar legal questions.

[40]See in relation to dispute settlement in the Sanitary and Phytosanitary (SPS) Chapter of the Trans-Pacific Partnership Agreement (TPPA) Wagner (2017), p. 467 ff.

[41]See Cottier (2004), p. 9.

[42]Agreement Establishing a Tripartite Free Trade Area among the Common Market for Eastern and Southern Africa, the East African Community and the Southern African Development Community (signed 10 June 2015, not in force yet https://treaties.dirco.gov.za/dbtw-wpd/images/20150610TripartiteFreeTradeAgreement.pdf. According to the South African Department of Trade and Industry, the Tripartite Free Trade Area (TFTA) was used as the basis for engaging in the African Continental Free Trade Agreement negotiations; see Mene (2018) Briefing by the

treaty establishing a hierarchy of treaties in relation to it and the treaties establishing its relevant contracting parties. In relation to the WTO Agreement, the 'Economic Partnership Agreement between the European Union and its Member States, of the One Part, and the Southern African Development Community EPA States, of the Other Part'[43] makes provision for a fork in the road provision and also prohibits parties to subject WTO obligations to the jurisdiction of arbitration bodies.[44] In other provisions of this agreement the jurisdiction of the WTO is ousted.[45] Similarly, provisions are found in the Preferential Trade Agreement Between the Common Market of the South and the Southern African Customs Union[46] where some disputes are only to be decided by the Dispute Settlement Understanding of the WTO whereas in others the parties have a choice[47] but in all instances, the obligations in terms of the WTO Agreement should be adhered to.

Department of Trade and Industry (DTI) to the National Council of Provinces' Trade and International Relations Committee on 8-08-2018 in relation to the ratification of the COMESA-EAC-SADC Tripartite Free Trade Area agreement—https://pmg.org.za/committee-meeting/26794/. The Tripartite Free Trade Area was launched in June 2015 and the negotiations concluded in May 2017; see Erasmus (2011), p. 1 ff. The regional economic communities are intended to be the 'building blocks' towards achieving wider integration within Africa. See African Union Media Advisory 'Press briefing of H.E. Issoufou Mahamadou, President of the Republic of Niger and champion of the Continental Free Trade Area (CFTA) Process' 4 July 2017 https://au.int/sites/default/files/newsevents/mediaadvisories/32638-ma-press_briefing_of_h_e_issoufou_mahamadou.pdf.

[43]L 250/44 *Official Journal of the European Union* 16 September 2016.

[44]'Art 95(1). Arbitration bodies set up under this Agreement shall not arbitrate disputes on a Party's rights and obligations under the WTO Agreement. 2. Recourse to the dispute settlement provisions of this Agreement shall be without prejudice to any action in the WTO framework, including dispute settlement action. However, where a Party has, with regard to a particular measure, initiated a dispute settlement proceeding under this Agreement or under the WTO Agreement, it may not initiate a dispute settlement proceeding regarding the same measure in the other forum until the first proceeding has ended. For the purposes of this paragraph, dispute settlement proceedings under the WTO Agreement are deemed to be initiated by a Party's request for the establishment of a panel under Article 6 of the DSU. 3. Nothing in this Agreement shall preclude a Party from implementing the suspension of obligations authorised by the Dispute Settlement Body of the WTO.'

[45]One example is found in article 32 where it is provided that anti-dumping and countervailing measures are governed by the relevant WTO agreements; but article 34.10 removes safeguard measures 'adopted under the provisions of this Article' from the jurisdiction of the WTO DSB: 'shall not be subject to WTO Dispute Settlement provisions'. There are many more similar examples in the treaty.

[46]http://www.sacu.int/docs/agreements/2016/mercosur-and-sacu-trade-agreement.pdf. Art 12: 'On matters related to customs valuation, the Signatory Parties shall refer to Article VII of GATT 1994 and the WTO Agreement on the Implementation of Article VII of GATT 1994.' Article 15 provides a bit differently 'In applying antidumping and countervailing measures, the Signatory Parties shall be governed by their respective legislation, which shall be consistent with Articles VI and XVI of the GATT 1994, the Agreement on Implementation of Article VI of GATT 1994 and the WTO Agreement on Subsidies and Countervailing Measures.'

[47]Annex V a 2. Article 2(7): 'Notwithstanding the foregoing provisions, disputes that may arise in connection with Chapter VIII [anti-dumping and countervailing measures] of this Agreement as well as Article 1 of Annex IV [safeguard measures] of this Agreement shall exclusively be submitted to the DSU'.

If the WTO ceases to exist and there remain references in treaties to the role of the WTO's dispute settlement body, amendments to these treaties would be required and these would be urgent in instances where for example the WTO's jurisdiction to deal with disputes had not been ousted or is compulsory.

4.2 *Overlapping Jurisdictions: Preferential Trade Agreements and the World Trade Organisation*

Article 103 of the Charter of the United Nations[48] provides that in case of a conflict between treaty provisions, the Charter takes precedence, making it clear what is to happen when conflicts do arise.[49] But there are many instances where, for example, the plurilateral trade agreements in southern Africa do not contain similar conflict provisions and also do not necessarily clash with the provisions of (for our purposes) the WTO agreements, but nevertheless contain dispute settlement mechanism(s) that may be invoked in cases of a violation of the treaty.

Due to the similarity of some of the provisions contained in the plurilateral as well as the WTO agreements and cross-references to the WTO agreements, questions as to the choice of forum arise.[50] Since the provisions of a plurilateral agreement may be similar to those of the WTO agreements, a violation of a treaty provision may amount to a breach or violation of both those treaties (if the complaining and offending parties are both members of the WTO as well as parties to the plurilateral agreement). In principle the dispute can be dealt with under either of the two agreements. Where one of the parties is not also a member of the WTO, the governance structures of the plurilateral agreement will apply as a matter of course.[51]

If one wants to argue that even in a post-WTO world the WTO agreements form (or should form) a so-called 'constitution' of the multilateral international trade regime, especially when in their treaty texts they note their relation to the WTO, extant or not, the dispute settlement mechanisms of preferential trade agreements (where all the members are or were indeed members of the WTO) should also be

[48] https://treaties.un.org/doc/publication/unts/no%20volume/part/un_charter.pdf.

[49] 'In the event of a conflict between the obligations of the Members of the United Nations under the present Charter and their obligations under any other international agreement, their obligations under the present Charter shall prevail.'

[50] Many have addressed this issue, either in general or in relation to specific treaties. See for example Henckels (2008), pp. 571–599; Petersmann (2008); Kuijper P-J (2010) Conflicting rules and clashing courts: the case of multilateral environmental agreements, free trade agreements and the WTO. ICTSD issue paper No 10; Koskenniemi (2006) and the sources they refer to.

[51] The implications that non-compliance with the WTO provisions may have on the legality of the agreements or the dispute settlement bodies established in terms of the agreements, will not be discussed in this contribution.

subject to the provisions of this constitutional framework.[52] But does that mean that there is (should be?) a hierarchy of dispute settlement bodies within this constitutional framework of international trade law? If the answer is in the affirmative, it means that the last say in all disputes relating to trade should lie with the dispute settlement body of the WTO or, in case of the WTO no longer existing, should be resolved through recourse to WTO created law, via the dispute resolution system of the relevant preferential trade regime. If one is to consider this to be a constitutional system, then clearly, as the panel found in *Turkey – Restrictions on Imports of Textiles and Clothing Products* the validity of the agreements as well as the provisions and the preferential trade agreement as such can (and should) be challenged when they deviate from the provisions of the WTO agreements.[53]

The sovereignty of states and their autonomy in concluding agreements, especially trade agreements, are severely impaired and limited by the practical consequences and legal effect of the provisions in the WTO, especially Article XXIV of the GATT. If all preferential trade agreements are to be tested against the WTO provisions, then all panel and Appellate Body findings relating to the interpretation of (particularly the provisions relating to the preferential trade agreements in) the WTO Agreements must be binding on *all parties* of the WTO, in a sort of Common Law or *erga omnes* manner, and not merely those involved in the dispute. It is only through this way that the jurisprudence on the law of the WTO and international trade law *in general* can evolve and can in actual fact be seen to be providing the constitutional framework of the international trading system.

If the WTO jurisprudence is indeed adding and supporting the constitutional framework, the interpretation of the WTO agreements and the outcomes of the disputes on particular issues should be considered as developing case law for purposes also of the international law on trade which should also be used in the interpretation of other international trade agreements and in the resolution of disputes in other fora such as the plurilateral fora—even in a post-WTO world.[54]

This would then mean that if one is dealing with a dispute in a Southern African Development Community trade panel for example, that relates to matters or provisions that use language that is the same as those contained in the WTO agreements, the Southern African Development Community panel should at least consider and give due regard to the interpretation given to that particular aspect in an adopted decision of the dispute settlement body, be it a decision of a panel or one of the Appellate Body. This would be a logical consequence of a developing 'customary law' of international trade supported by the constitutional framework of the WTO—even in a post-WTO world.

---

[52]It may even be that due to the increase in plurilateral agreements, that a new constitutional design is developing, but this is not an aspect that this contribution will delve into.

[53]WT/DS34/AB/R (adopted 22 Oct 1999) para 49 ff.

[54]See Wagner (2017), p. 467 ff for a similar argument in the relationship between the dispute settlement provisions in the SPS chapter of the TPPA and the WTO.

However, unless a hierarchy of international tribunals is established within the international economic law system, each treaty system will, and should, deal with disputes within its competence without having regard to the decisions of other tribunals unless it deals with the interpretation of particular norms that are common to the other treaty systems and thus contribute to the development of international economic (trade) law as well. If one could argue that a 'customary law of international trade' has developed perhaps even since the establishment of the WTO, then there will be scope for an argument that there should be cross-fertilisation between the different treaty systems' treatment of particular legal questions but before that happens, the scope for manoeuvring is much slimmer. But, in that way the law will continue to evolve—even after the WTO's dispute settlement system ceases contributing to it in a post-WTO world.

5 Conclusion

The rise of a renewed recognition of sovereignty seems to be here to stay and my dystopian view of the post-WTO environment does not see a move back to multilateralism in the form that it currently exists under the WTO or when it was formed a quarter century ago. It seems that the move towards plurilateralism and regionalism would be the way forward and indeed the way chosen already by both the members and non-members of the WTO.

With the rise in regionalism and preferential trade areas, it was commented that:

> [f]ragmentation is an obstacle to a "unified global order", which is supposed to be central to the notion of a world constitution. However, some commentators have postulated the idea that fragmentation gives rise to micro-constitutions, or "the emergence of a multiplicity of civil constitutions beyond the nation state".[55]

It seems to me that the idea of a unified global order and (super) globalisation cannot co-exist with the existence of sovereign states and as a result, other means of co-existence are in the process of being formed and this seems to be in the form of regional and mega-regional agreements, thus creating the "micro-constitutions" that is referred to above. A new form of economic or trade governance is being created not separate from but alongside the WTO. Accordingly, a closer relationship between the WTO dispute settlement system and those of regional organisations should in fact be the norm in a post-WTO world.

The development of governance systems (i.e. the dispute settlement mechanisms) in all of the agreements that are developing and in existence in the different regional agreements, in Africa at least, show signs, again, of a willingness to limit sovereignty. However, the African reality has shown that African states are not prone to engage each other in disputes and their view of sovereignty is perhaps much stronger

[55] Atilgan (2016), p. 138 (referring to Teubner 2010, p. 329).

in real terms than can be gathered from the number of agreements they conclude.[56] The same seems to apply in the developed world. But, through the vehicle of an emerging customary international trade law, initially developed by the WTO, these nominally independent systems will in fact find substantial harmonisation in a post-WTO world.

References

Atilgan A (2016) Global constitutionalism in the context of the third world: remarks in pursuit of a new paradigm. AJCCL 1:131

Cottier T, Schefer KN (1998) The relationship between World Trade Organization law, national and regional law. J Int Econ Law 1(1):83–122

Erasmus G (2009) Accommodating developing countries in the WTO: from mega-debates to economic partnership agreements. In: Steger DP (ed) Redesigning the World Trade Organization for the twenty-first century. Wilfried Laurier University Press, Ottowa, p 363

Erasmus G (2011) The Tripartite FTA: requirements for effective dispute resolution. In: Hartzenberg T et al (eds) Cape to Cairo: making the Tripartite Free Trade Area Work. tralac, Stellenbosch, p 1 ff

Henckels C (2008) Overcoming jurisdictional isolationism at the WTO – FTA nexus: a potential approach for the WTO. Eur J Int Law 19(3):571–599

Hu J (2004) The role of international law in the development of WTO Law. J Int Econ Law 7 (1):143–167

Lester S, Bacchus J (2019) Of precedent and persuasion: the crucial role of an appeals court in WTO disputes. Free Trade Bull 74:1–6

Matsushita M, Schoenbaum TJ, Mavroidis PC, and Michael (2015) The World Trade Organization Law, Practice, and Policy. Oxford, London

Mavroidis PC (2005) The General Agreement on Tariffs and Trade: a commentary. Oxford University Press, Oxford, p 230 ff

McRae D (2000) The WTO in international law: tradition continued or new frontier? J Int Econ Law 3(1):27–41

Messner D (2005) Global governance: Globalisierung im 21. Jahrhundert gestalten. In: Behrens M (ed) Globalisierung als politische Herausforderung. Global Governance zwischen Utopie und Realität. VS Verlag für Sozialwissenschaften, Wiesbaden, pp 27–54

Mitchell AD, Heaton D (2010) The inherent jurisdiction of WTO tribunals: the select application of public international law required by the judicial function. Mich J Int Law 31(3):561–621

Palmeter D, Mavroidis PC (1998) The WTO legal system: sources of law. AJIL 92(3):398–413

Pauwelyn J (2001) The role of public international law in the WTO: how far can we go? Am J Int Law 95(3):535–538

Pauwelyn J (2003) Conflict of norms in public international law. Cambridge University Press, Cambridge

Petersmann E-U (2008) Judging judges: from "principal-agent theory" to "constitutional justice" in multilevel "judicial governance" of economic cooperation among citizens. J Int Econ Law 11 (4):827–884

[56]For e.g., Erasmus (2011) states that there is a "phenomenon that governments are not keen to litigate against each other, especially in Africa.... Not a single SADC case involved a trade dispute between governments although there were instances where this could have happened" p. 91.

Rodrik D (2011) The globalization paradox: democracy and the future of the world economy. WW Norton, New York
Schlemmer EC (2019) Third-party governance in plurilateral trade-related agreements in southern Africa – overlapping jurisdictions and applicable law. TSAR 2019(2):226–251
Teubner G (2010) Fragmented foundations: societal constitutionalism beyond the nation state. In: Doublin P, Loughlin M (eds) The twilight of constitutionalism? Oxford University Press, Oxford, p 329
Van den Bossche P, Zdouc W (2013) The law and policy of the World Trade Organization. Cambridge University Press, Cambridge
Wagner M (2017) The future of sanitary and phytosanitary governance: SPS-plus or SPS-minus? J World Trade 51(3):445–470
WTO Secretariat (2017) A handbook on the WTO dispute settlement system. Cambridge University Press, Cambridge

Part IV
The Post-WTO: Specific International Economic Law Issues

The Concern with Non-concerns: For the End of Trade Dystopia

Leïla Choukroune

Contents

1 Introduction

While the World Trade Organisation (WTO) is questioned in its legitimacy and effectiveness, today's trade involves all aspects of human life and challenges States sovereignty, as much as it offers opportunities for growth and development. It is governed by norms of quasi-universal nature largely adopted and furthered during the past 70 years of existence of the General Agreement on Tariffs and Trade (GATT) and its institutionalised successor, the World Trade Organisation (WTO). Understood as a vehicle for greater prosperity through international integration, trade law is hardly questioned by mainstream international lawyers who still acknowledge its power to "regulate", "harmonise" and "adjudicate". In spite of the current World Trade Organisation (WTO) crisis, a large number of countries remain firm

Professor of International Law and Director of the University of Portsmouth Thematic Initiative in Democratic Citizenship.

L. Choukroune (✉)
Portsmouth Law School, University of Portsmouth, Portsmouth, UK
e-mail: leila.choukroune@port.ac.uk

M. K. Lewis et al. (eds.), *A Post-WTO International Legal Order*,
https://doi.org/10.1007/978-3-030-45428-9_12

supporters of a multilateral and a rules-based trade system. Even when departing from the WTO for its lack of effectiveness in trade reform (i.e. further trade liberalization), they rely on similar trade rules when growing alternative mega-regional deals. After all, the World Bank has demonstrated that "trade is an engine of growth that creates jobs, reduces poverty and increases economic opportunity [as] over one billion people have moved out of poverty because of economic growth underpinned by open trade since 1990."[1]

This is, however, without taking into consideration the very issue of the inequalities produced by trade liberalisation, which is at the core of the contestation of globalisation, a phenomenon seen as the product of world capitalism and indeed free trade. The immense echo of the research work of the Paris School of Economics on global inequalities and the resounding success of the book of the French economist Thomas Piketty, *Capital in the Twenty First Century*, are revealing of contemporary questionings.[2] Since the early 1990s indeed, the anti-globalisation movement has gained world prominence. It has taken multiple shapes and national expressions resulting in diverse political and economic evolutions from populism and the rise of extremism, to the contestation of multilateralism and international organisations, (mega)regionalism, renewed bilateralism, trade wars, or simply new forms of protectionism promoted in a paradoxical global campaign by the United States. As synthesised brilliantly by the Nobel prize winner in economics, Joseph Stiglitz's, "globalization is the field on which some of our major societal conflicts – including those over basic values – play out. Among the most important of those conflicts is that over the role of government and market."[3] In the same vain, for the Economist Dani Rodrik, the paradox of globalization poses an absolute challenge: "we cannot simultaneously pursue democracy, national determination, and economic globalisation."[4] With free trade and globalisation, the question of the State and its regulatory powers is posed with the greatest accuracy and a real sense of urgency.

What trade rules are we indeed talking about? The law "*as it is*"? Is a purely positivist approach to trade law relevant while there is much more to trade than trade? Why avoid a political and philosophical interrogation? What sort of international society does this technical trade law contribute to create or maintain? Far from the United Nations *utopia* for peace, trade law is fuelling a *dystopia* of unequals as conducive to the development of conflicts as it is prone to solve their technicalities on the basis of a long celebrated and now moribund Appellate Body.

The socio-economic and human aspects of trade have long been undermined by trade treaty-negotiators favouring this formal and mainstream legal approach focusing on tariffs or complex, if not obscure, non-tariffs barriers to trade taking the form of hyper technical norms. As if technique in isolation was the guarantee of prosperity. As if the international legal fragmentation denounced for the past 20 years was

---

[1]WTO (2019) Trade available at: https://www.worldbank.org/en/topic/trade/overview.

[2]Piketty (2014), p. 696; Piketty (2020).

[3]See Stiglitz (2007), p. xiv.

[4]See Rodrik (2011).

also a shield against interference in sovereign States' affairs. Anxious to protect their economic sovereignty, developing countries are indeed mistaking the need for human rights implementation with Imperial protectionism and the pursuit of neo-colonial objectives in disguise. While there is certainly some truth in the later, a rather cynical perspective on the virtues, but also the aims of trade, has resulted in the complete decoupling between norms and human realities. It has fuelled the fragmentation of international law, its justification, and deceived a civil society now rather opposed to global trade.

To address these pressing challenges and indeed reconcile trade objectives with other imperatives of States policies, recent treaties have adopted a language of rights, if not yet binding norms. The trend started in the US and Canada in the late 1980s with, for example, the inclusion of labour issues in the American General System of Preferences (GSP) and the adoption of the North American Agreement on Labour Cooperation (NAALC), the side agreement to the 1994 North American Free Trade Agreement (NAFTA). For the past 10 years or so, labour, gender, the environment, corporate social responsibility, and to a lesser extent human rights defined *per se*, are typically incorporated into the new generation of trade treaties - be it in their Preambles or in more precise special provisions.[5] So much so, that the EU, for instance, prides itself for the development of what it defines as a "Human Rights Clause", which often covers democratic principles and the rule of law envisaged as a way to engage in a constructive dialogue with trade partners, but also to enable the taking of specific measures in response to serious treaty breaches, that is the suspension of trade preferences.[6] This is yet to be seen. The integration of a "Human Rights Clause" has as much to do with a response to European civil society's quest for States' accountability than it has with a genuine defence of rights.

This dystopia of "unequals" that has been created under the pressure of financial globalisation and justifying the existence of parallel international law regimes will not be addressed if trade lawyers refuse to question the nature of trade law and keep referring to what is not "mainstream" as "non-trade concerns". Written against the backdrop of an interrogation on the utopian/dystopian nature the WTO regime, this short piece proposes to first critically address the concern with "non-trade concerns" and second to sketch the basis lines for possible change in a possible post-WTO environment.

[5]For an interesting historical perspective on the incorporation of labour in trade treaties, see for example, International Labour Organisation (ILO), Ebert FC and Posthuma A (2011) Labour Provisions, in Trade Arrangements: Current Trends and Perspectives, available at: https://www.ilo.org/wcmsp5/groups/public/%2D%2D-dgreports/%2D%2D-inst/documents/publication/wcms_192807.pdf. See also, US Congressional Research Service (2019) Labour Enforcement Issues in US FTAs, 23rd August 2019, available at: https://fas.org/sgp/crs/row/IF10972.pdf.

[6]See European Parliament Research Service (2019) Human Rights in EU Trade Agreements, The Human Rights Clause and Its Application, July 2019, available at: http://www.europarl.europa.eu/thinktank/en/document.html?reference=EPRS_BRI(2019)637975.

2 Setting the Scene

2.1 The Problem at the WTO

In a WTO context, the provisions dealing with what is not seen as mainstream or essential to trade are quite strangely referred to as "Non-Trade Concerns" (NTC). As if, for example, the issue of labour in the global supply chain was not "concerned" with trade and *vice versa*. As if trade was not producing the very "modern slavery" States now seem so keen to address as a component of their new and politically correct development and aid policies.[7] As if migrations, diplomatically called "the free movement of natural person" in a WTO language avoiding any reference to citizenship, residence or employment, did not matter.[8] The term itself is problematic: "Non-Concern". Why is the environment or gender equality a "concern" and not simply a reality or, even better, an opportunity? These "concerns" appeared in relation to the interpretation of the WTO Agreement on Agriculture (AoA), which is said to be flexible enough to provide for the protection of food security, rural development and poverty alleviation, and the environment.[9] In this context, the "multi-functionality" of agriculture already addressed by the Organisation for Economic Cooperation and Development (OECD) in its March 1998 Communiqué was stressed by the WTO itself on the basis of the Agreement on Agriculture Preamble:

> Noting that commitments under the reform programme should be made in an equitable way among all Members, having regard to non-trade concerns, including food security and the need to protect the environment; having regard to the agreement that special and differential treatment for developing countries is an integral element of the negotiations, and taking into account the possible negative effects of the implementation of the reform programme on least-developed and net food-importing developing countries; [. . .][10]

This apparently simple reasoning has nevertheless generated numerous heated debates from the early years of the WTO.[11] The absence of a clear definition of what could be a Non-Trade Concern participated to the confusion as well as developing countries' fears to see their trade policies impeded by externally imposed "Western" values and standards. In addition, recent cases such as the "seal dispute" have reactivated the debate on the basis of the interpretation of the GATT 94 Article

[7]See the UN data on modern slavery and its acknowledgment that it is a "feature" of our societies, 2 April 2019 at: https://news.un.org/en/story/2019/04/1035751.

[8]On "mode four" and trade in services, see the WTO at: https://www.wto.org/english/tratop_e/serv_e/mouvement_persons_e/mouvement_persons_e.htm.

[9]See WTO (2004) 'Non-trade' concerns: agriculture can serve many purposes, available at https://www.wto.org/english/tratop_e/agric_e/negs_bkgrnd17_agri_e.htm.

[10]See OECD, Ministerial communiqués related to agricultural policies, available at http://www.oecd.org/tad/agricultural-policies/ministerialcommuniquesrelatedtoagriculturalpolicies.htm#mar98.

[11]These include academic debates on NTC as reminded by Boisson de Chazournes (2016), pp. 379–381; See also, for an investment related perspective on environmental aspects: Boisson de Chazournes (2017), p. 371.

XX (General Exceptions) and the protection of public morals (Article XX (a)) and indigenous communities (Inuit) rights in particular.[12] Yet no consensus could be achieved in treaty drafting or case law on the very coverage of NTC.

Having this in mind, one can also expand the same sort of definition—or rather non-definition—to analyse the greater inclusion of Non-Investment Concerns (NIC) in international investment treaties and today's megaregional deals, which encompass a board vision of trade.

The following elements could be considered as falling under the banner of NIC: the right to regulate—despite its many and problematic meanings—human rights, development, labour, corporate social responsibility (CSR), the environment and anti-corruption. While certainly subjective, this list is based on today's most recurring treaty practices responding, even timidly, to pressing "societal" challenges treaty drafters and adjudicators do not yet dare to formulate in a rights and precisely human rights language. No matter their definition or absence of the same, NTC/NIC are not generally accepted.

2.2 *Between Sovereignty and Fragmentation: Justifying NTC*

States generally justify their reluctance to address NTC on the basis of two interrelated arguments: sovereignty and fragmentation.

As an example, and in reaction to the problematic increase of global trade disputes, India recently expressed its reluctance to see certain NTCs, including labour and the environment, introduced into the World Trade Organisation's purview. According to India's Commerce Secretary, developing nations are facing a double challenge when dealing with the WTO dispute settlement system: a lack of internal capacity to tackle complex technical issues such as trade remedies, and the progressive inclusion of labour and environment related decisions, settled in other fora, in the reasoning of the WTO's adjudicators.[13] This perspective is unfortunately not uncommon as it echoes other developing countries' approaches to international

---

[12]See Appellate Body Report., European Communities — Measures Prohibiting the Importation and Marketing of Seal Products, WT/DS400/AB/R (May 22, 2014) available at: https://www.wto.org/english/tratop_e/dispu_e/cases_e/ds400_e.htm. In this case, the Appellate Body upheld the Panel's finding that the EU Seal Regime is "necessary to protect public morals" within the meaning of Article XX(a) of the GATT 1994, but that the European Union had not justified the EU Seal Regime under Article XX of the GATT 1994 and in fact applied its exception in a discriminatory manner inconsistent with the GATT and the Agreement on Technical Barriers to Trade (TBT). For a synthetic perspective on the dispute, see: http://www.ictsd.org/bridges-news/biores/news/the-litmus-test-non-trade-interests-and-wto-law-after-seals; on interpreting the WTO agreements and developments in interpretation of the Article XX, see Trachtman (2014), pp. 323–327.

[13]On India's willingness and challenges to build up trade capacity, see Nedumpara (2016), pp. 33–51. See also Non trade Issues at the WTO: Lack of Capacity Worries India, The Hindu, 3 May 2016, available at http://www.thehindu.com/business/Economy/nontrade-issues-at-wto-lack-of-legal-experts-worry-india/article8548230.ece.

trade law and, at the same time, contributes to the artificial fragmentation of international law, which has characterized the past decades.[14] While developing and, to a lesser extent, emerging economies have traditionally associated their global attractiveness to a rather loose normative framework of protection for labour and the environment, hence creating a comparative advantage in trade, these disastrous views for a sound and sustainable development have been reinforced by the technicalization and strategic division of international law in many sub-disciplines eventually read in isolation to meet short term policy objectives. *Lex specialis* (specialized law), "self-contained" regimes, and regionalism have indeed been advanced as many explanations of the current international law fragmentation while, at the same time, *jus cogens*, "systemic integration" and repeated incantations to refer to the article 31 (3) (c) of the Vienna Convention of the Law of Treaties[15] (VCLT) are supposed to provide treaty drafters and judges with solutions in favour of a pluralistic and integrative vision of international law and integration of non-trade concerns in trade law.

It has been 20 years since Judge Guillaume, then President of the International Court of Justice (ICJ), stressed the issue of the "proliferation" of international law, and 15 years since the production of the International Law Commission (ILC) landmark report on "fragmentation".[16] The ILC explained, but never justified, trade law's apparent parallel existence. It actually stressed the irrelevance of "self-contained" regime:

> 191. The rationale of special regimes is the same as that of lex specialis. They take better account of the particularities of the subject-matter to which they relate; they regulate it more effectively than general law and follow closely the preferences of their members. Where the application of the general law concerning reactions to breaches (especially countermeasures) might be inappropriate or counterproductive, a self-contained regime such as, for instance, the system of persona non grata under diplomatic law, may be better suited to deal with such breaches. [...]
>
> 192. But no regime is self-contained. Even in the case of well-developed regimes, general law has at least two types of function. First, it provides the normative background that comes in to fulfil aspects of its operation not specifically provided by it. In case of dissolution of a State party to a dispute within the WTO dispute settlement system, for instance, general rules of State succession will determine the fate of any claims reciprocally made by and as against

[14]On fragmentation, see International Law Commission (2006) Fragmentation of International Law: Difficulties Arising from the Diversification and Expansion of International Law A/CN.4/L.682; as well as Petersmann (2013), pp. 921–970; See also, Choukroune (2016), pp. 179–215.

[15]Vienna Convention on the Law of Treaties, art. 31(2), May 23, 1969, 1155 U.N.T.S. 331

[16]See H.E. Judge Gilbert Guillaume, President of the International Court of Justice, Speech to the General Assembly of the United Nations (Oct. 30, 2001), available at: http://www.icj-cij.org/files/press-releases/5/2995.pdf; and ILC Analytical Study 2006, ILC Study Group on the Fragmentation of International Law. Fragmentation of International Law: Difficulties Arising from the Diversification and Expansion of International Law; Report of the Study Group of the International Law Commission, Finalized by Martti Koskenniemi. UN Doc A/CN.4/L.682; Add.1 and Corr. 1. New York: International Law Commission, 2006; and ILC Conclusions 2006. ILC, Report of the Study Group, Fragmentation of International Law: Difficulties Arising from the Diversification and Expansion of International Law: Conclusions (A/CN.4/L.702) (18 July 2006).

> the dissolved State. This report has illustrated some of the ways in which this supplementing takes place. Second, the rules of general law also come to operate if the special regime fails to function properly. Such failure might be substantive or procedural, and at least some of the avenues open to regime members in such cases are outlined in the Vienna Convention itself. Also the rules on State responsibility might be relevant in such situations.
>
> 193. Third, the term "self-contained regime" is a misnomer. No legal regime is isolated from general international law. It is doubtful whether such isolation is even possible: a regime can receive (or fail to receive) legally binding force ("validity") only by reference to (valid and binding) rules or principles outside it. In previous debates within the Commission over "self-contained regimes", "regimes" and "subsystems", there never was any assumption that they would be hermetically isolated from the general law.

And there is supposedly no "clinical isolation" as stressed by the now ritualistically cited decision of the Appellate Body: the "WTO agreement is not to be read in clinical isolation from public international law". It might well be indeed that:

> The general rule of interpretation [as set out in Article 31(1) of the Vienna Convention on the Law of Treaties] has attained the status of a rule of customary or general international law. As such, it forms part of the "customary rules of interpretation of public international law" which the Appellate Body has been directed, by Article 3(2) of the DSU, to apply in seeking to clarify the provisions of the General Agreement and the other "covered agreements" of the Marrakesh Agreement Establishing the World Trade Organization (the "WTO Agreement").[17]

However, the question is not so much about interpretation, but rather content of WTO law. When the de-coupling is intentionally embedded into the law there is not much for the adjudicator to interpret in a holistic fashion. The issue is not with interpretation but with the law itself.[18] A question is then whether these approaches would or should survive into a post-WTO environment or more likely a reformed WTO framework.

3 How to End Dystopia

Within the confines of what is meant to be a short piece, let us now sketch the basic lines for some possible avenues to end this trade law dystopia, not so much through "reconciling" opposed States' policy objectives, but rather in hierarchising ambitions. To take rights seriously indeed, one needs to take words seriously first, and depart from a pure cosmetic evocation of concepts. To achieve a genuine rights protection and produce a fair and just globalisation through trade, politics then has to be seen as an integral part of law making and implementation.[19]

[17]See Appellate Body Report, (1996) United States – Standards for Reformulated and Conventional Gasoline (US – Gasoline) at 17, DSR 1996:I 3, para. 16. (WT/DS2/AB/R).

[18]Ibid.

[19]On the reintroduction of politics to respond to fragmentation, see Koskenniemi (2007), pp. 1–30.

3.1 Take Words Seriously: Take Rights Seriously

Seventy years after the adoption of the Universal Declaration of Human Rights (UDHR), freedom, equality, democracy and the rule of law are still to be realised in most parts of the world. Across so much of the world people are fighting for their rights: the right to express freely their political opinions, the right to have access to justice, the right to be treated equally and with dignity. Despite greater corporate engagement and constructive dialogues with, for example, the UN Guiding Principles on Business and Human Rights,[20] the reality of global business and indeed trade has changed only at the margin. Human rights violations are still widespread, while new challenges are arising from globalisation backlashes, contested multilateralism and the unwillingness of world leaders to integrate rights at the core of legislation. The complete eradication of corporate abuses remains a *utopia*, but it is time to reflect upon the limitations and challenges we are all facing in advancing the human rights agenda in the trade *dystopia*.

One of these self-inflicted barriers is that of a metalanguage of poor effectiveness and complete conceptual vacuity. Without even realising it, trade lawyers as much as the human rights community, have embraced a consensual corporate language deprived of legal force. In using inappropriate and vague terms one creates unnecessary confusion on the objectives to be met. "Non-Concerns", "regulation", "right to regulate", "international rule of law", and "guidelines", among other terms, are systematically put forward but with what meaning and for what objectives? This creates a deceptive bureaucratic jargon inspired by managerial techniques leading to a voluntary and intended fragmentation of tasks aimed to dispatch authority for efficiency but creating *de facto* diminished responsibility and no accountability. It is for human being what greenwashing is for the environment. It is George Orwell's "Newspeak" supporting the most oppressive regimes, those which rely on the pauperisation of language and the ability to critically address and contest a situation. It "diminishes the range of thought." On the contrary, the language of rights is supported by the force of law. It is a powerful tool for human rights realisation. It is progressive and transformative. Taking words seriously will translate to into taking rights seriously. This may be even more so in the more fragmented world that would ensue the marginalisation of the WTO. The question is, and will be, that of the normativity of law and eventually its legitimacy.

3.2 Re-politicize Law

A WTO related interesting example of the disconnect between law and politics, stressing the need to take words and concepts seriously and so re-invest in a political

---

[20]See OHCHR (2011) UN Guiding Principles on Business and Human Rights HR/PUB/11/04 available at https://www.ohchr.org/documents/publications/guidingprinciplesbusinesshr_en.pdf.

vision of law, is the sanitised use of the term "development", an eminently political right.

The WTO Doha Development Agenda (DDA) was designed to support developing countries.[21] It commenced in 2001, at the Doha Ministerial Conference, under the Mandate of the then Director Mike Moore, with the idea of placing development at the centre of the trade negotiations.[22] In the Hong Kong Ministerial Declaration of 2005, members (re)emphasized the central importance of development to the Doha Round. The Aid for Trade Initiative was also launched to help developing countries build their supply-side capacity to expand trade.[23] At the Bali Ministerial Conference, in December 2013, a number of decisions were adopted under the developmental pillar to support least-developed countries' trade.

The provisions contained in the WTO for developing countries are known under the term "Special and Differential Treatment" (SDT). They consist in special rights allowing developed countries to treat developing countries more favourably than other WTO Members. As such, they are departures from key WTO principles such as Most Favoured Nation Treatment (MFN) or National Treatment (NT) and, indeed, the idea of reciprocity. These provisions are present throughout the WTO Agreement. In the GATT, the GATS, the TRIPS, the Agreement on Agriculture, the SPS, the TBT, etc. They have been acknowledged by the Doha Declaration as integral parts of the WTO agreements. Their wording is however vague if not ambiguous and developing countries are often not equipped to understand their potential usage and benefit. Their binding character is very much debated. For instance, the entire Part IV of the GATT includes provisions on the concept of non-reciprocal preferential treatment for developing countries but developing countries claim that Part IV is of no practical value as it does not contain any obligations for developed countries. The Committee on Trade and Development (CTD) is mandated to identify which of those special and differential treatment provisions are mandatory.

Some thus argue that these reforms are cosmetic, with the WTO failing developing countries even while the very basis of the advantages and benefits conferred to developing countries are now questioned. In 2019, the US expressed its opposition to the applications of WTO's developing country status and the possible advantages it confers. In a document entitled "An undifferentiated WTO: self-declared development status risks institutional irrelevance", the US argued as follows:

> Despite the great development strides made in the years since the WTO's inception, the WTO remains stuck in a simplistic and clearly outdated construct of "North-South" division, developed and developing countries. Each is a seemingly static set, regardless of economic, social, trade, and other indicators. This binary construct does not reflect the realities of 2019. Nor does it reflect how Members viewed development at the time the WTO was created. The

[21] See WTO at: www.wto.org/english/tratop_e/dda_e/dda_e.htm.

[22] The issue of developing countries in the WTO has fascinated international legal scholarship with a large production of books and papers. See for example, Trachtman and Chantal (2009), Shaffer and Melendez Ortiz (2010) and Alessandrini (2010).

[23] The 2019 WTO Review of Aid for Trade is available at: www.wto.org/english/tratop_e/devel_e/a4t_e/gr19_e/gr19programme_e.htm.

> preamble to the Marrakesh Agreement Establishing the World Trade Organization recognizes there are "needs and concerns at different levels of economic development," implying there could be many levels of development.
>
> (...)
>
> Self-declaration can lead to unpredictable and illogical results in the operation and implementation of existing WTO agreements. For example, Kazakhstan — ranked in UNDP's "Very High Human Development" quartile and having made no previous claim to developing Member status—claimed such status for the first time for the purposes of implementing its obligations under the Trade Facilitation Agreement. Some of the wealthiest WTO Members — including Singapore Hong Kong, China; Macao, China; Israel; the State of Kuwait; the Republic of Korea; United Arab Emirates; Brunei Darussalam; and Qatar — insist on being considered developing Members and can avail themselves of S&D provisions at their discretion – just like Sub-Saharan Africa.[24]

Unacceptable for some, and clearly targeted against China, the US document had the merit of pointing out the limits and incoherent nature of a self-declaration system in which Singapore can potentially be treated on the same basis as Ethiopia.[25] Some differentiation and categorization on the basis of UNDP or World Bank criteria introducing more complexity on the basis of per capita income, for instance, could indeed be referred to while taking into account the complexity of development.

That SDT needs to be terminated is another question but the superficial and technical character of WTO tools to address development in disconnect from its political nature and the interrogations it poses on power if not domination or imperialism is revealing.

The political approach developed in the decolonization period was to consider development as a right. The concept of the right to development has indeed informed the discussions of the international community for the past 40 years and in particular since the adoption of the UN General Assembly Resolution 41/128 on 4th December 1986. Present in the 1948 Universal Declaration of Human Rights (UDHR) already, the idea of development was meant to include more than economic growth, but it materialised with the New International Economic Order (NIEO) and decolonisation. It was indeed first recognized in 1981 in Article 22 of the African Charter on Human and People's Rights and its Article 22 (122), which provides that:

> All peoples shall have the right to their economic, social and cultural development with due regard to their freedom and identity and in the equal enjoyment of the common heritage of mankind.[26]

The right to development is now well recognized by a series of Declarations and programmes of actions for human rights and sustainable development (The Vienna Declaration and Programme of Action on Human Rights, The Rio Declaration on

---

[24]WTO (2019) An Undifferentiated WTO: Self-Declared Development Status Risks Institutional Irrelevance Communication from The United States (14 February 2019) WT/GC/W/757/Rev.1.

[25]On China's reaction, see: https://www.scmp.com/economy/china-economy/article/3020474/china-hits-back-donald-trumps-absurd-criticism-its-wto.

[26]African Charter on Human and People's Rights adopted in Nairobi June 27, 1981, entered into Force October 21, 1986.

Environment and Development, the Declaration on the Rights of Indigenous People notably). Some see the right to development as part of customary international law.

Eminently political and conceptually contested for its colonial legacy, development is not addressed by the WTO as a right but in a technical and superficial fashion only. Yet, developing countries are firmly attached to it for they feel it is a right indeed. In response to the US pressure, a group of heteroclite developing countries comprising China, India, South Africa, Venezuela, Laos, Bolivia, Kenya, Cuba and the Central African Republic have elaborated their defence of development as a right on, among other things, the basis of a quote from Thomas Jefferson "there is nothing more unequal than the equal treatment of unequal people" and argued:

> The world has indeed changed in many ways since the GATT and the establishment of the WTO, but in overall terms the development divide remains firmly entrenched. It is therefore of greater concern that some Members would attempt to ignore this reality in an effort to deprive developing Members of their right to develop.[27]

In a rigorous demonstration, they further argued that the GATT system was originally created *by* and *for* the developed world, which made sure to control the rules and amend them to its benefit. Rule makers *de facto* dominate international economic relations:

> [...] there were many instances wherein the developed Members secured exceptions and failed to adhere to even the fundamental principles of the multilateral trading system. Some of these exceptions were in place for decades, thereby undermining the rules and disciplines under the GATT/WTO. And during the Doha Round, many developed Members had secured country-specific carve-outs from rules that would have been generally applicable to them, for example country-specific carve-outs for some developed Members provided in the Draft Agriculture Modalities Text Rev.4, such as paragraphs 42 and Annex A of the Draft Modalities Text providing the United States an exception from the provision applicable for calculating product-specific limits on Blue Box, which gave the United States higher limits in product- specific support under Blue Box, particularly for corn, wheat, cotton and rice. In addition, exceptions for developed Members are also contained in the Nairobi Decision on Export Subsidies. (...). It is, thus, inaccurate and disingenuous of the United States to assert that all rules have applied only to a few (developed countries).[28]

While the world economy has progressed, the divide between the poorest and the richest is immense as inequalities are growing. These have to be measured not only on the basis of GDP or GNI, but also on per capita data for countries with immense populations like China and India, as well as on concrete access to education, health, culture, digital facilities, clean and sustainable environment, etc. More than two-thirds of WTO Members are developing countries.[29]

---

[27] WTO (2019) The Continued Relevance of Special and Differential Treatment In Favour Of Developing Members To Promote Development And Ensure Inclusiveness: Communication From China, India, South Africa, The Bolivarian Republic Of Venezuela, Lao People's Democratic Republic, Plurinational State Of Bolivia, Kenya And Cuba (26 February 2019) WT/GC/W/765.

[28] Ibid.

[29] See WTO, Who are the developing countries in the WTO? available at: www.wto.org/english/tratop_e/devel_e/d1who_e.htm.

Yet again, the inability to translate the right to development in clearly enforceable and binding norms is revealing of the true ambitions of an Organisation governed by liberalisation on the basis of norms created by and for a few. Hence the failure of the Doha round for its ambitions are contradictory and unachievable.

Now what is a political approach to international law and international trade law in particular? Whether it is based on jurisprudential currents such as Classical Realism, Third World Approaches to International Law (TWAIL), feminist approaches or the Integrated Marxist Approach to International Law (IMAIL) coined by B.S. Chimni, a political approach to international law does not artificially address "*law as it is*".[30] The political, cultural, social, philosophical or even psychological circumstances in which law is created and implemented are taken into consideration. Going even further, a political approach to law identifies objectives and creates hierarchies in ambitions. It is not about reconciling regimes, integration or systemic interpretation, it is about drafting, reading and engaging with the law as a tool to create a given type of society. It is about international law as a vehicle for a democratic and just world order. It is a disconnect with trade dystopia and its "Non-concerns" to reconnect with the United Nations *Utopia*, post-colonisation and possibly post-imperialism.

4 Conclusion

Are we soon going to be able to be less concerned with trade "Non-concerns" in a post-WTO world?

Some recent arbitral decisions in the investment context seem to timidly move towards the direction of a greater appreciation of Corporate Social Responsibility (CSR), if not entirely human rights as international law obligations, as illustrated in the *Urbaser* case (as concessionaire, Urbaser supplied water and sewerage services in the Province of Buenos Aires replacing in the context of water privatisation):

> 1195. The Tribunal may mention in this respect that international law accepts corporate social responsibility as a standard of crucial importance for companies operating in the field of international commerce. This standard includes commitments to comply with human rights in the framework of those entities' operations conducted in countries other than the country of their seat or incorporation. In light of this more recent development, it can no longer be admitted that companies operating internationally are immune from becoming subjects of international law. On the other hand, even though several initiatives undertaken at the international scene are seriously targeting corporations human rights conduct, they are not, on their own, sufficient to oblige corporations to put their policies in line with human rights law. The focus must be, therefore, on contextualizing a corporation's specific activities as they relate to the human right at issue in order to determine whether any international law obligations attach to the non-State individual.[31]

[30] See Chimni (2017).

[31] See *Urbaser S.A. and Consorcio de Aguas Bilbao Bizkaia, Bilbao Biskaia Ur Partzuergoa v. The Argentine Republic* (2016) Award ICSID Case No. ARB/07/26, para. 1195.

A solution could be to adopt a Human Rights Based Approach (HRBA), which not only encompasses essential human rights principles, but also proves an effective tool to international law reunification and coherent application from treaty drafting to dispute resolution. As applied to trade, an HRBA puts the discussion in another perspective, that of legal entitlements, rights holders can claim against the State and other non-State actors. Hence, for example, the provision of water and sanitation services to the most vulnerable and marginalized communities as in the *Urbaser* case, and many more to come including in India, is no longer a charitable act but a State's obligation to be fulfilled. Of course, one of the dangers of an HRBA could be the multiplication of rights deprived of concrete substance (the right to development as an example) and so possible application as hardly justiciable. This normative hyperactivity would prove counterproductive and so leads to the dilution of rights rather than to their fostering. However, an HRBA is not necessarily equivalent to rights inflation and eventual dilution. While HRBA re-politicizes international issues in calling for justice and equity, it can also be extremely concrete as based on a clear set of identified norms. Thus, HRBA makes rights justiciable. They can be invoked before domestic courts. There is a direct legal effect of trade treaties and a reconciliation of trade law with international law. Hence one departs from a mere superficial incorporation of poorly defined NTC to build trade around human rights. Priorities are reversed.

A post-WTO system is unlikely to take shape in today's geopolitical context. More likely we will stay in the grey area of contradictory ambitions until a new leadership emerges in North America and Europe particularly. We will see discussions on Plurilateral Agreements and other technical aspects of trade. A few more regional agreements will be negotiated but might not even come to life for they lack democratic support and their control mechanisms are in any case not as sophisticated as the flawed yet functional—if not blocked by the US—WTO. The future of the field is not really about procedural reforms of dispute settlement, the length of the Appellate Body decisions or their ambitions to "add or diminish rights", but rather should be about the content of the law and whether it reflects a just and fair approach to globalisation. Such a dramatic change in perspective would require an immense political will and a political vision of law. Yet, no matter what happens at the government levels, it is ample time for the international lawyers to re-invest the trade field with a critical mind rather than the protective gear of a hyper technicalization, which has deprived trade of its intellectual significance. None of us has chosen international law to rave about the technicalities of "zeroing".

References

Alessandrini D (2010) Developing countries and the multilateral trade regime: the failure and promise of the WTOs' development mission. Hart Publishing, Oxford

Boisson de Chazournes L (2016) WTO and non-trade issues: inside/outside WTO. J Int Econ Law 19(2):379–381

Boisson de Chazournes L (2017) Environmental protection and investment arbitration: Yin and Yang? ACDI - Anuario Colombiano de Derecho Internacional 10:371

Chimni BS (2017) International law and world order, a critique of contemporary approaches. Cambridge University Press, Cambridge

Choukroune L (2016) Human rights in international investment disputes: global litigation as international law re-unifier. In: Choukroune L (ed) Judging the state in international trade and investment law. Springer, Singapore, pp 179–215

Koskenniemi M (2007) The fate of public international law: between technique and politics. Mod Law Rev 70:1

Nedumpara J (2016) WTO, state, and legal capacity building: an Indian narrative. In: Choukroune L (ed) Judging the state in international trade and investment law. Springer, Singapore, pp 33–51

Petersmann EU (2013) Methodological pluralism and its critics in international economic law research. J Int Econ 15(4):921–970

Piketty T (2014) Capital in the twenty first century. Harvard University Press, Cambridge, p 696

Piketty T (2020) Capital and ideology. Harvard University Press, Cambridge

Rodrik D (2011) The globalization paradox, why global markets, states and democracy can't coexist. Oxford University Press, Oxford

Shaffer GC, Melendez Ortiz R (eds) (2010) Dispute settlement at the WTO: the developing country experience. Cambridge University Press, Cambridge

Stiglitz J (2007) Making globalization work, the next steps to global justice, p xiv

Trachtman J (2014) The WTO Seal Products Case: doctrinal and normative confusion. AJIL Unbound 108:323–327

Trachtman JP, Chantal T (eds) (2009) Developing countries in the WTO legal system. Oxford University Press, Oxford

The Rise of Import Substitution Subsidies and Local Content Requirements in a Dystopian WTO 2.0 Regime

James J. Nedumpara and Akshaya Venkataraman

Contents

1 Introduction

2020 is a decisive year for the future of the World Trade Organization (WTO). The non-appointment of new members to the Appellate Body has created an unprecedented crisis within the WTO. While the Uruguay round agreements of the WTO provide strict regulations across a range of disciplines in international trade, without the Appellate Body, the obligations are effectively toothless and unenforceable. As this crisis is unfolding, the WTO Members have the freedom to "appeal to the void"[1] to avoid compliance with their trade commitments. The opportunity of breaching

Respectively Professor and Head; and Senior Research Fellow at the Centre for Trade and Investment Law, Indian Institute of Foreign Trade. All views are personal.

[1]Pauwelyn (2019), pp. 297–321.

J. J. Nedumpara (✉) · A. Venkataraman
Centre for Trade and Investment Law, Indian Institute of Foreign Trade, New Delhi, India
e-mail: headctil@iift.edu; akshaya.ctil@iift.edu

M. K. Lewis et al. (eds.), *A Post-WTO International Legal Order*,
https://doi.org/10.1007/978-3-030-45428-9_13

WTO Agreements at will is bound to give way to a dystopian future of trade, where governments would be free to impose protectionist and trade distortive measures. In this context, this chapter examines the consequences of WTO Members resorting to trade distorting "local sourcing" or local content requirements (LCRs), under the guise of encouraging domestic production.

LCRs have a long history of being one of the most restrictive and trade distorting trade policy tools. As early as the 1920s, Canada had imposed LCRs which granted tariff reductions to manufacturers of automobile parts, who procured at least 50% of their inputs from local sources.[2] Australia, in the mid-1930s implemented an FDI policy which required utilisation of locally manufactured inputs.[3] Between the 1950s and the 1960s, Chile, Brazil and Argentina had promoted LCRs in the manufacture of commercial automobiles.[4] In the 1970s, the contracting parties of the Andean Pact implemented regional import substitution policies, and Norway implemented LCRs in the oil and gas industry.[5] In the 1980–1990s, Canada, Philippines, Thailand, India, Malaysia and China all imposed varying types of LCRs in the automobile industry.[6]

Notably, in 1984, a complaint by the United States under GATT 1947 led to the establishment of a GATT panel, widely known as the "Canada –FIRA dispute".[7] The GATT Panel held the LCRs imposed by Canada in the automobile industry as GATT inconsistent, especially with non-discrimination principles.[8] It is important to note that the GATT did not have specific provisions on LCRs, other than the broad principles of national treatment and the general prohibition on quantitative restrictions.

There is extensive literature on the economic impact of LCRs.[9] Some scholars argue that LCRs could potentially benefit sunrise industries and help mitigate the lack of economic incentives for technology driven industries such as renewables.[10] In other words, LCRs serve as a "lubricant" by generating local employment and

[2]WTO Council for Trade in Goods (2002) *TRIMs and Other Performance Requirements—Joint Study by the WTO and UNCTAD Secretariats, Part II, Addendum*, G/C/W/307/Add.1 para 9.

[3]Ibid., para 7.

[4]Ibid., paras 10, 8, 6.

[5]Ibid., para 4.

[6]Ibid., paras 21, 23, 14, 43, 11, 5–25.

[7]*Canada—Administration of the Foreign Investment Review Act*, Report of the panel, L/5504 (7 February 1984).

[8]Ibid., pp. 17–19.

[9]Hufbauer et al. (2013), p. 7. See also for instance Grossman (1981), p. 548; Kuntze JC, Moerenhout T (2013) Local Content Requirements and the Renewable Energy Industry – A Good Match? International Centre for Trade and Sustainable Development. ISSN 2225-6679.

Rivers N, Wigle R (2011) Domestic Content Requirement and Renewable Energy Legislation. Social Science Research Network; Krishna and Itoh (1988), pp. 107–125; Mussa M (1981) The Economics of Content Protection. National Bureau of Economic Research Working Paper No. 1457.

[10]Examined in Section III of this paper in more detail. See also, Shadikhodjaev (2018), pp. 147–193.

community development for harnessing the much needed governmental involvement in sectors where private sector participation is sub-optimal. There are good political economy reasons for LCRs, however, their economic impact is not as clearly visible and demonstrable as often claimed.[11]

1.1 The Economic Effects of LCRs

The economic impact of LCRs on domestic industry and the manner in which they have proliferated globally have often been the subject matter of detailed studies. In the early 1980s, Gene Grossman examined the economic effect of LCRs or what he called "domestic content protection and content preference policies".[12] Grossman's study found that domestic content protection policies have a long and continuing history of application, especially in semi-industrialised economies. Grossman concluded that content protection policies, despite their continued use, do not evidence a clear and measurable form of protection to the domestic industry; furthermore, it was even harder to assess the degree of protection. The apparent reasons were that the specific 'price effects' of LCRs would depend largely on other factors such as input substitution and market structures.[13] A subsequent study by Michael Mussa examined the impact of LCRs on a monopolistic industry.[14] The study confirmed that LCRs create distortions in productions and result in reduced incentives for growth in technical efficiency. The WTO and the UNCTAD conducted a joint study in 2002 on trade related investment measures.[15] The joint study notes that the "dynamic effects of an LCR on trade are . . . speculative."[16] The study notes that the long-term benefit of LCR measures would depend on the domestic producers who benefit from the market guaranteed by LCRs and whether they mature to become competitive at world market prices. In the absence of this, the study notes that LCRs could pose a risk of the entire domestic industry remaining uncompetitive.[17]

Most of the studies on LCRs confirm that LCRs do not necessarily contribute to fostering of domestic industry but may still have adverse impact on foreign goods. Importantly, the effectiveness of LCRs depend on a number of variables, such as market size and stability, restrictiveness of the measure, percentage of required domestic content, measures to additionally boost the domestic industry (for instance in the form of financial support) and the knowledge base and know-how of the

[11] Hufbauer et al. (2013), p. 8.

[12] Grossman (1981).

[13] Ibid, p. 602.

[14] Mussa (1981).

[15] WTO Council for Trade in Goods (2002) TRIMs and Other Performance Requirements – Joint Study by the WTO and UNCTAD Secretariats, Part II, Addendum. G/C/W/307/Add.1.

[16] Ibid, p. 64.

[17] Ibid, p. 64.

domestic industry which will substitute the foreign product as a result of the LCR measure.[18] A 2013 study by the Peterson Institute for International Economics ("Peterson Institute" or "PIIE") on LCRs also affirmed the view that the effectiveness of the LCRs depends on how additional incentives and policies are combined with LCR measures.[19]

Be that as it may, during the Uruguay round negotiations on the Agreement on Trade Related Investment Measures (TRIMS), developed countries such as the US, Japan and Switzerland sought a prohibition of all trade-related investment measures which were inconsistent with GATT or had an adverse trade impact.[20] Developing countries on the other hand argued that certain investment restrictions, for example performance requirements, were intended to 'channel foreign investment according to national development policy objectives' and thus could not be outrightly prohibited.[21] Nevertheless, the final text of the TRIMS Agreement provided very limited possibilities for the continued use of TRIMS. The WTO provides a strict three-pronged restriction on LCRs in trade in goods, set out in the General Agreement on Tariffs and Trade (GATT),[22] the Agreement on Subsidies and Countervailing Measures (SCM)[23] and the TRIMS.[24]

This proliferation of LCRs indicates that despite strict and binding WTO rules, WTO Members are not refraining from the use of LCRs. For example, the WTO panels and the Appellate Body have taken a tough position on LCRs. Cases such as *Brazil—Taxation*,[25] *Indonesia—Autos*,[26] *Canada—Autos*,[27] *India—Solar Cells*,[28]

---

[18]Kuntze and Moerenhout (2013), pp. 11–12.

[19]Hufbauer et al. (2013), p. 12.

[20]WTO Negotiating Group on Trade-Related Investment Measures (1987) Multilateral Trade Negotiations – the Uruguay Round Note by the Secretariat. MTN.GNG/NG12/3.3. ['TRIMS Negotiation Group'].

[21]TRIMS Negotiation Group (1987) MTN.GNG/NG12/2.

[22]General Agreement on Tariffs and Trade 1994, Marrakesh Agreement Establishing the World Trade Organization, Annex 1A. 15 April 1994. 1867 U.N.T.S. 187, 33 I.L.M. 1153 ['GATT 1994'].

[23]Agreement on Subsidies and Countervailing Measures, Marrakesh Agreement Establishing the World Trade Organization, Annex 1A. 15 April 15 1994. 1869 U.N.T.S. 14. ['SCM agreement'].

[24]Agreement on Trade-Related Investment Measures, Marrakesh Agreement Establishing the World Trade Organization, Annex 1A. 15 April 1994. 1868 U.N.T.S. 186 ['TRIMS Agreement'].

[25]*Brazil—Certain Measures Concerning Taxation and Charges*, -Report of the Appellate Body 11 January 2019, WT/DS472/AB/R. [*'Brazil—Taxation'*].

[26]*Indonesia—Certain Measures Affecting the Automobile Industry*, Report of the Panel,2 July 1998, WT/DS55/R, [*'Indonesia—Autos'*].

[27]*Canada—Certain Measures Affecting the Automotive Industry*, Report of the Appellate Body, 31 May 2000 WT/DS139/AB/R; WT/DS142/AB/R, [*'Canada—Autos'*].

[28]*India—Certain Measures Relating to Solar Cells and Solar Modules*, Report of the Panel, 16 September 2016, WT/DS456/R, [*'India—Solar Cells'*].

India—Autos[29] and *US—Renewable Energy*[30] demonstrate this approach. Again, in a string of cases in the last few years, WTO panels and the Appellate Body have sent a strong message by denouncing TRIMS adopted ostensibly for promoting global public goods such as encouraging renewable sources of energy and bridging the digital divide.[31] A collapse of the Appellate Body, coupled with the already booming use of LCRs in countries, will thus result in a return to the old and discredited import-substitution led industrial policies of the past. With this background, Sect. 2 of this chapter, examines the typology and characteristics of TRIMS. Section 3 maps the growth of LCRs around the world and examines such measures in the light of the existing WTO rules and jurisprudence. Section 4 sets out a comparative analysis of the framework governing LCRs under the WTO Rules on the one hand and the treatment of TRIMS under the RTAs and BITs on the other.

2 LCRs: Typology and Characteristics

LCRs take many different forms and can target multiple policy areas, including, for example, investment, trade and tax regulations or government procurement policies. Each of these types of LCR measures targets slightly variant policy goals. A report by Peterson Institute has classified LCRs broadly into six categories.[32] LCRs that act as a condition to participate in public tenders and access the local procurement market are categorised as *Public Procurement LCRs*. On the other hand, *Investment sector LCRs* typically operate as a precondition for the investment to occur i.e. joint stock requirement. *Market access LCRs* set conditions for preferential market access in terms of reduced tariffs, import licensing schemes, etc. *Business operations and financial support LCRs* encompass preferential financing schemes and tax schemes based on the use of local goods and services and the finance of production of capital goods destined for exports. *Export related LCRs* stipulate export promotion preferences based on the use of local inputs, thereby generating additional trade rather than restricting trade.[33] LCRs form a part of the larger group of measures that are typically referred to as performance requirements or localisation requirements.

While these are the broad types of LCRs that are typically implemented, it is relevant to note that the level of sophistication of LCRs has constantly been

---

[29] *India—Measure Affecting the Automotive Sector*, Report of the Appellate Body, 19 March 2002 WT/DS146/AB/R, ['*India—Autos*'].

[30] *United States—Certain Measures Relating to the Renewable Energy Sector*, Report of the Panel, 27 June 2019, WT/DS510/R, ['*US—Renewable Energy*'].

[31] See, *Canada—Certain Measures Affecting the Renewable Energy Generation Sector*, Report of the Appellate Body, 06 May 2013, WT/DS412/R, ['*Canada—Renewable Energy*']; Panel Report, *India—Solar Cells*; Appellate Body Report, *Brazil—Taxation;* etc.

[32] Cimino et al. (2014), Policy Brief: PB14-6.

[33] Ibid.

evolving.[34] In view of the flexible nature of their design and structure, LCRs can be implemented for virtually any sector, and any good or service.[35]

3 Rise in LCRs Globally

Despite these persistent criticisms, LCRs continue to find favour with governments. The two most often made arguments in favour of LCRs are that they allow for protection of infant industries and contributes to job creation. A report by European Centre for International Political Economy (ECIPE) notes that "by imposing LCRs governments might try to promote general political goals like maintaining or improving the domestic employment, attracting FDI and companies from high-value added and R&D intense industries, and increasing the access to foreign technology."[36] A report by the OECD on countries that implemented LCR measures post the 2008 financial crisis notes that job-creation is a common short-term reason for employing LCRs in an industry.

Particularly in the context of the renewable energy sector, there is a view, rather an impressionistic view, that by requiring firms to use certain percentage of local inputs, demands for clean industries will increase, spurring green job creation in the short term.[37] More particularly in the renewable energy sector, which is a technology intensive sector, LCRs may facilitate transfer of technology to the domestic industry given that businesses which are forced to utilise local products may transfer technology to sustain the quality of the end-product.[38] Another argument made in favour of increasing LCRs in the renewable energy sector is that more LCRs are likely to increase the number of new businesses and players in the global market with the requisite capabilities, which in turn will lead to lowering of 'green technology costs' and increasing transfer of green energy technology.[39]

LCRs also appear to generate political visibility for measures aimed at increasing employment rates and fostering sunrise industries. In an environment of increasing protectionist economic policies around the world,[40] LCRs may prove to be a handy

---

[34]Deringer H et al. (2020) The Economic Impact of Local Content Requirements: A Case Study of Heavy Vehicles, 4. Ecipe.org. https://ecipe.org/publications/the-economic-impact-of-local-content-requirements/.

[35]United Nations Conference on Trade and Development (2014) Local Content Requirements and the Green Economy United Nations Publication (2014) UNCTAD/DITC/TED/2013/7, 4. https://unctad.org/en/PublicationsLibrary/ditcted2013d7_en.pdf.

[36]Deringer et al. (2020), p. 8.

[37]Farrell (2011), p. 8.

[38]Lewis and Wiser (2005).

[39]Kuntze and Moerenhout (2013), p. 6.

[40]Gunnella V, Quaglietti L (2019) The Economic Implications of Rising Protectionism: A Euro Area and Global Perspective. Issue 3, ECB Economic Bulletin https://www.ecb.europa.eu/pub/economic-bulletin/articles/2019/html/ecb.ebart201903_01~e589a502e5.en.html#toc1.

tool for governments looking to promote domestic industry in the short run. The growing populist political climate of countries has also impacted the economic policies, be it the UK's decision to exit the European Union, Turkey's growing emphasis on protectionist trade policies, the long-continuing trade war between the United States and China or the "make-local" policies of several governments.

Subsequent to the 2008 economic crisis, LCR measures once again came to the forefront of government policy making in a number of countries.[41] The OECD estimates that between 2008 and 2014, more than 146 localisation measures had been implemented by nearly 40 countries and economies in response to the 2008 financial crisis.[42] The report notes that nearly 67% of the LCRs implemented in the period between 2008 and 2014 were in countries with employment rates over 6%. The percentage of LCRs implemented, the report notes, increased to nearly 80% if LCRs specifically targeted at industrial inputs are examined.[43] The OECD report further states that the countries which implemented LCRs in this period accounted for approximately 52% of exports globally.[44]

The Peterson Institute's study, referred to earlier, noted that quantifiable LCRs, taken together, affected more than $373 billion in goods and services trade flow in 2010 alone. This survey identified 117 LCR measures imposed by countries since 2008.[45] A paper published in 2018 by the ECIPE notes that despite the existence of binding WTO rules, LCRs "have quietly returned and been transformed into new types that are always one step ahead [of] the trade regulation framework."[46]

Despite the difficulty in capturing LCRs implemented by various provincial and local government agencies, a database maintained by *Global Trade Alert*, provide some rough statistics on LCRs. According to *Global Trade Alert*, the countries which utilise LCRs most prominently are Argentina, Brazil, China, India, Indonesia, Russia, Saudi Arabia, and the US (Fig. 1).[47]

With the evolution of the renewable energy sector and the growing focus on "green development", LCRs have found a central role in the policies of many governments. Kuntze and Moerenhut in their 2013 study of LCRs note that China, the Canadian provinces of Ontario and Quebec, Spain, Brazil, Turkey and South Africa have adopted requirements of 30–70% local content in the wind energy industry.[48] These LCRs are implemented as either conditions of subsidisation or as

[41] Shadikhodjaev (2018), pp. 147–193.

[42] Trade and Agriculture Directorate (2015).

[43] Ibid., p. 17.

[44] Ibid., p. 18.

[45] Hufbauer et al. (2013), p. 37.

[46] Deringer et al. (2020), p. 8.

[47] For instance, the latest Trade Policy Review Report for Saudi Arabia notes that the Saudi Export Programme provides export financing and guarantees to exports with at least 25% local value added—WTO, *Trade Policy Review—Kingdom of Saudi Arabia,* Report of the Secretariat, 29 February 2016, WT/TPR/S/333.

[48] Kuntze and Moerenhout (2013), Table 5, p. 30.

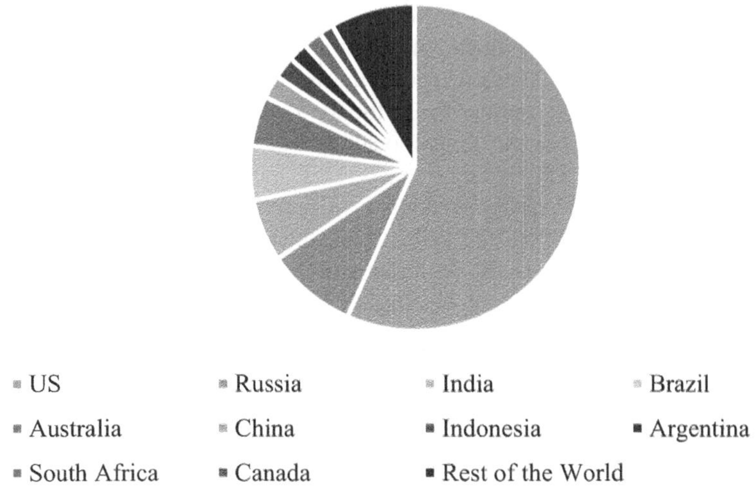

Fig. 1 Countries imposing LCR. Source: Global Trade Alert Database, WTO Documents Online

part of tender requirements or, most commonly, as part of feed-in tariff requirements.[49] Similarly, Italy, France, Turkey, India and the US have LCRs in the solar energy sector.[50] These are only a few examples of countries which use LCRs as a tool of green industrial development.

There are reports that Argentina has set progressive local content requirements that 35% of renewable energy equipment and related services must be sourced domestically by 2020.[51] Brazil, known for its import substitution policies, continues to employ LCRs in certain industries, even though percentages of LCRs have reduced over time. In 2017, the Brazilian National Petroleum Agency announced revised local content rules in the exploration and production phases of oil and natural gas projects of 50% in onshore projects and 18% in offshore projects.[52] Brazil also employs LCRs in the broadcasting and telecommunication sector.[53] Without enforceable WTO rules, there is no effective check on the impulse to take similar industrial measures which have an adverse effect on trade.

These growing trends are not just applicable to the renewable industry sector. In the most recent meeting of the WTO TRIMS Committee held on the 6 June 2019,

---

[49]Ibid., p. 30.

[50]Ibid., p. 30.

[51]Spatuzza A (2017) Argentina sets 35% renewable energy local-content by 2020. Recharge News. https://www.rechargenews.com/transition/argentina-sets-35-renewable-energy-local-content-by-2020/2-1-178926.

[52]'Brazil: Recent Oil and gas Reforms. 2019. US Commercial Service. https://www.export.gov/article?id=Brazil-Recent-Changes-to-Brazil-s-Oil-Gas-Sector-May-Attract-More-Business-Opportunities.

[53]WTO *Trade Policy Review—Brazil*, Report by the Secretariat, 12 June 2017, WT/TPR/S/358, 26 & Table 2.3 at 2.35.

issues concerning LCRs implemented by certain Members were discussed.[54] Specifically, the US, EU and Japan highlighted concerns with respect to China's LCRs on goods related to cybersecurity measures and procurement of technology.[55] The US, EU, Japan, Chinese Taipei and Switzerland have also pointed to measures which are in place in Indonesia, spanning across the energy, industry, agricultural, pharmaceutical and retail sectors and the varying types and percentages of LCRs imposed in such sectors.[56] Russia's legislation on fisheries (which provides subsidies in the form of fishing quotas to companies using Russian ships) and Argentina's legislations granting fiscal incentives to companies using Argentinian auto-parts were also questioned in this meeting.[57] As noted previously, in April 2019, the European Union sought a request for consultation with Turkey on the grounds that Turkey had implemented prohibited LCRs in its pharmaceutical industry, along with other trade restrictive investment measures.[58] A Panel to review the dispute was established in September 2019.[59] Even if a WTO Panel were to adjudicate in favour of the EU, it remains to be seen how such a panel report will be adopted to ensure Turkey's compliance, without an effective Appellate Body.

A few years ago, India announced 'Make in India' as one of its driving economic goals. 'Make in India' is an initiative aimed at promoting manufacturing and production domestically.[60] The initiative has, however, only resulted in local content requirement policies applicable within government procurement schemes (which are currently permitted within the WTO regime).[61]

---

[54]WTO, Committee on Trade-Related Investment Measures, 06 June 2019, *Minutes of the Meeting* G/TRIMS/M/46, pp. 1–5.

[55]Ibid.

[56]Ibid., pp. 8–28.

[57]Ibid., pp. 37–44.

[58]The European Union has alleged that the measures implemented by Turkey force 'foreign producers of pharmaceuticals' to locate their production activities domestically to avail social security reimbursement schemes available to medicines in the Turkish healthcare system. Since this social security reimbursement scheme includes the majority of medicinal products consumed in Turkey, the EU has argued that the exclusion of the foreign pharmaceutical companies creates an 'anti-competitive barrier' vis-à-vis domestic Turkish manufacturers of pharmaceuticals.

[59]*Turkey—Certain Measures concerning the Production, Importation and Marketing of Pharmaceutical Products*, Request for Consultation. WT/DS583/1 (2 April 2019) https://www.wto.org/english/tratop_e/dispu_e/cases_e/ds583_e.htm.

[60]Department of Industrial Policy and Promotion, Ministry of Commerce and Industry (2017) Public Procurement (Preference to Make in India), Order 17 (P-45021/2/2017-B.E.-II, 2017); See also—Press Trust of India. 2018. Government mandates preference to India-made vehicles in public procurement. Economic Times. https://economictimes.indiatimes.com/news/economy/policy/government-mandates-preference-to-india-made-vehicles-in-public-procurement/articleshow/67009970.cms?from=mdr. Press Trust of India (2018) Providing Local Content percentage made mandatory for Railway procurement process. Economic Times. https://economictimes.indiatimes.com/industry/transportation/railways/providing-local-content-percentage-made-mandatory-for-railways-procurement-process/articleshow/62579507.cms?from=mdr.

[61]Ibid.

Despite the lack of conclusive evidence on the positive effect of LCRs, they have made a significant comeback in the past decade, even with a strict regime led by the WTO. Given how extensively LCRs have been used in the past to protect and grow the domestic industry, it appears that the utilisation of LCRs is likely to rise manifold in the near future without an effective WTO.

4 Taming LCRs: A Comparison of Frameworks

4.1 The Existing WTO Framework Regulating LCRs

The WTO Agreements provide a strong framework for disciplining LCRs. LCRs in the trade of goods is subjected to restrictions set out in the GATT, the SCM and the TRIMS. The General Agreement on Trade in Services (GATS) sets out restrictions on LCRs in trade in services. As early as in 1997, LCRs imposed by Indonesia in its auto industry were challenged before the WTO.[62] Article III of the GATT which sets out the principle of 'national treatment' is designed "to avoid protectionism in the application of internal tax and regulatory measures."[63] Article III prohibits a WTO Member from according less favourable treatment to imported products as compared to like products of national original in respect of all laws, regulations and requirements affecting internal trade[64] and specifically prohibits the imposition of any quantitative regulation, which requires the utilisation of 'local products' in a specified amount or proportion.[65] The TRIMS Agreement prohibits investment measures that conflict with Articles III or XI of the GATT. Investment measures that set out or prescribe LCRs are inherently considered as trade-related and thus prohibited, as they "always favour the use of domestic products over imported products, and therefore affect trade."[66] The SCM Agreement prohibits a specific kind of LCR measure. Article 3.1(b) read with Article 3.2 of the ASCM prohibits 'import substitution subsidies' i.e. subsidies which are contingent on the use of domestic over imported goods and includes *de jure* as well as *de facto* subsidies.[67]

The disputes brought before the WTO DSB which concern LCRs have all thrown up new interpretative challenges, as the interplay between various WTO agreements has been a novel issue.[68] Annexure 1 of this Chapter identifies some of the key WTO

[62] *Indonesia—Autos*, Panel Report.

[63] See *Japan—Taxes on Alcoholic Beverages*, Report of the Appellate Body, 4 October 1996, WT/DS8/R, ['*Japan—Alcoholic Beverages II*'] p. 16.

[64] See Article III:4, GATT 1994.

[65] See Article III:5, GATT 1994.

[66] Panel Report, *Indonesia—Autos*, para 14.82.

[67] Appellate Body Report, *Canada—Autos*, paras 140–143.

[68] LCRs are often implemented in conjunction with subsidies granted by the state, or as a part of government procurement which lead to questions on the interplay of the WTO Agreements.

disputes or consultations which relate to LCRs in goods. A measure, for instance, could incentivise the use of domestic content but may not fall within the definition of 'subsidies' and thus would be permitted within the WTO regime.[69] In another instance, purchase of electricity by government only from solar power developers who used domestically manufactured solar cells/and or modules, would not fall within the 'government procurement' exception of Article III:8 since the discriminated product was solar cell or modules and the product 'procured by the government' was electricity.[70] Such cases indicate, that despite the expansive restriction on LCRs under the WTO Agreements, the design, structure and the architecture of the LCR measure would determine its potential WTO consistency or inconsistency.

The WTO Agreements undeniably provide the strictest regime on LCRs.[71] As a result of the findings of Appellate Body or the Panel, Members have almost completely discontinued or revoked LCR measures that were challenged.[72] Given the nature of remedies available in WTO, which are prospective rather than retrospective, it is possible that Members have taken LCRs only for short duration. But most respondent Members have complied with the DSB rulings.

It is also possible that detecting LCRs is not often straightforward as governments camouflage LCR schemes in innocuous looking programmes.[73] For example, the *Buy America* programme of the US was extended to projects under the Water Development Act, 2013 under which certain eligible projects could avail loans and loan guarantees from federal agencies if they used US produced iron, steel and manufactured goods.[74] Similarly, in 2012–2013, it was reported that China encouraged companies using local produced inputs by linking the obtaining of approvals with such LCR policies.[75]

It is, thus, not surprising that despite this trinity of agreements curtailing local content measures, such measures have spread over the past two decades.[76] Furthermore, many Members of the WTO may refrain from disputing LCR measures at the DSB partly because it can be expensive to bring cases through dispute settlement

[69]See Appellate Body Report, *Canada—Renewable Energy.*

[70]See Panel Report, *India—Solar Cells.*

[71]See Annex 1 for the list of WTO disputes dealing primarily with LCRs.

[72]For example, India notified the WTO on 14 December 2017 that it had withdrawn the LCRs under the Jawaharlal Nehru National Solar Mission which were found as WTO inconsistent in *India—Solar Cells.*

[73]For example, in *Brazil—Taxation,* the incentive schemes granted benefits only to 'accredited' companies. Accreditation required localisation of business or sourcing of local goods. Each of the incentive schemes and the underlying rules had to be individually examined to establish that there was indirect LCR for availing the benefit of the incentives.

[74]European Commission Directorate-General for Trade (2013) Eleventh Report on Potentially Trade Restrictive Measures, 27. https://trade.ec.europa.eu/doclib/docs/2014/november/tradoc_152872.pdf.

[75]Nedumpara and Raturi (2013), p. 13.

[76]Santos (2012), pp. 551–632.

procedures. In addition, many Members may have similar policies back home.[77] Interestingly, when the US challenged India's domestic content requirements on solar cells and modules in 2013, India challenged various local renewable energy subsidy measures in the US without delay. Further, in the vast majority of cases, when investment incentives are coupled with LCRs, complaints do not materialize, as the multinational firms receiving the incentives typically prefer to receive the benefit and comply with the LCR regime rather than bringing up the matter to the notice of their respective governments. Moreover, some governments do not consistently publish their performance requirements and instead reach a private understanding with the firm. Countries continue to implement LCRs not only in connection with their investment incentives but also in new forms. Certain types of LCRs—namely, LCRs relating to technology transfer, intellectual property licensing, and localization of data centres—have become increasingly popular and a possible "escape route" from the disciplines under TRIMS.[78]

Despite these shortcomings, the WTO Covered Agreements have still been more effective than any other alternative regime on LCRs. In particular, the illustrative list of the TRIMS, which was negotiated with the intention of expanding the GATT, removes some of the ambiguities associated with identifying LCRs.[79] A commentary on the Punta del Este declaration[80] and the negotiation of the Uruguay Round states that:

> [o]ne reason for [the] resistance [to TRIMS negotiations] is that TRIMS (at least if construed broadly), along with other new issues on the Uruguay Round agenda, expand the scope of the GATT system beyond its traditional jurisdiction. These new issues potentially involve a significant expansion of the scope of activities governed by the basic principles (non-discrimination, open markets, fair trade) that inform the GATT and its agreements. Instead of regulating trade at the borders of each member country in the form of tariff reductions and other agreements, a multilateral agreement on [trade related investment measures] would widen the scope of the GATT framework beyond "border measures". This new level of regulatory oversight of domestic trade through GATT standards restricts the prerogatives of national and (local) government in the regulation of trade policy.[81]

In the absence of an enforcement mechanism for the WTO Agreements and its jurisprudence on LCRs, governments seeking to implement import substitution trade policies will have unfettered ability to impose mandatory LCRs across sectors. As noted by Louis Henkin, "International law aims at nations which are in principle law-abiding but which might be tempted to commit a violation if there were no threat of undesirable consequences."[82] Hitherto, taking into consideration the potential

---

[77]Cimino et al. (2014).

[78]Ibid.

[79]Fennell and Abellard (1993), p. 2002.

[80]Ministerial Declaration (1986) General Agreement on Trade and Tariffs Punta Del Este Declaration. http://www.sice.oas.org/trade/Punta_e.asp.

[81]Fennel and Abellard (1993), p. 2003.

[82]Henkin (1979), pp. 320–321.

challenges, governments used to phase out or modify LCRs over shorter periods of time. In the absence of a binding WTO system, Members will be free to impose LCRs indiscreetly. Member states will be free to impose LCRs without any explicit or implied sunset clauses.

4.2 The Framework Regulating LCRs Under BITs and RTA

In the absence of enforceable WTO Agreements, trade between countries will effectively be governed by regional and mega-regional trade agreements. However, RTAs do not provide a sufficiently strong protection against LCR measures. In fact, many have argued that RTAs may in fact indirectly have the effect of localising multi-stage production. 'Rules of Origin' clauses, common in most RTAs, make 'only qualifying originating goods – typically, goods produced with substantial domestic or regional content – eligible for preferential treatment.'[83] RTAs thus often act as a form of 'regional local content requirements'.

It is relevant to note that there appears to be a paucity of information on the total number of RTAs in force and how many of them contain prohibitions on LCRs in trade in goods. However, studies conducted on investment chapters of PTAs and the performance requirements they contain provide some indication. A WTO Staff Working Paper which studies a set of 230 RTAs notes that 111 RTAs out of the 230 contain certain disciplines on investment. Of the 111, the study notes that 70% contain restrictions on performance requirements.[84] However, it is important to make a distinction here between LCRs applicable to the trade in goods sector which are prohibited under the TRIMS and LCRs which appear as conditionalities for investment. As noted previously, there is a lack of conclusive evidence on the number of RTAs which contain prohibitions on LCRs in the trade of goods. Without a cohesive set of prohibitions on LCRs in goods applicable across the board, it is difficult to claim that the framework of RTAs will achieve the same level regulation as in the TRIMS or the SCM.

Moreover, dispute resolution under RTAs is not considered very effective. McDougall notes that "there is very little dispute settlement activity under traditional RTAs" which focus on economic relations (economic integration agreements like the EU and Andean Community being an exception to this).[85] McDougall identifies

[83]Shadikhodjaev (2018), pp. 147–193.

[84]Crawford JA, Kotschwar B (2018) Investment Provisions in Preferential Trade Agreements: Evolution and Current Trends. Staff working Paper ERSD-2018-14. 18–19 & Fig 3. https://www.semanticscholar.org/paper/Investment-provisions-in-preferential-trade-and-Crawford-Kotschwar/.

[85]McDougall R (2018) Regional Trade Agreement Dispute Settlement Mechanisms: Modes Challenges and Options for Effective Dispute Resolution. International Centre for Trade and Sustainable Development (ICTSD). 7. http://e15initiative.org/wp-content/uploads/2015/09/Regional-Dispute-Settlement-Mechanisms-Robert-McDougall-RTA-Exchange-Final.pdf.

that lack of information regarding disputes, appointment of adjudicators, lack of a body of case law or informal precedent, and the lack of institutional support as some of the possible reasons for the lack dispute settlement activity under RTAs.[86] The effectiveness of the provisions in RTAs restricting LCRs is dependent on how dispute settlement mechanisms under these RTAs would fare in the absence of the WTO Appellate Body.

Restrictions on LCRs which are set out in investment chapters of RTAs fare slightly differently. As previously noted, the WTO Staff Working Paper points out the presence of performance requirements in almost 70% of the PTAs examined.[87] The trends identified by this study indicate that none of the PTAs entered into by the EU and Central Asia countries as of 2017 contained provisions restricting performance requirements, and only about 50% of the PTAs entered into by South Asia, Middle East and North African countries contained prohibitions on performance requirements. On the contrary, all the PTAs entered into by North American countries and over 75% of the PTAs entered into by East Asia and Latin American countries contained restrictions on performance requirements.[88]

Nevertheless, the scope of these prohibitions on performance requirements is set out in the investment chapters and is typically applicable to foreign investment as opposed to trade in goods. Therefore, without the Appellate Body, there is no clear, equally effective and enforceable alternative to the GATT, TRIMS or the SCM.

In a similar vein to investment chapters in PTAs, a few Bilateral Investment Treaties (BITs) also contain provisions with restrictions in investment. Most new generation BITs are generally silent on performance requirements, i.e. they make no express reference either to restrictions under the TRIMS or restrict LCRs through other express provisions.[89] A memorandum published by TradeLab, Geneva, in 2019, corroborates these findings, and notes that investment treaties between developing countries, particularly those concluded after 2013, are silent on addressing performance requirements.[90]

Some investment agreements incorporate the TRIMS agreement by affirmation or explicit reference.[91] Some international Investment Agreements (IIAs) which incorporate the TRIMS and as a consequence prohibit LCRs includes the Canadian—Costa Rica Bit of 1998, the Canada—Kuwait BIT of 2011, the China—Canada BIT

[86]Crawford and Kotschwar (2018), p. 11.

[87]Ibid., p. 18 [Figure 3].

[88]Ibid., p. 35 [Table 2].

[89]Nikièma SH (2014) Performance Requirements in Investment Treaties, Best Practices Series International Institute for Sustainable Development, p. 7.

[90]Yuerong AK et al. (2019) Prohibitions on Performance Requirements in Investment Treaties' TradeLabs. https://www.tradelab.org/single-post/2019/01/23/Prohibitions-on-Performance-Requirements-in-Investment-Treaties.

[91]Ibid., para 68.

of 2012, ASEAN-Korea Investment Agreement of 2009, and the ASEAN Comprehensive Investment Agreement.[92]

The memorandum notes that agreements which do set out restrictions, also provide a host of exceptions. These exceptions range from general treaty exceptions[93] and sector specific exceptions[94] and some are drafted in fact to allow host states to confer "advantages" to investors upon complying with performance requirements.[95] One seminal investor—state arbitration dealing with LCR prohibitions is *Lemire v Ukraine* which dealt with a Ukrainian measure requiring '50% of the total broadcasting time of every radio station in Ukraine to play music produced in Ukraine'.[96] The case is an example of how the range of exceptions built into prohibitions on performance requirements dilute their impact. The tribunal in *Lemire v Ukraine* held that the requirement did not violate the prohibition on performance requirement in the US-Ukraine BIT, on the ground that Ukraine imposed the restriction not to protect local industries and restrict import but rather to promote Ukraine's cultural inheritance.[97] Thus, despite the measure in effect being an LCR, the tribunal took the view that since the objective of the measure was not to create a trade barrier, it would not fall foul of the prohibition on LCR.[98]

This case is an interesting reflection of the wide range of flexibilities available to arbitral tribunals under BITs in interpreting and applying prohibitions on LCRs wherever they do exist. BITs, it thus appears, offer very little in the way of restrictions against the growing tide of LCR measures. While most agreements do not include explicit prohibition on LCRs, it is possible that other investment protections such as the standard of 'fair and equitable treatment' may be interpreted to prevent performance requirements. In *Lemire v Ukraine*, the Tribunal acknowledged the potential for a claim on breach of the FET standard as a result of the 50% locally made music requirement, but since a breach of the relevant article was not claimed by the Claimant, the Tribunal did not make a finding.[99] Nevertheless, there are relatively few ISDS cases to come out of BITs which deal, directly or indirectly, with performance requirements. In over 800 investor-state disputes only a handful relate directly or indirectly to performance requirements.[100] Furthermore, all known

---

[92] Article VI of the Canada—Costa Rica BIT, Article 9 of the China—Canada BIT, Article 9(1) of the Canada—Kuwait BIT, Article 6 of the ASEAN Korea Investment Agreement 2009, and Article 7(1) of ASEAN Comprehensive Investment Agreement.

[93] Yeurong et al. (2019) para 3.4.1.

[94] Yeurong et al. (2019) paras 3.4.2–127.

[95] Yeurong et al. (2019) paras 130–131.

[96] *Joseph Charles Lemire v Ukraine*, ICSID Case No. ARB/06/18, (14 January 2010) ['*Lemire v Ukraine*'].

[97] Ibid, para 510.

[98] Ibid, paras 505, 510.

[99] Ibid, para 507.

[100] Yeurong et al. (2019) para 2.

disputes of performance requirements under BITs involve agreements negotiated by Canada or the US and a majority of them are under the NAFTA.[101]

Therefore, at present, both RTAs and BITs appear to be ineffective in regulating the rising tide of LCRs. In the absence of the economic pressure that a multilateral arrangement provides, dispute settlement under RTAs do not have the same deterrent effect that the WTO DSB has.[102] A collapse of the Appellate Body, and a possible lack of enforcement of the removal of WTO inconsistent LCRs, will leave unbridled freedom for several WTO Members to continue to implement egregious LCRs and import substitution policies.

4.3 LCRs Within a (Post) WTO Regime

The WTO Covered Agreements and the principles negotiated and agreed to therein have been incorporated and adopted across most regional trade agreements, particularly those relating to trade in goods. National treatment, MFN treatment, and the general exceptions are recognised as principles fundamental to governing free trade. Thus, while a WTO 2.0 may result in rethinking on some WTO disciplines,[103] the underlying fundamental principles of the GATT and the GATS are likely to continue. The key feature of a WTO 2.0 which could lack what the existing WTO possesses is likely to be the dispute settlement mechanism.

The growth of LCRs must then be viewed in light of a new trade regime dominated by proliferating RTAs and a WTO 2.0, both lacking the teeth (based on the historical experience thus far) for a strong, strictly enforceable dispute settlement system, the hallmark of WTO 1.0.

One must not lose sight of the fact that there is an increasing amount of literature in support of local content requirements, which could impact the way rules around LCRs are negotiated in trade agreements in the future. In 2015, Timothy Meyer argued that LCRs implemented at the level of local governments were essential for the protection of public goods and increasing public welfare. He argued for a re-examination of WTO rules on non-discrimination and proposed that a distinction must be made between 'welfare increasing LCRs' and 'welfare decreasing LCRs' and that Article XX General Exceptions must be interpreted to permit 'politically necessary', proportional and justifiable LCR measures by local governments. This argument is a part of a growing scholarship pushing for the protection of some policy

[101]Nikièma (2014) para 3.1.

[102]Cimino et al. (2014) para 4.

[103]For instance—the development agenda and the enabling clause are at the forefront of WTO reform discussions, Member States are pushing for considering rules on E-Commerce, fisheries subsidies have continued to be an important issue since the Doha round of negotiations etc.

autonomy in developing countries[104] for the promotion of public welfare and sustainable development.

A WTO 2.0 with a weak dispute settlement system will expand space for policy autonomy for Member States, allowing them to adopt LCRs for multiple purposes—sometimes for good, sometimes for the worse. Given the growing emphasis on climate change in international conversations on trade governance, a WTO 2.0 may even lead to renegotiation of some of the principles underpinning the WTO Agreements to accommodate such policy concerns.

5 Conclusion

The Uruguay round agreements of the WTO provide the strongest regulation of trade-hindering LCRs. Despite the condemnation and phaseout of trade distorting LCRs pursuant to the TRIMS Agreement, they have increasingly been employed by countries since the global financial crisis in 2008. The world is entering a new decade which has been prefaced by increasing pushback against globalisation, the rise of protectionist economic policies and rejection of the regulatory oversight by international bodies such as the WTO. In this legal, political and economic climate, several WTO Members are brazenly resorting to LCRs. While studies on the effects of LCRs have not provided a consensus on beneficial impact of these measures, governments have found such measures particularly appealing to their political audience and sun-rise industries.

This growing tide of LCRs can only be checked through the strong enforcement of the TRIMS-specific provisions under the WTO. If the Appellate Body of the WTO were to not revive or unless some equally effective appeal mechanism replaces the Appellate Body, the effectiveness of the GATT, TRIMS and SCM Agreement will also diminish, if not disappear. As this chapter has demonstrated, the dispute settlement mechanisms under the existing RTAs are ill-equipped to deal with this problem. In that scenario, the coming decade will witness an unchecked and unbridled use of local content based industrial policy measures.

Acknowledgements The authors are grateful to Colin B. Picker and another anonymous referee for helpful comments.

[104]See for instance, Santos (2012)—in which he presents ways in which developing countries can utilise the gaps in WTO Agreements to carve out space for policy autonomy. He uses the example of Brazil to highlight how it has successfully managed to implement import substitution industrialisation policies.

Annexure 1: Tale of Key WTO Disputes on LCRs

S. No	DS number	Name of the dispute	Status	WTO agreement provisions
Appellate Body Report or Panel Report circulated				
1.	DS510	*US—Renewable Energy*	*Panel Report*: 27 June 2019	GATT: Art III.4, XVI:1 SCM: Art 3.1(b), 3.2, 5(a), 5(c), 6.3(A), 25 TRIMS: Art 2.1
2.	DS497/ DS472	*Brazil—Certain Measures Concerning Taxation and Charges*	*Appellate Body Report*: 13 December 2018	SCM: Art 3.1(b), 3.2 TRIMs: Art 2.1, 2.2, Annex GATT: Art I:1, II:1, III:4, III:5
3.	DS456	*India—Solar*	*Appellate Body Report*: 16 September 2016	GATT: III:4, TRIMS: Art 2.1 SCM: 3.1(b), 3.2, 5(c), 6.3 (a), 6.3(c), 25
4.	DS426/ DS412	*Canada—Renewable Energy*	*Appellate Body Report*: 06 May 2013	GATT: Art III:4, III:5, XXIII:1 SCM: 1.1, 3.1(b), 3.2 TRIMs: Art 2.1
5.	DS438/ DS444/ DS445	*Argentina—Measures affecting the Importation of Goods*	*Appellate Body Report:* 15 January 2015	GATT: Art III.4, VIII, X:1, X:2, X:3; TRIMs: Art 2, 6.1 And ors
6.	DS342/ DS340/ DS339	*China—Measures Affecting Imports of Automobile Parts*	*Appellate Body Report*: 12 December 2008	GATT: Art III, II, X; SCM: Art 3, 3.1(b), 3.2 TRIMs: Art 2, 2.1 Protocol of Accession
7.	DS334	*Turkey—Measures Affecting the Importation of Rice*	*Panel Report*: 21 September 2007	GATT: III, X, XI TRIMs: Art 2.1, Annex 1 And ors
8.	DS175/ DS146	*India—Measures Affecting Trade and Investment in the Motor Vehicle Sector/Measures affecting the Automotive Sector*	*Appellate Body Report*: 19 March 2002	GATT: Art III, XI TRIMs: Art 2
9.	DS142/ DS139	*Canada—Autos*	*Appellate Body Report*: 31 May 2010 *Article 21.3(c) Arbitration Report*: 04 October 2000	GATS: Art II, VI, XVII GATT: Art I.1, III.4, XXIV SCM: Art 3 3.1(a), 3.2 TRIMs: Art 2
10.	DS54/ DS55/ DS59/ DS64	*Indonesia—Autos*	*Panel Report*: 2 July 1998 *Article 21.3 (c) Arbitration Report:* 07 December 1998	SCM: Art 3.1(b), 28.2 TRIMs: Art 2, 5.4 GATT: Art I:1, III:2, III:4, X:1, X:3(a)

(continued)

S. No	DS number	Name of the dispute	Status	WTO agreement provisions
Under consultation				
1.	DS583	*Turkey—Pharmaceutical Products[EU]*	*Request for Consultations*: 02 April 2019	GATT: Art III.4, X:1, X:2, X:3, XI:1 SCM: Art 1.1, 3.1(b) TRIMS: Art. 2.1 TRIPS: Art 3.1, 27.1, 28.2, 39.1, 39.2
2.	DS563	*United States—Certain Measures Related to Renewable Energy*	*Request for Consultations*: 14 August 2018	GATT: III:4 TRIMS: Art 2.1, 2.2 SCM: Art 3.1(b), 3.2
3.	DS459/ DS452	*European Union and Certain Member States—Certain Measures on the Importation and Marketing of Biodiesel and Measures Supporting the Biodiesel Industry*	*Request for Consultations*: 15 May 2013	GATT: Art I:1, III TRIMs: Art 2.1, 2.2 SCM: Art 3.1(b), 3.2, 5(b), 5(c), 2.3, 1.1, 6.3(a) And ors
4.	DS195	*Philippines—Measures Affecting Trade and Investment in the Motor Vehicle Sector*	*Request for Consultations*: 23 May 2000	SCM: Art 3.1(b) TRIMs: Art 2.1, 2.2, 5.2, 5.5 GATT: Art III:4, III:5, XI:1
Settled or Terminated				
1.	DS359/ DS358	*China—Certain Measures granting Refunds, Reductions or Exemptions from Taxes and other Payments*	*Settled or terminated (withdrawn, mutually agreed solution)*: 07 February 2008	GATT: Art III:4 SCM: Art 3, 3.1(b), 3.2 TRIMs: Art 2, 2.1, Annex 1 Protocol of Accession

References

Cimino C, Hufbauer GC, Schott JJ (2014) A proposed code to discipline local content requirements. Peterson Institute for International Economics, Washington, D.C. Policy Brief: PB14-6

Farrell J (2011) Maximizing jobs from clean energy. New Rules Project 28:8

Fennell WA, Abellard DA (1993) Trade related investment measures. In: Stewart TP (ed) GATT Uruguay round: a negotiating history (1986–1992), vol IIb. Kluwer, Deventer and Boston, p 2002

Grossman GM (1981) The theory of domestic content protection and content preference. Q J Econ 68:548

Henkin L (1979) How nations behave. Law and foreign policy. Columbia University Press, New York, pp 320–321

Hufbauer GC et al (2013) Introduction: LCRs the phenomenon. In: Hofbauer GC, Schott JJ (eds) Local content requirements: a global problem, vol 102. Peterson Institute for International Economics, Washington, D.C, p 7

Krishna K, Itoh M (1988) Content protection and oligopolistic interactions. Rev Econ Stud 55 (1):107–125

Lewis J, Wiser R (2005) Fostering a renewable energy technology industry: an international comparison of wind industry policy support mechanisms. Ernesto Orlando Lawrence Berkeley National Laboratory, Environmental Energy Technologies Division, Berkeley

Nedumpara JJ, Raturi R (2013) 2012–2013 survey of trade policy developments in key economies. Centre for International Trade & Economic Laws, New Delhi, p 13

Pauwelyn J (2019) WTO dispute settlement post 2019: what to expect? J Int Econ Law 22 (3):297–321

Santos A (2012) Carving space for policy autonomy for developing countries in the World Trade Organisation: the experience of Brazil and Mexico. Va J Int Law Assoc 52(3):551–632

Shadikhodjaev S (2018) Local content requirements and industrialization. In: Industrial policy and the World Trade Organization: between legal constraints and flexibilities. Cambridge University Press, Cambridge, pp 147–193

Trade and Agriculture Directorate (2015) Trade committee emerging policy issues: localisation barriers to trade. Organisation for Economic Co-operation and Development (OECD), Paris. TAD/TC/WP(2014)17/FINAL 17

A Development-Driven Post WTO World

Sonia E. Rolland and David M. Trubek

Contents

Respectively a Professor of Law at Northeastern University School of Law (Boston, USA); and a Voss-Bascom Professor of Law and Dean of International Studies Emeritus at the University of Wisconsin-Madison.
This paper is reprinted in part and adapted in part from Rolland SE, Trubek DM (2019) Emerging Powers in the International Economic Order. Cambridge University Press, Cambridge, pp. 187–211.

S. E. Rolland (✉)
Northeastern University School of Law, Boston, MA, USA
e-mail: s.rolland@northeastern.edu

D. M. Trubek
University of Wisconsin-Madison, Madison, WI, USA
e-mail: dmtrubek@wisc.edu

M. K. Lewis et al. (eds.), *A Post-WTO International Legal Order*,
https://doi.org/10.1007/978-3-030-45428-9_14

1 Introduction

After the fall of the Soviet Union and the opening of China, a new world economic order emerged. It was built on four pillars: the World Trade Organization (WTO), a network of bilateral investment treaties, policies of the international financial institutions, and regional and bilateral free trade agreements (FTAs). This order stressed the importance of free markets and open economies, and imposed restrictions on many forms of state intervention in the economy. It facilitated the growth of global trade and enabled an increasing flow of capital across borders.

Emerging economies chafed at some of the limitations imposed by this regime. But, in the aggregate, they benefited from it. The BRICS and other emerging countries developed new export sectors fuelled in part by foreign direct investment (FDI), and expanded their exports to developed and developing markets. This in turn gave a stimulus to domestic markets, which grew rapidly. As they became industrial powerhouses, leading emerging economies began to catch up with the older industrialized nations. As they grew, their share of the world economy increased to the point where it now constitutes almost 60% of world GDP.

While millions were lifted out of poverty, not all within emerging countries benefited from this economic transformation. The increased economic wealth also did not necessarily accrue to all developing countries, nor did it necessarily translate into equitable redistribution policies, or into social, health, educational and other empowerment opportunities for the segments of the population that were vulnerable or that did not benefit directly from economic gains.

Although many countries benefited from the new environment, China stands out. Enjoying growth rates without precedent in world history, in a short time China has created the largest economy in the world (when adjusting for purchasing power parity)[1] or second-largest economy at official exchange rates. It has eclipsed the other BRICS: the International Monetary Fund estimated that in 2018 Chinese GDP would be larger than that of the other four BRICS combined.[2] As a result it emerged as a unique challenger to US economic dominance, and the influence on global governance that came with it.

International economic law has played a crucial role in this development. The order has frequently been described as "rule-based." Various bodies of legal rules have cemented this new, relatively open capitalist economic order. The rules of the WTO helped developing countries open their economies, and facilitated access to developed country markets. Bilateral investment treaties (BITs) added some security for FDI, although it is hard to find conclusive evidence that it had a causal effect on capital flows. These legal regimes were buttressed by FTAs.

---

[1]World Bank, International Comparison Program database, https://data.worldbank.org/indicator/ny.gdp.mktp.pp.cd?end=2017&start=1990&view=chart.

[2]International Monetary Fund (2018) GDP based on PPP. In: April 2018 Economic Outlook. https://www.imf.org/external/datamapper/PPPSH@WEO/OEMDC/ADVEC/WEOWORLD.

This world order is undergoing a fundamental transformation both in terms of who the influential players are and the governance norms and structure they seek to pursue. The 2008 financial crisis has had lasting and ongoing socio-economic effects in developed countries, including a worsening of income inequality. It has fuelled a rise in populism and its attendant rejection of multilateralism and embrace of defensive protectionism and unilateralism. The United States, in particular, is eschewing its role as guarantor of the post-World War II rule-based global economic order. Meanwhile, China is consolidating its economic and political power with a recommitment to state capitalism that, in many ways, runs counter to the ethos of Bretton Woods cum WTO. This has fuelled a reaction from the United States which has tried to use massive tariffs to pressure China to fully open its markets and reduce the role of the state in the economy. As the nature of US and Chinese policies change, and the relationship between the US and China becomes more combative, other countries including other emerging countries and the poorest countries alike are affected.

This chapter argues that overcoming the current disintegration of international economic relations would require a pluralist world order. By this, we mean a world order where economic integration and interdependence command some common normative and institutional features, but not through a unitarian project as the WTO had envisioned. The international economic law system has always included some pluralism. The WTO attempted to bring in a more unified system and succeeded to some extent, but also generated a significant measure of discontent in the process. De facto pluralism has now taken hold in many ways, both in trade and investment law. While the WTO is viewing such developments with some angst, we argue that pluralism creates opportunities to preserve a law-based international economic system. However, a stable and fair pluralist system would require architectural coherence and a legitimate normative bedrock. This chapter explores what forms pluralism could take, institutionally and normatively.

Section 2 briefly presents pluralism as a foundational principle for a future world order. Section 3 outlines the normative and institutional parameters of what such an order could comprise, setting out two paradigms for regionalism: regional and topical. Section 4 asks how we can build a stable and fair pluralist system.

2 Pluralism As the New Normal

A regime that reflects global economic integration but seeks to better serve its most disempowered constituents should maintain some basic rules for global trade while allowing greater flexibility for emerging economies to follow development strategies of their choice. Such a regime would be "pluralist" in several senses. First, it would be normatively pluralist, understood as lacking a single normative order governing international economic relations. At every level of effective regulation, it would be sensitive to different normative and strategic views, and it would not seek to impose a "one size fits all" approach to economic ordering, nor enshrine a mainstream, orthodox approach to economic relations. Second, it would be institutionally pluralist, looking to regional groupings and plurilateral agreements among consenting states to bear more of the burden of transnational regulation while also making room for private ordering. Thirdly, it would be pluralist in the sense used by Francis Snyder to refer to a situation where there are overlapping layers of governance requiring mechanisms to avoid conflicts among these levels.[3]

There are various indications pointing toward the emergence of such a regime. The first is the exploitation of de jure and de facto flexibilities in the current order. This can be seen as implementation of pluralism *avant la lettre*. The extensive use of safeguard duties and trade remedies (anti-dumping and countervailing duties), the use of subsidies which are often ultimately found to run afoul of WTO disciplines and the resurgence of industrial policy programs backed by the state, standstill agreements on bringing claims against bailouts in the wake of the 2008 crisis, delays in implementing the findings of the WTO's dispute settlement system all illustrate the use of de jure and de facto flexibilities by developed and developing countries alike. The second is the spread of multiregional agreements, including the Comprehensive and Progressive Agreement for Trans-Pacific Partnership (CPTTP) and Regional Comprehensive Economic Partnership (RCEP), as well as less consolidated regional groups such as those developing in Latin America and Africa. Third are the agreements that have been negotiated under the auspices of the WTO, such as the Trade Facilitation Agreement (now in force) and the Environmental Goods Agreement, or worked out on its sidelines, such as the proposed Trade in Services Agreement, which are either optional or include variable geometry agreements, all in departure to the traditional single undertaking approach.

Perhaps these developments can be the basis for a new pluralist international economic order. Such a regime would need to be more flexible than the current system, but it would have to meet certain standards and include core commitments. To ensure it would be development-friendly, such a regime must meet the fundamental needs of the emerging economies for market access and policy flexibility. They need to maintain access to the developed markets that have helped spur export-led growth; they want more freedom of policy choice. They want room to experiment with development policies and to be able to craft policies acceptable to their populations. Second, the regime must offer developed countries reasonable access to emerging markets whilst protecting the latter against destabilizing trade shocks. That means that emerging economies will have to accept some restrictions on their ability to protect domestic industry, while developed countries must be able to limit trade shocks and provide support for those displaced. The challenge is to craft a system that combines maximum flexibility within these core commitments.

[3] Snyder (2010).

3 Two Paradigms for Pluralism

We see two paradigms for pluralism, which are not mutually exclusive, and in practice are likely to coexist. First, a comprehensive "regional" type of pluralism offers a clublike economic integration model where parties subscribe to broad-ranging and deep trade and investment disciplines, but the structure has no universal membership aspiration. The RCEP and CPTPP illustrate this approach. Second, a topical pluralism comprises agreements on specific issues or areas of economic relations, where the integration ambition is shallow, in that the subject matter of the agreement is defined narrowly and specifically, but the membership aspires to be as open and numerous as possible. Plurilateral agreements within the WTO and instruments such as TiSA illustrate this approach. This section explores the nature, features and implications of each of these two paradigms for international economic relations, with particular reference to emerging economies.

3.1 "Regional" Pluralism

This model of economic relations aims to regulate deeply on a range of subject matters, but eschews any aspiration to universal membership. In fact, it is understood that members may participate in a variety of trade or investment agreements outside of the group. Such groupings reflect the traditionally horizontal and decentralized nature of public international law. In that respect, they contrast with the WTO, which posits itself as a "first amongst others" forum requiring any outside commitments by its members to be "WTO-compatible," that is, subordinated to WTO rules and standards. These regional groupings may or may not become preferred forums for negotiation of trade arrangements: this would be determined by economic and political factors, not by legal rules requiring exclusivity.

3.1.1 Normative Nature

As Andrew Lang has pointed out, much of international economic law takes as its standard a particular model of a market economy, and its rules are designed to ensure that such a model will eventually prevail everywhere.[4] State intervention is circumscribed in the name of providing a "level playing field" for private economic actors. This approach has been rejected by many emerging economies: they wish to preserve policy space to experiment with different economic strategies and avoid being pushed into policies that could cause domestic unrest. Market-oriented rules in international economic law clash with those wishes in many ways. Achieving full normative pluralism would involve a willingness to accept different forms of

---

[4]Lang (2019), pp. 677–719.

economic ordering rather than use international economic law as a straightjacket. A number of flexibilities exist in the current trade regime that recognize, to some extent, the reality of pluralism in political economy and development strategies.[5] And there are de facto flexibilities including knowing breaches of trade rules where a country simply implements a policy that is likely to get challenged but can continue it in effect until the conclusion of the dispute settlement process, typically several years after its inception.[6] Emerging economies want not only to preserve those flexibilities; many would like to transform de facto exceptions into new de jure rules more accepting of different forms of economic organization.

"Regional" pluralism offers opportunities for different groups to enshrine different understandings of economic governance and developmental concerns. Existing regional trade agreements already offer a range of approaches to the trade and development nexus. For instance, self-reliance is at the core of several African trade groups, particularly when dealing with industrial policy provisions.[7] African trade pacts also often emphasize "equitable development"—the notion that economic benefits expected from liberalization require a distributional policy not only between nations but also those affecting domestic constituencies and concomitant reforms in domestic governance.[8] Agreements involving ASEAN members and

[5]See, e.g., Shaffer (2019), pp. 183–191; Rodrik (2011); Dani Rodrik D (2008) Second-Best Institutions. NBER Working Paper 14050, pp. 7–8. Available https://www.nber.org/papers/w14050.

[6]E.g., India's Nehru National Solar Mission program challenged at the WTO India—Certain Measures Relating to Solar Cells and Solar Modules, Appellate Body Report, WT/DS456/AB/R (14 Oct 2016). See also Brazil's INOVAR auto program challenged at the WTO Brazil—Certain Measures Concerning Taxation and Charges, Appellate Body Report, WT/DS472/AB/R; WT/DS497/AB/R (13 Dec 2018).

[7]See, e.g., Art. 99(a) Treaty Establishing the Common Market for Eastern and Southern Africa (COMESA) (Kampala, 5 Nov 1993; 2314 UNTS 265) (objectives of cooperation in industrial development include the promotion of "self-sustained and balanced growth"); Art. 79 Treaty for the Establishment of the East African Community (EAC Treaty)(Arusha, 30 Nov 1999; 2144 UNTS 255) (members shall take steps in industrial development to "promote self-sustaining and balanced growth"); Art. 26.2(a) Treaty of the Economic Community of West African States (ECOWAS) (Cotonou, 24 Jul 1993; 2373 UNTS 233) (to promote industrial developments, members shall "foster self-sustained and self-reliant development"); Art. 5.1(d) Treaty of the Southern African Development Community, as Amended (SADC) (Windhoek, 17 Aug 1992; 32 ILM 116) (objectives include promoting "self-sustaining development on the basis of collective self-reliance, and the interdependence of Member States"); Preamble, Charter of the South Asian Association for Regional Cooperation (SAARC Charter) (Dhaka, 8 Dec 1985) (noting that cooperation "would contribute significantly to national and collective self-reliance").

[8]Art. 6(d) COMESA; Art. 5.2 EAC (objectives include "accelerated, harmonious and balanced development and sustained expansion of economic activities, the benefit of which shall be equitably shared"); Art. 7.1(f) EAC (principles include the "equitable distribution of benefits" of operation); Preamble, ECOWAS ("Accepting the need to share the benefits of economic cooperation and integration among Member States in a just and equitable manner . . . "); Art. 2(b) SACU (objectives include creating "effective, transparent and democratic institutions which will ensure equitable trade benefits to Member States"); Art. 2(g) SACU (objectives include facilitating "the equitable sharing of revenue arising from customs, excise and additional duties levied by Member States");

some Caribbean trade agreements are mindful of intragroup economic disparities and the need for asymmetric commitments to address developmental and economic gaps between members.[9]

The Asia-Pacific context offers an interesting microcosm of regional pluralism. First, a number of groupings co-exist, with different but overlapping memberships. Seven of the eleven CPTPP members are also in negotiations for the RCEP. Conversely, seven of the fifteen RCEP negotiating parties are members of the CPTPP. All members of the CPTPP are also members of the Asia-Pacific Economic Cooperation forum (APEC), as are all RCEP negotiating parties except for Laos, Cambodia and Myanmar. All Association of Southeast Asian Nations (ASEAN) members are parties to either the CPTPP or the RCEP, and the organization has concluded a number of free trade agreements with other participants of RCEP and CPTPP.

Second, beyond membership, the overlap of topical coverage of these groupings is another significant feature. All agreements endorse general non-discrimination rules such as most-favored-nation clauses and national treatment clauses. They also regulate a vast array of topics, making them good examples of the depth of regulation that characterizes "deep" regional integration amongst a relatively small number of member states.

Preamble, Cartagena Agreement (community will "lead to the balanced, harmonious, and shared economic development of their countries"); Art. 1 Cartagena Agreement (objectives are to "promote the balanced and harmonious development of the Member Countries under equitable conditions"); Art. 60(f) Cartagena Agreement (objectives of industrial development include "equitable distribution of benefits"); Art. 3.1(b) SAARC Charter ("ensuring equitable benefits to all Contracting States, taking into account their respective levels and pattern of economic development").

[9]Preamble, CARICOM; see also Preamble, SACU ("Mindful of the different levels of economic development of the Member States and the need for their integration into the global economy"); Preamble, Agreement Establishing the ASEAN–Australia–New Zealand Free Trade Area (Chaam, Phetchaburi, 27 Feb 2009) ("Considering the different levels of development among ASEAN Member States and between ASEAN Member States, Australia and New Zealand and the need for flexibility, including special and differential treatment"); Preamble, South Pacific Regional Trade and Economic Cooperation Agreement (Tarawa, 14 Jul 1981; 1240 UNTS 66) ("Mindful of the differing economic potential of Forum Island countries and the special development problems of the Smaller Island countries"); Art. 144 COMESA; Art. 1 Cartagena Agreement (the agreement also seeks "to reduce existing differences in levels of development"); Preamble, CARICOM ("the persistence of disadvantage, however arising, may impact adversely on the economic and social cohesion in the Community"); Art. 1.6 ASEAN Charter (purposes include narrowing the development gap within ASEAN); preamble para 9 and Art. 1(d) Framework Agreement on Comprehensive Economic Cooperation among the Governments of the Republic of Korea and the Member Countries of the Association of Southeast Asian Nations (ASEAN–Korea) (Jeju-do, 2 June 2009); preamble paras 2 and 7, Arts. 1(d) and 2(d)–(e) Framework Agreement on Comprehensive Economic Cooperation between ASEAN and the People's Republic of China (ASEAN–China) (Phnom Penh, Nov. 4, 2002); preamble para 6 Framework Agreement on Comprehensive Economic Cooperation between the Republic of India and the ASEAN (ASEAN–India) (Bali, 8 Oct 2003).

The vast topical overlap among these deep economic integration schemes could suggest a lack of normative diversity. After all, if the agreements cover the same topics, and many states participate in both agreements, are we really expecting a different normative ethos and regulatory output from each agreement? The counter point could be that if members saw fit to engage in the regulation of the same topic in different fora, it may also be indicative that they wished to do so somewhat differently across platforms. While the CPTPP seems to embody elements of the one-size-fits-all approach resisted by many emerging countries, observers believe that the RCEP, when it is finalized, may be more accepting of diverse economic models and strategies. For example, CPTPP includes restrictions on SOEs and WTO + IP rules, while RCEP will have neither. We can therefore think of the CPTPP and RCEP as reflecting elements of normative pluralism.

Even within a particular agreement there may be opportunities for flexibility and differentiation of commitments, which is another expression of pluralism. For example, the CPTPP proceeds on the basis of a single common core agreement addressing all the topics at stake in the negotiations, with individual state commitments modulated in a series of side instruments and annexes. The CPTPP's main agreement is complemented by no less than 25 side instruments including different sets of parties. Additionally, 103 country-specific annexes and a few more common annexes also form a part of the agreement.

Such procedurally different approaches to negotiations reflect different substantive understandings of economic regulation. This may help to explain why there is apparently no appetite for consolidating these various groupings into a single pan-Asian pact.

3.1.2 Institutional Features

There may have been a time when one could imagine the WTO evolving into an exclusive, unitary and comprehensive site for global regulation of trade and related matters, with supportive institutions. But that is not how things have materialized. Inability to agree on many issues stalled new rulemaking in the WTO; the dispute settlement system, long the institutional crown jewel of the organization, is threatened logistically (due to insufficient resources to deal with the high volume and complexity of cases) and politically. Deep "regional" agreements stand in sharp contrast to the multilateral economic governance project at the WTO.

There is no necessary relationship between the normative features of regional pluralism and its institutional features, but they can come together, and the deeper integration project inherent in regional pluralism would naturally lend itself to the creation of supportive institutions. In practice, we observe somewhat looser levels of institutional integration in regional pluralism than at the WTO. Dispute settlement processes perhaps provide the most salient illustration. A core feature of the WTO is its mandatory and exclusive dispute settlement system: members must use it, to the exclusion of any other dispute resolution forum. The WTO offered different types of dispute settlement, including a quasi-adjudicatory system with the panels and the

Appellate Body; single-step arbitration, mediation, good offices, and diplomatic negotiations; but if negotiations fail, members favor the quasi-adjudicatory process virtually exclusively.

The CPTPP is more flexible, and not exclusive. Most notably, it allows complaining parties to choose which forum they wish to use to resolve disputes arising under the CPTPP and another trade agreement.[10] This a direct challenge to the exclusivity and mandatory rules of the WTO, but it may be seen as a response to the Mexico—Taxes on Soft Drinks[11] dispute, where a dispute arising under the North American Free Trade Agreement (NAFTA) eventually spilled over into the WTO system but the WTO panel and AB refused to take into account the NAFTA elements of the dispute. ASEAN and APEC agreements are typically devoid of adjudicatory or arbitration options for dispute settlement, but the RCEP parties have been negotiating a dispute settlement chapter.

3.2 Topical Pluralism

Another type of pluralism eschews deep multifaceted economic governance in favor of ad hoc, stand-alone agreements on specific issues or topics. Plurilateral agreements at the WTO and on its sidelines illustrate this approach. For instance, the Agreement on Government Procurement is separate from the single undertaking and deals with a specific subject matter. WTO members are free to subscribe to it or not, and have a great degree of latitude in defining which domestic entities might be covered by the agreement.[12] Participation in one agreement is not generally conditional upon participation in other agreements, and withdrawal is therefore less complex too. Although the Agreement on Government Procurement is conditional on WTO membership, parties may withdraw at any time with 60 days' notice without losing their WTO membership. The ASEAN and APEC illustrate another take on topical pluralism. Rather than having a single comprehensive agreement with complex schedules of commitments by individual members, they have accumulated, over the years, dozens of separate, mostly self-contained instruments on different topics. Such topical pluralism, then, is fluid over time because it makes it easier for countries to extract themselves from an agreement that no longer suits their needs, unlike participation in a deep integration "regional" agreement.

As a rulemaking enterprise, topical pluralism offers flexibility. Amendments to such agreements or renegotiations are likely easier to undertake in a limited time frame, which makes this type of regulation nimbler and more apt to respond to changes in political, economic, technical or technological circumstances. The Agreement on Government Procurement offers an illustration of topical pluralism in

[10] Art. 28.4 CPTPP.

[11] AB Report, Mexico—Taxes on Soft Drinks, DS308/AB/R (7 Oct 2005).

[12] Agreement on Government Procurement, Art. XXIV.

action. It was originally developed as part of the 1979 Tokyo Round of trade negotiations and entered into force among its state parties in 1981. It became the Agreement on Government Procurement (GPA) 1994 at the time of the conclusion of the WTO, then underwent a broad revision between 1997 and 2012 when the Protocol of Amendment was finalized. It entered into force just 2 years later in 2014 and currently includes forty-seven parties (including the EU, which represents 27 member states),[13] with a further ten members in the process of acceding, and another 21 having observer status. The Trade Facilitation Agreement, although ostensibly within the framework of the single undertaking at the WTO, operates in practice much like a plurilateral agreement. Negotiations on the Trade in Services Agreement between 23 WTO members also pertain to topical pluralism.

Because topical pluralism results in agreements or institutions that are limited in scope and have no universal membership ambition, it may be more responsive to technological innovation. For instance, it is reasonable to contemplate future stand-alone deals on block chains or cryptocurrencies, even as negotiations on the GATS are stalled, and the CPTPP and RCEP may also lack the ability to engage in such topical negotiations on a short time horizon.

In some cases, regulatory projects that we could recognize as manifestations of topical pluralism fail. The Anti-Counterfeiting Trade Agreement (ACTA) provides a case in point. Like TiSA, it was meant as an effort to bypass the logjammed WTO negotiations, and to respond to the threat caused by a global intellectual property piracy economy reportedly worth at least USD $500 billion annually[14] and often connected to organized crime, money laundering and terrorism financing.[15] However, scrutiny by civil society, and concerns over both the process and the substance of the agreement led to its effective abandonment, after Japan was the only state to ratify and the EU Parliament declined to consent to ratification in 2012. Here, the expression of pluralism resulted in a rejection of a topical regulation.

Topical pluralism is a way to make international economic ordering more responsive to popular will. One of the complaints against the trade regime is that normative commitments like WTO+ disciplines on intellectual property have proliferated in deeper "regional" agreements where they are bundled with numerous other topics and issues, making it hard for opposition to specific measures to crystalize. The failure of the proposed ACTA treaty illustrates this point: the focus on one particular topic for regulation allowed a more targeted and vocal mobilization by civil society constituencies who opposed the treaty and industries who promoted it. These same constituencies found it much harder to challenge provisions like WTO+ IP rules that were embedded in much larger frameworks. Hence, the normative subtext of topical

[13]Miles T (27 Nov 2018) WTO Agrees in Principle to Keep Britain in Procurement Deal. Available via Reuters. https://uk.reuters.com/article/uk-britain-eu-wto/wto-agrees-in-principle-to-keep-britain-in-procurement-deal-envoy-idUKKCN1NW1WN.

[14]OECD/EUIPO (2016) Trade in Counterfeit and Pirated Goods: Mapping the Economic Impact. https://doi.org/10.1787/9789264252653-en.

[15]See, e.g., Chow (2003), pp. 473–484.

pluralism must be read both in the regulatory output that is created and the potential output that is cast aside.

For emerging countries, topical pluralism offers opportunities for what we could call project-based developmentalism. Agreements or institutions meant to achieve a particular developmental objective or project, without seeking an all-encompassing economic integration, are well-suited to this paradigm. For instance, an agreement on the development of an integrated transportation network and infrastructure in Africa illustrates the potential for topical pluralism to achieve a particular development project.

The increasingly blurred lines between public aid to development, development finance, and foreign direct investment may also find new regulatory venues with topical pluralism. Infrastructure projects in Africa, Latin America and Asia involve a mix of public and private agreements, often implemented by a corresponding mix of government actors, private entities or government-sponsored semiprivate actors, in the case of SOEs. The Belt and Road Initiative (BRI) is perhaps the most prominent example of such project-based developmentalism involving public-private partnerships. It ostensibly aims at developing infrastructure in the participating countries. Although it involves major transfers of goods and services across borders, it is not governed by a single trade or investment agreement, but leverages a number of trade and investment instruments along with domestic regulation. It largely relies on special domestic laws and machinery for disputes. It is implemented through government contracts as well as private contracts. Disputes might be heard in domestic courts in China that will be created specifically to adjudicate such international commercial and investment projects. Plurilateral agreements focusing on BRI projects could set substantive safeguards on the modalities for investment, finance and trade, as well as standards for disputes and possibly alternative fora.

4 How to Build a Development-Oriented Pluralist System?

The emergence of pluralism in all its senses is a challenge: normative pluralism narrows the bite of any system of rules, as they must be flexible enough to accommodate fundamental diversity. Regional pluralism means there will be no single source of norms and no uniform system of disputes settlement; topical pluralism takes fragmentation even further.

The need to rethink international economic law is a major undertaking and will require input from a host of stakeholders. Emerging economies will play an important role and are already engaged in experimenting with new forms of trade and investment agreements. Regardless of the shape that pluralism takes, it should have the capacity to regulate a variety of approaches to development in order to garner legitimacy with the different political economy strategies that prevail throughout the world. This is not to say that anything goes, in an anarchic, law-less fashion. Rather, a stable and equitable pluralist system must include principles and rules for recognizing and supporting a range of development models. Section A offers some thoughts on that issue. Another problem that we can anticipate in a pluralist environment is the need for principles to police the boundaries of the component parts of the system. As discussed above, the overlap between topics and regulated entities is bound to create a complex, decentralized legal architecture. Section B further explores this matter. Lastly, Section C asks where a pluralist system leaves a WTO 2.0.

4.1 What Normative Governing Principles for a Development-Oriented Pluralist System?

As it became clear in the late 1990s that conceiving of trade law as a self-contained regulatory domain separate from the rest of international law was untenable, we witnessed the emergence of a sort of buffer zone called "non-trade issues": those topics pertaining to public international law that rubbed against "purely" trade matters (though it is still a guess what the latter might be). Non-trade issues encompass labor, environment, public health, education, governance and corruption, social welfare policies and more. While recognizing the inevitable intersection between trade and non-trade issues was a critical first step, legal tools to manage the relationship are minimal and blunt. In the WTO context, article XX and XXI of the GATT and their counterparts in the GATS, article 2 of the TBT agreement, and similar provisions enshrine some level of recognition that topics outside of the trade realm may overlap with trade topics. However, they have been interpreted to subordinate the non-trade issues to what are perceived as trade obligations. The trade obligation is the rule, and the non-trade concerns might at times be interpreted to be acceptable exceptions. Similar dynamics are at play with respect to international investment regulation.

Voices from emerging economies and elsewhere have called for an end to this practice. This effort to equalize trade and non-trade concerns can be seen in calls for more policy space, and in recent efforts to outline a "right to regulate" as a way to legitimize the call for policy space and make it enforceable.

A pluralist system must go beyond granting flexibilities at the margins of a normatively uniform system. Rather, it must inherently recognize a variety of political economy approaches as legitimate and it must provide mechanisms for dealing with policy clashes. The WTO tried to do the latter, but current discontent with the institution suggests that its solution is no longer viable.

Rather than offering a grand theoretical solution, this section examines the range of legal tools that are available to grapple with this issue.

– *Protecting policy space: rules of conflicts, positive lists, negative lists*

If "non trade" concerns are to be treated equally with trade issues, then their scope and extent must be reflected more pervasively in trade agreements. This could be done through a conflict of law-type of approach establishing a presumption that any legitimate public policy in certain areas trumps trade concerns. Negative lists can serve to exclude certain regulatory domains. For instance, an increasing number of trade and investment agreements include prudential carve-outs in the area of financial services, to allow states concerned about the stability of their financial markets to decide on the level of control they wish to assert over financial flows. Agreements based on positive lists give states the option to progressively subject sectors or industries to trade rules on an opt-in basis. This can be useful to help a state differentiate between its competitive industries and its sectors that are developing and still need state support and shielding from global competition.

– *Temporary adjustments: safeguards and exceptions*

Developing countries tend to face balance of payment difficulties or temporary sectoral crises as a result of the major socio-economic transformations that they are undergoing. Currently, options for buffering such crises exist within the trade regime but can be more limited in the investment law regime, which is problematic. Some coordination, harmonization and increased coherence across the law and policy of trade institutions, international financial institutions and international investment law is needed.

– *Addressing the impact of developmental policies on other trade partners: actionable/non-actionable, justiciable, self-judging, compensable?*

Currently, the WTO generally does not require damages for a state to have standing when a discipline has allegedly been breached, the theory being that breaches of the rules affect the system as a whole, even in the absence of a particular damage. By contrast, international investment law cares less about enforcement of the rules for their own sake, and more about damages. Another way to approach the question of political economy diversity is to think about how much reviewability, justiciability and compensation would be available for states' measures in future agreements.

As for reviewability, the WTO currently offers a tiered system, whereby some actions are reviewable by specific committees (balance of payment measures, for instance), separate from potential claims in dispute settlement. Some issues are also excluded from dispute settlement claims (for instance, non-actionable subsidies), while other measures are allowed but subject to compensation to adversely affected members (actionable subsidies, tariff renegotiations), and others are subject to withdrawal of a measure if the latter is found to be incompatible with trade disciplines. Within the range of measures subject to discipline, some benefit from greater state discretion than others (compare national security under GATT Article XXI, the protection of exhaustible natural resources under GATT article XX(g) and the protection of public health under GATT article XX(b)). This range of options is laudable, and could inform states' negotiations in other trade and investment agreements. Even at the WTO, however, a reallocation of these various standards of review seems to be necessary.

The US-China Trade Policy Working Group Joint Statement put forward by a group of legal scholars and economists under the leadership of Jeffrey S. Lehman,

Dani Rodrik and Yang Yao offers a paradigm shift in how to balance international trade commitments and other policy objectives or needs.[16] It explicitly situates itself as an alternative to the current convergence model and a way to get beyond the US-China debate over decoupling versus integration. The authors propose categorizing policies into four "buckets" depending on the type and magnitude of spill-over effects one country's policy has on other trading partners. While the policies that are likely to create the gravest distortions, such as beggar-thy-neighbour policies are prohibited, other types of policies fall into three remaining categories that would trigger "bilateral discussions and adjustments", "domestic adjustments" and call for "multilateral governance", respectively. While this approach borrows elements from the WTO's current trade remedy system, it is designed to apply to any policy, whether currently covered by trade agreements or merely in more or less formal negotiations, such as issues pertaining to the digital economy. As a result, it bypasses the debates about whether a domestic policy is legitimate, for WTO purposes, and who the decision-maker or interpreter might be regarding the legitimacy issue. It only concerns itself with the effects of a given policy on other countries or territories. Inherently, it therefore enables various and divergent political economy and developmental models to co-exist while seeking to create a system to address the allocation of costs that various policies might have.

4.2 *How to Police Legal Conflicts Among Component Parts of a Pluralist Order?*

Our two paradigms for pluralism, "regional" large membership but shallow integration and "topical" limited subject matter with a deeper regulation for smaller groups of members with a common interest, presume the co-existence of a variety of regulatory spheres. A critical issue would then be to allow for the smooth operation of these separate, yet overlapping systems. Much has been written on the potential and actual conflicts raised by the "spaghetti bowl" of regional trade agreements, and the WTO's role requirement that RTAs be WTO compatible.[17] Some have also examined the relationship between WTO obligations and other international rules.[18] Yet the topic remains under-theorized while the pressure to resolve these issues is ever increasing.

Adding to the complexity is the relationship between domestic and international law dispute settlement. In international investment law, for instance, the use of investor-state dispute settlement to essentially avoid or overrule domestic judicial

[16]The US-China Trade Policy Working Group Joint Statement (2019) US-China Trade Relations: A Way Forward. https://rodrik.typepad.com/US-China%20Trade%20Relations%20-%20A%20Way%20Forward%20Booklet%20%28for%20print%29.pdf.

[17]E.g., Matsushita (2019).

[18]Pauwelyn (2003).

processes has raised serious legitimacy concerns and is prompting a redrafting of international investment agreements by several countries seeking to protect the finality of domestic judicial decisions.[19]

Yet another consideration is the types of entities that are regulated, and their standing to challenge rules or bring disputes seeking to enforce the rules. While trade law operates largely on a state-to-state model, the channelling of corporate interests and others through state negotiations and disputes is a contentious matter which fuels the system's legitimacy crisis. Investment law allows both for state-to-state disputes and for investor-state disputes, but grants little by way of recourses to other affected constituencies such as civil society, population groups, workers, consumers, etc.

A pluralist system must rethink the role of all affected constituencies in policing the rules and challenging them.

4.3 What Would Pluralism Mean for a WTO 2.0?

The current position of the WTO as a sort of first amongst equals for international trade regulation is neither effective, nor tenable. The WTO needs to abandon the idea of a unitarian trade regime for its diverse members. It should also abandon the notion of being the final arbiter on trade and increasingly other matters. However, the WTO's *acquis* is valuable and is here to stay for its 164 members as well as the 22 accession candidates. Each of these themes is discussed in turn.

To move away from a unitarian ethos, the WTO should reorient its understanding of trade and development and design a new role for itself in relation to other economic law systems. Recent developments, including the US-China trade conflict, show that the effort to herd all states' political economies towards a common liberal, capitalist ethos has reached its limit. Nonetheless, there are a number of things that the WTO could do in the new global economic order that is emerging.

First, the WTO could proceed with those programs and policies that are compatible with the nascent pluralist order such as plurilateral agreements and variable levels of commitments within agreements tied to domestic capacity. Pluralism could be the escape valve that allows states to pursue alternative strategies, thereby alleviating the pressure on the WTO to deliver agreeable policies to all its members on a broad range of topics.

Second, the WTO could take the lead in designing a new way to weigh trade and non-trade costs and benefits, both economically and legally, perhaps along the lines of The US-China Trade Policy Working Group Joint Statement. Such a system could be used in WTO processes and adopted by other trade groups.

---

[19]For instance, the *White Industries* case prompted widespread outcry in India and precipitated a review of its model BIT. White Industries Australia Limited v. The Republic of India. Available via UNCTAD Investment Policy Hub, http://investmentpolicyhub.unctad.org/ISDS/Details/378. Ranjan (2014), pp. 419–450; Hanessian and Duggal (2016), pp. 216–226.

Third, the WTO could embrace experimentation, something that is currently curtailed by the one-size-fits-all neo-liberal ethos. It has already successfully done so with the Agreement on Trade Facilitation. This Agreement enshrines tiered commitments related to developmental capacity, complemented by a built-in funding mechanism that recognizes the cost of implementation better than any other trade agreement has done before. The speed at which it has been ratified by WTO members testifies to the positive response to this type of topical regulation, which is separate from the rest of multilateral negotiations and is premised on a new approach to balancing commitments for a diverse membership.

Freed from the single undertaking in negotiations, a WTO 2.0 could move towards more limited agreements, both topically and in terms of membership, with a different balance of trade liberalization and development priorities. The recent agreement between 16 WTO members, including all the EU states, for a gap-filling appeals mechanism until the Appellate Body situation can be resolved is another example of such variable geometry experimentation. This accord, involving Australia, Brazil, Canada, China, Chile, Colombia, Costa Rica, the European Union, Guatemala, the Republic of Korea, Mexico, New Zealand, Norway, Panama, Singapore, Switzerland and Uruguay,[20] commits its signatories to use the arbitration mechanism of Article 25 of the Dispute Settlement Understanding as an avenue for appealing a panel report. Such arbitrations awards are then adopted by the Dispute Settlement Body per the normal reverse consensus decision-making procedure, and eventually open the door to implementation monitoring and potential retaliation, should compliance by the losing party not be forthcoming.

The agreement is open to any other WTO member wishing to avail itself of this procedure. The list of original signatories is also revealing of some deeper political dynamics at the WTO. While China, Brazil and a number of other developing countries which have historically been supportive of the role of the WTO in governing international trade relations joined, India is conspicuous by its absence. As with many other negotiation topics, India has established itself as a fiercer critic of the WTO as currently shaped.

Experimentation may be particularly important at a time when the WTO is facing a serious crisis and undertaking a significant internal reform effort. Indeed, if it no longer had to bear the responsibility of being the core and ultimate backstop for all trade issues, the WTO might be freed to explore new productive avenues for relevant, legitimate and equitable trade regulation.

At the same time, the WTO has a vast legal *acquis* that is likely to endure. The *acquis* has two values. From a technical, legal perspective, other trade agreements must be WTO-compatible with respect to obligations of WTO members. Second, normatively, the WTO can influence other regimes informally, particularly if it acts as an experimental venue through plurilateral agreements. A WTO 2.0 would

[20]Statement by Ministers, Davos, Switzerland, 24 Jan 2020. https://trade.ec.europa.eu/doclib/docs/2020/january/tradoc_158596.pdf.

therefore become one regulatory venue amongst others, serving as a formal and informal regulatory source.

In theory, the WTO had a role in avoiding conflicts with other trade agreements with GATT article XXIV and GATS article V. However, the supposed WTO compatibility of free trade agreements is questionable in many cases and, at any rate, the WTO review mechanism for free trade agreements and customs union has been a failure. A WTO 2.0 should not be tasked with organizing the pluralist economic law realm. Rather, a WTO 2.0 could participate in designing rules for governing relations between various trade agreements, along with states and other international organizations.

The WTO's legal *acquis* has and continues to influence the drafting of free trade agreements, and it now also inspires some provisions in international investment agreements. The WTO has generated an epistemic community among negotiators, civil servants, scholars, practitioners, industry and policy-makers worldwide. This community could play a major role in working out the complexities of a pluralist international economic order and the WTO could play a significant role in strengthening such a community through a variety of measures including technical assistance programs, research grants, conferences, databases. Current illustrations of such efforts include the annual WTO Public Forum conference bringing together a range of public and private stakeholders, and the vast repository and database resources it offers through its websites, including information regarding trade commitments in non-WTO agreements. This kind of information dissemination work and its accompanying epistemic ecosystem has played a significant role in the growth of the EU. A WTO 2.0 could expand this kind of activity.

The WTO is facing an existential crisis as a result of the political and economic changes of recent years. To maintain its relevance in the international economic order, it will need to rethink its role in the world and reorient how it treats members' shifting priorities. Because of changes on the world stage, there may be a window of opportunity to move in new, more developmentally-friendly directions. Three inflection points stand out in this respect. The US has withdrawn its leadership; a more powerful and assertive China has indicated support for global order while insisting on the right to maintain heterodox strategies; and the EU has maintained its commitment to multilateralism. Of course, some may fear that by moving in such a direction, the WTO would lose influence, becoming just another relatively powerless version of UNCTAD. But there are reasons to think such would not be the case. First, the WTO involves the major economic and political players whereas UNCTAD faltered on that front. Second the WTO is institutionally, legally and culturally entrenched in a way that UNCTAD never was. We may indeed be at a turning point in the relation between trade and development: only time will tell.

References

Chow DCK (2003) Organized crime, local protectionism, and the trade in counterfeit goods in China. China Econ Rev 14(4):473–484

Hanessian G, Duggal K (2016) The 2015 India Model BIT: is this the change the world wishes to see? ICSID Rev 32(1):216–226. https://doi.org/10.1093/icsidreview/siw020

Lang A (2019) Heterodox markets and 'market distortions' in the global trading system. J Int Econ Law 22(4):677–719. https://doi.org/10.1093/jiel/jgz042

Matsushita M (2019) The WTO shares the governance of international trade with FTAs and other international organizations. In: Paradise lost or found? The post-WTO international legal order (Utopian & Dystopian possibilities). University of Tokyo, Tokyo, 9–10 January 2019

Pauwelyn J (2003) Conflict of norms in public international law: how WTO law relates to other rules of international law. Cambridge University Press, Cambridge

Ranjan P (2014) India and bilateral investment treaties – a changing landscape. ICSID Rev 29 (2):419–450. https://doi.org/10.1093/icsidreview/sit052

Rodrik D (2011) The globalization paradox: democracy and the future of the world economy. Norton, New York

Shaffer G (2019) Bargaining over policy space in trade negotiations. In: Santos A, Thomas C, Trubek DM (eds) World trade and investment law reimagined. Anthem, New York, pp 183–191

Snyder F (2010) The EU, the WTO and China: legal pluralism and international trade regulation. Hart, Oxford

Saving the World Trade Order from the Bottom Up: A Role for Preferential Trade Agreements

Peter-Tobias Stoll

Contents

Professor of Law and Jean-Monnet Chair, Director at the Institute for International Law and European Law, Head of the Department for International Economic and Environmental Law at the Georg-August-University Göttingen.

P.-T. Stoll (✉)
Institute for International Law and European Law, Georg-August-University Göttingen, Göttingen, Germany
e-mail: pstoll@gwdg.de

M. K. Lewis et al. (eds.), *A Post-WTO International Legal Order*,
https://doi.org/10.1007/978-3-030-45428-9_15

1 Introduction

When looking back, it appears that for about a quarter of a century—almost a human generation—international economic law practitioners and academics have lived in paradise. With the 1995 establishment of the World Trade Organization, they got a world trade rulebook and a world trade court. Now, many feel that this paradise may be lost. Obviously, the bold actions and the erratic course of a rather strong and influential WTO member have caused such fears. But should a single member be allowed to ban the rest from paradise? And indeed, can such a fragile thing be called a paradise in the first place? The defence for the WTO is rather modest, both in support and magnitude. It appears that there is doubt as to what to defend. What is the WTO good for and is it worth defending?

One way to find an answer to this question is to hypothetically assume that the WTO would cease to be relevant or, indeed, would cease to exist altogether. Here, such a hypothesis will be applied to the rapidly growing number of "preferential", "regional" or "free" trade agreements, as the WTO envisages under Art. XXIV GATT, Art. V GATS or the Enabling Clause and which shall jointly be referred to here as "preferential trade agreements" (PTAs). Lately, the debate has focused on discussing PTAs as rivals to the WTO in world trade governance and their potential to undermine and compromise its virtues, most importantly non-discrimination. In turn, it has been questioned whether the WTO is able and willing to effectively control these developments. By contrast, here, PTAs will be regarded from a different perspective, inquiring whether they can support or even substitute for the WTO multilateral trade system as they stand, or whether they could, at least, be further developed in this direction.

After a quick look at PTAs and their evolution, the analysis will focus on certain areas of activity and functions of the world trade order. These include market access, non-tariff-barriers and governance, including implementation, dispute settlement and negotiations. In debating these issues, two strands of discussions will be seen, which may shed a light on whether trade agreements could save the world trade order from the bottom up. One concerns the "multilateralization of regionalism", quite a topical debate around 2010. The second concerns spillover effects, through which trade agreements could be seen as providing benefits to third parties. As will be shown, the ensemble of PTAs and possible improvements contribute to the world trade order but would hardly be fit to take over essential core functions of the WTO.

2 Preferential Trade Agreements: A Mapping Exercise

Over the last decades, we have witnessed a mushrooming of preferential trade agreements both in terms of numbers and complexity. Today, slightly more than 300 trade agreements (302) are in force and 481 notifications have been made to the WTO.[1] The complexity of the resulting ensemble of treaty relationships and its evolution have been described in some detail elsewhere.[2] In our specific context of a bottom-up contribution to the world trade order, what is relevant are the structure, contents and the rationale of these agreements as well as their interactions with the WTO.

2.1 *The Momentum for Regionalism and Its Limits*

In WTO nomenclature, the majority of the agreements discussed here are called "regional" trade agreements.[3] This terminology correctly points to the fact that regionalism was an early driver of such agreements and that they still form the predominant class of trade agreements in terms of ambition and progress. This notable development started with the establishment of the EEC (1958), EFTA (1960) and the Central American Common Market (1961). The 1980s and 1990s have seen the conclusion of a whole number of further agreements, such as the Latin American Integration Association (LAIA) in 1981, the Gulf Cooperation Council (GCC) in 1981, the Andean Community in 1988, the Southern Common Market (Mercosur) in 1991, the Australian New Zealand Closer Economic Relations Trade Agreement (ANZCERTA) in 1983 or the ASEAN Free Trade Area (AFTA) in 1993. The year 1994 saw the establishment of an especially rich number of important agreements, namely the North American Free Trade Agreement (NAFTA), the European Economic Area (EEA), the Common Market for Eastern and Southern Africa (COMESA), the Commonwealth of Independent States (CIS) and the Economic Community of Western African States (ECOWAS).

All in all, today, such regional arrangements exist all over the world. Especially in recent times, we have witnessed a further completion and consolidation of such systems by way of accession of additional States, of bridging of sub-regional agreements and by way of stepping up to even more ambitious levels of integration. In most cases, such advances have been introduced by additional agreements. Thus,

---

[1] See: WTO, Regional Trade Agreements Database at https://rtais.wto.org/UI/publicsummarytable.aspx, last updated 12 December 2019. A comprehensive overview and analysis is provided in: WTO (2011) World Trade Report 2011. The WTO and Preferential Trade Agreements: From Co-Existence to Coherence, Geneva.

[2] Carpenter (2009), pp. 13–27; Fiorentino et al. (2016), pp. 28–76; Lester et al. (2016).

[3] For a reference to and the text of agreements referred to in this paper see generally the WTO Regional Trade Agreements Database at https://rtais.wto.org/UI/PublicMaintainRTAHome.aspx.

in most regions, a whole thicket of agreements exist. In terms of ambition, the agreements by far surpass multilateral standards of trade regulation. They are driven by the idea of economic integration, which often envisages some type of a common market, and close cooperation in other areas of economic governance, including financial services, competition, and investments. They also come along with advanced structures for policy dialogue and adjudication. Furthermore, such regional trade regimes are embedded in a context of regional cooperation in other dimensions, including security and foreign policy issues, human rights, development, resource management and environmental protection.

No doubt, these schemes existed long before the establishment of the WTO and can be seen as a welcome complement—just in line with the expectations that can be seen to underlie Art. XXIV GATT. They work well to bring about open markets and advanced regulation. However, in view of a possible bottom-up strategy, their contribution is limited. They can be expected to maintain open markets and regulation at regional level. However, they are rooted in regional history, politics and culture. Thus, it would be difficult to see how they could be enlarged to also cover other areas and countries outside such regional context.

2.2 *Distant Bilateralism*

Besides regionalism, a second type of agreements exists, which are typically concluded bilaterally. They are characterized by distance in geographical and political terms. Often, they are concluded between parties from two very different regions of the world. Also, they are typically characterised by their lack of will or ambition for further integration. Thus, "free trade agreements" (FTAs) is the term best suited to them. Their development is much more recent and started in the late 1990s and thus after the establishment of the WTO. Such agreements originally were much less elaborate and basically envisaged the establishment of a free trade area and the elimination of tariffs. Such agreements were concluded along trade routes or supply chains, as is particularly true for Asian countries and by parties with much trade activity or in a special geographical situation, as is true for Singapore and Chile, which were later seen as "hubs". Large trade blocs, too, engage in this regard. The US maintains such agreements with 14 partners. The EU had originally been hesitant to conclude such agreements for fear that this would undermine the multilateral system. However, in 2006, the European Commissions' "Global Europe" paper made a turnaround and advocated the conclusion of a whole set of free trade agreements.[4] Indeed, from that point onwards, the EU started several negotiations

[4]COM (2006) Communication from the Commission to the Council, the European Parliament, the European Economic and Social Committee and the Committee of the Regions Global Europe: Competing in the World a Contribution to the Eu's Growth and Jobs Strategy. COM (2006) 567 final of 4.10.2006.

to partner up with a large number of countries around the world, including the US, Canada, Japan, Korea, Vietnam, Singapore, Mexico, India and others. Meanwhile, this type of agreement has gained importance, as signified sometimes by calling these agreements "deep" agreements. They often contain important additions to WTO disciplines and envisage cooperation in competition policies and in the areas of non-tariff barriers standards and regulations. Recently, they also involve investment policies and protection and even chapters on sustainable development, environmental protection and labour standards. In these latter areas, they also envisage the participation of civil society.

Clearly, the growing number of bilateral agreements and their further development is driven by a dynamic of competition. States and trade blocs around the world compete for potential partners and favourable conditions.

While, as has been seen, the WTO and regionalism can go along quite easily, the developments concerning bilateral agreements have been met with quite some concern. As not least the 2006 EU paper indicates, these developments can be seen as a reaction to the WTO's inability to make progress with the Doha round. Also, such agreements, when they proliferate further, could indeed undermine the WTO's principle of non-discrimination and also result in an erosion of traditional preferences, most importantly those afforded to developing countries under the Enabling Clause. Nevertheless, under a bottom-up perspective as discussed here, these agreements could be a promising basis, if we see them as some sort of a network.

2.3 Plurilateralism: The Comprehensive and Progressive Agreement for Trans-Pacific Partnership—CPTPP

A potentially promising dynamic is reflected by the recently established CPTPP, which joins eleven parties from across the Pacific within a far-sighted and progressive agreement. Because of the number of parties, who come from formerly distinct regional contexts, the CPTPP might be seen as a forerunner for larger—even "plurilateral" regimes, which emerge outside the traditional patterns of regional integration and "small" bilateralism. The existence of a number of ties in terms of trade routes and supply chains has probably prompted this agreement. Also the emergence of the agreement might have been helped by the early initiative of the US, which abandoned the project with the coming into office of the current administration after an earlier iteration of the agreement (the Trans-Pacific Partnership, TPP) had been already finalized. It is an open question whether such favourable conditions would promote this type of agreement also in other areas of the world.

2.4 Linking Regional Trade Blocs: The Transregional Dimension

Another and potentially even more promising avenue for a "bottom-up" approach is the development of various initiatives to link trade blocs of different regions. A number of such agreements are under way or have even already been established. As examples, the EU-Cariforum (2008), EU-CAFTA (2012) and EFTA's agreements with SACU and the GCC may be mentioned. In 2018, a Memorandum of Understanding was concluded between ASEAN and the Eurasian Economic Union on economic cooperation.[5] On 28 June 2019 and after almost 20 years of negotiation, MERCOSUR and the EU agreed "in principle" on a comprehensive trade agreement as part of a larger association agreement.[6]

One particularly ambitious and demanding project has been to set up a trade agreement between the EU and ASEAN. Negotiations started in 2000 but were suspended in 2009. However, talks continue on a broader scale of topics with the aim of a strategic partnership and the EU aims to intensify negotiations with particular States of the ASEAN region, which is seen as a stepping stone towards a future comprehensive EU-ASEAN arrangement. A similar development could occur regarding the relations between the EU and the Andean Community. The EU has concluded a free trade agreement with three of the Andean Community's four member states, while the fourth one, Bolivia, currently receives preferential market access via the EU's Generalized System of Preferences.[7]

2.5 Preferential Trade Agreements: Conclusion

Regional trade agreements are by and large compatible with the WTO system but have a natural limit posed by their focus on regional integration. Bilateral agreements, for their part, are not confined to geographic regions. However, their sheer number increases the fragmentation of international trade law. Two more recent developments, "plurilateral" trade agreements between more than two states and trans-regional agreements concluded between two regional integration organizations, could serve to mitigate the concerns of fragmentation while managing to overcome the inherent limits of regionalism.

---

[5]See ASEAN and EEC (2018) Memorandum of Understanding between the Association of Southeast Asian Nations and the Eurasian Economic Commission on Economic Cooperation https://asean.org/storage/2018/11/MOU-between-ASEAN-and-the-EEC_Signed-English.pdf.

[6]See European Commission (2019) New EU-Mercosur trade agreement. The agreement in principle, Brussels, 1 July 2019, https://trade.ec.europa.eu/doclib/docs/2019/june/tradoc_157964.pdf.

[7]See European Commission (2019) Countries and Regions, Andean Community https://ec.europa.eu/trade/policy/countries-and-regions/regions/andean-community/.

3 Market Access and the Multilateralization of Regionalism

Providing market access through the reduction or elimination of tariff barriers is the original and still vital function of the international trading system. The multilateral part of this system envisages binding tariffs and their further reduction on a most-favoured nation basis. In times of bold unilateral tariff increases imposed to persuade several WTO members to agree to "deals", the vital importance of securing market access and equal treatment everywhere and for all is evident.

The various trade agreements mentioned above are different: they offer more liberalization for a small and exclusive number of parties. So far, PTAs have been seen by many as a welcome "preferential" addition to multilateral market access provided for by the WTO.[8] Assuming that the latter would become less reliable or even assuming its non-existence, the question would arise as to what extent this ensemble of trade agreements could support or substitute WTO-type market access or at least could be developed in this direction.

To date, PTAs seem unfit to meet this challenge. While they govern significant portions of world trade in economic terms, a closer look reveals that this is mainly true for regional trade. Imagining a map of world trade, the many customs unions and free trade areas created by those agreements would look like separate spots or like a patchwork. Market access on these terms is clearly not for all and everywhere. Also, the imaginary map of the ensemble of agreements invites a visual illusion: while it suggests that goods and services could move around in a market access network built by agreements, in reality all these connections are carefully separated by origin and respective rules. However, a number of avenues have been explored below to broaden the market access under those agreements.

3.1 Bilateralism à la BIT: A Merely Theoretical Option

Firstly, and more as a theoretical starting point, one could imagine a world of bilateralism. In such a scenario, states or customs territories would conclude as many separate agreements as they deem necessary to meet their trade needs. This vision comes close to the fabric of international investment protection with its many bilateral investment treaties. Already at first glance, it is obvious that such bilateralism would importantly further fuel fragmentation, which already to date is a problem, and which is often referred to under the term "spaghetti bowl". If the appetite for "deep" rules would make its way into more and more agreements, this scenario would be close to absurdity. The situation would become even more absurd

[8] See, however, the caution warranted by the Nairobi Ministerial Declaration: "We reaffirm the need to ensure that Regional Trade Agreements (RTAs) remain complementary to, not a substitute for, the multilateral trading system.", WT/MIN(15)/DEC 19 December 2015 para 28.

if we were additionally to assume a non-WTO scenario where no disciplines apply in view of permissible forms of the control of market access, including rules of origin.

3.2 Enlarging Existing Agreements: The Accession Option

A more promising avenue could be to open up existing agreements for accession by additional parties. This way, new parties would become parties to the existing customs unions or free trade areas and enjoy market access without having to conclude separate agreements with any of the parties. Likewise, market access for pre-existing parties would be enlarged, because it would cover an additional customs territory. Quite a number of agreements explicitly welcome accessions.[9] Accessions to agreements without explicit accession clauses might also be feasible by way of an amendment, if parties so agree. Indeed, some regional agreements have seen accessions in recent years.[10] These accessions helped to consolidate market access in regions. Within the group of typically bilateral agreements as described above, accessions have rarely taken place thus far. Presumably, the bilateral culture of such agreements, as well as the carefully negotiated reciprocal trade concessions, are not supportive of inviting additional parties.

3.3 Creating New and More Encompassing Agreements

Another way of improving market access would be to create new and additional agreements with a larger number of customs territories. The CPTPP could serve as a role model in this regard. However, so far, it remains the only significant example. Will we see more in times of a weakened or absent multilateral system? Beyond the culture of regionalism, the promotion of such agreements would have to rely on the persuasive power of the rational argument that "bigger" agreements have a number of advantages, most notably larger market access. Of course, common economic interest in trade routes and supply chains would help. But would it promote the clustering of relations, which so far often have been strictly bilateral? Furthermore, there is a chance that such more inclusive agreements would center around one or two major economic powers, like e.g. the US-CAFTA-DR FTA, which is formally plurilateral regarding membership but is in reality very much dominated by one party.

[9]Crawford JA (2012) Market Access Provisions on Trade in Goods in Regional Trade Agreements. WTO Staff Working Paper ERSD-2012-20, pp. 28–44.

[10]For example, the 2012 EU-Colombia-Peru FTA was acceded to by Ecuador in 2016.

3.4 *Linking Existing Schemes of Liberalization at Intra-regional and Trans-regional Levels*

A more comprehensive way of enlarging market access would be to link existing agreements in a way that economic operators within one regime could also enjoy access to markets in another regime. Indeed, we see schemes like this emerging within regions, as is true for Europe, the African continent and for Latin America. Linking existing regional trade blocs across the world could be seen as a silver bullet for achieving market access as close as possible to a multilateral dimension by way of a bottom-up strategy. The EU-MERCOSUR trade agreement can be held as a forerunner in this regard. Art. X of the trade part of the agreement envisages "regional integration" by "facilitat[ing] the movement of goods and services between and within the two regions". In this regard:

> goods originating in a signatory Member State of MERCOSUR that are released for free circulation in the European Union ... shall benefit from free movement of goods within the territory of the European Union ... under the conditions established by the Treaty on the Functioning of the European Union; (Art. X (2)a)

whereas

> the signatory Member States of MERCOSUR shall apply to goods originating in the European Union ... that are imported in its territory from another signatory Member State of MERCOSUR, customs procedures that are no less favourable than those applicable to goods originating in that signatory Member State of Mercosur. (Art. X (2) b)[11]

3.5 *MFN Clauses in PTAs as a Means to Spread Market Access*

Another vision of increasing market access would be to allow parties of one agreement to become involved in an agreement that is subsequently concluded by only one of them with a third party. In general, market access is only provided for within an agreement and distinct from other arrangements with other parties. However, sometimes, trade agreements include so-called most-favoured nation clauses, which allow parties to participate in benefits of an agreement that one of them subsequently concludes with a third party. Probably, such clauses are inserted to ensure that the competitive advantage of market access concessions made in one agreement is not put into question by one of the parties subsequently engaging in an even more beneficial deal with a third party.

---

[11]European Commission (2019) EU-Mercosur Association Agreement, Trade Part of the Agreement. Following the Agreement in Principle announced on 28 June 2019, https://trade.ec.europa.eu/doclib/docs/2019/july/tradoc_158143.%20Regional%20Integration%20Clause.pdf.

Of course, this kind of benefit by most-favoured nation treatment falls short of full membership to a subsequent agreement with a third party. Nevertheless, one could imagine such most-favoured nation treatment to importantly amplify the effect of market access concessions granted under partly overlapping trade agreements. And, of course, parallels to the world of investment law are obvious where similar MFN clauses exist and produce a significant networking or "multilateralization" effect.[12]

There is a lot of variation between those clauses, relating to their coverage, their effect and the conditions upon which such treatment is granted. In rare cases, such an effect takes place automatically, whereas other clauses envisage that reciprocity has to be granted. Still other clauses require some sort of negotiations and agreement.[13]

However, the idea of such most-favoured nation clauses in FTAs has also been met with criticism. Some fear that such clauses could discourage parties from concluding additional agreements for fear of having to share benefits subsequently with their partners from pre-existing agreements. Moreover, considerable doubts have been voiced as to whether such sharing can be limited to parties of pre-existing preferential agreements. The point has been made that other WTO Members can legitimately ask for similar treatment under the more general MFN principle of the WTO, as Art. XXIV GATT cannot exempt those MFN clauses.[14]

Notwithstanding such shortcomings and concerns, overall, it cannot be doubted that MFN clauses have the potential to further promote market access. This is particularly so in a non-WTO scenario, where concerns about the applicability of Art. XXIV as an exemption from general WTO most-favoured nation treatment would not be relevant.

3.6 In Conclusion: Multilateralization of Regionalism and Its Limits

The various options considered here in view of enlarging and advancing market access were all part of the larger discussion of "multilateralization of regionalism", which has been mentioned before and took place some ten years ago.[15] Interestingly, "multilateralization" was called for in this discourse to remedy the inherent problems of the growing system of PTAs rather than to care for the WTO, which was still going strong at the time. Indeed, because of the notorious spaghetti-bowl issues and the considerable fragmentation, some sort of clustering or "multilateralization" was recommended. On an optimistic note, one thus could conclude that today, there is a double momentum for "multilateralization". In this scenario parties could be persuaded to use all the above options both because there is an inherent need to reform

[12]Schill (2009).

[13]Crawford (2012).

[14]Kim (2014), p. 443.

[15]Baldwin and Low (2009).

the current ensemble of PTAs and because a more multilateral-type of market access is called for in times of a contestation of the WTO or in a non-WTO scenario.

However, in the end, a "bottom-up" approach to achieving multilateral market access by means of further developing preferential agreements is like driving with a flat tyre: Even in sum, the market access opportunities provided for in this way would by far fail to achieve what the WTO MFN system is achieving. Richer and politically more relevant players will be able to arrange for market access swiftly and to ask for preferences according to their wishes. Others will experience difficulties, lose existing preferences in what may be called preference erosion and will no longer enjoy any protection against the erratic course of trade policy of some strong actors in the field. If we take the WTO out of the picture entirely, there would be no MFN and no disciplining exceptions, such as Art. XXIV GATT and Art. V GATS. In such a scenario, bold bilateralism would prevail.

4 NTBs, Standards and Spillover Effects

With the successful reduction and elimination of tariffs and quotas, the many non-tariff barriers to trade became more visible. They include all sorts of regulations which are applied at the border or in the market and make trade difficult and burdensome. Preventing protectionist abuse of standards and providing open regulatory environments for global value chains is the coming most challenging task in international trade regulation and policy. For quite some time, PTAs have been playing a significant role in this regard as witnessed by the conclusion of "deep" agreements containing specific and exhaustive rules or even whole chapters on these issues.[16]

The point is sometimes made that while being "preferential" in market access, trade agreements are somehow open in regard to regulatory issues and can even produce beneficial "spillover effects" for the world trade community at large. This would, of course, provide important support for the "bottom-up" approach.

4.1 Multilateral Disciplines of Regulatory Action: Can They Be Preserved by PTAs?

Trade law addresses standards in two ways: it disciplines the scope and extent of unilateral regulatory action and provides for mechanisms to facilitate trade between different regulatory environments. The former issue importantly relies on multilateral rules. Art. XX and XXI GATT and the SPS and TBT agreements set up a framework to prevent the excessive or protectionist use of unilateral exercises of the

[16]Mathis (2016), pp. 142–168.

right to regulate. They do so by defining permissible policy goals and conditions for related measures. In EU parlance, this set of rules can be described as pursuing "negative integration".

Moreover, most modern PTAs mirror those WTO rules with a few additions on procedures and cooperation. In the case of a weakening or even absent WTO regime, those rules would still stand. At first glance, this looks like a rather effective entrenchment of multilateral rules. However, aside from a possible change in PTA language, this effect is questionable when dispute settlement comes into play. Very likely, complaints in the agreements' proper dispute settlement mechanisms will be blocked by explicit exclusions. Such exclusions are provided for in many recent PTAs to prevent dispute settlement parallelism and to pave the way to WTO settlement as the more appropriate forum to hear cases relying on WTO treaty language. If the route to WTO dispute settlement becomes more rocky, the effective enforcement of these disciplines will become altogether critical and may easily end up in a double fault.

4.2 Convergence of Regulatory Environments: Decentralized and Multilateral Benefits

While being strong in setting outer limits to the right to regulate, the WTO does not play much of a role in promoting coherence among regulatory environments. At the global level, the Codex Alimentarius and the ISO play a role in promoting harmonization in the field of food and feed and technical standards.

Besides these laudable, but altogether limited endeavours, the task to facilitate trade among different regulatory environments is taken care of at bilateral or plurilateral levels. Mutual recognition agreements are concluded for that purpose in great numbers on a bilateral basis or at regional levels and address issues like equivalence and conformity assessments. The more recent "deep" PTAs often build on such agreements and contain additional elements and mechanisms, which may even amount to what has been called regulatory cooperation. WTO rules play a limited role in this regard, which is confined to safeguarding transparency, calling on members to engage in cooperation and in participation. One can conclude at this point that convergence of regulatory regimes is an issue which is dealt with at decentralized levels anyway, and would not be much affected if the WTO were to become less relevant or even left out of the picture.

4.3 Spillover Effects: The Larger Picture

While relying on cooperation at bilateral or plurilateral levels, this type of activity is hardly confined to producing "preferential" effects or resting on exclusivity. As seen, the elimination of tariffs and quotas among parties takes place on a "preferential" basis and the parties to the PTA will be keen not to share those benefits with third parties. However, when parties agree on common standards on the basis of PTAs or MRAs, they often have an interest in disseminating their standards around the world. This is often seen as a "positive spillover effect" as third parties can export to more than one market under the same standards.[17]

As this may indicate, PTAs are not necessarily driven by preference only. Besides granting preferential market access as a core function, trade agreements also contain parts that surpass the logic of exclusivity. They might be driven by an essential interest in propagating their standards in a run to compete with other trade blocs in determining the world's future rules on products and services.

Sometimes, non-exclusivity might also result from WTO rules. This is true for intellectual property because of the fact that the TRIPs Agreement lacks a most-favoured nation treatment exception along the lines of Art. XXIV GATT and Art. V GATS. In other cases, it might not be worthwhile to invest the effort in preferential treatment. Also, PTAs might produce beneficial effects for third parties *de facto*, as is true for disciplines on subsidies and their application, which will also benefit third parties. Lastly, third parties may benefit from disciplines on labour standards and environmental protection as contained in sustainable development chapters in a number of more recent PTAs, as this might help to preserve a level playing field.

As has been emphasized, such effects, sometimes called "spillover effects," can indeed deliver important services to the larger trade community. However, the nature and extent of such effects are worth a closer look.

4.3.1 Spillover Effects: de facto or de iure?

When looked at in some detail, it appears that the legal nature and extent of such beneficial effects varies significantly. In the area of intellectual property, the position of third states and their nationals is very strong. It relies on most-favoured nation treatment and national treatment under Arts. 3 and 4 of the TRIPs agreement, which—as has been seen—do not contain an exemption for preferential agreements along the lines of Art. XXIV GATT or V GATS or the Enabling Clause. What is more, national treatment is even seconded by the respective WIPO Conventions, which contain similar clauses on national treatment.

In the case of standards and regulations, the mutual recognition of conformity assessments or even of the equivalence of standards themselves within a PTA is helpful for their parties, as they may export to the members of the PTA on the same conditions. Thus, by meeting conditions on conformity assessment or standards as

[17] See generally Pauwelyn (2017), pp. 61–74.

defined within a PTA, industries in third countries can often export to all the members of the PTA on a uniform basis.[18]

Again, different is the kind of benefit delivered to third parties by effective control of subsidies within a PTA. Certainly, this is a *de facto* benefit. However, third parties do not have any entitlement to initiate enforcement action in this regard within and under the rules of a PTA. While the continued applicability of WTO subsidies rules through reference made to them in a PTA is good news in a non-WTO scenario, third parties have no means to initiate or enforce their application. The same—just a *de facto* benefit—applies in view of provisions in PTAs on labour standards and environmental protection.

4.3.2 Participation: An Open Question with Regard to Standards

These diverse spillover effects, whether accruing *de facto* or *de iure*, are certainly relevant for upholding some disciplines and governance in scenarios in which multilateral rules are less effective or absent altogether. However, that does not mean that third parties necessarily endorse these effects in a particular case. This will, probably, not pose much of a problem regarding intellectual property, subsidies and sustainable development commitments. However, any sort of regulatory cooperation within a PTA may impact export industries in third parties. Third parties may be concerned about PTA joint action in the field of regulation. They may understand these activities to reflect industry practice and market expectations among PTA members rather than taking into account the conditions prevailing in potentially quite different environments. While the WTO lacks a mandate to engage in achieving conformity among regulatory environments themselves, it envisages at least some sort of participation to give third parties a voice in regulatory activities in other Members, as Art. 4 of the SPS Agreement and Art. 2 of the TBT Agreement illustrate.

5 The Governance Question

In the international trade order, many substantive elements such as market access are embedded in a system of governance for implementation, dispute settlement and negotiations. In general, these diverse systems of governance are charged to serve their proper regimes and respective institutional and procedural rules. The question, therefore, arises as to how governance functions of trade agreements could contribute to multilateral governance in a scenario of substantially weakened or non-existent WTO governance.

[18]In detail, however, some restrictions may apply as mutual recognition may be confined to trade in products originating in one of the PTA members. For instance, Art. 4 of an MRA between New Zealand and Iceland, Liechtenstein and Norway from 19.4.1999 states: "1. This Agreement shall apply to products originating in the Parties to the Agreement according to the non-preferential rules of origin.". https://lovdata.no/dokument/TRAKTATEN/traktat/1999-04-29-1.

5.1 *Implementation*

Most trade systems have specific institutions and procedures in place for implementation, which administer, guide and promote implementation and compliance. At the WTO level, a number of councils, committees and other bodies are charged with this task. Their work is importantly supported by the complex and manifold notifications on the policies and actions of Members. In addition, many of these notifications, discussions and decisions by WTO bodies are publicly available and thus provide for a high level of transparency. Implementation is also a key element in dispute settlement and is also supported by the Trade Policy Review Mechanism.

PTAs have similar devices at hand, often less sophisticatedly designed. This is due to the fact that the relevant institutions and procedures do not need to accommodate more than two parties at a time, and that the limited regional or bilateral setting promotes a spirit of cooperation. These governance structures support the PTAs and compliance with their rules. As has been seen, these rules provide for some limited market access and also have "spillover" effects and furthermore, often "mirror" WTO rules. In these confines, they also would be supportive to a bottom-up strategy. Conversely, however, it should be noted that by its notification and transparency provisions, the WTO also supports implementation at regional/bilateral levels, which would fail in a scenario as discussed here.

5.2 *Dispute Settlement*

In addition to implementation, dispute settlement is an important governance element of the international trade order. It serves three objectives, namely the settlement of disputes, enforcement and compliance, and the further clarification of the pertinent rules. The WTO dispute settlement mechanism includes a panel procedure and an additional appellate review. As is well known, the latter is currently blocked, as, as of 10 December 2019, the number of members fell below the necessary quorum of three, when the term of two Members expired without any decision taken as to their replacement. While, certainly, the blockade of the nomination of new members and of the appellate procedure as such is regrettable, the panel stage of the WTO dispute settlement is still working.

Moreover, other trade agreements are equipped with dispute settlement mechanisms. A few advanced regional systems have courts in place, as is true for e.g. the EU, Mercosur, African regimes and the Eurasian Union, some of which are very fruitful in generating jurisprudence. The majority of PTAs, however, provide for less-elaborated mechanisms, which come close to the WTO panel stage procedure and lack an appellate review. Also, and as is often highlighted, they are not very active.

There is quite an overlap between the two levels of WTO and PTA dispute settlement. While, formally, the different dispute settlement bodies only apply the rules of the respective multilateral, regional or bilateral agreements, rules are sometimes similar and the measures at dispute often relate to different rules at both levels. That has been particularly worrisome in the case of NAFTA, where complaints have been brought to NAFTA dispute settlement and to the WTO in sequence or even in parallel. As a consequence, recent PTAs tend to exclude the applicability of their own dispute settlement for chapters which mirror or are close to WTO rules, or contain a "fork in the road" provision which precludes bringing the same dispute to both the PTA and the WTO.[19] In sum, there is a strong tendency to favour WTO dispute settlement, which is further promoted by the reputation of the WTO as an experienced and reliable dispute settlement agency. Thus, under today's conditions, the WTO delivers an important service to PTAs by doing much of the dispute settlement work. In a non-WTO scenario, PTA parties would have to strengthen their own proper dispute settlement mechanisms significantly by removing the aforementioned limitations and by submitting more cases to these PTA dispute settlement mechanisms. Nonetheless, if this is done, the applicable rules and their interpretations would stem from and relate to the agreements at hand only, potentially bringing about or increasing fragmentation from a multilateral point of view.

5.3 Negotiations and Forum Functions

Furthermore, apart from implementation and dispute settlement, there is a need for a viable, effective and sustainable international forum to reflect on and further develop rules to cope with changing realities. Regarding the WTO, this is often referred to as a forum function. Indeed, according to Art. II:1 of the WTO agreement:

> [t]he WTO shall provide the common institutional framework for the conduct of trade relations among its Members in matters related to the agreements and associated legal instruments

and shall:

> provide the forum for negotiations among its Members concerning their multilateral trade relations in matters dealt with under the agreements . . . The WTO may also provide a forum for further negotiations among its Members concerning their multilateral trade relations (Art. III:2)

5.3.1 Negotiation and Innovation

As is well known, the most prominent and probably overly ambitious negotiation project of the WTO, the Doha Round, has been, by and large, blocked for over a decade.[20]

[19] Stoll (2019b), pp. 229–244.

[20] Stoll (2019a), p. 74.

As is often highlighted, today, new rules for international trade are primarily introduced through PTAs. Also, it can be observed that such new rules sometimes spread around. It should be noted, however, that this innovation takes place when new agreements are being concluded and that we know little about innovations taking place within the operation of existing ones. One could thus conclude that a weakened or non-existent WTO would have fewer repercussions on this innovation function. However, notwithstanding its actual impasse, the WTO has the potential to act as a forum to translate these new rules to the multilateral level.

5.3.2 Forum Function

Aside from negotiations, trade regimes provide a forum for political discourse, which might address issues of implementation, dispute settlement and negotiations. In a scenario with a weaker or even absent WTO, institutions in trade agreements at the regional or bilateral level would still work. So far, they generally focus on their own matters. In a few cases and with regard to certain specific topics, they provide for coordination or joint action in view of WTO forums.[21]

However, in order to support or replace the forum function provided by the WTO, PTAs would have to take ownership over a broad range of issues of a multilateral dimension. As an example of the issues at stake, the 2008 financial crisis comes to mind. In that situation, a policy dialogue in the WTO helped to prevent WTO members from closing their markets. It is hard to believe that institutions of regional or bilateral agreements could or would have engaged in a similar way because of a lack of both the mandate and the legitimacy. It is even harder to imagine that they could join forces in some way to coordinate and take action.[22]

6 Conclusion

Could the world trade order be secured by the rapidly growing number of PTAs, if we take the WTO out of the picture for the sake of argument? This timely question is a difficult one. And perhaps, these difficulties are telling.

First, having taken the WTO as a given for quite some time, it is useful to reiterate its main purposes and benefits. It is a system providing for non-discriminatory market access for everyone everywhere based on mutual concessions, delivered through an organization where everybody has a say. This is an impressive bulwark against bilateralism, power politics and a strong businesses, traders and smaller and

[21]See CETA, Art. 7.4 (1)(a): agricultural trade, (b): fisheries subsidies, Art. 23.7 (1)(b): labour standards; Art. 24.12 (1)(b): multilateral environmental agreements; EU-Japan, Art. 4.12: customs cooperation, Art. 18.3: regulatory cooperation.

[22]See Bown (2017), p. 109.

developing countries. As stated above, even a far more developed combination of preferential market access will be like driving with a flat tyre: manageable and even enjoyable for rich drivers only.

Second, preferential agreements have their place in the world trade order. They produce some beneficial services for the wider community, including promotion of coherence of standards and regulations. However, the prospects of world standards and regulatory cooperation should not let us forget the virtues of the WTO in setting outer limits for unilateral regulatory action. If GATT Art. XX and related disciplines fail, we are likely to see imports conditioned by labour standards and all other sorts of "fairness" virtually overnight.

Third, the WTO and PTAs are more closely related than one would assume at first glance. PTAs contain innovative rules, which the WTO could take up later, if it were to get over its various blockades. In turn, PTAs rely on the WTO not only for its dispute settlement mechanism but also, more importantly, for its ability to keep a minimum level of coherence and non-discrimination in what would otherwise become a formidably fragmented order. Most importantly, however, the WTO is the only forum where global trade issues can be addressed—with a say for everybody. If we take the WTO out of the picture for analytical reasons, these few insights would suggest that we need to urgently join forces to build such a paradise again—possibly by ironing out some of its shortcomings. If the WTO did not exist, it would have to be invented.

References

Baldwin R, Low P (eds) (2009) Multilateralizing regionalism. CUP, Cambridge

Bown CP (2017) Mega-regional trade agreements and the future of the WTO. Council of Foreign Relations. Global Policy 8(1):107–112

Carpenter T (2009) A historical perspective on regionalism. In: Baldwin R, Low P (eds) Multilateralizing regionalism. CUP, Cambridge, pp 13–27

Fiorentino RV, Crawford JA, Toqueboeuf C (2016) The landscape of regional trade agreements and WTO surveillance. In: Baldwin R, Low P (eds) Multilateralizing regionalism. CUP, Cambridge, pp 28–76

Kim JB (2014) Entrenchment of regionalism: WTO legality of MFN clauses in preferential trade agreements for goods and services. World Trade Rev 13:443

Lester S, Mercurio B, Bartels L (eds) (2016) Bilateral and regional trade agreements: case studies. CUP, Cambridge

Mathis J (2016) Regulatory regionalism in the WTO: are 'deep integration' processes compatible with the multilateral trading system? In: Lester S, Mercurio B, Bartels L (eds) Bilateral and regional trade agreements: commentary and analysis. CUP, Cambridge, pp 142–168

Pauwelyn J (2017) Not as preferential as you may think: how mega-regionals can benefit third countries. In: Rensmann (ed) Mega-regional trade agreements. Springer, Cham, pp 61–74

Schill SW (2009) The multilateralization of international investment law. CUP, Cambridge

Stoll PT (2019a) A Washington wake-up call and hybrid governance for world trade. QIL, Zoom-Out 63:59–81

Stoll PT (2019b) The WTO dispute settlement system and regional trade tribunals: the potential for conflict and solutions. In: do Amaral Júnior A, de Oliveira Sá Pires L, Lucena Carneiro C (eds) The WTO dispute settlement mechanism. Springer, Cham, pp 229–244

A New International Trade Framework for Digital Assets

Rolf H. Weber

Contents

1 Introduction: Utopia and Dystopia in the WTO Context

As widely acknowledged, the World Trade Organization (WTO) is confronted with manifold challenges, originally coming from the political environment of increasing nationalism, but having a substantial influence on the normative framework. Technological advances lead to the situation that classifications as discussed in and introduced by the Uruguay Round are outdated to a remarkable extent; the adaption

Professor of International Business Law at the Law Faculty of the University of Zurich, and practicing attorney at-law in Zürich, Switzerland.

R. H. Weber (✉)
Law Faculty, University of Zurich, Zürich, Switzerland
e-mail: rolf.weber@rwi.uzh.ch

M. K. Lewis et al. (eds.), *A Post-WTO International Legal Order*,
https://doi.org/10.1007/978-3-030-45428-9_16

of the regime would need the consensus of a much larger number of countries as for the implementation of the WTO more than 25 years ago. Therefore, disruptive technologies can impact the present normative situation in form of a stagnation in the foreseeable future or even in a disruptive way.[1]

A "disruption" as such, often known from natural sciences, is also not a new phenomenon in social sciences. In the context of the search for the ideal social order several disciplines have developed a number of imaginable models in the past, for example the so-called concept of utopia and of dystopia. Notwithstanding the fact that at the origins the social order at large was targeted, an analogous application can also be taken into account in the context of the international trade regime. Therefore, the respective notions need to be described.

(i) *Utopia* (literally translated as "no-place") refers to a non-existent society having been coined more than five hundred years ago by Sir Thomas Morus as the title of his well-known book "Utopia" (1516).[2] In the perception of Morus, the term utopia describes an imaginary place where social, political and moral aspects are considered to be perfect. (ii) In contrast, *dystopia* (literally translated as "not-good place"), linked to dehumanization, totalitarian governance or other declines in society, reflects the situation of an undesirable community. Many subgenres of fiction deal with dystopian societies for calling attention to real-world issues such as corruption in politics, environmental pollution, religious wars or unethical behaviour.

During the last 50 years efforts have been undertaken to better incorporate *utopian projects* into the structure of legislative and regulatory (international and national) regimes. Initially qualified as "Framework of Utopia" by Robert Nozick,[3] more recently autonomous cultural arrangements were assessed through the lens "From Apology to Utopia" (Martti Koskenniemi)[4] by outlining the international legal order's descriptive and normative concerns. Similar to utopian projects some 70 years ago the voices pointing to *dystopian societies* became louder, for example in "Nineteen Eighty-Four" (George Orwell)[5] showing a totalitarian invasive super State or in "Fahrenheit 451" (Ray Bradbury)[6] addressing the burning of books to create apathy and disinterest in the general public.

By transferring these different utopian/dystopian scenarios to the present uncertainties of the international trade regime the question arises whether the future regulatory framework leaves some room for a forward-looking normative

---

[1]See the introduction of Picker and Nakagawa (2020), pp. ... Recently, the Economist (30th November 2019, 61) used the article title "Global trade: It's the end of the World .... Trade Organisation as we know it, and America feels fine".

[2]More T (Morus) (1516/1869) Utopia, Libellus vere aureus, translated into English in 1551 by Robinson R and Burnet G. Alex Murray & Sons, London.

[3]Nozick (1974).

[4]Koskenniemi (2009), pp. 562–573.

[5]Orwell (1949).

[6]Bradbury (1953).

environment between the "no-place" model (utopian perspective) and the "not-good place" concept (dystopian perspective). Therefore, efforts are needed which could help to avoid the biblical situation of a "Menetekel" (i.e. a "writing on the wall")[7] constituting the threat that the days of the organization (the "kingdom") are limited (to be counted). The potential approaches can be more general or more specific. In this article, the respective discussion is led with respect to digital assets as concrete example, addressing the almost unsurmountable challenges caused by digital assets in the present WTO regime and developing ideas how a new normative framework could be designed.

As an introductory starting point for the design of the normative environment,[8] the observation must be recalled that the international trade regime cannot exist without a minimal legal order that does have a social impact. Therefore, concepts and designs need to be transformed into reality. Such kind of perception was not obvious in the past: (i) Plato understood his democracy proposal in his treatise "Republic" as an utopian idea.[9] (ii) Morus envisaged in his novel "Utopia" a paradise on a fictional island in the Atlantic Ocean on which an ideal society could exist. (iii) In the nineteenth Century, many social movements in Europe searched for various forms of utopian environments; the non-existing society as understood by the term "utopia" converged into an ideal society in these theoretical models.[10]

2 Tensions Between New Developments and Old Categories

2.1 Technological Advances

The Internet in its original form has been established more than 50 years ago and the involvement of civil society and businesses in the Internet goes 25 years back. The Internet has dramatically changed the communication tools and opened the door for new business models mainly executed on virtual platforms. The multi-sided markets offer new opportunities for international trade. All these developments cause major legal tensions and frictions.[11]

During the last few years, the distributed ledger (blockchain) technology (DLT) got established as an alternative infrastructure. Communications and assets in the form of tokens can be transported in an anonymous way. So far, the regulatory environment and the governance in the DLT context appear to be underdeveloped.[12]

---

[7]In "Book of Daniel" in the Bible (5:30–31), the writing on the wall is described in the context of king Belshazzar's feast.

[8]For a general overview to these questions see Weber (2016a), p. 198.

[9]Plato (1942).

[10]See also Weber (2014), p. 107.

[11]For a general overview Peng (2019), pp. 1–27.

[12]For a general overview see Weber (2017), pp. 1–6.

This fact appears to be unsatisfactory since data usually represents a value; in whatever (digital) form such a value is transferred, the DLT technology increases efficiency at low costs (and often also security) of the transaction.

Apart from the traditional fixed line and the expanding mobile networks, new inventions are attempting to facilitate the transmission of data. The aim is to provide reasonably fast, high-quality connections to almost everyone around the globe. Instead of the familiar terrestrial technology the following new technological developments are noteworthy: (i) The US firm OneWeb plans to launch 648 small relatively simple satellites into low orbits of 1200 km providing a latency similar to that offered by a fixed line connection.[13] (ii) SpaceX of Elon Musk intends to use about 4000 satellites at a similar altitude of the orbit having very sophisticated functions.[14] (iii) Rival technologies (for example developed by Facebook's Connectivity Lab) try to plug specific gaps in the existing infrastructure; special drones should provide basic access to a small number of sites free for users.[15] (iv) Google has also started to experiment with drones: the project "Loon" envisages to grid the earth with a swarm of thousands of helium-filled balloons containing solar powered wireless transmitters.[16]

In parallel to the new technological developments of the digital infrastructures, new appearances can also be seen in the "hardware" context. Products and services (i.e. tangible assets) are tokenized as digital units; thereafter, the values can easily be transferred in the form of such tokens. Mostly, even if a common definition has not yet been established, the term "digital assets" or "crypto assets" is used for such kind of values.[17]

2.2 *Limited Suitability of GATT and GATS*

The General Agreement on Tariffs and Trade (GATT) has been negotiated in the late fifties of the last century and partly adapted during the Uruguay-Round (1986–1993). The General Agreement on Trade Services (GATS) was a new "invention" of the Uruguay-Round. Looking at the time of the respective

[13]Winkler G (2015) Greg Wyler's OneWeb Satellite-Internet Company Secures Funding. The Wall Street Journal, 14 January 2015. http://www.wsj.com/articles/greg-wylers-oneweb-satellite-internet-company-secures-funding-1421278832.

[14]Majumdar D (2015) Why the Time Seems Right for a Space-Based Internet Service. MIT Technology Review, 27 January 2015. http://www.technologyreview.com/news/534361/why-the-time-seems-right-for-a-space-based-internet-service/.

[15]Simonite T (2014) Facebook's Drones Will Battle Google's Balloons to Spread Internet Access. MIT Technology Review, 27 March 2014. http://www.technologyreview.com/view/525951/facebooks-drones-will-battle-googles-balloons-to-spread-internet-access/.

[16]Simonite T (2015) 10 Breakthrough Technologies 2015: Project Loon. MIT Technology Review, 18 February 2015. https://www.technologyreview.com/s/534986/project-loon/.

[17]For an overview see Blanke (2014).

negotiations, it is obvious that the contract parties to the GATT and the GATS could not take into account the changes caused by the Internet and the digitization since the society was living in an analogue world. Therefore, it is not surprising that the rules do not easily comply with the needs of the digital environment.

2.2.1 History and Notion

As mentioned, during the Uruguay-Round e-commerce was still at its infancy stage; the launch of the online giants Amazon and eBay marked the official "birth" of e-commerce. Consequently, neither the GATT nor the GATS provide a legal definition of the term "e-commerce" or the term "digital trade". The 1998 adopted "Work Programme on E-Commerce" describes the term e-commerce as "the production, distribution, marketing, sale or delivery of goods and services by electronic means".[18] In the meantime, many voices suggest that the term "digital trade" can be used analogously.

The contents provided by online trade mostly lack physical attributes and mostly are offered on a temporary basis. In practice, online trade frequently covers items having similarities to the rendering of services. Thus, at first glance, digital trade appears to be classifiable as "trade in services".[19] The term "services" itself, however, is relatively vague and it is not clear whether it also encompasses electronically supplied services. The definition in article I:3(b) GATS only states that the notion of "services" incudes "any services except services supplied in the exercise of governmental authority". The services sectoral classification list (W/120) containing a comprehensive list of all services (sub-)sectors covered by the GATS, does not make any exact mention of digital trade and does provide only little guidance for the treatment of e-commerce under the GATS.

The same appreciation holds true for the term "digital assets" (or "crypto assets"); the notion of this new form of assets is about 5 years old and is related to the distributed ledger technology (blockchain).[20] Digital assets are usually expressed in the technological form of a so-called "token" being a data package which is encrypted and contains the relevant information about the asset. The contents of tokens can be manifold, from currencies to securities, commodities and minerals. Therefore, different asset classes exist not necessarily having the same regulatory treatment.

---

[18]General Council, Work Programme on Electronic Commerce, 25 September 1998, WT/L/274, para 1.3.

[19]See Weber (2015), p. 324 with further references.

[20]See for example Mougayar (2016), pp. 39 et seq.

2.2.2 Difficulties in Classifying Digital Assets

In contrast to the GATT, the GATS is based on the so-called positive-list-approach meaning that only those services appearing on the applicable list are subject to the GATS commitments. Therefore, following the positive-list-logic, new services are not automatically covered by the GATS; moreover, Member States have to actively agree on an obligation and notify the respective commitments. In view of the fact that many new services have appeared since the conclusion of the GATS, the international trade in services framework is not applicable to a broad scope of the services sector, except if specific digital services do fall into an existing category such as "telecommunication services" (for example e-mail, online information and data base retrieval).[21]

Trade in services under the GATS is classified in four categories, depending on the territorial presence of the supplier and the consumer, namely cross-border supply (mode 1), consumption abroad (mode 2), commercial presence (mode 3), and presence of natural persons (mode 4). Digital transactions are usually characterized by the fact that no legal or natural person needs to be present in order to deliver the service. Thus, mode 3 and mode 4 are of little relevance in this context. However, the question of whether to classify a certain digital service as GATS mode 1 or GATS mode 2 has often proven to be difficult. Case law (for example US-Gambling and China-Audiovisual Services) suggests that digital trade in services falls within the commitments of GATS mode 1.

The digitization is also transforming goods, i.e. they can be stored, used and distributed in a digital form. These so-called digital assets are intangible goods, the most prominent examples being downloaded e-books or streamed music plays, e-tickets, or software. Whereas it appears to be uncontested that products purchased online and delivered physically fall in the scope of the GATT, the legal situation is less clear if the end-product itself is delivered electronically: Is a film downloaded online "like" a film bought as a DVD? What about a film streamed online? The classification systems of both, the GATT (Harmonized System, HS Code) as well as the GATS (Services Sectoral Classification List, W/120), do not provide any guidance on how to classify digital trade.[22]

Digital assets need to be processed on some kind of carrier media: An application software ("App") can only be used on a mobile device like a smartphone or a tablet; an e-book, an e-reader, and music download are of no use without a speaker or a music-player. These carrier media are tangible goods and are listed in the HS System (for example HS number 8523). Therefore, the legal qualification of the carrier media is quite clear, but the challenge concerns the delineation between the end of the carrier media and the beginning of the digital asset: If a video game console provides for online-games, audio-visual content and computer services, which legal

[21]Weber (2015), p. 324.

[22]See also Note by the Secretariat: Services Sectoral Classification List, MTN.GNS/W/120 (10 July 1991).

framework does apply? The qualification as good under the GATT might be confronted with the reservation of Member States that digital products can enshrine politically sensitive contents (particularly audio-visual or cultural products).[23]

So far, Member States have not reached consensus on the appropriate classification of digital assets. Some voices seem to favour a classification under the GATT, basing their arguments on reasons of the durability of a digital asset (in contrast to services) and its inseparability from a physical carrier medium. In addition, the fact that a digital asset does not have distinguishable physical attributes and is invisible and intangible does not per se exclude the applicability of the GATT as the qualification of electricity shows (HS Code 2716.000). However, other voices propose a classification under the GATS, arguing that digital assets delivered electronically cannot be considered "like" those products physically delivered.[24] Denying the need for a clear position, even hybrid solutions (GATS classification and GATT treatment) have been suggested under the Work Programme,[25] notwithstanding the fact that this middle course approach does not appear to be practical from a legal point of view and would further undermine the WTO legal framework.

The WTO itself is well aware of the existing problems and efforts have been initiated to remedy the situation. In the context of the 11th Ministerial Conference (December 2017, Buenos Aires), a short "Joint Statement on Electronic Commerce" has been adopted inviting the participating Member States to do further work on digital trade.[26] Most developed countries have agreed to this Joint Statement; China did it in the almost last minute. However, no concrete outcome can be seen for the time being even if several proposals have been submitted and discussed in WTO fora. The World Trade Report 2018 of the WTO also intensively addressed digital trade pointing to the further transformations of the global trade regime; as a result of the investigations, the WTO pleads for a technology-induced reshaping of the regulatory environment.[27]

2.2.3 Servitization of Manufacturing

Apart from the classification discussions (goods/services), in the digital trade context the term "servitization" has been invented in order to qualify those "manufacturers" that bundle or integrate services with the goods they produce and sell.[28] Thereby, goods are becoming more and more linked to one another as a complete package, a

[23]Weber (2015), pp. 325–326 with further references.

[24]Weber (2015), p. 326.

[25]Wunsch-Vincent (2006), pp. 61–62.

[26]WTO, WT/MIN(17)/60 of 13 December 2017.

[27]WTO (2018), pp. 130 et seq.

[28]In connection with the photocopier industry see Visintin (2014), p. 23.

fact that is particularly shown in the context of the Internet of Things.[29] An example nicely showing the challenges is 3D printing; similarly, the question can be asked whether a smart/intelligent "product" must be considered as good or as service. Therefore, the "servitization of manufacturing" will be part of the future design of new global value chains.

Traditionally, legal doctrine starts from the concept of the "predominant purpose" test (goods-oriented or services-oriented "products") and assesses the characteristics of digital assets such as intangible/heterogeneous/inseparable/perishable (non-storable).[30] However, even with these additional characteristics the dilemma of the classification cannot be easily overcome. Moreover, the taxonomy becomes more complicated and existing tensions will remain hard to overcome. In addition, such an approach is only able to cover the "product-like" assets, not the data often having a substantial value in the supply chain and in particular in services-oriented markets (such as financial or e-health markets).

This assessment appears to be equally justified since a hybrid regulatory approach (involving governments, multistakeholder organizations, and the private sector) for the development of WTO rules has so far never been realized. The WTO rules typically do not refer to private standards or industry best practices although they are commonplace in the digital world.[31] Nevertheless, the WTO has liaised with some multilateral institutions in the financial and environmental field; a similar approach could be implemented also in Internet matters. Such kind of cooperation would be a first step into the direction of a broader concept of rule-making, but not improve the participation of civil society and of the private sector in order to reach a more balanced evaluation of the "disruptive" developments.

3 Dystopia: New Wine in Old Skins or "Lawless" Regime

A dystopian assessment of the given difficulties in bringing the digital assets into the classification regime of the present WTO regime could come to the conclusion that the historical baggage of the existing WTO framework would be too heavy to break down the legal goods/services silos.[32] Such an approach (called "no-good-place") would lead to the consequence that the available classifications will have to be stretched in one or the other way in order to make the respective provisions of the GATT or the GATS, respectively, applicable to transactions with digital assets.

[29]See also Trachtman JP (2019) The Internet of Things Cybersecurity Challenge to Trade and Investment: Trust and Verify?, pp. 1 et seq. https://papers.ssrn.com/sol3/papers.cfm?abstract_id=3374542.

[30]For further details see Peng S-y (2019) A New Trade Regime for the Servitization of Manufacturing, Paradise Lost or Found? The Post-WTO International Legal Order (Utopian & Dystopian Possibilities), University of Tokyo Workshop, pp. 1–2.

[31]See Mitchell and Mishra (2019), pp. 389–416; Pauwelyn (2014), pp. 739 et seq.

[32]Peng (2019, n. 30), p. 6.

Such an approach appears to be unsatisfactory and resembles the situation that new wine is filled into old skins. Technology is always faster than legislative processes (often coined as "regulatory lag"); consequently, the WTO regime would become a never ending stretching exercise (with delays). In addition, it is hard to see how data constituting a value could be covered by an even extended regulatory regime, apart from the fact that national data ownership laws and data protection laws would eventually also play an important role.

If the WTO regime should fall apart, Regional Trade Agreements (RTA) would still remain in existence. A large number of bigger and smaller RTA is in place in all geographic regions of the world.[33] However, as the word "region" tells, these agreements only apply in a specific geographic area; enterprises domiciled in a country not belonging to the RTA are deprived from the preferential treatment rules. Therefore, the RTA lead to an undesirable fragmentation of global trade. Experience has shown that the increase of the trade volume is larger on the global than on the regional level; consequently, RTA cannot replace the WTO framework.

For international (cross-border) trade the lack of a common global understanding (at least in respect of the main legal principles) leads to an almost "lawless" situation. Since national regulations often do not meet the requirements of global trade, the role of private actors might become more important. However, experience has shown that it is difficult to identify sufficiently clear legal contours in a completely "privatized" environment. Even in case of a certain degree of standardization in the international trade transactions between businesses the legal stability as a vital characteristic of law is not given; respective uncertainties of the normative framework would jeopardize international trade. Therefore, a dystopian development leading to a "not-good place" appears to be undesirable.

4 Utopia: Dream of a Digital Assets Framework

4.1 Need for a Bottom-up Approach

An utopian approach would envisage building a new digital assets regime in the form of a freshly established cooperative arrangement encompassing those States, international organizations and private actors that are willing to engage in such an undertaking. Assuming that the WTO stagnates and that the unfinished business resulting from the Uruguay-Round can reasonably not be completed since it would be a "winding and bumpy road",[34] a new approach appears to be unavoidable.

---

[33] Weber (2015), pp. 334 et seq.; Burri and Polanco (2020), pp. 193 et seq.; Willemyns (2020), pp. 223 et seq.

[34] Peng (2019, n. 30), p. 7.

From a structurally theoretical perspective, a new regulatory framework can be implemented by applying a top-down or a bottom-up approach.[35] (i) A top-down approach necessarily requires the establishment of a global agency and the implementation of a central authority which is unlikely to happen if the WTO should stagnate. (ii) A bottom-up process is based on a step-by-step model encompassing the major entities and individuals concerned with the respective tasks and challenges. During the last few years, collaborative processes through a bottom-up model gained increased acceptance; experiences made in different forms lead to improved deliberation and decision-making processes. An approach encompassing the interested public bodies, industry organizations and private actors also appears to be suitable in the international trade context.

The new "buzzword" for such kind of collaborative approach is "multistakeholderism".[36] The multistakeholder approach must rely on the motivated participation by those with interests, capacities and needs. Appropriate strategies leading to the desired legitimacy should include the following elements[37]: (i) openness, (ii) transparency, (iii) accessibility, (iv) accountability, (v) credibility, (vi) consensus-orientation, (vii) availability of complaint/appeal structure, and (viii) resistance against capture. Even if in the context of the distributed ledger technology and of the digital assets the present situation appears to be relatively far away from a multistakeholder regime, in the medium term it is unavoidable that the different stakeholders (regulators, standardization organizations, industry associations, users' groups, etc.) attempt to achieve a minimal structural framework allowing to exchange information, develop suitable standards and implement harmonizing rules. The first discussions conducted in academic circles and in a few industry associations of how to legally qualify digital assets are a promising start; the further work must be taken up on a higher and broader level.[38]

Obviously, major challenges of such an approach are not to be overlooked, particularly in respect of the legitimacy of the normative framework. The legitimate stakeholders of the regulatory processes need to reach the justification of authority giving the addressees of the norms the trust that their own values are represented in a decision-making context (so-called "right to rule"). Since a source-oriented perception of legitimacy looking at the authority in democratic States might not suffice, a procedural approach encompassing a result-oriented type of legitimacy appears to be appropriate; based on the "discourse-principle", the approval of the potentially affected private and public actors can be assumed if the participation in a rational discourse leads to a validation.[39]

---

[35]For further details see Weber (2017), pp. 3–4.

[36]Raymond and DeNardis (2015), pp. 572 et seq.

[37]For a general overview see Weber (2016b), p. 251.

[38]See also Weber (2017), p. 4, with further references.

[39]Weber (2016a), p. 208; see also Fukuyama (2014), pp. 524–548.

4.2 *Procedures for Standardization*

A standardization of the international trade terms is of utmost importance. Apart from regulations of States, the standardization can also be promoted by way of "private rule-making". Such an approach is relevant if international organizations (mainly the WTO) are "blocked" and if national legislators are not the most suitable regulators. An efficient involvement of all potentially concerned actors in the self-regulatory processes is needed to establish a level playing field being suitable for the development of standards and for the promotion of competition and innovation. The concerned market participants (i.e. private and partly also public actors) through existing or newly formed trade associations as well as the (public) trade negotiators would be best positioned to develop a framework which reflects the given commercial realities as well as the digital business models.

A crucial function in such a bottom-up process could be played by the International Standardisation Organisation (ISO); in an almost "lawless" environment standards gain a high value for the market participants. The ISO appears to be particularly suitable to standardize the concept of digital assets classes since it already is involved in the standard-building and in the governance-design of blockchain, being the technical infrastructure of digital assets.[40] National standardization organizations are equally active in this field: Australian experts elaborated on proposals for standards governing the distributed ledger technology[41] and German experts addressed the topic of standard terms for smart contracts.

In addition, sector-specific organizations for example in the fields of maritime shipping, land transportation or digital customs handling might also gain importance by way of implementing guidelines for international trade. The "Single Window" project in East Asia standardizing electronic customs formalities is a good example.[42] The Organisation for Economic Cooperation and Development (OECD) as institution of the more developed countries as well as the World Economic Forum (WEF) as private body equally support standardization efforts, at least by preparing reports that show how different advances can be made interoperable ("Tokenisation of Assets and Potential Implications for Financial Markets",[43] "Building Value with Blockchain Technology"[44]).

---

[40]ISO (2016) Technical Committees, ISO/TC 307, Blockchain and Distributed Ledger Technologies. https://www.iso.org/committee/6266604.html.

[41]Standards Australia, Blockchain & Electronic Distributed Ledger Technologies: New Field of Technical Activity. http://www.standards.org.au/OurOrganisation/Events/Documents/Blockchain%20NFTA%20Information%20Sheet.pdf.

[42]For further details see Weber (2011), pp. 1–24.

[43]OECD (2020) The Tokenisation of Assets and Potential Implications for Financial Markets, Report of January 2020. http://www.oecd.org/finance/The-Tokenisation-of-Assets-and-Potential-Implications-for-Financial-Markets.htm.

[44]WEF (2019) Building Value with Blockchain Technology: How to Evaluate Blockchain's Benefits, Report of 16 July 2019. http://www3.weforum.org/docs/WEF_Building_Value_with_Blockchain.pdf.

As outlined, the development of standards encompasses organizational aspects and substantive elements. The first step consists in the aforementioned identification or establishment of the most suitable standardization body; the second step must be devoted to the discussions and negotiations of the appropriate contents of the standards. Such an approach will not be stable within a short time frame, i.e. legal instability cannot fully be avoided. Nevertheless, this utopian dream appears to be more appealing than a dystopian disappointment.

4.3 Taxonomy of Digital Asset Classes

The WTO legal framework does not regulate aspects of ownership and property (with the exception of acknowledging intellectual property rights), its focus is on transactional issues. Property remains the domain of the Nation States. The challenge with digital assets consists in the fact that data and tokens are not tangible and, therefore, national property laws do not easily apply.[45] A new digital assets regime could be based on a fresh notion of "ownership" more relying on "factual control" than on a traditional property understanding. Obviously, this aspect does not only concern international trade but generally transactions with digital assets; however, a new global trade regime could join forces with the efforts on national and regional levels to qualify digital asset as particularly values.

The contents of digital assets (or crypto assets) can be manifold; examples are crypto currencies, crypto tokens, crypto shares, etc.[46] Since money, shares and other products have already been classified separately in the traditional business life, a similar approach must also be taken in the context of digital assets. Therefore, a taxonomy of asset classes needs to be developed making sense for international trade.[47]

Financial market authorities have already developed categories and classifications. For example, FINMA, the Swiss regulator, distinguishes between the following three main token designs based on the underlying economic function[48]:

- *Payment tokens:* Such tokens are intended to be used as a means of payment for acquiring goods or services or as a means of money or value transfer; payment tokens do not give rise to any claim against their issuer.
- *Utility tokens:* Such tokens are intended to provide access digitally to an application or service by means of a blockchain-based infrastructure.

[45]For further details see Thouvenin et al. (2017), pp. 111–145; Agar (2019), pp. 61 et seq.

[46]See also Burniske and Tatar (2017), pp. 31 et seq.

[47]The OECD-Report on the tokenization of assets (2020), pp. 11 et seq., does not address the taxonomy issues in detail.

[48]FINMA Guidelines for enquiries regarding the regulatory framework for initial coin offerings (ICOs) of 16 February 2018. https://www.finma.ch/en/news/2018/02/20180216-mm-ico-wegleitung/.

- *Asset tokens:* Such tokens represent assets, for example a debt or equity claim on the issuer (or a claim related to physical assets to be traded on the blockchain); asset tokens can promise a share in future company earnings or future capital flows similar to equities, bonds or derivatives.

Reality seldom corresponds to theoretical categories. Therefore, the mentioned token classifications are not mutually exclusive and hybrid tokens do occur in different business models. Obviously, hybrid tokens make asset classifications difficult. Furthermore, the categories developed in the context of financial markets do not necessarily need to correspond to the international trade requirements.

4.4 Contents of Standards for Digital Assets

Governmental regulations of all political levels (international, regional, national) and self-regulatory rule-making are confronted with the task of designing the contents of the standards. Since the likelihood of successful international developments is not very high, the following list of issues is mainly addressed to the above mentioned standardization organizations.

Relevant regulatory topics for the design of a legally stable environment regarding digital assets are for example[49]:

- *Definition of a digital asset:* The regulatory framework should be introduced with a description of the term "digital asset" encompassing the relevant technological elements (such as hash, encryption, etc.).
- *Conditions for the establishment of a registry:* Digital assets can only be transferred and traded in a structured way if their roots are reflected on a registry; the conditions how the registrar is implementing the registry must be set (for example secure infrastructure, access to data, etc.).
- *Effects of the registration:* The entry of a digital asset into the registry needs to have certain legal effects; amongst others, the registration should evidence ownership by an individual or a company, protect the trust of third persons in the correctness of the registration and build a pre-condition of a valid transfer of a digital asset.[50]
- *Transfer requirements:* The regulatory framework must state the requirements for the transfer of digital assets (for example form of transfer, delisting in the previous registry and entry into the new registry, etc.).
- *Nullification of a digital asset:* As with physical goods, the "loss" of a digital good cannot be excluded; such a "loss" mainly occurs if the entitled person does

[49]Recently a similar regulatory approach has been chosen by the Swiss legislator: see Botschaft des Bundesrates zum Bundesgesetz zur Anpassung des Bundesrechts an Entwicklungen der Technik verteilter Register vom 27. November 2019, Bundesblatt 2020, pp. 233 et seq.

[50]See for example Botschaft des Bundesrates (ibid.), pp. 285 et seq.

not anymore know his/her private key or the successors of a decreased person are not aware of it. A nullification procedure is already known in case of "disappeared" securities; similar rules might be advisable.

- *Liability rules:* The provider of the registry and possibly also the provider of the technological infrastructure should be obliged to comply with reasonable diligence standards; non-compliance therewith must have liability consequences.

The above mentioned regulatory topics are not exclusive but appear to be the most important issues. In a bottom-up approach the respective rules for digital assets could be developed by self-regulatory bodies; at a later stage, successful rules would be available to be taken over by governmental regulators.

4.5 Possible Roadmap

Under the assumption that the WTO stagnates and that an appropriate regulatory framework for digital assets will not be developed and designed by an international rule-maker in the near future, utopian alternatives need to be taken into account, not at least with the help of academia. In a nutshell, a roadmap could encompass the following steps:

- *Definition of the relevant issues:* Digital assets are a "new world"; therefore, the working-out of the relevant issues is the first important task. Academia is called to identify the theoretical framework for digital assets in international trade.
- *Involvement of appropriate organizations:* Due to the lack of an international legislator or regulator dealing with digital assets, those globally active organizations and associations are to be addressed that are able to promote the standardization of the terms and characteristics of digital assets (for example the International Standardisation Organisation).
- *Development of substantive standards:* Knowing the organizational actors being involved in the processes, expert groups are to be appointed that are knowledgeable and experienced to develop the above mentioned substantive principles. Thereby, a multistakeholder approach makes sense; if businesses are involved, the likelihood increases that the adopted standards will be applied in practice.

Even if such kind of utopian approach with the described possible roadmap is not easy to be realized, the chances exist that the presently endangered international trade regime can be replaced by an appropriate and modern framework for digital assets. The efforts undertaken by the involved organizations and associations in developing an appropriate private rule-making can be made fruitful for international legislators at a later stage.

References

Agar N (2019) How to be human in the digital economy. MIT Press, Cambridge
Blanke T (2014) Digital asset ecosystem. Elsevier Science, Amsterdam
Bradbury R (1953) Fahrenheit 451. Ballentine Books, New York
Burniske C, Tatar J (2017) Cryptoassets. McGraw Hill, New York
Burri M, Polanco R (2020) Digital trade provisions in preferential trade agreements: introducing a new dataset. JIEL 23(2):187–220
Fukuyama F (2014) Political order and political decay. Profile Books, New York
Koskenniemi M (2009) From Apology to Utopia: the structure of international legal argument, 3rd print. Cambridge University Press, Cambridge
Mitchell AD, Mishra N (2019) Regulating cross-border data flows in a data-driven world: how WTO law can contribute. JIEL 22(3):389–416
Mougayar W (2016) The business blockchain. Wiley, Hoboken
Nozick R (1974) Anarchy state and Utopia. Basic Books, New York
Orwell G (1949) Nineteen eighty-four. Secker & Warburg, London
Pauwelyn J (2014) Rule-based trade 2.0? The rise of informal rules and international standards and how they may outcompete WTO-treaties. JIEL 17(4):739–751
Peng S-y (2019) The rule of law in times of technological uncertainty: is international economic law ready for emerging supervisory trends? JIEL 22(1):1–27
Picker C, Nakagawa J (2020) An introduction to Utopian and Dystopian post-WTO regimes and environments. In: Picker C, Nakagawa J, Stoll P-T, Kolsky Lewis M, Neuwirth RJ (eds) The post-WTO international legal order. Paradise lost or found? Springer, Berlin, pp …
Plato (1942) Apology – Crito – Phaedo – Symposium – Republic: five great dialogues, 1942 translated by Jowett B. Random House, New York
Raymond M, DeNardis L (2015) Multistakeholderism: anatomy of an inchoate global institution. Int Theory 7:572–616
Thouvenin F, Weber RH, Früh A (2017) Data ownership: taking stock and mapping the issues. In: Dehmer M, Emmert-Streib F (eds) Frontiers in data science. CRC Press, Boca Raton, pp 111–145
Visintin F (2014) Photocopier industry: at the forefront of servitization. In: Lay G et al (eds) Servitization in industry. Springer, Berlin, pp 23–43
Weber RH (2011) Legal framework for the single window concept in ASEAN: a successful movement towards trade facilitation in East Asian countries. Asian J Law Econ 2(4):1–24
Weber RH (2014) Realizing a new global cyberspace. Schulthess, Zurich
Weber RH (2015) Digital trade and E-commerce: challenges and opportunities of the Asia-Pacific regionalism. Asian J WTO Int Health Law 10:321–348
Weber RH (2016a) Elements of a legal framework for cyberspace. Swiss Rev Int Eur Law 26:195–215
Weber RH (2016b) Legal foundations of multistakeholder decision-making. Zeitschrift für Schweizerisches Recht I:247–267
Weber RH (2017) Regulatory environment of the ledger technology. Comput Law Rev Int (CRi) 18(1):1–6
Willemyns I (2020) Agreement forthcoming? A comparison of EU, US, and Chinese RTAs in times of plurilateral e-commerce negotiations. JIEL 23(2):221–244
WTO (2018) World Trade Report 2018, the future of world trade: how digital technologies are transforming global commerce. WTO, Geneva
Wunsch-Vincent S (2006) The WTO, the internet and trade in digital products: EC-US perspectives. Hart Publishing, Oxford

The manufacturer's authorised representative in the EU is Springer Nature Customer Service Centre GmbH, Europaplatz 3, 69115 Heidelberg, Germany. If you have any concerns regarding our products, please contact ProductSafety@springernature.com

Printed and bound by CPI Group (UK) Ltd, Croydon, CR0 4YY
30/09/2026
02225323-0005